Seán MacBride

Seán MacBride

A Republican Life
1904–1946

Caoimhe Nic Dháibhéid

Liverpool University Press

First published 2011 by
Liverpool University Press
4 Cambridge Street
Liverpool L69 7ZU

This paperback version published 2014

British Library Cataloguing-in-Publication data
A British Library CIP record is available

ISBN 978-1-84631-658-6 cased
ISBN 978-1-78138-011-6 paperback

Typeset in Scala by Koinonia, Manchester

Printed and bound by CPI Group (UK) Ltd, Croydon, CR0 4YY

Contents

Acknowledgements

It is a very great pleasure to acknowledge the help and support of a number of people and institutions who made this work possible. My first debt of gratitude is to Richard English, who supervised the doctoral thesis on which this book is based, offering guidance, encouragement, advice and friendship throughout the project and beyond. Margaret O'Callaghan was also an invaluable source of support and insight.

A Queen's University Belfast Studentship provided the funding for my doctoral studies, and the School of Politics, International Studies and Philosophy and the Institute of Irish Studies offered stimulating academic environments both to pursue the research for this book and complete its writing. More recently, Fitzwilliam College Cambridge has been a generous and welcoming home.

Other individuals have helped me greatly in a variety of ways: Paul Bew, Jessie Blackbourn, Dominic Bryan, Marie Coleman, Roy Foster, James Greer, Brian Hanley, Alvin Jackson, Patrick Maume, Shaun McDaid, Deirdre McMahon, Audra Mitchell, Tina Morin, Colmán Ó Clábaigh, Eunan O'Halpin, Senia Pašeta, Simon Prince, Jennifer Regan-Lefebvre, Kacper Rekawek and Graham Walker. The support of Alison Welsby at Liverpool University Press has been greatly appreciated.

I would also like to thank a number of libraries and archives who have assisted me with my research: the National Archives of Ireland, the National Archives of the United Kingdom, the National Library of Ireland, the New York Public Library, the Burns Library at Boston College, the Public Record Office of Northern Ireland, the staff of the University College Dublin Archives Department, and Commandant Victor Laing at the Irish Military Archives. I also would like to specially thank the staff of the McClay Library at Queen's University Belfast, in particular Diarmuid Kennedy of Special Collections and Florence Gray of the Inter-Library Loans section.

My wider family has been a source of great support: Kieran McDaid arranged at short notice an archival visit which would otherwise have been difficult, while Brighdín McDaid and Vera McElhinney provided a refuge when needed. I especially wish to thank Phelim and Michelle McDaid, who were unfailingly hospitable hosts in Dublin and graciously allowed me to frequently impose on them. My sisters, Ailbhe, Róisín, Bríd and Niamh, have helped me more than they know. I owe an enormous debt to Colin Reid, who was a valuable soundboard for ideas, and provided thoughtful and perceptive criticism at all stages. For this, and for much else, I am grateful. Finally, I wish to thank my parents, Fergus and Bridie, for the unstinting love, support and encouragement they have always shown to me. This book is dedicated to both of them.

Caoimhe Nic Dháibhéid

Cambridge
November 2010

Abbreviations

ASU	Active Service Unit
BMH	Bureau of Military History
DORA	Defence of the Realm Act
GAA	Gaelic Athletic Association
GHQ	General Headquarters
IMA	Irish Military Archives
IPP	Irish Parliamentary Party
IRA	Irish Republican Army
IRB	Irish Republican Brotherhood
L&H	Literary and Historical [Society]
NAI	National Archives of Ireland
NARA	National Archives and Records Administration, College Park, Maryland
NAL	National Archives, London
NLI	National Library of Ireland
NYPL	New York Public Library
O/C	Officer Commanding
PRONI	Public Record Office of Northern Ireland
QUB	Queen's University Belfast
RIC	Royal Irish Constabulary
RUC	Royal Ulster Constabulary
TD	Teachta Dála
UCC	University College Cork
UCD	University College Dublin

Introduction

'Death of an evil man'. The title of Seán MacBride's obituary in the *Sunday Telegraph*, on 17 January 1988, was breathtakingly direct. The article itself was equally hard-hitting, describing MacBride as a 'murderer ... [with] a psychopathic inability to understand those with whom he disagreed', and claiming that two principles 'guided his entire political life. The first was hatred of Great Britain; the second a worship of violence.'[1] The following day, a cardinal, seven bishops and a papal nuncio concelebrated MacBride's funeral mass at Dublin's Pro-Cathedral. Among the congregation were the President of Ireland, the Taoiseach, leaders of all Irish political parties, and members of the diplomatic corps. There were also representatives of a vast number of organisations that had reason to remember Seán MacBride: the African National Congress, the Palestine Liberation Organisation, the Ancient Order of Hibernians, the 1916–1921 Club, Fianna Éireann, Sinn Féin, Republican Sinn Féin, the Irish Congress of Trade Unions, the Irish Anti-Apartheid Movement, Trócaire, Amnesty International, and the Irish Campaign for Nuclear Disarmament. Completing the attendance were members of the Irish judiciary and bar, writers and journalists, and the rock group U2.[2]

In the years after his death, MacBride – who had in his lifetime earned the notable distinction of winning both the Nobel and the Lenin Peace Prizes – received further accolades. The International Peace Bureau created the Seán MacBride Peace Prize in his honour; the Irish section headquarters of Amnesty International was renamed Seán MacBride House; and there was created Seán MacBride Square in Wexford Town, Sean MacBridestraat in Amsterdam, and Seán MacBride Street in Windhoek, Namibia, bisecting Robert Mugabe Avenue.

MacBride in Scholarly Literature

The binary nature of responses to MacBride's death mirrored the duality of his life: French-born but fervently Irish nationalist in identity; an internationally renowned humanitarian activist but wedded to his militant Irish republican roots; Nobel Peace Laureate but Chief-of-Staff of the Irish Republican Army (IRA). Despite his international fame, including the dubious honour of lending his name to the

---

1 *Sunday Telegraph*, 17 January 1988.
2 *Irish Times*, 19 January 1988.

1

ill-advised MacBride Principles,[3] Seán MacBride remains best known in Irish political history for his leadership of the political party Clann na Poblachta and his period as Minister for External Affairs in the inter-party government of 1948 to 1951. A number of incidents marked his ministerial career: the repeal of the External Relations Act, the somewhat haphazard declaration of the Republic of Ireland, and the Mother and Child crisis which led to the collapse of the coalition government in May 1951. The constitutional stage of MacBride's political career is well served in scholarly literature.[4] MacBride also features centrally in Eithne MacDermott's valuable study of Clann na Poblachta and in John Horgan's biography of Noël Browne.[5] By comparison, MacBride's earlier incarnation as boyish revolutionary, leading IRA member, and advocate for the republican movement remains relatively untouched. A tangential figure in a number of important studies of the mid-century IRA, the first biographical treatment of MacBride came in 1993, with Anthony Jordan's slim, impressionistic volume.[6]

In 2007, Elizabeth Keane's *Seán MacBride: A Life* appeared.[7] Claiming to be 'the most authoritative discussion to date on Seán MacBride's political and personal life', Keane's study is heavily weighted towards MacBride's ministerial career, to which the bulk of the narrative is devoted. In addressing MacBride's life before 1946, Keane relies heavily and uncritically on MacBride's posthumously published memoir, supplemented by general surveys on twentieth-century Ireland. Accordingly, much important detail is omitted or misinterpreted and key episodes in MacBride's narrative are missed. This book therefore represents the first scholarly attempt fully to investigate, chronicle and analyse MacBride's life and political career prior to his reinvention as a constitutional politician. MacBride's early career merits such serious study for a number of reasons. Although he played only a minor role during the Irish War of Independence, his exalted parentage afforded him access to key figures within the revolutionary movement. This duality of revolutionary identity singles MacBride out: he was representative of the IRA rank and file while simultaneously occupying a privileged position. Equally, MacBride's individual narrative during the post-revolutionary years offers a wider perspective

3 Kevin McNamara, *The MacBride Principles: Irish America Strikes Back* (Liverpool: Liverpool University Press, 2009).
4 Ronan Fanning, 'The response of the London and Belfast governments to the declaration of the Republic of Ireland, 1948–9', *International Affairs*, vol. 58, no. 1 (1981); R. J. Raymond, 'Ireland's 1949 NATO decision: a reassessment', Éire-Ireland, vol. xx, no. iii (Fomhar, 1985); Francis McEvoy, 'Canada, Ireland and the Commonwealth: the declaration of the Irish republic, 1948–9', *Irish Historical Studies*, vol. xxiv, no. 96 (November, 1985); E. McKee, 'Church-state relations and the development of Irish health policy: the mother-and-child scheme, 1944–53', *Irish Historical Studies*, vol. xxv, no. 98 (November, 1986), pp. 159–94; and David McCullagh, *A Makeshift Majority: The First Inter-party Government, 1948–51* (Dublin: Institute of Public Administration, 1998).
5 Eithne MacDermott, *Clann na Poblachta* (Cork: Cork University Press, 1998); John Horgan, *Noël Browne: Passionate Outsider* (Dublin: Gill & Macmillan, 2000).
6 Anthony Jordan, *Seán MacBride: A Biography* (Dublin: Blackwater Press, 1993). For the IRA of the 1920s and 1930s, see Richard English, *Radicals and the Republic: Socialist Republicanism in the Irish Free State* (Oxford: Clarendon Press, 1994); and Brian Hanley, *The IRA, 1926–1936* (Dublin: Four Courts Press, 2002).
7 Elizabeth Keane, *Seán MacBride: A Life* (Dublin: Gill & Macmillan, 2007).

on the lingering violence in the newly formed southern state and the ideological, political and strategic dilemmas confronting the republican movement. Finally, a consideration of MacBride's wartime activities adds nuance to the scholarly literature charting Ireland's experience of neutrality and intelligence links with external agencies during the Second World War.

A Note on Sources

'Sean MacBride invited neither historian nor biographer to examine his life.'[8] As Keane and others have identified, the primary difficulty confronting MacBride's biographer is the unavailability of a personal archive. While MacBride's private papers exist, they were bequeathed to his secretary Caitriona Lawlor, allegedly on the proviso that they should not be deposited in a publicly accessible archive.[9] The problems posed by the lack of a personal archive have been eased somewhat by the publication of MacBride's memoir, *That Day's Struggle*, in 2005, but this too has provided difficulties of its own. A collection of oral reminiscences transcribed and cross-checked, the memoir is by turn episodic, inaccurate and self-aggrandising. Although it contains some valuable insights, particularly in terms of political psychology, it represents very much the MacBride of the 1970s, anxious to stake his place in the chronology of the republican movement and at pains to deflect the criticism of former comrades. This book, therefore, has sought throughout to subject MacBride's later opinions to rigorous historical scrutiny, and also to locate MacBride within contemporary archival material.

The book is structured in three broad sections. Chapters One to Four explore MacBride's political formation from continental boyhood in Paris to the upheavals of revolutionary Dublin and imprisonment during the Civil War. Chapters Five and Six probe the period 1926 to 1937, in which MacBride rose to the leadership of the IRA, becoming Chief-of-Staff in 1936, while occupying a median position between the vehemently divided left and right wings of the republican movement. The final section (Chapters Seven to Nine) examines MacBride's activities from 1938 to 1946, both as a respected barrister and as a central link between the IRA and agents of Nazi Germany. The latter war years saw MacBride laying the foundations for a political career: urging republican participation in the democratic institutions of the Irish state, sharply criticising government actions towards republican prisoners, and finally mobilising popular discontent to springboard the formation of a political party under his leadership. A brief epilogue chronicles MacBride's subsequent political and humanitarian career.

8   *Irish Times*, 7 December 2004.
9   Keane, *Seán MacBride*, pp. 241–2; Michael Hopkinson, 'Review article: biography of the revolutionary period': Michael Collins and Kevin Barry', *Irish Historical Studies*, xxviii, no. 111 (May 1993), p. 316; *Irish Independent*, 11 February 1989.

1

'The Centre of Delight of the Household':[1] 1904–1916

On 26 January 1904, Pope Pius X received a telegram from Mary Barry O'Delaney, Irish nationalist and propagandist, announcing that the future King of Ireland had been born. The wires between Paris, Dublin and America buzzed that night and over the following days, as messages arrived from across the Irish nationalist community, saluting the birth of the 'President of Ireland'.[2] The child in whom so much hope was invested was John Seaġan MacBride (afterwards Seán), born in Paris to John MacBride and Maud Gonne. He was the only child of their marriage, which after less than a year was already displaying signs of irretrievable breakdown. Marked out from birth by his parents as one who would do great work for Ireland, his birth and early life in the heart of the republican aristocracy exposed him to a particular kind of radicalism: part old-school Fenian nationalism, part romantic mysticism, part cosmopolitan struggle against the wider forces of imperialism. MacBride's immediate family history provides an illuminating lens through which to examine the intersections between Irish republicanism, nationalism and culture at the turn of the twentieth century, intersections which definitively shaped the contours of his early life.

'A great red-haired yahoo of a woman' and a 'drunken vainglorious lout'[3]

Retaining custody of her son after her separation from her husband, Maud Gonne was the dominant figure in Seán MacBride's early life, a unique figure who combined the wealthy sophistication of upper-class English society with a decidedly bohemian non-conformity and a passionate attachment to the cause of Irish nationalism.[4] Born on 21 December 1866 in Farnham, Surrey, Maud Gonne was the eldest daughter of Captain Thomas Gonne of the 17th Lancers, and Edith

---

1 Ella Young, *Flowering Dusk: Things Remembered Accurately and Inaccurately* (London: Dobson, 1945), p. 109.
2 Margaret Ward, *Maud Gonne: Ireland's Joan of Arc* (London: Pandora, 1990), p. 85.
3 Louis Purser on Maud Gonne, quoted in R. F. Foster, *W. B. Yeats: A Life: I: The Apprentice Mage* (Oxford: Oxford University Press, 1997), p. 91; W. B. Yeats, 'Easter 1916', *The Major Works*, ed. Ed. Larrisey (Oxford: Oxford University Press, 1997), pp. 85–6.
4 Anna MacBride White and A. Norman Jeffares (eds.), *Always your Friend: The Gonne-Yeats letters 1893–1938* (London: Hutchinson, 1992), p. 5; C. Innes, *Women and Nation in Irish Literature and Society 1880–1935* (Hemel Hempstead: Harvester Wheatsheaf, 1993).

Cook. Her father's family were prosperous wine importers in London, who, as Gonne was at pains to point out, had come from Ireland via Portugal in the seventeenth century.[5] Her early adulthood was spent immersed in Anglo-Irish garrison society, but an apparently Damascene conversion to Irish nationalism followed soon after, prompted by the plight of evicted tenant families in 1885. [6] Gonne herself explained some sixty-five years later to M. J. MacManus, literary editor of the *Irish Press*, that it was these events 'which changed the whole course of my life by changing me from a frivolous girl, who thought of little but dancing and race meetings, into a woman of fixed purpose'.[7] This drastic change of political perspective coincided with the death of her father shortly afterwards; it should also be seen in the light of her blossoming relationship with the married French Boulangist politician, Lucien Millevoye.[8] Over the following decade, Gonne combined her activities within Irish nationalism with her affair with Millevoye, giving birth to two children: Georges Sylvère, born in January 1890, and Iseult, born in August 1894.[9] Early activism on behalf of evicted tenants in Donegal and the Irish treason-felony prisoners in Britain were soon followed by more extensive politico-literary pursuits: she attended meetings of the Contemporary Club where through the Fenian John O'Leary she met the young poet William Butler Yeats on 30 January 1889.[10] Yeats was instantly infatuated, remembering in his memoirs that she had 'a stature so great she seems of a divine race';[11] his affections were not, however, reciprocated, Gonne encouraging Yeats to sublimate his romantic frustration into the creation of a new literature for a new Ireland. In spite of this imbalance in their relationship, the friendship endured war, revolution and political polarisation until Yeats's death in January 1939.

As the liaison with Millevoye fizzled out, and Iseult grew old enough to be left with a nursemaid, Gonne increased her efforts on behalf of the advanced nationalist movement. She was intimately involved with both the protests surrounding Queen Victoria's visits to Ireland in 1897 and 1900,[12] and the preparations for the centenary celebrations of 1798, also beginning a close association with Arthur Griffith, for whose publication the *United Irishman* she contributed numerous

5   See C. A. Balliett, 'The lives – and lies – of Maud Gonne', *Éire-Ireland*, vol. 14 (Fall 1979), pp. 17–44 for an in-depth examination of Maud Gonne's presentation of her family background.
6   Maud Gonne MacBride, *A Servant of the Queen: Reminiscences* (London: Gollancz, 1974, first published 1938), p. 32.
7   Boston College, Burns Library, M. J. MacManus Papers, MS86–36, Box 1, Folder 15, Maud Gonne MacBride to M. J. MacManus, 22 January 1950; Gonne MacBride, *A Servant of the Queen*, pp. 41–2.
8   Ward, *Maud Gonne*, pp. 11–12.
9   A. Norman Jeffares, 'Iseult Gonne', in Warwick Gould (ed.) *Poems and Contexts: Yeats Annual 16* (Basingstoke: Palgrave, 2004), pp. 197–200. Georges Sylvère died of meningitis in 1891.
10 Ward, *Maud Gonne*, pp. 22–4.
11 W. B. Yeats, *Memoirs*, ed. Denis Donoghue (London: Macmillan, 1974, first published 1972), p. 40.
12 See Andrea Bobotis, 'Rival maternities: Maud Gonne, Queen Victoria and the reign of the political mother', *Victorian Studies* (Autumn 2006), pp. 63–83; Senia Pašeta, 'Nationalist responses to two royal visits to Ireland, 1900 and 1903', *Irish Historical Studies*, vol. xxxi (1999), pp. 488–504; and Janette Condon, 'The patriotic children's treat: Irish nationalism and children's culture at the twilight of empire', *Irish Studies Review*, vol. 8, no. 2 (2000), pp. 167–78.

articles.[13] The committee formed to coordinate resistance to the royal visit of 1900 provided the basis of Inghinidhe na hÉireann, a women's movement whose object was 'to work for the complete independence of Ireland'.[14] Gonne was also a leading member of the Irish Transvaal Committee, established to provide a conduit for goods, an ambulance corps and volunteers to the Orange Free State, while a vigorous anti-recruiting campaign further stirred up Boer fever.[15] She was an extremely well-known figure across the political spectrum in Ireland, combining the notoriety attached to a politically active woman with her striking appearance to create an unforgettable impression, while her voracious energies made her a central player within advanced nationalism, both political and cultural. For all her professional success, however, on the personal front, Gonne was coming to something of a crossroads. Her liaison with Millevoye was effectively at an end, and the strain of maintaining a proper façade for her unconventional household in Paris was beginning to tell. Her growing friendship with Griffith and close involvement in nationalist pro-Boer activities made it unsurprising that she met John MacBride, who was energetically carving out a name for himself at the head of the Irish Brigade in the Transvaal.

If Maud Gonne represented the privileged and romantically nationalist side of Seán MacBride's heritage, then his father, John MacBride, offered a hard link to the Fenian past. John MacBride's life is less richly documented than that of his estranged wife, but for a time he was among the foremost members of the advanced nationalist movement in Ireland, and a close associate of senior figures in the Irish Republican Brotherhood (IRB). In documents prepared for his legal team during his divorce from Maud Gonne in 1904, John MacBride sketched a highly subjective, self-aggrandising account of his life and background, claiming descent from dead generations of Irish nationalists:

> His great-grandfather took part in the insurrection of 1798; his grandfather followed the fortunes of the Young Irelanders who first struggled for the estab-lishment of an Irish parliament and ultimately drifted into revolution; his father and uncles were members of the Irish Revolutionary Brotherhood of 1867... Irish patriotism was therefore, so to say, in his blood.[16]

John MacBride's father, Patrick MacBride, was in fact an Ulster-Scots Protestant from Glenhesk in County Antrim, a sea captain and trader; one of his regular stops was Westport, County Mayo, where he met and married Honoria Gill. The couple set up home and business at the Quay in Westport, and later had five sons, all of whom were raised in the Catholic faith of their mother: Joseph, Patrick Junior, Anthony, Francis and John, who was born on 8 May 1868.[17] John MacBride

13 Karen Steele, *Women, Press & Politics during the Irish Revival* (New York: Syracuse University Press, 2007), p. 78ff.

14 Gonne MacBride, *A Servant of the Queen*, p. 291; Pašeta, 'Nationalist responses to two royal visits to Ireland', pp. 493–4.

15 Donal P. McCracken, *Forgotten Protest: Ireland and the Anglo-Boer War* (Belfast: Ulster Historical Foundation, 2003, first published 1989), p. 39ff.

16 National Library of Ireland [NLI], Fred Allan Papers, MS 29819.

17 Anthony Jordan, *Major John MacBride: MacDonagh and MacBride and Connolly and Pearse* (Westport: Westport Historical Society, 1991), p. 3.

received a typically nationalist education at the Christian Brothers School in Westport, and at St Malachy's College in Belfast. Working in Dublin, having already been sworn into the IRB, he moved decisively into the more radical circles of advanced nationalist opinion; membership of the Young Ireland society, an IRB-infiltrated organisation, brought him into contact with John O'Leary, Arthur Griffith and Fred Allan.[18] A signal of his growing extremism may be seen in his alignment with the Irish National Alliance, an extremist organisation comprised of Clan na Gael renegades, old Stephensites, a resurrected cabal of Invincibles, and a London-headed association of regular IRB dissidents.[19] He soon attracted the attention of Dublin Castle, however, and by 1895, he remembered, he 'could not go anywhere without having a brace of detectives on my heels'.[20] This, along with youthful wanderlust, contributed to his decision to emigrate to South Africa along with Arthur Griffith.

When the Second Boer War began in 1899, the Irish republicans in the Transvaal quickly mobilised to form the 'Irish Brigade', in which John MacBride was second in command, adopting the rank of major. The brigade operated effectively as a commando unit and, by all accounts, MacBride soldiered well and was a capable leader of his men, despite the establishment of a rival Irish unit.[21] Ireland, however, was never far away; in the midst of his participation in a fully fledged imperial war, MacBride found himself at the centre of a bitter provincial battle: the by-election in South Mayo of 1900. When Michael Davitt resigned his Westminster seat, partly in protest at British actions in the Transvaal, advanced nationalists in Ireland, led by Griffith and Rooney, proposed that John MacBride contest the election, thereby striking a blow against the British war effort and in favour of Irish separatism. Griffith and Rooney attempted to have MacBride stand unopposed, arguing to the dominant Irish Parliamentary Party (IPP) that, if elected, MacBride would be prevented from taking his seat on account of his treasonable activity in the Transvaal, and a further by-election would then be held, allowing the IPP candidate to win through.[22]

This proposal did not meet with the approval of the IPP hierarchy, and the little-known figure of John O'Donnell was prevailed upon to stand for the IPP against MacBride. A nasty campaign ensued: vitriolic insults traded in the press, intimidation on both sides, and at least one incident of stoning.[23] But the strength

18 NLI, Fred Allan Papers, MS 29817, Notebook written by John MacBride, 1905; Leon Ó Broin, *Revolutionary Underground: The Story of the Irish Republican Brotherhood, 1858–1925* (Dublin: Gill & Macmillan, 1976), pp. 36–40.

19 Ó Broin, *Revolutionary Underground*, pp. 59–63; Owen McGee, *The IRB: the Irish Republican Brotherhood from the Land League to Sinn Féin* (Dublin: Four Courts Press, 2005), pp. 241–3.

20 NLI, Fred Allan Papers, MS 29817, Notebook written by John MacBride, 1905.

21 Donal P. McCracken, *MacBride's Brigade: Irish Commandos in the Anglo-Boer war* (Dublin: Four Courts Press, 1999), pp. 29–30.

22 Patrick Maume, *The Long Gestation: Irish Nationalist Life 1891–1918* (Dublin: Gill & Macmillan, 1999), pp. 34–5.

23 John O'Leary was a prominent supporter of MacBride, writing to O'Brien 'What can any obscure O'Donnell or any other do just now for Mayo or for Ireland which is comparable to what that man is doing who is actively engaged in putting bullets into the bodies of Englishmen in South Africa?' NLI, Fred Allan Papers, MS 26758, John O'Leary to William O'Brien, 24 February 1900.

of the IPP electoral machine pulled through: O'Donnell polled 2,401 votes to MacBride's 427 on a turnout of less than twenty-five per cent.[24] As the war dragged on, however, and the superior number of the British Army began to tell, the Irish Brigade was forced to disband. The Boer government arranged for the men of the Irish Brigade to receive passage to Trieste, and onwards to America, and for each to receive a small sum of money. Major MacBride went to Paris, to meet his family and friends. Among their number was his former comrade in Langlaate goldmine, Arthur Griffith, and Griffith's close associate, Maud Gonne.

Marriage and Divorce

Although the paths of Maud Gonne and John MacBride had crossed in the past – they had both been members of the Celtic Literary Society, and Gonne had been a prominent member of the Irish Transvaal Committee – it was in Paris in late 1900 that they really made each other's acquaintance. Along with Arthur Griffith and other members of the Paris Young Ireland Society, she was on the platform at Gare de Lyon to greet the 'wiry, soldierly-looking man, with red hair and skin burnt brick-red by the South African sun'.[25] That first evening, MacBride and Gonne sat up all night, talking of the war in the Transvaal, of the state of revolutionary activity in Ireland, and of MacBride's planned lecture tour of America. Their burgeoning relationship appears to have been entirely constructed upon their shared commitment to advanced Irish nationalism; personal attraction played a decidedly secondary role.[26]

Whatever the psychological motivation for their relationship, their romance blossomed during the lecture tour of the United States in the spring of 1901, on which Gonne joined MacBride some three months in. The tour had mixed success: MacBride's stilted speeches failed to really stir the crowds who turned out to greet the Boer War hero, while Gonne's attacks on the United Irish League cut little ice with Irish-American audiences accustomed to supporting constitutional Irish nationalism.[27] But the tour bore fruit of a more personal nature: by June 1902, having spent more and more time in each other's company, Gonne agreed to MacBride's proposal of marriage. MacBride claimed later that the idea to marry was entirely his wife's:

> One evening she told me that she would place her whole future life in my hands to direct as I would wish if I would only make her my wife, that she had suffered greatly and wanted to try and be a good woman. I was moved by her tears, felt very sad for her, and thinking I was doing a good act for my country and for herself I consented to marry Maud Gonne. I was foolish.[28]

---

24 McCracken, *MacBride's Brigade*, p. 76.

25 Gonne MacBride, *A Servant of the Queen*, p. 319.

26 See Ward, *Maud Gonne*, p. 69 on Maud's Electra-like preference for soldierly men; and Foster, *The Apprentice Mage*, p. 284 on John MacBride's 'incarnation of 'the authentic and uncompromising Irish nationalism to which [Maud Gonne] had dedicated her life'.

27 Nancy Cardozo, *Maud Gonne: Lucky Eyes and a High Heart* (London: Gollancz, 1979), pp. 205–6.

28 NLI, Fred Allan Papers, MS 29817, Notebook written by John MacBride, 1905; Gonne MacBride, *A Servant of the Queen*, p. 342; Foster, *The Apprentice Mage*, p. 284.

While this account was written from the jaundiced perspective of an ex-husband, Gonne's letters to her close family indicate a weariness with solitude which is in keeping with MacBride's version.[29] Equally important, marriage to MacBride provided a conventional environment in which to raise Iseult, whose illegitimacy was already proving difficult in polite society. With the security of married life, Gonne could take Iseult out of the quiet convent school at Laval, and could even travel back to Ireland with her daughter without fear of ostracism. However, Iseult disliked MacBride intensely, and reacted negatively to news of the impending union.[30] Moreover, in her autobiography, Gonne recalled the opposition of count-less friends and family; it seems that almost everyone who knew the couple predicted disaster for their union. It is indicative of the stubborn nature of both parties to the marriage that this flood of letters from the closest of family and friends did not give them pause.

First in the sequence of events leading up to the wedding was Gonne's recanting of the Protestant 'heresy'; this took place on 15 February 1903 in the Chapelle des Dames de Saint Thérèse at Laval; two days later, Gonne was received into the Catholic Church. The wedding ceremony took place in the Church of Saint-Honoré d'Eylau, and at the British consulate, as required under French law. It has been described as 'a new form of political theatre':[31] the union of Ireland's Joan of Arc and the Boer War hero was replete with a theatricality entirely of its moment. Echoes of the military experience of MacBride were to be found throughout the proceedings: the ceremony was conducted by Father van Hecke, former chaplain to the Irish Brigade, and the green flag of the brigade was carried by the best man, Victor Collins. Due weight was given to Gonne's political activism, and the blue emblem of Inghidhine na hÉireann was carried alongside the brigade's flag.[32] The newlyweds departed on honeymoon to Spain, apparently on a secret mission to assassinate King Edward VII; this came to nothing, apparently stymied by a combination of faulty intelligence and MacBride's drunkenness. The wedding trip came to an abrupt end, and the couple packed up and returned to France the following morning.

Following that inauspicious start to their married life, further indications of the rapidly growing distance between the couple were found in Gonne's frequent and lengthy visits to Ireland during the summer of 1903, where she coordinated the activities of Inghnidhne na hÉireann in opposition to the visit of Edward VII to Dublin. Dedicated as she was to her nationalist activities, they also provided her with a means of escaping the nightmare that was becoming her marriage. The difference in social status between the couple quickly told: the major very much resented his financial dependence on his wife, and even her wedding gift

29 To her sister, Maud Gonne wrote, 'Neither you nor anyone on earth quite knows the hard life I have led, for I never told of my troubles ... now I see the chance, without injuring my work, for a little happiness and peace in my personal life and I am taking it.' Maud Gonne to Kathleen Gonne Pilcher, n. d. [1903?] quoted in Balliett, 'The lives – and lies – of Maud Gonne', pp. 31–2.
30 Gonne MacBride, *A Servant of the Queen*, p. 348. See also Jeffares, 'Iseult Gonne', p. 207.
31 Foster, *The Apprentice Mage*, p. 286.
32 *United Irishman*, 28 February 1903, cited in Ward, *Maud Gonne*, p. 78.

to him of £3000 was viewed as an affront to his old-fashioned masculinity.[33] But that summer Gonne also realised she was pregnant, and returned to her husband, her daughter, and her responsibilities in Colleville. These, then, were the circumstances into which John Seaġan MacBride was born, on 26 January 1904. From the beginning, Gonne treasured her son, at long last a replacement for the lost Georges.[34] But where her grief for 'Georginet' had to be largely concealed, her devotion to her second son could be fully expressed. He would remain the very centre of her focus over the coming years, as her marriage disintegrated into divorce and her fashionable Parisian existence transmuted into lonely exile.

Intending that her son be christened in Ireland, Gonne brought him to Dublin in April 1904. Fearing arrest, Major MacBride could not travel with his family, although he arranged for his mother and brothers to be present at the baptism, which took place at the Church of the Three Patrons in Rathgar on 1 May. The veteran Fenian John O'Leary stood as Seán's godfather, although the ceremony almost did not take place when the parish priest objected to O'Leary's participation.[35] However, the breakdown of the MacBride-Gonne marriage was gathering speed. That summer, Gonne evidently gave a full and frank confession to her husband of her personal history before their marriage, including her liaisons with Millevoye and others, and the illegitimate children she bore the Boulangist politician. The effect of this account was to turn MacBride even more strongly against her: 'I knew she had led an evil life before our marriage but did not know it was as bad as I found out afterwards ... She is a vile woman. "Woman", it is a disgrace to womanhood to call her by that holy name.'[36]

Gonne's visits to her friends in Ireland and London continued, but in autumn 1904, events took a more serious turn. In addition to the usual tales of MacBride's drunken carousing in the company of similarly exiled Irishmen, her closest friend in Paris, Madame Avril, informed her that Iseult had been molested by MacBride.[37] It was in the wake of this allegation, coupled with reports of similar attacks upon female members of the household, that the marriage entered its final stages. When MacBride finally decided to risk travelling to Ireland to visit his family, Gonne took her opportunity to begin the process of dissolving their union. The disintegration of their union exploded onto the nationalist political and literary landscape, and the public rehearsal of their private differences, charges and counter-charges, and the most intimate details of their personal lives fuelled gossip in Dublin, London and Paris.[38]

---

33   NLI, Fred Allan Papers, MS 29819.
34   NLI, Fred Allan Papers, MS 29817, John MacBride notebook.
35   Michael Farrell, 'The extraordinary life and times of Seán MacBride: Part I', *Magill*, vol. 6, no. 3 (Christmas 1982), p. 17; Uinseann MacEoin, *Survivors: The Story of Ireland's Struggle as Told through some of her Outstanding Living People Recalling Events from the Days of Davitt, through James Connolly, Brugha, Collins, Liam Mellows, and Rory O'Connor to the Present Time* (Dublin: Argenta Publications, 1980), p. 107ff.
36   NLI, Fred Allan Papers, MS 29817, John MacBride notebook, 1905.
37   MacBride White and Jeffares (eds.), *The Gonne-Yeats Letters*, p. 183.
38   For more on the detail of the Gonne-MacBride divorce case, including reactions within nationalist Ireland, see Caoimhe Nic Dháibhéid, '"This is a case in which Irish national considerations must be taken into account": the breakdown of the MacBride-Gonne marriage, 1904–1908', *Irish Historical Studies*, xxxvii, no. 146 (Nov. 2010), pp. 64–87.

While nationalist and literary circles buzzed with news of the affair, in Paris, the divorce dragged on. After John MacBride rejected proposed terms for settlement and custody arrangements, Gonne formally appealed to the law courts on 3 February 1905. The documents lodged at the Civil Tribunal in Paris made public for the first time at least some of the charges against MacBride, including his 'jealous, suspicious and violent temper ... his intemperate habits, his unbridled licentiousness, [and] his unscrupulous immorality'. In greater detail, the application charged that on Christmas night 1903 (when Gonne was eight months pregnant), MacBride arrived inebriated with a friend to the marital home in Passy and 'picked a quarrel with his friend and was looking in his pocket for a revolver when the petitioner intervened and succeeded, after having received several kicks from her husband, in dragging him into the bedroom'. Various other charges of drunkenness followed, as well as allegations of mental cruelty to his wife. More seriously, at least in the eyes of French law (which did not consider drunkenness alone grounds for divorce), it was alleged that MacBride had made improper advances towards female members of the household.[39]

MacBride's defence largely consisted of presenting testimonials as to his fine character (thereby refuting the charges of immorality and drunkenness) and a counter-suit for separation. As the case dragged on through 1905 and into 1906, Irish media interest failed to abate, and weekly reports were carried in the principal nationalist newspapers. When the *Irish Independent* repeated in full the charges Gonne had preferred against MacBride, including the allegations of adultery and immorality, he sued for libel. This added a further dimension to an already complex set of legal proceedings: in order to sue in a Dublin court, MacBride had to prove Irish citizenship. However, the French court had established MacBride as a South African citizen (owing to his citizenship oath during the Boer War). This was essential in order for the divorce case to be tried under French law. The complications arising from this addition to the legal mixture resulted in further delays to the resolution of the Paris proceedings.

A final verdict arrived at last on 8 August 1906. The judge ruled that, resulting from MacBride's successful establishment of Irish nationality and domicile during the *Independent* libel case, only a legal separation could be granted. Under the terms of this separation, Gonne was granted sole custody and guardianship of her son, while MacBride was to be permitted 'the right of visiting the child at his [ex-]wife's house every Monday, and when the child shall be over six years old [the court] allows the father to have him for one month in the year'.[40] Gonne appealed the provision for monthly visits, and in January 1908 succeeded in having these suppressed. The right to weekly visits were upheld, although these were described by Gonne as 'a dead letter', owing to MacBride's apparent lack of interest in seeing his son during the previous three years since the marriage had foundered.[41]

39   NLI, Fred Allan Papers, MS 29,816, Petition of Maud Gonne MacBride to the President of the Civil Tribunal, Paris, 3 February 1905.

40   MacBride White and Jeffares (eds.), *The Gonne-Yeats letters*, Maud Gonne to W. B. Yeats, 8 August 1906, pp. 232–3.

41   Janis Londraville and Richard Londraville (eds.), *Too Long a Sacrifice: the Letters of John Quinn and Maud Gonne* (London: Associated University Presses, 1999), Maud Gonne to John Quinn, 25 March 1908, p. 37.

In the event, the visitation arrangements were rarely acted upon. MacBride decided to rebuild his life in Ireland, and risked arrest by openly returning. The new Liberal government seems to have allowed him to live in relative peace, although the authorities kept a close eye on his activities. Seeking an income, he attempted unsuccessfully to reinvent himself as a journalist before finally securing a position as Water Bailiff to Dublin City Corporation.[42] He retained his involvement in the IRB, however, and in 1911 was appointed to its Supreme Council, representing his home province of Connaught. He was soon replaced by Seán MacDiarmada, as a secret clique began to prepare for the rebellion to come in 1916. Although he had been present at a September 1914 meeting where a decision was taken to assist Germany during the war, as IRB plans solidified for a rebellion against British rule, MacBride was evidently kept in the dark.[43] But his involvement in the rising of 1916 would transform his reputation within Irish republicanism and his place within his son's memory.

Early Childhood

The rancorous divorce of his parents was the defining feature of Seán MacBride's early life and cast a hideous shadow over his childhood. The inadequacy of the final divorce settlement, from a legal perspective, meant that John MacBride could theoretically challenge for custody under Irish law, should Gonne be proved to be domiciled in Ireland. Initially, Gonne had hoped to raise her family in Ireland, but the judgement handed down by the French court effectively made this impossible. The possibility that her son might be snatched from her, either legally or outside the confines of the law, was a constant worry. Gonne extracted a harsh revenge on her former husband by effectively sabotaging his relationship with his son: in making French the sole language of her household, she made meaningful conversation between the two practically impossible.[44] In later life Seán MacBride recalled the inadequacy of his relationship with his father, noting that there 'was not much [contact]. I saw him three or four times, in summer periods ... and I used to get occasional postcards from him.'[45]

MacBride's memoir, *That Day's Struggle*, opens in 1916 with the execution of his father in the aftermath of the Easter Rising, largely skipping over his childhood in France.[46] However, the detail of the first twelve years of his life can be reconstructed using his mother's correspondence, biographical detail relating to his half-sister Iseult Gonne, and a variety of memoirs in which Maud Gonne's Passy household makes a cameo appearance. Whereas Iseult suffered much as a child from her mother's frequent absences, in the wake of the traumatic divorce case Gonne severely curtailed her political activities, and was a much more stable presence in the home. Another constant figure was M. Barry O'Delaney, who had

42 Jordan, *Major John MacBride*, p. 90; Ó Broin, *Revolutionary Underground*, p. 137.
43 Ó Broin, *Revolutionary Underground*, p. 156; McCracken, *MacBride's Brigade*, pp. 106–12.
44 Balliett, 'The lives – and lies – of Maud Gonne', p. 40.
45 'Seán MacBride Remembers', RTÉ television documentary, originally broadcast 1989.
46 Seán MacBride, *That Day's Struggle: A Memoir 1904–1951*, ed. Caitriona Lawlor (Dublin: Currach Press, 2005), pp. 16–17.

featured in the divorce trial. The family divided their time between Passy and the summerhouse at Colleville, where the children could escape the congestion of Paris. Whether in Paris or Colleville, there was a constant stream of visitors; the most habitual guest was Yeats. In 1908, he and Maud Gonne apparently rekindled their spiritual marriage, and embarked upon a brief physical affair before settling back into their old platonic relationship. Although Yeats disliked young children, and preferred the dreamier Iseult, he did teach MacBride how to fly a kite on the beaches of Normandy. Another literary visitor was the novelist James Stephens, described by MacBride as 'the idol of my youth'; he befriended the boy and took him on outings to stamp shops and *pâtisseries* in Paris.[47]

Political activists were also regular figures in the Passy household, of an Irish and international flavour. Callers included Madame Cama, the writer Rabindranath Tagore, and a young student named Jawaharlal Nehru.[48] Arthur Lynch, commander of the second Irish Brigade during the Boer War, was a fairly regular visitor, as was Roger Casement.[49] Casement called to see Maud Gonne each time he passed through Paris, and they discussed Irish affairs openly. The pungency of nationalist views were tempered somewhat by the frequent presence of Gonne's English relations, her sister Kathleen Pilcher and her cousin May Bertie-Clay. Both women had married high-ranking British army officers and, as such, they and their young families represented an alternate perspective on world affairs. Despite the divergence of political opinion, Gonne remained on good terms with her relatives, and Iseult and MacBride benefited from exposure to another milieu.

If the household in which MacBride spent his childhood was remarkable for its singularity, MacBride himself was equally peculiar as a child. From birth there were concerns for his health, which grew more pronounced as he advanced in years. As a baby he was extremely attached to his mother and reacted hysterically if she disappeared from sight. More worryingly, the least excitement could cause him to lose consciousness: 'If he was toddling after his mother and a door was banged by the wind she would find him unconscious behind it.' Madame Dangien, the governess, later confided in Iseult that the French doctors, to whom MacBride had been taken in an attempt to get to the bottom of the fainting fits, had not thought he would live past his seventh birthday.[50] In addition to his already delicate constitution, MacBride was a sickly child. He contracted influenza in January 1909; altogether more serious was his bout of appendicitis in 1912. Gonne was stricken with fear, the illness of MacBride bringing back painful memories of the death of Georges. Iseult, who was probably jealous of the close bond between her mother and MacBride not to speak of the regularity of their relationship, felt that the symptoms were psychosomatic, and that her brother 'could work up a temperature when his mother was going away'.[51] At any event, it was decided to operate

47 MacBride, *That Day's Struggle*, p. 17.
48 Farrell, 'The extraordinary life and times of Seán MacBride', p. 18.
49 MacBride, *That Day's Struggle*, p. 16.
50 A. Norman Jeffares, Anna MacBride White and Christina Bridgewater (eds.), *Letters to W. B. Yeats & Ezra Pound from Iseult Gonne: A Girl that knew all Dante Once* (Basingstoke: Palgrave, 2004), pp. 17 and 33.
51 Jeffares, MacBride White and Bridgewater (eds.), *Letters to W. B. Yeats & Ezra Pound from Iseult Gonne*, p. 33.

despite Gonne's reluctance, and the appendix was duly removed. While he was still convalescing, MacBride contracted measles and, in later years, chickenpox, regular bouts of gastroenteritis, and assorted mystery complaints.[52]

Education and War

Along with his health, MacBride's education was a matter that would preoccupy his mother for much of his childhood. Initially, he was schooled at home with his sister. Iseult, who was receiving instruction from Yeats, also took it upon herself to tutor MacBride in art, poetry and literature.[53] Being schooled at home made for much flexibility in his early childhood, and the family was able to switch homes from Paris to Colleville without overly disrupting his education. He also received religious instruction: Gonne's close association with the convent in Laval meant that both Iseult and MacBride were exposed at an early age to a devout and rigorously intellectual French Catholicism. They attended the Easter ceremonies of 1910 at Bayeux Cathedral, and were regular visitors to the mysterious medieval monastery-fortress of the Mont St-Michel.[54] A year later, there was an even more important event in MacBride's religious development, when the family journeyed to Italy. There, they attended a private mass with Pope Pius X, received holy communion from his hands, and were presented with holy medals.[55] Gonne used this opening as an opportunity to enlist Vatican support for her latest project: the provision of free meals for Dublin schoolchildren, which had run into opposition from the Irish hierarchy.[56]

Although Gonne retained her fear that John MacBride might stage a kidnapping of her son, her anxiety had abated somewhat by the summer of 1910, when she spent two months in the west of Ireland with the children. Moreover, they took a house in Mulranney, County Mayo, a short distance from the MacBride homestead in Westport, where they visited family members.[57] Despite the bitterness of the legal proceedings following the disintegration of the MacBride-Gonne marriage, cordial relations were evidently resumed between the two families at this point. However, this was all contingent on the non-appearance of John MacBride, who apparently remained in Dublin throughout the summer.

As he grew older, MacBride needed a more formal education than daily lessons with a governess. Gonne placed him at a Jesuit college, the renowned St-Louis de Gonzague at rue Benjamin Franklin, in time for the beginning of the school year in September 1911. MacBride thrived in this challenging environment: Gonne

---

52 MacBride White and Jeffares (eds.), *The Gonne-Yeats Letters*, p. 316ff; Londraville and Londraville, *The Letters of John Quinn and Maud Gonne*, Maud Gonne to John Quinn, 11 April 1912, p. 96. Barry O'Delaney kept the removed appendix as 'a souvenir of her glory boy'.

53 Young, *Flowering Dusk*, p. 102.

54 MacBride White and Jeffares (eds.), *The Gonne-Yeats Letters*, Maud Gonne to W. B. Yeats, 28 September 1907, p. 246.

55 MacBride, *That Day's Struggle*, illustration 7; Jeffares, MacBride White and Bridgewater (eds.), *Letters to W. B. Yeats and Ezra Pound from Iseult Gonne*, p. 25.

56 Londraville and Londraville (eds.), *The Letters of John Quinn and Maud Gonne*, Maud Gonne to John Quinn, 17 June 1911, p. 77; Ward, *Maud Gonne*, pp. 98–101.

57 Ward, *Maud Gonne*, p. 97.

writing: 'My little Jean is making alarming progress at school; I do all I can to inculcate idleness and prevent the master putting him in a higher class than his age warrants.'[58] She also saw to it that he received an adequate 'Irish' education, instructing him herself in Irish history during the summer holidays at Colleville:

> I was to do one hour [of] Irish history a day with her, and she had all the Irish history books. I wasn't particularly enthusiastic, I might as well tell you, because it used to cut into my holiday programme so to speak ... but she insisted on this and I learned quite a lot of Irish history from her.[59]

In teaching him Irish history, Gonne imparted to her son a reflexive, atavistic hatred of British misdeeds in Ireland, and a belief that Ireland's historical troubles were solely due to British malfeasance. She also arranged for MacBride to receive Irish lessons, although these were rather less of a success. Being almost wholly Francophone, it was difficult for MacBride to summon up any enthusiasm for learning the Irish language, and his tutor also fell short: 'A Frenchman who knew Irish used to come and give me occasional lessons ... I always felt that he really didn't know an awful lot himself.'[60] MacBride never adhered to the Irish-Ireland ethos which gained currency among Irish nationalists at the beginning of the twentieth century, and the language question never really interested him. He always had trouble with Irish, and when Fianna Fáil deputies in 1948 attempted to embarrass the English public school- and Trinity-educated Noël Browne by submitting Dáil questions in Irish, they could probably have had more success targeting his party leader.[61]

It was still hoped that the family would be able to return to Ireland at some point, and Gonne contacted Patrick Pearse in 1914, with a view to enrolling MacBride at St Enda's, the innovative school he had established at Rathfarnham, County Dublin. MacBride recalled being brought to Dublin to be interviewed by Pearse in early 1914, where Pearse and his mother 'had a long discussion, first of all about my schooling, what courses [and] languages I should do and what education I should receive'.[62] Then the conversation switched to Irish politics, and MacBride, focusing largely on the smell of fresh paint from recent renovations, lost interest. But the sudden outbreak of the First World War in August 1914 meant that all their plans had to be changed.

In July 1914, Gonne travelled with Iseult and MacBride to Arrens, a small village in the Pyrennées. There they were joined by Helena Molony; initially the little group enjoyed an idyllic month, walking in the mountains and dining in the village inn, but the war clouds were gathering. The outbreak of war was signalled to the villagers in the most dramatic fashion, and hugely impressed 10-year-old MacBride:

> There is in France and in other countries on the continent of Europe a thing called a *tocsin* ... whenever a disaster threatens an area, the church bell is rung,

58 MacBride White and Jeffares (eds.), Maud Gonne to W. B. Yeats, n.d. January 1912, p. 307.
59 'Seán MacBride Remembers'.
60 'Seán MacBride Remembers'.
61 John Horgan, *Noël Browne: Passionate Outsider* (Dublin: Gill and Macmillan, 2000), p. 60.
62 MacBride, *That Day's Struggle*, p. 16.

in a particular rhythm ... I'd never heard it, neither had any of the children ever heard it, but they knew of it from their parents ... and the minute the church bell rang, the *tocsin*, they <u>fled</u> in every direction and I fled home as well. This was the start of World War I.[63]

Gonne was completely overwhelmed by the outbreak of war, describing it to Yeats as 'race suicide', and 'an inconceivable madness which has taken hold of Europe'.[64] She soon pulled herself together, however, and by the end of the month was effectively running a makeshift hospital at Argelès-sur-mer, a fashionable resort on the Mediterranean, where the casino had been commandeered to cope with the train-loads of wounded arriving from the front.[65] Gonne was a regular Red Cross nurse, while Iseult and Helena Moloney were employed as helpers. MacBride too played his part, acting as a messenger boy in the wards, fetching cigarettes and sweets for the convalescent soldiers. But he also had a more serious task, removing amputated limbs from the surgical theatres, getting a 'fairly early taste of war and death and destruction', to which he quickly became inured.[66]

They remained in Argelès until Christmas 1914, before returning to a subdued and grieving Paris. MacBride returned to school in January, while his mother and sister resumed their duties at Paris-Plage within the sound of cannon fire on the front.[67] Their own extended family did not escape the horror of war: Tommy Pilcher, Gonne's nephew, was killed in March 1915 at Neuve-Chapelle, and Henri Millevoye, Iseult's half-brother, also died in battle at the end of September 1915.[68] As the new year dawned with no sign of the war abating and attempts to secure a passport to return to Ireland having failed, the family resigned themselves to spending the duration of the conflict in France. Gonne revealed to John Quinn that she intending leaving Europe when peace finally came:

> I believe after this war I shall come to America with Iseult and the boy and get naturalised, for Europe won't be a place to live in for generations. If the allies win, only England and Russia will be strong and the vilest jingoism and imperialism *à la* Rudyard Kipling will prevail.[69]

But the actions of a small group of rebels in Dublin on Easter Monday changed the direction of all their lives.

---

63 'Seán MacBride Remembers'.
64 MacBride White and Jeffares (eds.), *The Gonne-Yeats Letters*, Maud Gonne to W. B. Yeats, 26 August 1914, pp. 347–8.
65 Ward, *Maud Gonne*, p. 107.
66 'Seán MacBride Remembers'.
67 Jeffares, MacBride White and Bridgewater (eds.), *Letters to W. B. Yeats and Ezra Pound from Iseult Gonne*, p. 46.
68 MacBride White and Jeffares (eds.), *The Gonne-Yeats Letters*, Maud Gonne to W. B. Yeats, 1 October 1915, pp. 356 and 359.
69 Londraville and Londraville (eds.), *The Letters of Maud Gonne and John Quinn*, Maud Gonne to John Quinn, 4 February 1916, p. 166.

2

'Fighting the Tans at Fourteen':[1] 1916–1918

Ireland's seismic political transformations from the years 1916 to 1923 were paralleled by a similar period of immense personal change for MacBride. His relatively tranquil existence in Paris, albeit somewhat disrupted by wartime privations, came to a sudden end as news of the Easter rebellion filtered through. His life over the following eight years would change utterly: first, a massive psychological readjustment, as John MacBride's execution transformed him in the eyes of his estranged wife and son from feared bogeyman to revered martyr. Second, Maud Gonne's urge to be in the thick of the action drove the family first to London, then on to Dublin, MacBride thus forced to leave behind forever the security of his childhood home and his first language in exchange for a peripatetic existence in what was effectively a foreign country. This sense of displacement was reinforced by the imprisonment of his mother in Holloway Prison. MacBride was then shipped around from trusted family friend to casual acquaintance, his half-sister unable or unwilling to care for him. Eventually, he settled down to a thoroughly eccentric education at the hands of a Benedictine maverick. These were destabilising years, politically and personally: MacBride's own physical and emotional upheavals mirrored by wider turmoil in Ireland.

Easter Rising

John MacBride was not part of the inner sanctum of the IRB which planned the Rising of 1916; on Easter Monday, he was on his way to meet his brother ahead of a family wedding, and happened upon Thomas MacDonagh and his Second Battalion of Irish Volunteers at Stephen's Green.[2] On account of his military experience, MacBride was appointed second-in-command to MacDonagh as the Volunteers seized the Jacob's biscuit factory. A calm, unruffled, soldierly figure amid the chaos of Jacob's, his stoicism helped to soothe the consternation caused by news of Pearse's capitulation on Easter Saturday, and the Second Battalion

---

1 Seán MacBride quoted in *Sunday Independent*, 14 September 1980.
2 T. M. Healy, *Leaders and Letters of My Day: Volume II* (London: Thornton Butterworth, 1928), p. 563. On the Easter Rising, see especially Charles Townshend, *Easter 1916: The Irish Rebellion* (London: Penguin, 2006) and Fearghal McGarry, *The Rising: Ireland: Easter 1916* (Oxford: Oxford University Press, 2010).

marched in formation to a formal surrender. Glad to have had 'the privilege of two days against the tyranny of the British government, one in South Africa, and, thanks be to God, today one in Ireland', MacBride was court-martialled on 4 May 1916, where his previous record against the British in South Africa was brought to the court's attention. The expected death sentence was passed, although MacBride made a forceful impression on the court. W. E. Wylie, a Dublin barrister appointed to represent the accused, later recalled that 'General Blackadder told me the next day that when in South Africa he thought of McBride [sic] as about the lowest thing that crawled but "damn it! I'll never think of him now without taking my hat off to a brave man."'[3] John MacBride was executed by firing squad in Kilmainham Gaol on 5 May.

Seán MacBride spent the Easter holidays, as usual, with his mother and half-sister in Colleville; there, news reached them of the unfolding drama in Dublin. The family hastily returned to Paris in early May, as reports of the executions filtered through. There is some confusion as to how exactly 12-year-old Seán learned of his father's death. In a letter to Florence Farr, W. B. Yeats places the family at home together as word came through:

> When [Maud] heard the news of her husbands [sic] execution she went to Iseult, paper in hand and looking pale and said 'MacBride has been shot' and then went to her little boy who was making a boat and said, 'your father has died for his country – he did not behave well to us – but now we can think of him with honour and then said to Iseult 'Now we can return to Ireland.'[4]

But by Seán MacBride's own account, news of the execution reached him while at school in St Louis de Gonzague.[5] What seems to have made the most significant immediate impression was the rector's inclusion of John MacBride in the weekly ceremony commemorating the fallen fathers, brothers and uncles of the pupils in the Great War:

> The name of my father was read out and the rector made a very eloquent speech, and indeed I always felt gratitude towards him then, saying that my father had been executed by the British, who were the allies of the French, but who had occupied Ireland and treated Ireland as a colony, and that the Irish people were fighting for their liberation. It was a small nation like Belgium, fighting for its own freedom, and my father had been one of the Irish patriots that had risen against Britain and deserved their respect and their prayers.[6]

An enormous adjustment was required on the part of MacBride in the wake of the executions: brought up to fear and revile his father, communication between

---

3 National Archives London [NAL], 89/30/2, W. E. Wylie Papers, Unpublished memoir, p. 30; Memorandum from Maxwell to Asquith, reproduced in Brian Barton, *From Behind a Closed Door: Secret Court Martial Records of the 1916 Easter Rising* (Belfast: Blackstaff Press, 2002), p. 215.
4 W. B. Yeats to Florence Farr, 19 August [1916], quoted in R. F. Foster, *W. B. Yeats: A Life: II: The Arch-poet* (Oxford: Oxford University Press, 2003), p. 55.
5 Seán MacBride, *That Day's Struggle: A Memoir, 1904–1951*, ed. Caitriona Lawlor (Dublin: Currach Press, 2005), p. 13.
6 'Seán MacBride Remembers', RTÉ television documentary, originally broadcast 1989.

father and son had been desultory in the years following the final separation of John MacBride and Maud Gonne, effectively reduced to a sporadic 'written correspondence'.[7] But John MacBride's participation in the events of Easter week not only secured for him a position in the republican pantheon, but also a revered place within his son's memory. For his son, the key importance of the Easter rebellion lay in the complete rehabilitation of his father's reputation. Maud Gonne too was obliged to come to terms with the effective beatification of all those who were executed in the rebellion; her unflinching hatred of her estranged husband was transmuted into a stoic acceptance of his transformation. Her letters to Yeats reveal the shift in her thinking: 'Major MacBride by his death has left a name for Seagan to be proud of. Those who die for Ireland are sacred. Those who enter Eternity by the great door of Sacrifice atone for all – in one moment they do more than all our effort.'[8] Similarly, to her old friend John Quinn she wrote, '[John MacBride] has died for Ireland and his son will bear an honoured name. I remember nothing else.'[9]

Return to Ireland

In the wake of the Rising, Maud Gonne decided that the family should return to Ireland. With her estranged husband safely out of the way, there could be no nasty custody battle for her son, and the long-standing desire to have him educated in Ireland could come to pass. But on 18 November 1916, their Parisian lives packed up and ready for the journey to Ireland, the family discovered that they were to be permitted to travel only as far as England, on the orders of the War Office.[10] Maud Gonne immediately wrote to Lloyd George to demand an explanation, and attempted to enlist the help of several of the Irish MPs, with rather desultory results:

> John Redmond replied 'he could not interfere in such a matter.' Tim Healy replied that John Redmond was the only person who could help if he *would*. John Dillon said he would do his best. Stephen Gwynn wrote me a long letter saying that being at the front himself he could not do much but if I were willing to support Redmond in Ireland he would try![11]

With little help forthcoming, they were forced to resume their lives between Paris and Colleville as 1916 passed into 1917. Having relinquished their comfortable apartment in anticipation of the return to Dublin, they squeezed into a tiny attic flat where, in the freezing winter, life seemed grim. Iseult wrote to Yeats

---

7 MacBride, *That Day's Struggle*, p. 13.

8 Anna MacBride White and A. Norman Jeffares (eds.), *The Gonne-Yeats letters, 1893–1939: Always Your Friend* (London: Hutchinson, 1992), M. Gonne to W. B. Yeats, 11 May 1916, p. 375.

9 Janis Londraville and Richard Londraville (eds.), *Too Long a Sacrifice: The Letters of John Quinn and Maud Gonne* (London: Associated Universities Press, 1999), Maud Gonne to John Quinn, 11 May 1916, p. 169.

10 Londraville and Londraville (eds.), *The Letters of John Quinn and Maud Gonne*, M. Gonne to J. Quinn, 24 November 1916, p. 181.

11 Londraville and Londraville (eds.), *The Letters of John Quinn and Maud Gonne*, Maud Gonne to John Quinn, 11 March 1917, p. 186.

describing the mood in the family: 'At meals Moura [Maud Gonne] talks of war, I of the cold weather, Bichon [Seán] of his school and we all conclude "When will it ever end!"'[12] Iseult's letters to Yeats provide a useful snapshot into family life at this point, with an emerging portrait of the 13-year-old MacBride: 'He is nearly as tall as we are, speaks with a man's voice and has at last acquired some smoothness and grace of manner.'[13] War-time shortages had begun to tell, compounded by Maud Gonne's losses on the French stock exchange, and by spring 1918 the family were in Colleville, 'living on the potato field [she] planted ... and the torpedoed fish and coal, wood etc. washed up treasures the sea brings us'.[14]

By the summer of 1917, the bulk of the 'political prisoners' having been released, Gonne chafed ever more strongly against the apparent intransigence of government policy. She wrote to Major Lampton, head of the English Passport Office in France: 'I suppose as all the Irish Sinn Féin prisoners have now been released and allowed to return to Ireland, the English War Office will make no further difficulties to my return home.'[15] In spite of her fear that she and her children would be interned on reaching Southampton, she was anxious to get Seán to Ireland in time for the beginning of the school year and, accompanied by Yeats, they sailed to England on 17 September. The return to Britain was not without incident: they were searched at Southampton and served with a notice under the Defence of the Realm Act prohibiting their journey to Ireland.[16] The excitement of the return – Yeats wrote of Maud 'in a joyous and self-forgetting condition of political hate the like of which I have not yet encountered' – was tempered by Iseult's deep depression following her refusal of Yeats's proposal of marriage the previous month.[17]

With emotional turmoil and high political feeling running through the family, Yeats feared that Gonne would attempt 'something wild'. He was relieved, therefore, when she announced her intention to remain in London for the time being, studying design at London Central College Art School and renting a flat in King's Road, Chelsea.[18] These London days were later recalled by MacBride as 'a type of double-life', in which restored relations with the Gonne relatives mingled with new, more exciting contacts with Patricia Lynch and the Pankhurst sisters.[19] His first taste of the exoticism of parliamentary life came in December 1917, when the *Irish Independent* – which had regularly commented on the Gonne-MacBride family's limbo-like existence in London – reported on the visit of 'an interesting

12 A. Norman Jeffares, Anna MacBride White and Christina Bridgwater (eds.), *Letters to W. B. Yeats & Ezra Pound from Iseult Gonne: A Girl that knew all Dante Once* (Basingstoke: Palgrave, 2004), Iseult Gonne to W. B. Yeats, [?] February 1917, p. 77.
13 Jeffares, MacBride White and Bridgewater (eds.), *Letters to W. B. Yeats & Ezra Pound from Iseult Gonne*, Iseult Gonne to W. B. Yeats, n.d., July 1917, p. 85.
14 NAL, CO904/208, Report dated 3 September 1916; Londraville and Londraville (eds.), *The Letters of John Quinn and Maud Gonne*, Maud Gonne to John Quinn, 30 July 1917, p. 206.
15 NAL, CO904/208, Maud Gonne to Major Lampton, 30 June 1917.
16 NAL, HO144/1465/321387, War Office Memorandum, 27 September 1916.
17 W. B. Yeats to Augusta Gregory, 8 September 1917, quoted in Foster, *The Arch-poet*, p. 91; Yeats proposed to George Hyde-Lees on 24 September 1917; they were married on 20 October.
18 Foster, *The Arch-poet*, p. 92; Margaret Ward, *Maud Gonne: Ireland's Joan of Arc* (London: Pandora, 1990), p. 116.
19 MacBride, *That Day's Struggle*, p. 14.

young visitor' to Westminster in the company of Arthur Lynch MP, who gave 'Seaghan Gonne MacBride' a tour of the House of Commons and a place in the Distinguished Strangers' Gallery. The youthful guest was described as 'an attractive and promising-looking lad [who] speaks English with a slight French accent. He has learned a little of the Irish language. So far, he has been educated in France but he proposes to continue his studies in Ireland.'[20] Iseult, too, appeared to settle into a new life, securing a position – through Yeats's intervention – at the School of Oriental Languages and later as an assistant to Ezra Pound on the journal *The Little Review*.[21]

While Iseult was reasonably content in carving out something of an independent existence in London, for Maud Gonne, the return to Ireland was imperative. This was hampered by the constant presence of two Scotland Yard detectives, who shadowed their every move. Thirteen-year-old MacBride was enlisted in attempting to outwit the detectives: he shadowed them in their turn, and observed that instead of waiting for Gonne while she took her customary Turkish bath in Russell Square, they were in the habit of passing the time in a nearby pub. In January 1917 a plot was duly devised: Gonne entered the Turkish baths as normal, but emerged a short time later disguised as an old woman, 'her hair powdered white with a little blue hat ... a man's stiff collar, a dowdy grey coat, and a worn grey fur muff and collar.' She travelled on the mail train to Dublin and arrived unmolested, her disguise apparently so effective that her old friend Helena Molony failed to recognise her.[22] It appears that MacBride travelled ahead of her to Dublin, staying in the interim with Dr Kathleen Lynn.[23] The British authorities had anticipated her flaunting of their order, and even her probable disguise, but decided that it was 'a pity to make a martyr out of her by arrest or prohibition'. Her presence at the funeral of Dora Sigerson Shorter at Glasnevin Cemetery was noted, but no attempt to arrest or deport her was made.[24]

Life in Dublin

Buying a house at 73 Stephen's Green, Gonne returned to the old certainties of her previous life, embroiled in political and, to a lesser extent, cultural activities. She and her son slotted neatly into the turbulent Dublin of 1918, MacBride especially enjoying the vibrant atmosphere of the salons that continued to operate amid the darkening political landscape. Of particular pleasure was the regular Sunday night gathering at George Russell's, 'a must for everybody in Dublin who was

20 *Irish Independent*, 18 December 1917.
21 A. Norman Jeffares, 'Iseult Gonne' in Warwick Gould (ed.) *Poems and Contexts: Yeats Annual 16* (Basingstoke: Palgrave, 2005) pp. 235ff.
22 Jeffares, MacBride White and Bridgewater (eds.), *Letters to W. B. Yeats & Ezra Pound from Iseult Gonne*, Iseult Gonne to W. B. Yeats, [n.d.] January 1918, p. 95; Ward, *Maud Gonne*, p. 117.
23 Iseult Gonne's letter to Yeats quoted above clearly indicates that Seán left for Dublin before his mother; Seán's later account, given credence by Elizabeth Keane in *Seán MacBride: A Life* (Dublin: Gill & Macmillan, 2007), states that he followed on a prearranged signal. MacBride, *That Day's Struggle*, p. 15.
24 NAL, HO 144/1465/321387, Home Office to Aliens Officer, 20 December 1917; NAL, CO904/208, report dated 9 January 1918.

worthwhile'.[25] But coupled with the delightful eccentricities of old literary Dublin was an insistent subversive note: Maud Gonne's Wednesday-night salon was an explicitly political gathering, and she soon resumed her old pattern of addressing meetings and rallies. Lily Yeats noted the effect on MacBride, writing to her brother that he 'is being bred up and trained for martyrdom'.[26] MacBride's first personal brush with the forces of the Crown came in March 1918, during the trial of Laurence Ginnell on the charge of 'using language inculcating cattle-driving'.[27] As Ginnell was taken down to begin his sentence, his wife waved a republican flag, supported by Gonne. As constables attempted to remove her, Seán MacBride joined the fray: 'He was immediately grappled with by detectives and other police constables, but he made a vigorous fight, striking out right and left.' Order was restored after a brief interval, with the removal of Mrs Ginnell and 'the young MacBride, who continued struggling all the way'.[28]

If MacBride's first brush with the law was but an exciting interlude, events swiftly took a more serious turn. On 19 May 1918, two days after the arrest of seventy-three prominent 'Sinn Féiners' on the spurious pretext of the 'German plot', Maud Gonne was detained, later writing to Edward Shortt, the new Irish chief secretary, that she was 'kidnapped in the streets of Dublin on 19 May by five suspicious-looking ruffians who had no warrant'.[29] She had been returning from one of George Russell's regular evenings, along with her son, Dulcibella Barton and Joseph King MP. As she was bundled away in a police van, MacBride ran behind the vehicle, later following her to the Bridewell where he brought along food and his mother's warmest fur coat.[30] The next day, she was deported to Holloway Prison, where she joined fellow female prisoners Constance Markievicz and Kathleen Clarke in the venereal disease wing.[31] MacBride thus entered into a period of intense anxiety: to all intents and purposes, he was alone in the world. His father was dead, his mother imprisoned, his half-sister busy with her own life in London. He was wholly dependent on the charity of friends. Notwithstanding his youth and his precarious position, he embarked on a vigorous campaign for the release of his mother. On 20 May, the day Gonne was transported to England, he visited the headquarters of the British military in Ireland, demanding to see his mother. A report was later sent to Shortt (probably from Major Price, then Director of Military Intelligence in Ireland):

25 'Seán MacBride Remembers'.
26 NAL, CO904/208, report on lecture to Irish Citizen Army by Maud Gonne, 11 March 1918; Lily Yeats is quoted in Ann Saddlemyer, *Becoming George: The Life of Mrs W. B. Yeats* (Oxford: Oxford University Press, 2002), p. 151.
27 *Meath Chronicle*, 14 December 1918'; *Freeman's Journal*, 27 March 1918. On Ginnell's history of radical agrarian agitation see Paul Bew, *Conflict and Conciliation in Ireland, 1890–1910: Parnellites and Radical Agrarians* (Oxford: Clarendon Press, 1987), pp. 165–8.
28 *Freeman's Journal*, 27 March 1918.
29 NAL, HO 144/1465/321387, Maud Gonne MacBride to Edward Shortt, 26 June 1918.
30 Bureau of Military History [BMH], WS317, part 2, Witness Statement of Maud Gonne MacBride; Jeffares, MacBride White and Bridgewater (eds.), *Letters to W. B. Yeats & Ezra Pound from Iseult Gonne*, p. 201. For a detailed account of the experiences of the Holloway internees, see Seán McConville, *Irish Political Prisoners, 1848–1922* (London: Routledge, 2003), p. 631ff.
31 MacBride White and Jeffares (eds.), *The Gonne-Yeats Letters*, p. 394.

As [Seán MacBride's] actions were suspicious, he was searched and was found to be carrying a small revolver which did not work and two revolver cartridges which did not fit the revolver, and a knuckle-duster, police (pattern) whistle, and Boy Scout mobilisation scheme. He was deprived of these articles and turned out of HQ. He appeared to be about eighteen years of age.[32]

Underneath the letter, an anonymous commentator noted, 'I should think that this lad is quite capable of doing some silly and possibly dangerous thing to get notoriety.'[33]

Although in the immediate aftermath of Gonne's arrest, MacBride remained in Dublin in the care of George Russell, he was determined to be close to his mother, and on 25 May travelled to London and on to his sister's apartment in Chelsea.[34] For her part, Gonne vigorously protested her innocence, but the terms of her imprisonment in Holloway were harsh: interned without charge, kept in a cramped cell for twenty-three hours per day, her letter writing writing restricted to three half-pages a week, and an even more restrictive policy regarding visitors. Her chief concern was her son, declaring that she was 'wild with anxiety about Seaġan' and that she intended to go on hunger strike unless she be allowed see him: 'If I die, my death will give America and the world a striking example of English justice.'[35] MacBride immediately applied for permission to visit his mother, writing a series of letters to the Home Office and the prison authorities, arguing successfully that he needed to see her in order to finalise arrangements for his schooling.

This was becoming something of a problem for all concerned: effectively, the boy had not received any formal education since the summer of 1916. Around this time he received some lessons from Ezra Pound, a young American poet who had begun to move in Yeats's circle; the lessons were evidently rather unsuccessful, Pound later recalling that 'Shawn or Sewan or however he spells it Sua Eccelenza McB/ has probably never forgiven me for trying to lam some Ovid into his VERY allergic head/and probably never approved of art and letters ANYhow.'[36] Thus the question of his education was becoming a rather acute issue by the summer of 1918; this problem would not be resolved until the beginning of 1919, by which time he had missed two-and-a-half years of school. Permission to visit his mother was finally granted in the middle of June 1918, the authorities noting that '[t]his visit is to be allowed in the presence of discreet and reliable officers, and is to be confined to matters relating to the boy's education and personal affairs (Mrs MacBride is to be warned of this. If the conversation touches on politics or Irish affairs … [the] interview must be stopped at once).'[37]

32 NAL, CO904/208, GHQ to Chief Secretary, 19 June 1918. MacBride was in fact 14 years old.
33 NAL, CO904/208, unsigned commentary, 19 June 1918.
34 Jeffares, MacBride White and Bridgewater (eds.), *Letters to W. B. Yeats & Ezra Pound from Iseult Gonne*, Iseult Gonne to W. B. Yeats, 25 May 1918, pp. 102–3.
35 NAL, HO144/1465/321387, Maud Gonne MacBride to Iseult Gonne, 15 June 1918; MacBride White and Jeffares (eds.), *The Gonne-Yeats Letters*, Maud Gonne MacBride to W. B. Yeats, 14 June 1918, p. 395.
36 Jeffares, MacBride White and Bridgewater (eds.), *Letters to W. B. Yeats & Ezra Pound from Iseult Gonne*, p. 137.
37 NAL, HO144/1465/321387, unsigned report dated 18 June 1918.

While the anxieties of mother and son may have been somewhat allayed by the visit, which took place on 8 July, the question of MacBride's education continued to pose problems. Iseult, reluctantly cast in the role of guardian, found her brother stubborn on the issue, writing to Yeats that, 'the child has come back [to London] with his head packed with rubish [sic] and will hear of nothing for the present but resuming his former life in Dublin'.[38] Dublin, however, was considered much too dangerous for the fourteen-year-old, his sister commenting perceptively that '[he] is both too intelligent, too active and too young to be in the midst of it.'[39] An interim solution of sorts was found in July 1918, when Yeats brought MacBride back to Ireland to spend the summer with him and his wife George.

'The most remarkable boy I have met'

During his stay with the Yeatses at Ballinamantane House in County Galway, Seán was tutored by the village schoolmaster at Gort, and received supplementary classes in Irish, French and Latin from Claude Chavasse, an Anglo-French eccentric who wore only kilts and refused to speak English. Yeats was also making enquiries as to the suitability of a number of Irish schools, considering 'Clongowes ... the best as it is not so rough as most and the teaching is good. Castleknock is a good school but to[o] near Dublin and its political excitement.'[40] The name of one school was recurrent: Mount St Benedict in Gorey, County Wexford. At this point, however, that school was firmly ruled out by the presence of Victor Collins among its teaching staff. Collins had been John MacBride's best man and drinking companion in Paris, and had publicly taken his old friend's side during the divorce proceedings. Contrary to Elizabeth Keane's arguments that after the death of John MacBride, 'Collins's connection with Mount St Benedict was no longer important', it is clear that his presence at the school was still sufficient reason to disqualify it as a suitable place in which to educate Seán MacBride as late as the summer of 1918. [41] Despite the ongoing problem of schooling, MacBride's summer with the Yeatses was largely a success, Yeats writing to Quinn of a 'gentle solitary boy[,] and whether he has talent or not it is impossible to say for he is still too much the boy, thinking of what he does and sees but not forming judgement'.[42] By August, Yeats was writing to Gonne that MacBride was 'the most remarkable boy I have met – self possessed and very just, seeing all round a question and full of tact'.[43]

The arcadian tranquillity of that summer was soon jolted by yet more upheaval in London: this time centred on Iseult, whose relations with her flatmate Iris

38 Jeffares, MacBride White and Bridgewater (eds.), *Letters to W. B. Yeats & Ezra Pound from Iseult Gonne*, Iseult Gonne to W. B. Yeats, n. d. [late May 1918], p. 104.

39 Jeffares, MacBride White and Bridgewater (eds.), *Letters to W. B. Yeats & Ezra Pound from Iseult Gonne*, Iseult Gonne to W. B. Yeats, 23 July 1917, p. 106.

40 Jeffares, MacBride White and Bridgewater (eds.), *Letters to W. B. Yeats & Ezra Pound from Iseult Gonne*, p. 204; MacBride White and Jeffares (eds.), *The Gonne-Yeats Letters*, W. B. Yeats to Maud Gonne MacBride, 18 August 1918, p. 395.

41 Keane, *Seán MacBride*, p. 34.

42 W. B. Yeats to John Quinn, 23 July 1918, quoted in Foster, *The Arch-poet*, p. 127.

43 MacBride White and Jeffares (eds.), *The Gonne-Yeats Letters*, W. B. Yeats to Maud Gonne MacBride, 18 August 1918, p. 396.

Barry had deteriorated beyond repair. However, Iseult's intense fear of conflict made her reluctant formally to sever their relationship. Through her letters to her brother, word of this rupture reached Yeats, and he and his wife left for London at the beginning of August, leaving MacBride at nearby Tullyra, in the care of Edward Martyn, whose eccentric asceticism added yet another layer to the boy's disjointed upbringing.[44]

Maud Gonne's imprisonment remained the most immediate focus of her friends and family, and as the summer of 1918 passed with no prospect of release, they waged a concerted campaign. Influential voices within the British establishment were enlisted in support of her release, and a number of questions about the legality of her imprisonment were asked in Parliament.[45] MacBride was at the heart of this campaign, having insisted upon travelling back to London at the beginning of September 1918. The three women in Holloway were briefly joined by Hanna Sheehy Skeffington, Irish suffragette and widow of the murdered Francis, who was arrested while returning from America. Upon her imprisonment, Sheehy Skeffington promptly embarked on a hunger strike, and she was soon released under the Prisoners Discharge for Health Act.[46] Seán arranged to visit Sheehy Skeffington in Dublin on 2 September en route back to London, presumably anxious to hear news of his mother, writing that 'the treatment [in Holloway] looks very good for an English prison'.[47] Although Sheehy Skeffington was liable to rearrest under the terms of the Act, her success in securing even a temporary release was tempting to her fellow prisoners.

Maud Gonne's health was already displaying the strain of imprisonment; the prospect of her refusing food was deeply worrying to her family and friends, and added a new impetus to the campaign for her release. MacBride wrote a constant stream of letters to the prison authorities, applying for permission to visit, appealing that a lung specialist should examine his mother, and warning of her intention to hunger strike:

> She has now lost about 2 stone – 28 lbs – in weight and I must say that by her general appearance she struck me to be very ill. This treatment [by the authorities] and her state of health I am very afraid will lead to a hunger strike as she has already announced me [sic] this intention. In the present state of things in Ireland it would be most regrettable that a second Thomas ASH [sic] tragedy should occur.[48]

A visit by Dr Tunnicliffe, pulmonary consultant at King's College Hospital, was permitted on 22 October; his report on the state of Maud Gonne's health made sobering reading:

44 MacBride White and Jeffares (eds.), *The Gonne-Yeats Letters*, p. 395. See Madeleine Humphreys, *The Life and Times of Edward Martyn: An Aristocratic Bohemian* (Dublin: Irish Academic Press, 2007).

45 Particularly by Joseph King, who persistently queried the legality of Maud Gonne's internment and her isolation from her family. See *Hansard*, fifth series, vol. 106, col. 1589; vol. 107, col. 168; vol. 108, col. 34.

46 Margaret Ward, *Hanna Sheehy Skeffington: A Life* (Cork: Attic Press, 1997), p. 216.

47 National Library of Ireland [NLI], Sheehy Skeffington Papers, MS 24,103, Seán MacBride to Hanna Sheehy Skeffington, 22 August 1918.

48 NAL, HO 144/1465/321387, Seán MacBride to Home Office, 11 September 1918.

In my opinion Mrs MacBride's condition at the present time is due to a recrudescence of her former pulmonary tuberculosis, situated most probably at the base of her left lung. If the disease is to be arrested she requires active medical and open-air treatment in a suitable climate without delay.[49]

Armed with such a report, the campaign gathered sway: Stephen Gwynn intervened to arrange a meeting between Yeats and Chief Secretary Shortt, at which it was suggested that the British government would allow Gonne to return to live in France, although it was unlikely that she would consent to such an arrangement.[50] Letters from friends and sympathetic observers flooded the authorities: among those writing on her behalf were Ezra Pound, John Quinn, George Russell, Horace Plunkett, Joseph King, and T. P. O'Connor.[51]

Release

MacBride's experience of battling with the British authorities – the inflexibility and hostility he encountered – contributed to a growing political extremism and a hastily coagulating Anglophobia. Certainly, the months he spent in Ireland in early 1918 seem to have had a decided effect, which were noticeable to those who had known him in his gentler days. Ezra Pound, whose affair with Iseult almost definitely soured any relationship he had with Seán, commented of his former pupil that he 'was quite intelligent when [his mother] brought him from France, but the months in Ireland have ruined his mind and left him, as might be expected at his age, doomed to political futilities. He is a walking give-away of the real state of feeling there.'[52] The Welsh poet Arthur Symons, also an admirer of Iseult's, described Seán as 'a nihilist revolutionary student', further noting the stormy relationship between brother and sister, recording one monumental argument during the course of which Iseult threw Seán down the stairs at Woburn Buildings.[53] In a marked shift from his earlier more favourable impressions, Yeats grew to firmly disapprove of MacBride's increasingly headstrong temperament, writing to George Russell that 'Seugan [sic] has no fixed habits or discipline. Iseult has done her best.'[54]

Such a lack of discipline arguably stemmed largely from his rootless existence during most of 1918 and the absence of parental authority. This situation was transformed on 29 October 1918, when Maud Gonne was released from Holloway

49 NAL, HO 144/1465/321387, Report of Dr Tunnicliffe, 22 October 1918. For details of Maud Gonne's troubled medical history, see Caoimhín S. Breathnach, 'Maud Gonne MacBride (1866–1953): An Indomitable Consumptive', *Journal of Medical Biography*, vol. 13, no. 4 (2005), pp. 232–40.

50 MacBride White and Jeffares (eds.), *The Gonne-Yeats letters*, W. B. Yeats to Maud Gonne MacBride, 4 October 1918, pp. 397–8.

51 NAL, HO 144/1465/321387; NAL CO 904/208; Londraville and Londraville (eds.), *The Letters of John Quinn and Maud Gonne*, John Quinn to Iseult Gonne, 7 November 1918, p. 219.

52 New York Public Library [NYPL], John Quinn Papers, Ezra Pound to John Quinn, 15 November 1918.

53 K. Beckson, 'Arthur Symons' "Iseult Gonne": a previously unpublished memoir' in W. Gould (ed.) *Yeats Annual 7* (Basingstoke: Macmillan, 1990), pp. 202–4.

54 W. B. Yeats to George Russell, 14 December 1918, quoted in Foster, *The Arch-poet*, p. 693.

Prison on grounds of ill-health, and transferred to a nursing home; on 7 November she left the nursing home and returned to Woburn Buildings. Disregarding orders to remain in England, she and her children returned to Dublin some time after 20 November.[55] But the return was not the peaceful event they had wished for. While she had been imprisoned, Gonne had agreed to Yeats's proposal that he should rent her Stephen's Green house and his assurance to her that '[s]hould you be released and allowed to live in Ireland we will move out which strangers would not.'[56] But when the Gonne MacBrides arrived, George Yeats was seven months pregnant and dangerously ill with influenza. Her husband turned Gonne away at the door, perhaps understandably: 'with a heavily pregnant wife seriously ill, the risk of a military raid could not be taken'.[57] Gonne was furious, calling Yeats 'an unpatriotic coward',[58] and the ensuing quarrel was serious enough to threaten almost forty years of friendship. Iseult judged that 'they have both behaved as badly as they could', and as the dispute divided literary Dublin, recorded that 'Russel [sic] and I are the only two who refuse to take sides with this only difference that Russel says [they are] both right and I maintain they are both wrong.'[59] The family found lodgings with friends until George had recovered enough to move out of 73 Stephen's Green; a reconciliation was slowly effected, but something of the old friendship had been lost, and Gonne and Yeats were never as close again.

For MacBride, the return to Dublin meant a return to the excitement of political upheaval. The upcoming general election was awaited with anticipation, and MacBride became involved in Constance Markievicz's electoral campaign in the winter of 1918, in the St Patrick's constituency of Dublin City. Although MacBride's duties were largely monotonous – 'mainly typing copies of the register – the routine, humdrum work of elections'[60] – he relished the political engagement, his sister noting that 'in the midst of electioneering [he] seems to show sound sense and perhaps this complete immersion in political life may be his salvation.'[61] The day of the count, however, made a significant impression on him: but it was the pathos of the defeated IPP candidate rather than the significance of Markievicz's victory, the first female MP elected to Parliament, which remained:

> I felt sorry for William Field, who was an older man and looked battered and woebegone. He proceeded to get up from his seat and walk out from the Court House, passing me by quite closely. He was knocked down and immediately a number of people started kicking him on the ground. I jumped in there. I was

55 Beckson, 'Arthur Symons', pp. 202–4; Jeffares, MacBride White and Bridgewater (eds.), *Letters to W. B. Yeats & Ezra Pound from Iseult Gonne*, Iseult Gonne to Ezra Pound, n.d. November 1918, p. 140.

56 MacBride White and Jeffares (eds.), *The Gonne-Yeats Letters*, W. B. Yeats to Maud Gonne MacBride, n. d. September 1918, p. 396.

57 Foster, *The Arch-poet*, p. 135.

58 Londraville and Londraville (eds.), *The Letters of John Quinn and Maud Gonne*, p. 216.

59 Jeffares, MacBride White and Bridgewater (eds.), *Letters to W. B. Yeats & Ezra Pound from Iseult Gonne*, Iseult Gonne to Ezra Pound, n.d. [late November 1918], p. 141; 8/9 December 1918, p. 143.

60 MacBride, *That Day's Struggle*, p. 22.

61 Jeffares, MacBride White and Bridgewater (eds.), *Letters to W. B. Yeats & Ezra Pound from Iseult Gonne*, Iseult Gonne to Ezra Pound, n. d. [early December 1918], p. 142.

furious, absolutely ... This was a man who had been their representative for a long time, who, I am sure, had done some good work in his day, who had not been particularly obnoxious, and who knew he was fighting a losing battle. I have always remembered it since.[62]

The election results appeared emphatic: Sinn Féin winning 73 of Ireland's 105 seats to the IPP's six.[63] But after the heady excitement of the winter election, however, a curious lethargy appeared to set in: the motley nature of those united under the Sinn Féin banner had yet to really agree a political programme, the men of violence had not yet emerged, and Seán MacBride had to go back to school.

Mount St Benedict

The question of his schooling had long consumed his mother: an Irish education was one of the things Maud Gonne most desired for her son. Although war, rebellion and imprisonment had intervened, it was finally possible to select a suitable place in which to educate MacBride, bringing to an end a period of somewhat chaotic tutoring that had lasted since September 1917. The school that was eventually chosen for him was Mount St Benedict in Gorey, Co. Wexford. It is likely that the school's location, far from the growing turmoil of Dublin, was one of the deciding factors in its favour. As its name suggests, it was a Benedictine foundation, a sister-school to the famous Downside Abbey, where upper-middle-class Irish Catholics had been sending their sons for generations. It was essentially a labour of love of its founder and headmaster, John Francis Sweetman, a member of a renowned Catholic nationalist family with long-standing links to the Catholic hierarchy and Sinn Féin.

Sweetman, or 'the Reverend man' as he was known to his students, was himself a product of Downside, and after having acted as chaplain to the British forces in South Africa in 1900, returned to teach at the abbey.[64] The ethos of the school was liberal: 'The boys are given a wide measure of freedom in order that, by being trained in habits of personal responsibility, they may be fitted to exercise the greater freedom of the university and afterlife.'[65] The transformation in Irish political opinion in the months following the Easter Rising was also felt at the Mount, and whereas Dom Francis was previously 'most enthusiastic to persuade anyone who was available to join the British army', the school soon gained a reputation

62 Jeffares, MacBride White and Bridgewater (eds.), *Letters to W. B. Yeats & Ezra Pound from Iseult Gonne*, Iseult Gonne to Ezra Pound, n. d. [early December 1918]; *Irish Times*, 16 December 1918.

63 Brian M. Walker (ed.), *Parliamentary Election Results in Ireland, 1918–92: Irish Elections to Parliamentary Assemblies at Westminster, Belfast, Dublin, Strasbourg* (Dublin: Royal Irish Academy, 1992), pp. 4–9.

64 Aidan Bellenger OSB, 'The post-Reformation English Benedictines and Ireland: conflict and dialogue', in Martin Browne and Colmán Ó Clabaigh O.S.B. (eds.), *The Irish Benedictines: A History* (Dublin: Columba Press, 2005), p. 150.

65 Printed material relating to Mount St Benedict, quoted in Bellenger, 'The post-Reformation English Benedictines and Ireland', p. 151.

as the ideal place to receive an Irish nationalist education.[66] Other old boys of Mount St Benedict, many of them contemporaries of MacBride, included Mac and Aodhagán O'Rahilly; James and Brian Dillon, sons of the leader of the IPP; four Sweetman brothers from Glendalough; Owen Gwynn, son of Stephen, the former MP for Galway; Cecil Salkeld; and the sons of Tom and Kathleen Clarke.[67]

Accordingly, MacBride was sent there in January 1919, to receive formal lessons before he sat the matriculation examinations for the National University. He was reluctant to leave the excitement of Dublin, Lily Yeats writing to Quinn that 'the boy has consented to go to school, on condition that he can leave at the end of a month if he doesn't like it. Isolde [*sic*] says he feels as if a statesman was asked to go to school.'[68] Whereas the presence of Victor Collins among the staff had ruled Mount St Benedict out the previous year, the major's old friend had departed for America in early 1919, apparently among the entourage of Eamon de Valera.[69]

Although MacBride had been initially unenthusiastic about the school, he soon found it was to his liking. His French Jesuit education stood him in good stead, and he was permitted to miss French and mathematics lessons, using the spare time to deliver telegrams for the local post office which doubled, fortuitously, as the school tuck shop.[70] That summer, it seems that MacBride spent some weeks at the Irish college at Ring, County Waterford, presumably in an attempt to improve his Irish, a language with which he had always had difficulty and with which he felt no particular affinity. Andrews noted MacBride's 'difficulty in settling down in the Gaelic-speaking environment', rather sarcastically recalling that MacBride's 'stay was cut short by an urgent summons from the Lord Mayor of Cork, Terence MacSwiney, who wished to consult him on some urgent national business'.[71] Of course, MacSwiney was not yet Lord Mayor, merely a leading figure in the Cork IRA, and MacBride quite possibly inflated a run-of-the-mill errand into 'urgent national business'. Whatever the circumstances of his departure from Ring, it was his last attempt to come to grips with the Irish language.

A more serious aspect to MacBride's time at the Mount was his involvement in an 'attack' on a local Royal Irish Constabulary (RIC) barracks, when a group of schoolboys terrorised the policemen inside with homemade explosions from matches, nails, keys and metal pipes. This incident was not merely tolerated by the school authorities: after the police came to the school to investigate, Sweetman was 'chuckling away to himself about it, not exactly encouraging us but more or less saying to "about time somebody put the RIC out of this country"'.[72] The reputation that the school had begun to carve out for involvement in such matters contributed to its ultimate failure as an institution. One former pupil noted in an

---

66 *Irish Times*, 16 September 1981.
67 MacBride, *That Day's Struggle*, p. 17; Maurice Manning, *James Dillon: A Biography* (Dublin: Wolfhound Press, 1999), pp. 20–1; Bellenger, 'The post-Reformation English Benedictines and Ireland', p. 153.
68 Lily Yeats to John Quinn, 7 January 1919, quoted in Saddlemyer, *Becoming George*, p. 197.
69 William O'Brien and Desmond Ryan (eds.), *Devoy's Postbag, 1871–1928* (Dublin: Academy Press, 1979, first published 1953), p. 531
70 MacBride, *That Day's Struggle*, p. 17.
71 C. S. Andrews, *Dublin made me* (Dublin: Lilliput Press, 2001, first published 1979), p. 130.
72 MacBride, *That Day's Struggle*, p. 19.

unpublished memoir that '[it] is the duty of school authorities to keep boys out of politics: at the Mount the tendency was in the opposite direction … sermons were preached and demonstrations were staged.'[73]

The school was raided a number of times during 1919 by the British military, and the resultant negative publicity in the local area led the Bishop of Ferns to formally request that the Downside authorities close Mount St Benedict. It had been a unique institution: during its short lifespan it educated prominent figures in Irish public life in the first half of the twentieth century, and achieved a notoriety perhaps more than it merited. Its methods, 'somewhere between eccentricity and inspiration', provided a fitting end to MacBride's decidedly haphazard schooling; his formal education was patchy at best.[74] But, in 1920, aged sixteen and intending to enter the National University, he returned to an increasingly turbulent Dublin where the lure of revolutionary activities would soon take precedence over his university career.

73 J. A. James, 'The light and warmth within' (unpublished manuscript), quoted in Bellenger, 'The post-Reformation English Benedictines and Ireland', pp. 152–3.
74 Bellenger, 'The post-Reformation English Benedictines and Ireland', p. 151.

3

Seán MacBride's Irish Revolution
1919–1921

MacBride's participation in the violent events which shook Ireland from 1919 onwards formed the basis of his political and personal identity in the years that followed. Within post-Treaty IRA circles, MacBride was certainly regarded as 'having the well-deserved reputation of having a good IRA record', despite his relative youth.[1] A recent publication notes that by current standards, MacBride would be 'stigmatised as a child soldier ... and his recruiters would be guilty of war crimes'.[2] MacBride's revolution was somewhat slow to start, however. His schooling in Wexford removed him from much of the early activities of the Dublin IRA; and when he did return and join their ranks, it was as a very junior member. In so far as MacBride's revolution can be held as emblematic of anything, it is the revolution of an adolescent, desperately eager to please, who achieved middle rank and was involved in a respectable number of ambushes without achieving the fame of a Dan Breen or an Ernie O'Malley. Indeed, such an experience is arguably the more commonplace for Ireland's revolutionary heroes. MacBride's story from 1919 to 1921 is that of a young man trying to find a place for himself in the country and the circumstances he had been brought up to consider his birthright: fighting the British in Ireland.

The initial stages of what came to be known as the War of Independence rather passed MacBride by. While he was at school in Wexford, events elsewhere were assuming a momentum of their own: the inaugural meeting of Dáil Éireann in January 1919 was given an unexpected resonance by the murder of two policemen the same day in County Tipperary. This, however, is not to suggest that the republican leadership in Dublin had ordered or even sanctioned the attack. The new Dáil government pinned the majority of its hopes on securing international support for the reaffirmed Republic of Ireland. Business during its early sessions – MacBride attended the third sitting, on 10 April – included an appeal for recognition from (and admission to) the Paris Peace Conference.[3]

---

1 C. S. Andrews, *Dublin Made Me* (Dublin: Lilliput Press, 2001, first published 1979), p. 236.
2 William A. Schabas, 'Ireland, the European Convention on Human Rights and the personal contribution of Seán MacBride', in John Morison, Kieran McEvoy and Gordon Anthony (eds.), *Judges, Transitions and Human Rights* (Oxford: Oxford University Press, 2007), pp. 251–74.
3 See Dáil pass issued to Seaġán Gonne MacBride, 10 April 1919 reproduced in illustration 10, Seán MacBride, *That Day's Struggle: A Memoir 1904–1951*, ed. Caitriona Lawlor (Dublin:

Fianna Éireann

The reconstruction of MacBride's movements during the early stages of the revolutionary period poses definite challenges, among these his failure to provide a witness statement to the Bureau of Military History. This is exacerbated by the unreliability of MacBride's later reminiscences, preserved mainly in his posthumous memoir and in interviews recorded toward the end of his life. The kindest judgement on these would be that the passage of time had obscured the clarity of his recollections; a harsher critic might conclude that his accounts are wholly unreliable. An illustration of this unreliability can be seen in MacBride's assertion that he was 'fighting the Tans at fourteen',[4] predating the arrival of the Black and Tans in Ireland by some two years. Other dubious claims include his alleged internment for six weeks in 1918: 'I was in jail for the first time when I was fourteen. Charge? No charge. My father had been executed and I was put in jail for good measure.'[5] As we have seen, he spent most of 1918 alternating between Dublin, Galway and London, and while he had come to the attention of the authorities, there is no record of his having been interned along with his mother. Accordingly, the need for verification is paramount – an approach which the author of the only extant biographical study does not appear to have taken. In writing her account of MacBride's revolutionary career, Elizabeth Keane relies entirely on his published memoir. Scant supplementary material, archival or otherwise, seems to have been consulted, resulting in a verbatim reproduction of MacBride's own version, which condenses the entire period of 1918 to 1923 into ten rushed pages.[6]

In his memoir, MacBride claimed to have been a member of the IRA as early as 1918. Given the transitory nature of his life in 1918, particularly after the arrest and imprisonment of his mother, it is unlikely that MacBride was a fully fledged Volunteer at this point. The more probable sequence of events is that MacBride became a member of Fianna Éireann shortly after his arrival in Ireland, although this was interrupted by the arrest and imprisonment of his mother. On his return to Ireland and schooling in Wexford, MacBride resumed his activities in the Fianna, and at some point, either in late 1919 or early 1920, was incorporated into the Volunteers, in time for the beginning of his university education. Progression from the Fianna into the Volunteers proper was commonly made around the age of eighteen. MacBride was not unique, however, in making the transition at an earlier stage: Todd Andrew and Kevin Barry are but two examples of those who transferred before their eighteenth birthdays. This progression – Fianna Éireann in 1918, moving into the IRA in early 1920 – is confirmed by Seán MacEntee's file on MacBride's political history, compiled sometime in 1947.[7]

But what of MacBride in the Fianna? In an interview recorded towards the end of his life, MacBride claimed to have participated in the Fianna procession at the

Currach Press, 2005).

4   *Sunday Independent*, 14 September 1980.

5   *Sunday Tribune*, 4 January 1981.

6   Elizabeth Keane, *Seán MacBride: A Life* (Dublin: Gill and Macmillan, 2007), pp. 35–45.

7   University College Dublin Archives [UCDA], Seán MacEntee Papers, 'Synopsis of political history of Seán MacBride SC, Roebuck House', P67/539(1).

funeral of Thomas Ashe, who had died in the Mater Hospital after an attempt at force-feeding resulted in a perforated oesophagus.[8] This is simply impossible: Ashe's death occurred on 25 September 1917, shortly after MacBride's arrival in London from Paris along with his mother and sister, but long before their defiance of the DORA order forbidding them passage to Ireland. MacBride's membership probably began some time early in 1918, and was likely influenced by George Irvine, a Fermanagh-born schoolteacher, captain in the Fourth Battalion of the Dublin Brigade and 1916 veteran, who tutored MacBride sporadically in 1918 in Irish language and history.[9] Fianna meetings at that point were largely comprised of lectures on aspects of Irish history and interminable drilling exercises. More exciting were weekends spent in the Dublin mountains: '[i]t was quite good fun, with the added thrill that the RIC was always chasing us. We used to be very disappointed if the RIC or the military didn't arrive at some stage of our camping expedition to chase us all away again.'[10] Soon, though, this excitement too began to pall, and MacBride was itching to leave the boys' organisation and join the men in the IRA.

The Dublin Brigade

Partially the subject of Joost Augusteijn's survey of the Volunteers, the Dublin Brigade formed the over-arching military structure for the IRA in Dublin. Divided into four city battalions, which in turn were subdivided into thirty-eight companies, by 1920 the Brigade adjutant reported a strength of 1,550 men (although later estimates put the fighting strength at no more than 1,150).[11] Operations on the ground in Dublin during this early period were mostly confined to securing weaponry and intensive patrolling. Specific instructions were given to all companies 'to report the movements of British troops and to carry revolvers. We were, however, specifically instructed not to attack or provoke the British troops in any way except [if] we were attacked ourselves and in such an eventuality we were permitted to use our arms.'[12]

The relative dearth of offensive action in Dublin was somewhat mirrored in the country at large, where casualty figures throughout the year remained relatively low: one study notes that fifteen men from the Royal Irish Constabulary (RIC) were killed as a result of 'political violence' for the whole of 1919, a figure which pales in comparison with 178 the following year.[13] The outlawing of Dáil Éireann

---

8   'Seán MacBride Remembers', RTÉ television documentary, originally broadcast 1989.
9   MacBride, *That Day's Struggle*, pp. 20–1; Bureau of Military History [BMH], WS 265, Witness Statement of George Irvine.
10 MacBride, *That Day's Struggle*, p. 21.
11 Quoted in Joost Augusteijn, *From Public Defiance to Guerrilla Warfare: The Experience of Ordinary Volunteers in the Irish War of Independence, 1916–1921* (Dublin: Irish Academic Press, 1996), pp. 25, 97. See also BMH, WS 340, Witness Statement of Oscar Traynor; and D. O'Kelly, 'The Dublin scene', in *With the IRA in the Fight for Freedom: 1919 to the Truce* (Tralee: the Kerryman, n. d.), p. 27.
12 BMH, WS 508, Witness Statement of Dermot O'Sullivan.
13 Richard Abbot, *Police Casualties in Ireland, 1919–1922* (Cork: Mercier Press, 2000), pp. 48, 169.

in September 1919 was a decisive moment in escalating the pattern of violence; with GHQ increasingly more amenable to the idea of force, the hawks within the movement, particularly at local level, forced the pace.

MacBride's transfer into the IRA proper most likely occurred in early 1920, shortly after the Volunteer Executive authorised attacks on Crown forces. While MacBride's membership of the Fianna made it likely that he would transition into the IRA at some point, far more important in this regard was his relationship with the Fitzgerald family of 173 Brunswick Street, three of whom were active Volunteers. As members of the Fianna, Leo and Jim Fitzgerald had participated in the Easter Rising, and by September 1920 the family home was the subject of military searches.[14] The Fitzgeralds were contracted to carry out renovations of the Gonne MacBride house on Stephen's Green, and the older sons seem to have very much taken the younger MacBride under their wing, bringing him with them to tinker around in their family garage. Soon he was a willing new recruit to B Company, Third Dublin Battalion.

The territory covered by this company was south-east of the city centre, operating primarily around Brunswick Street and Mount Street, busy thoroughfares for British military vehicles leaving Beggar's Bush Barracks. This was some distance away from MacBride's home at Stephen's Green, but his choice of company was equally determined by his anxiety to keep his IRA membership secret from his mother as it was influenced by his new friends, the Fitzgeralds. Membership of a local company would have been almost impossible to keep under wraps; as it was, his university studies provided as useful a cover from his mother as it did from Crown forces. In 1986, MacBride told Margaret Ward, his mother's biographer, that Gonne only discovered her son's secret IRA life when a gun he was cleaning in the attic accidentally went off; the bullet passing through the floorboards and narrowly missing a priest convalescing there after a nervous breakdown.[15]

While Gonne's attentions were directed elsewhere, and at home distracted by Iseult's elopement with Francis Stuart, Seán was becoming embroiled in 'B$_3$', as his company was known within IRA GHQ. Most of his early activities were taken up by training and drilling, much as with the Fianna the year before: 'At that time there was a lot of drilling, lessons on revolvers, rifles, even machine guns, and regular classes ... we had endless parades. We were sent out two by two, walking about the various streets, making a report on everything we saw.'[16] While incessant drilling was tedious, and concrete training in the handling of weapons scant across all IRA units, the repetition did, as Charles Townshend has noted, reinforce the importance of discipline within the movement.[17] The relative lack of military action experienced by MacBride and his comrades in B Company during much of 1920 was not unusual in terms of the wider Dublin Brigade. In addition, for most of the year, MacBride was juggling IRA activism with university studies, as a law

14   P. Quinn, 'The Battle of Brunswick Street' in *Dublin's Fighting Story, 1916–21: Told by the Men who Made It* (Tralee: The Kerryman, n.d.); *Irish Times*, 10 September 1920.
15   Margaret Ward, *Maud Gonne: Ireland's Joan of Arc* (London: Pandora, 1990), p. 127.
16   MacBride, *That Day's Struggle*, p. 21.
17   Charles Townshend, *The British Campaign in Ireland, 1919–1921* (Oxford: Oxford University Press, 1975), p. 61.

and agriculture student at University College Dublin.

University College Dublin

When Seán enrolled in University College Dublin in early 1920, the institution was in the midst of its most serious crisis since the apparent resolution of the university question in 1908. The problems posed initially by the Great War, then by the Easter Rising and the deteriorating security situation in Dublin, placed the college authorities in an extremely difficult position. MacBride matriculated at UCD to study law and agriculture, harbouring dreams of becoming a gentleman farmer dabbling in law on the side: 'I started off with a strange idea of being a farmer and a lawyer, of having a small farm in the country, living from the farm, and doing an occasional law case, for interest, or to be able to vindicate justice from time to time.'[18] Keane argues that MacBride's choice of subjects was 'probably influenced by his mother's experience with the legal system in Britain and Ireland'; MacBride himself claims to have had, even at this early stage, 'a sense that justice was important'.[19] Whatever his interest in law and the abstract ideal of justice, this did not necessarily equate to his being a dedicated and diligent student – by his own admission he 'was not working very hard'.[20] Todd Andrews, a contemporary at UCD, remembered the curious sense of detachment from the normal sequence of university life that the disrupted political scene had wrought, remarking that he 'felt that with the country in such turmoil ... the moment of truth in the form of an examination day would never arrive. I think that was the general feeling of the young people who were really committed members of the IRA.'[21]

MacBride's increasing involvement with the IRA was equally as much of a distraction as the more traditional diversions of the college Literary and Historical Society, a debating society of which he was an enthusiastic member. The functioning of the L&H was rendered more difficult in the years 1920 to 1922, especially during periods of curfew, but although inaugural meetings were suspended for that period, regular Saturday meetings continued to take place. John Farrell was secretary of the L&H for the session 1920–1921; his committee included James Dillon and Seán MacBride, later described as 'the best committee of all time'.[22] The committee meeting room, located in the basement of Earlsfort Terrace, was a favourite haunt of the inner circle of the L&H, and was especially frequented by those students who played bridge: MacBride, Dillon, Sars Hogan and John Farrell among them. Farrell later recalled how one bridge session was interrupted by a raid by British authorities:

> men in uniform who would, no doubt, have been well content to get their hands on Niall MacNeill or Seán MacBride. Not unduly brusquely, they shepherded us up the stairs and into the centre hall where we sat down on the tiles and went

18 MacBride, *That Day's Struggle*, p. 34.
19 Keane, *Seán MacBride*, p. 36; MacBride, *That Day's Struggle*, p. 34.
20 'Seán MacBride Remembers'.
21 Andrews, *Dublin made me*, pp. 131–2.
22 John Farrell, 'Curfew – Part I', in James Meenan (ed.), *Centenary History of the Literary and Historical Society of University College Dublin, 1855–1955* (Tralee: The Kerryman, 1956), p. 172.

on with the game. James Dillon cut the cards for Niall, who dealt first to Seán, while the enemy looked on.[23]

The question of student involvement in the IRA was one that exercised MacBride in later years. His position was essentially that there was a surprisingly low number of students participating in the revolutionary struggle:

> The whole country at that stage had reached boiling point, all the young people had joined the IRA, but there were very few in UCD in the IRA, very, very few ... the surprising thing was [how few] students were involved with the republican movement at that period. Normally it should have been the centre of republican revolutionary activity but it wasn't.[24]

How far does this contention hold up? Joyce Nankivell, an Englishwoman resident in Dublin during 1920, noted that there were two types of Volunteers: 'a youthful, cheeky type belonging to the National University, and there was a dirtier, rather more prepossessing type, drawn from the errand boy'.[25] This latter, known variously as the 'shop-boy' or the 'corner-boy' was something of a commonplace in contemporary accounts of the IRA. Peter Hart has compiled detailed statistics on the composition of the IRA in the Dublin metropolitan area for 1917–1923, and found that of a sample of 507 ordinary Volunteers in 1920–1921, only three were students. Of a sample of eighty-six IRA officers in the same period, there was just one student.[26] These findings would appear to confirm MacBride's assertion of the lack of revolutionary fervour among the student body of UCD, but other biographies of known IRA activists point to a clear UCD link during the War of Independence: Todd Andrews, Niall MacNeill, Michael Rynne, Richard Mulcahy, Rory O'Connor and, famously, Kevin Barry and Frank Flood.

The degree to which student members of the IRA associated with each other may help to explain MacBride's impression of the university's remoteness from the political upheavals of the period. Todd Andrews recalled the reluctance on the part of revolutionary active students to socialise with each other:

> In the College, there were a number of students who were known to be IRA men, but unless they were in the same Company or Battalion, they never spoke or associated with each other on the basis of their common allegiance to the IRA and if they were friendly, it was for altogether different reasons.[27]

This tendency seems to have been present in MacBride's IRA connections within the university: his friendship with Michael Rynne came through the common bond of membership of the L&H, his acquaintance with Niall MacNeill through their shared fondness for bridge. Furthermore, the fact that MacBride deliberately joined an IRA Company some considerable distance from both his home at 73 Stephen's Green and the university district around Earlsfort Terrace, and in

---

23 Farrell, 'Curfew', p. 170.

24 'Seán MacBride Remembers'.

25 Joice Nankivell and Sydney Loch, *Ireland in Travail* (London: John Murray, 1922), pp. 55–6.

26 Peter Hart, *The IRA at War, 1916–1923* (Oxford: Oxford University Press, 2005, first published 2003), p. 119, table 11.

27 Andrews, *Dublin made me*, p. 158.

a predominantly working-class area, made it less likely that he would encounter fellow company members at the university. Nevertheless, the presence of the IRA was felt sufficiently within student life for the Student Representative Committee to co-opt a member of the IRA from each faculty onto their body.[28]

The first serious interruption to MacBride's studies came on 26 September 1920, when he was arrested with Constance Markievicz and Maurice Bourgeois, a French journalist on a fact-finding mission to Ireland. MacBride offered to drive Bourgeois down to Maud Gonne's cottage in Glenmalure, County Wicklow, and Markievicz hitched a lift. They were arrested on their return to Dublin, and stopped on the Highfield Road because the car had a broken tail-light.[29] All three were taken to the Bridewell and then to Mountjoy. Bourgeois was soon released, his diplomatic credentials standing him in good stead. Constance Markievicz, as a member of the outlawed Dáil Éireann, was sentenced to two years' hard labour, and remained in Mountjoy until the truce of July 1921.[30] MacBride was initially detained for some time; in what appears to have been an attempt to obtain incriminating evidence, the family home at Stephen's Green was raided shortly after the arrest.[31] The family expected a court martial, but MacBride was unexpectedly released at 4.30 pm on 8 October. The arrest was something of a secret delight to MacBride, who at last was appearing to live up to his illustrious republican heritage. As far back as 1918 the 14-year-old had spoken 'of arrest as necessary to his political career'; this, at least, was one ambition fulfilled.[32] The most serious consequence of the arrest was that he missed half of his university examinations – although he performed well in the March examinations, obtaining 76 per cent and placed fourth in his class[33] – beginning a pattern of wholesale disruption that would end in 1922 with the abandonment of his studies.[34]

MacBride's short-lived detention was quickly followed by an important episode in the history of UCD during the Irish revolution: the execution of Kevin Barry, an 18-year-old medical student, for his part in a lethal ambush on Crown forces. As Barry passed into martyrdom on 1 November 1920, MacBride was, by his own account, surprised at the muted response within the college: '[n]ormally one would expect the national university of a country, when one of its students had been hanged, to have reacted. Instead of that, there was virtually no response from the student body.'[35] Wishing to make a protest, he and some other like-minded law students forced their way up onto the roof of Earlsfort Terrace and raised a tricolour

28 Dónal McCartney, *UCD: A National Idea: The History of University College* (Dublin: Gill & Macmillan, 1999), p. 106.

29 Mark Sturgis, *The Last Days of Dublin Castle: the Mark Sturgis Diaries*, ed. Michael Hopkinson (Dublin: Irish Academic Press, 1999), p. 46.

30 *Irish Times*, 4 and 29 December 1920.

31 *Freeman's Journal*, 28 September 1920. See also *Irish Times*, 2 October 1920.

32 New York Public Library [NYPL], John Quinn Papers, Ezra Pound to John Quinn, 20 November 1918.

33 Anna MacBride White and A. Norman Jeffares (eds.), *The Gonne–Yeats Letters, 1893–1939: Always your Friend* (London: Hutchinson, 1992), Maud Gonne MacBride to W. B. Yeats, 21 March 1921, p. 422.

34 *Freeman's Journal*, 28 September 1920.

35 MacBride, *That Day's Struggle*, p. 23.

to half-mast. He was subsequently 'hauled up ... by the president of the University College and threatened with expulsion'.[36] While the sincerity of MacBride's protest may be accepted, his claims that the student population were uninterested in Kevin Barry's execution are rather more difficult to sustain. Dónal O'Donovan, a relative of the Barry family, noted in his biography of Kevin Barry that at nine o'clock on the morning of his execution, a Mass was said in the University Church for repose of the soul of Kevin Barry.[37] Celia Shaw, a fellow student, noted in her diary that she had 'never experienced anything like the surging fury which the news pronounced'.[38] John Mowbray, another student, remembered that later on the afternoon of 1 November, 'a group of Auxiliary policemen searched university buildings for arms and documents.'[39] After the Barry execution, MacBride resumed his studies, albeit with regular and increasing interruptions from his IRA commitments. In an interview with Tim Pat Coogan, MacBride remembered quickly shifting from his IRA activities to his student persona:

> When we'd see a patrol or a lorry coming along we'd fire on it, or lob a bomb, and fire on them when they'd jump out. Then we'd run like hares, dump the revolvers and I'd get back to college. The professors weren't too keen on what we were doing, but it didn't matter. So long as I got back quickly to Earlsfort Terrace I could pretend I was there when the ambush took place.[40]

The impact of these interruptions was profound: MacBride is not listed as a graduate of UCD in any calendars after 1922, and his successful completion of the King's Inns' examinations and subsequent career at the bar was undertaken without the background of a university degree.

Darkening Clouds

On the personal front, life grew somewhat troubled within the Gonne-MacBride household in 1920. Maud Gonne's illness for much of the previous year, probably suffering the effects of the turbulent previous five years – war, rebellion, bereavement (her beloved sister Kathleen had died in January), coupled with her imprisonment – contributed to the broken nature of family life, although some degree of continuity with their old lives was provided by the figures of Barry O'Delaney and Josephine Pillon. In the autumn of 1920, the top floor of the house on Stephen's Green was rented out to Dorothy Macardle, another addition to the household of women.[41] The most serious event, however, was Iseult Gonne's disastrous relationship with Francis Stuart, a cold, precocious, would-be writer eight years her junior. The couple eloped to London in January 1920, just after Seán had stood as godfather in absentia for Stuart's reception into the Catholic Church, and returned in

---

36   'Seán MacBride Remembers'.
37   Dónal O'Donovan, *Kevin Barry and his Time* (Dublin: Glendale, 1989), p. 165.
38   Quoted in McCartney, *UCD*, p. 106.
39   John Mowbray 'Curfew – Part III', in Meenan (ed.), *Centenary History of the Literary and Historical Society*, p. 177.
40   T. P. Coogan, *Michael Collins* (London: Arrow Books, 1990), p. 143.
41   BMH, WS 457, Witness Statement of Dorothy Macardle.

April to be married.[42] The disastrous nature of the marriage revealed itself during the summer of 1920: furious arguments and mutual destruction of each other's possessions paled into insignificance once Stuart began depriving Iseult of food and locking her up for hours at an end. When events reached a nasty climax in July, Maud Gonne sent for Yeats, who proved surprisingly practical, mediating between the Gonnes and the Stuarts for a separation agreement, and arranging medical treatment for Iseult, who was pregnant.

Despite all that had passed between them, Iseult was unwilling to end the relationship; the best concession her distraught mother and Yeats could extract from the couple was an agreement that Stuart should provide Iseult with an income and leave her in peace while the pregnancy advanced.[43] MacBride's own thoughts on Iseult's unhappy marriage are unrecorded, beyond his reply to Geoffrey Elborn in 1986 when the latter requested an interview for his biography of Stuart. MacBride replied: 'Francis Stuart treated Iseult disgracefully, and I will have nothing to do with you or your book.'[44] Maud Gonne was, understandably, utterly distracted by Iseult's troubles through most of 1920. In early 1921, she was invited to sit on the executive of the newly formed Irish White Cross; her day-to-day activities included coordinating relief efforts for the affected Dublin population and agitating on behalf of prisoners and prisoners' families.[45] As far as she was concerned, her son was safely occupied at university in Dublin. Her attention elsewhere, this formed the context within which MacBride was able to conceal his IRA membership throughout most of the War of Independence.

During the second half of 1920, the security situation throughout Ireland was in a state of rapid degeneration: ambush, counter-ambush, raid and reprisal contributed to an atmosphere of escalating terror, particularly in the small towns of provincial Ireland. Yet, the British authorities had reason to believe that, in Dublin at least, the tide had turned in their favour: the IRA in the capital had been largely quiescent since the summer, the last time it had launched a successful attack on British forces. This, however, changed dramatically on the morning of 21 November, when fourteen British agents – although the original targets were as many as forty – were assassinated, most unarmed, some asleep in bed with their wives and girlfriends. Later that afternoon, Auxiliary forces entered Croke Park during a Gaelic football match; amid scenes of pandemonium, Crown forces opened fire on players and crowd, killing fourteen in their turn.[46] But the turbulent events of that day – known afterwards as 'Bloody Sunday' – rather passed

42 A. Norman Jeffares, Anna MacBride White and Christina Bridgwater (eds.), *Letters to W. B. Yeats & Ezra Pound from Iseult Gonne: A Girl that knew all Dante Once* (Basingstoke: Palgrave, 2004) pp. 118–19.
43 A. Norman Jeffares, 'Iseult Gonne' in Warwick Gould (ed.) *Poems and Contexts: Yeats Annual 16* (Basingstoke: Palgrave, 2005), pp. 246–8; R. F. Foster, *W. B. Yeats: A Life: II: The Arch-poet* (Oxford: Oxford University Press, 2003), pp. 172–6.
44 Geoffrey Elborn, *Francis Stuart: A Life* (Dublin: Raven Arts, 1990), p. 7.
45 See BMH, WS 317, Witness Statement of Maud Gonne MacBride.
46 For a full account of the planning and execution of the Bloody Sunday attacks, see Michael Foy, *Michael Collins's Intelligence War: The Struggle between the British and the IRA, 1919–1921* (Stroud: Sutton, 2006); and Anne Dolan, 'Killing and Bloody Sunday, November 1920', *Historical Journal*, vol. 49, no. 3 (2006), pp. 789–810.

MacBride by.

The men chosen for the job were not confined solely to members of the Squad; effectively they were the cream of the entire Dublin Brigade, from across a number of battalions. MacBride, however, was not among their number, for all his later boasts of directing ambushes, leading squads and running Active Service Units.[47] One might be tempted to offer his youth as an excuse – aged just sixteen in November 1920 – but many of the participants in the attacks on Bloody Sunday were little older: Charles Dalton a year older at seventeen, Vinny Byrne and Todd Andrews nineteen, Seán Lemass barely twenty. As it was, MacBride's activity on Bloody Sunday was limited to an evening spent in Lennox Robinson's flat off Nassau Street.

In conjunction with Ernie O'Malley, MacBride was in search of a safe house, as warnings not to sleep in usual places circulated the Dublin Brigade the previous night; Robinson, Iseult's would-be suitor, had offered MacBride a bed, should he ever need one, little imagining his offer would ever be taken up. This though, of all nights, was a dangerous one to sleep at home: the British response to the morning's events was in full sway, and lorry-loads of Auxiliaries and Black and Tans were combing the streets of Dublin. On the stairs outside Robinson's flat, O'Malley told MacBride of his intention to fight, should there be a raid. Armed with two revolvers and a grenade, he showed the younger man, unfamiliar with the more exotic Parabellum, the workings. O'Malley's determination not to be taken easily would play itself out two years later, in different circumstances and with different enemies, in the Humphreys' home on Ailesbury Road.[48] Inside the flat, the duo were welcomed and fed; later, they were joined by Thomas MacGreevy, poet and future director of the National Gallery. It was a curious evening; Beethoven on the pianola, stilted attempts at conversation and MacGreevy's monological reminiscences of the Great War mingled with jarring noises from outside.[49]

Following the events of Bloody Sunday, MacBride became involved in the preparation of the defence for some of the prisoners arrested in the aftermath. He was a very junior assistant to Michael Noyk, the resident republican solicitor who, along with Bob Briscoe, was one of the few Jews in the republican movement.[50] Noyk represented virtually every IRA prisoner in Dublin in the period from 1919 to 1921, for which offence his offices in College Green were regularly raided in search of incriminatory papers.[51] MacBride operated as a sort of unpaid intern within Noyk's offices, with the 'very junior role of gathering evidence, gathering state-

47 MacBride, *That Day's Struggle*, p. 29; 'Seán MacBride Remembers.'

48 Ernie O'Malley, *On Another Man's Wound* (Tralee: Anvil Press, 1990, first published 1936), p. 209; MacBride, *That Day's Struggle*, p. 25. For an account of O'Malley's dramatic capture during the Civil War, see Richard English, *Ernie O'Malley: IRA Intellectual* (Oxford: Clarendon Press, 1998), pp. 19–21.

49 O'Malley, *On Another Man's Wound*, pp. 209–10.

50 Cormac Ó Gráda, *Jewish Ireland in the Age of Joyce* (Princeton: Princeton University Press, 2006), p. 13; Patrick Maume, *The Long Gestation: Irish Nationalist Life, 1891–1918* (Dublin: Gill & Macmillan, 1999), p. 52. See also Liam Ó Briain's appreciation of Noyk after his death, *Irish Times*, 24 October 1966.

51 *Irish Times*, 22 March 1921; David Foxton, *Revolutionary Lawyers: Sinn Féin and the Crown Courts in Ireland and Britain, 1916–1923* (Dublin: Four Courts Press, 2008).

ments, preparing the statements, attending consultations and finding witness-es'.[52] One case in particular made a deep impression on him: that of Thomas Whelan, a fellow member of the Third Battalion. Whelan had been 'lifted' during the raids that followed Bloody Sunday, and was held in Kilmainham awaiting court martial for the murder of Captain G. T. Baggally, a British GHQ officer and Great War amputee. Michael Foy and Anne Dolan have both recently identified the men involved in the murder of Baggally at Baggot Street as Mattie MacDonald, Pat McCrae, Jimmy Griffin, Ben Byrne, Jack Keating and Seán Lemass; Thomas Whelan, evidently, was not among their number.[53]

The evidence in Whelan's favour appeared decisive, with alibis confirming his attendance at mass on the morning in question.[54] Noyk and his legal team, including MacBride, considered the evidence to be strongly in Whelan's favour and believed that Whelan would be acquitted. Accordingly, when plans were made for the famous escape from Kilmainham of February 1921, Noyk was approached to give his legal opinion as to which of the prisoners would be most likely to 'get off'. MacBride remembered the deliberations:

> It was a question of making a choice ... We knew from the evidence and from the inside information which we had. Especially in one particular case – I think Whelan was the man – we knew he had not been involved in the ambush and could not be involved. We advised that he was not in danger, and therefore he was one of the prisoners who could be left behind.[55]

Those selected to escape were O'Malley, Patrick Moran and Frank Teeling. O'Malley, who had yet to be charged, was of vital importance to the success of the war effort in provincial Ireland; Teeling's guilt was certain, as he had been apprehended while armed, climbing over the wall of the house in which Lieutenant MacMahon lay dead.[56] Moran's was a different case. He was charged with the murders of Lieutenants Ames and Bennett, but Noyk was certain of his innocence, and of 'a watertight defence'. Moran was certainly innocent of that particular double murder, and a whole raft of witnesses testified that he had been in south Dublin that morning, miles away from the scene of the shootings. However, Moran was part of the unit that entered the Gresham Hotel on 21 November and shot two different British officers. Moran, confident that he would be acquitted, eventually opted out of the escape, Simon Donnelly took his place, and along with O'Malley and Teeling, slipped to freedom on 14 February 1921.[57]

The calculations were wrong for both Moran and Whelan. Although evidence to their being elsewhere was presented before the courts martial, the testimony of

52 MacBride, *That Day's Struggle*, p. 31.
53 Foy, *Michael Collins's Intelligence War*, p. 158; Dolan, 'Killing and Bloody Sunday', p. 799.
54 National Library of Ireland [NLI], Michael Noyk Papers, MS 36233(1), Statement of Thomas Whelan. Statement of Alicia Kennedy; MS 36223(3), Statements of W. Lacy and E. Vaughan; BMH, WS 707, Witness Statement of Michael Noyk.
55 MacBride, *That Day's Struggle*, p. 31.
56 Sturgis, *The Last Days of Dublin Castle*, p. 115.
57 Tim Carey, *Mountjoy: The Story of a Prison* (Cork: Collins Press, 2000), p. 193. See also Witness Statement of Dermot O'Sullivan, who remembered that Paddy Moran 'believed no Court could find him guilty.' BMH, WS 508.

British officers was accepted instead. Moran's case was undermined by a photograph of him in Volunteer uniform, displaying a revolver; Whelan had naively boasted of his Volunteer regimental affiliation to the Governor of Mountjoy Prison.[58] Both men were convicted as charged, and sentenced to be hanged along with four other Volunteers arrested after the Drumcondra ambush of 31 January 1921. The customary campaigns for clemency were launched, appeals to the Attorney-General made in the House of Commons, and threats issued to Dublin Castle 'of what will happen if an innocent man is hanged'.[59] On 12 March the relatives of the condemned men gathered at Maud Gonne's house on Stephen's Green; MacBride was despatched to bring Michael Noyk to meet the families. Recalling the events some thirty years later, Noyk remembered:

> As we were walking up Grafton Street, I saw three obviously British intelligence officers in mufti, walking along, and out of the corner of my mind I recognised Commandant Maye – the commandant of Kilmainham Jail – who was wearing a flaming yellow pullover. I never saw a more villainous look on a man's face. He evidently thought that MacBride, at a distance, was Teeling or O'Malley. They were both fair-haired.[60]

Such a mistake was hard to comprehend, as both O'Malley and Teeling were much older than 17-year-old MacBride, by seven and four years, respectively. Furthermore, both the older men had distinctive features, O'Malley with a shock of red hair, Teeling walking with a slight limp. Whatever the circumstances, Noyk pulled MacBride into a friendly tobacconist shop to take shelter until the British officers had passed, and the two continued to Stephen's Green to 'a very harrowing scene' with the prisoners' families.[61] It was, however, a close escape. Another near miss had occurred the previous week, on the night of 4 March, when a section of the Prince of Wales Volunteers (South Lancashire Regiment) raided 73 Stephen's Green. The object was 'to arrest John MacBride'. Seán, luckily, was 'dining the night of the raid and on account of 9 o clock curfew was sleeping with his friends'.[62] Having missed their quarry, the military departed with 'one map, various pamphlets, a copy of handbook for rebels and some correspondence'.[63] Iseult was less fortunate than her brother; eight months pregnant at the time of the raid, her daughter Dolores was born three days later.[64] By this point, MacBride had evidently come to the attention of the British authorities; that the house on 73 Stephen's Green was raided specifically to arrest him might indicate that, *pace*

---

58 BMH, WS 707, Witness Statement of Michael Noyk.

59 Sturgis, *The Last Days of Dublin Castle*, p. 141; *Irish Times*, 11 March 1921.

60 BMH, WS707, Witness Statement of Michael Noyk.

61 BMH, WS707; O'Malley, *On Another Man's Wound*, pp. 262–63; English, *Ernie O'Malley*, pp. 2–3; Charles Dalton, *With the Dublin Brigade* (London: Peter Dalton, 1929), p. 42.

62 National Archives London [NAL], WO 35/83, Daily Reports of Raids, 4/5 March 1920; MacBride White and Jeffares (eds.), *The Gonne–Yeats Letters*, Maud Gonne MacBride to W. B. Yeats, n. d. [March 1921], p. 423.

63 NAL, WO 35/83, Daily Reports of Raids, 4/5 March 1920.

64 Jeffares, MacBride White and Bridgewater (eds.), *Letters from Iseult Gonne to W. B. Yeats and Ezra Pound*, p. 226, n. 2. Dolores Stuart died four months later from meningitis. See Iseult's letter to Yeats of [29] July for a moving account of the baby's death, p. 122.

Noyk, Commandant Maye and the other officers on Grafton Street did not mistake MacBride for another, more famous, rebel, but sought him on his own account.

On 13 March, Seán Kavanagh, a fellow prisoner in Mountjoy to where the condemned men had been moved, saw through the spyhole of his cell six empty coffins being brought up from the carpenter's workshop.[65] The following morning, the executions were duly carried out, the *Irish Independent* featuring a photograph of Maud Gonne at the front of the gathered crowd outside Mountjoy alongside the sorrowing Mrs Whelan, Thomas's mother. Whelan and his mother had become celebrity figures in the days leading up to the execution: his filial devotion, his devout Catholicism and her traditional Connemara dress adding up to an almost idealised portrait of Irish mother and son, a Gaelic *pietà*.[66] Whelan's execution made a deep impression on MacBride, 'because it showed how unreliable British court martial could be at that period. Indeed, it showed how unreliable judicial systems could be in regard to capital punishment.'[67]

Equally unreliable, however, were IRA courts martial dealing with alleged spies and informers. MacBride claimed to have intervened to prevent the execution of an ex-servicemen in B Company's area, 'having come to the conclusion that he was too dim-witted to be a spy for anybody'. Having arranged for a medical examination, MacBride spirited the prisoner away, who was duly committed to Grangegorman Hospital. If this was indeed the case, the life of the prisoner had in all probability been saved. The IRA was not slow to target ex-servicemen. The general campaign of boycotting and harassment, punctuated by the occasional murder, was taken to a new level by Michael Collins's assertion in the spring of 1921 that there 'was no crime in detecting and destroying, in wartime, the spy and the informer'. This statement was followed by a marked increase in the number of ex-servicemen executed in March 1921, and may well coincide with MacBride's case mentioned above. In later years, MacBride conceded that IRA actions against alleged informers was designed '*pour encourager les autres*', a euphemism for the campaign of terror in which republicanism dealt so well. He also admitted that in many instances IRA 'justice' was skewed: 'I think that probably many people were executed as a result of this kind of drumhead court martial who probably should not have been executed and shot by the IRA.'[68] This professed distaste for the arbitrary nature of court martial justice was not, however, an enduring feature of his republican career: in 1929 MacBride was arrested in the backroom of a pub outside Tullamore, County Offaly, officiating as prosecutor at the court martial of a local member of the IRA.[69]

65 Kenneth Griffith and Timothy O'Grady (eds.), *Curious Journey: An Oral History of Ireland's Unfinished Revolution* (London: Hutchinson, 1982), p. 215

66 *Irish Independent*, 14 March 1921, 18 March 1921; *Freeman's Journal*, 16 March 1921.

67 MacBride, *That Day's Struggle*, p. 31.

68 MacBride, *That Day's Struggle*, p. 33.

69 UCDA, MacEntee Papers, 'Synopsis of political history of Seán MacBride SC, Roebuck House', P67/539(1).

The Battle of Brunswick Street

On the day that Thomas Whelan and the five other Volunteers were hanged, MacBride participated in what became known as 'the Battle of Brunswick Street,' the only military operation in which it has been possible to identify his involvement during the War of Independence. It was a sizeable ambush, yet Keane reduces it to one paragraph lifted entirely from MacBride's own memoir, failing to understand its significance both in terms of the Bloody Sunday executions and the wider pattern of IRA campaign in Dublin.[70] The Battle of Brunswick Street, described as 'probably the fiercest engagement witnessed in the streets of Dublin since the beginning of the present trouble',[71] occurred in the context of an apparent reinvigoration of the Dublin Brigade following the advances gained by Crown forces during the winter of 1920. This was prompted largely by the accession of Oscar Traynor to the command of the Dublin Brigade; among his proposals to increase the fighting potential of the IRA in the capital was the formation of an Active Service Unit, with a target strength of 100 men from all four city battalions. The introduction of the company patrol was a further contributing factor to the improvement in the performance of Dublin units. Where previously Volunteers had been instructed to avoid firing on with Crown forces unless provoked, now they were actively pursuing violent engagements. A tenfold increase in operations was the result.

A company patrol of B Company was ordered on the evening of 14 March 1921, following the hangings in Mountjoy that morning. This was no coincidence; John Donnelly, wounded that evening, remembered the mood: 'On that day Frank Flood and five others ... were executed, and we went out that night for reprisals.'[72] In his memoir MacBride does not note the emotive circumstances of 14 March, merely commenting that 'we were told that our job was to protect the Catholic Working Man's Club in Great Brunswick Street. There was to be a battalion council meeting'.[73] The headquarters of Eamon de Valera's Third Battalion during Easter Week, 144 Great Brunswick Street was a Volunteer location of long standing; it was still an IRA meeting place and the subject of constant Volunteer patrols. An important meeting may indeed have been taking place that evening, but more important are the instructions given to the members of B Company that evening: 'All enemy to be engaged and if possible wiped out. In the event of a patrol coming into contact with enemy, all patrols to concentrate on that sector of the area to be in the fight.'[74]

It appears certain that, far from hoping to fire on whatever Crown forces happened to be passing, B Company took definite steps to ensure that the enemy would pass number 144. Shortly after eight o'clock, 'Captain Peadar O'Meara suggested to Seán Dolan to throw a bomb at College Street [police] station.'[75] Unluckily for Dolan, the bomb he was preparing to launch exploded prematurely and when

70   Keane, *Seán MacBride*, p. 37.
71   *Freeman's Journal*, 16 March 1921.
72   BMH, WS 626, Witness Statement of John Donnelly.
73   MacBride, *That Day's Struggle*, p. 26.
74   UCDA, Richard Mulcahy Papers, P7A39, 'Report on the Brunswick Street Action, 14 March 1921'; Quinn, 'The Battle of Brunswick Street', p. 159.
75   BMH, WS 626, Witness Statement of John Donnelly.

the police rushed out amidst shattering glass, 'they found him lying on the tram tracks in the deserted street with his left foot completely severed from the leg'.[76] Dolan and his foot were removed to Mercer's hospital. The incident, however, had the intended result, with two tenders of Auxiliaries – the feared F Company – and an armoured car roaring down Great Brunswick Street towards the waiting IRA squads. MacBride was among this number; as it was his first significant military action, he was paired with the more experienced Leo Fitzgerald, stationed at the corner of Sandwith Street under Lieutenant Seán O'Keeffe.[77] In the darkness, the IRA opened fire on the approaching vehicles, provoking panic among the troops. The ensuing gun battle lasted for some time, some residents claiming to have heard up to 100 shots and machine-gun fire over a period of some hours. In this measure, the Battle of Brunswick Street is largely dissimilar to prior skirmishes between Dublin IRA units and Crown forces, previously confined to small-scale attacks or 'intelligence' operations. Arguably, the events of 14 March bear more resemblance to the 'flying column' ambushes of Cork and Tipperary than to the normal patterns of urban guerrilla warfare. Furthermore, the mobilisation of such a large number of Volunteers – Augusteijn references thirty-eight – can be viewed as prefiguring the large-scale attack on the Custom House later that year.[78]

The outcome of that night was bloody: the final death-toll stood at seven. Two Auxiliaries were seriously injured, both succumbing to their wounds the following day. 34-year-old Section Leader Bernard Beard from Staffordshire, formerly Briga-dier-General in the Hundred and Twelfth Infantry Division and winner of the Military Cross, was shot in the neck and the head; 28-year-old James O'Farrell, a Dublin native, was also a Great War veteran, having served in the Royal Dublin Fusiliers and received a commission as lieutenant in the Tank Corps. He was shot twice in the back and died in theatre at George V Hospital.[79] Three civilians were also killed – the first, 41-year-old David Kelly, manager of the Sinn Féin bank and brother of Sinn Féin Alderman Thomas Kelly. On hearing the police vehicles pass his house at 132 Great Brunswick Street, he went to warn the IRA units and was caught in cross-fire – 'riddled with bullets' as John Donnelly described it.[80] Thomas Asquith, an elderly caretaker of Messrs Frame iron works, was shot in the abdomen outside his house. He lay bleeding to death beside his distraught wife for two hours before his body was removed. Stephen Clarke, an ex-serviceman, was on his way home to nearby Rostrevor Terrace after visiting his mother, when he strayed into the firing line. Instead of rushing for cover, he stopped to assist 70-year-old May Morgan who was seriously wounded, and was shot through the neck as he picked her up.[81]

76 *Irish Independent*, 15 March 1921.
77 MacBride, *That Day's Struggle*, p. 26; Quinn, 'The Battle of Brunswick Street', p. 159. The Crown vehicles numbered three, not five or six as Keane states. Keane, *Seán MacBride*, p. 37.
78 Augusteijn, *From Public Defiance to Guerrilla Warfare*, p. 167.
79 NLI, Michael Noyk Papers, MS 36,227, Courts-Martial of John Donnelly and Thomas Traynor, Statement of Third Prosecution Witness [identity undisclosed]; Abbot, *Police Casualties in Ireland*, pp. 208–9.
80 BMH, WS 626, John Donnelly Witness Statement; *Irish Independent* 17 March 1921; *Irish Times*, 17 March 1921.
81 *Freeman's Journal*, 16 March 1921; *Irish Independent*, 16 March 1921.

The IRA sustained numerous casualties that night, apart from the wounded Seán Dolan in Mercer's Hospital. Martin O'Neill was wounded and carried to safety, leaving a long trail of blood on the road; John Donnelly was discovered lying wounded with a 'bulldog' revolver and three live rounds. He, along with Tom Traynor, was arrested and court-martialled for the murders of Beard and Farrell. Both convicted as charged, Traynor was hanged on 22 April, while Donnelly was still in prison awaiting execution at the time of the Truce. Bernard O'Hanlon, a Dundalk native aged seventeen, who had been recently released from arrest after Bloody Sunday, was wounded and died later in hospital. Leo Fitzgerald, MacBride's partner, was also killed. His death occurred in the heat of battle, as the pair fired from their positions towards the Auxiliaries:

> Suddenly I became conscious that there were a lot of sparks hopping off the pavement around us ... Then I realised that these were bullets, hitting off the paving stones. I looked up and saw an armoured car about twenty or thirty yards away, firing directly at us on the ground. By this stage I realised that our position was untenable.[82]

Urging Fitzgerald to retreat, he put out his hand to shake him but 'his head was blown to pieces, my hand full of blood and brain matter'.[83] MacBride retreated into Erne Terrace, and hid there, covered in Fitzgerald's blood until first light. Returning home to wash and change his clothes, he was confronted with his first experience of death. The execution of his father was a mere abstraction, a romantic end to a figure he had never known; the soldiers dying in the French war hospitals similarly remote Fitzgerald's death was different; a close friend, killed alongside him, MacBride had to explain to the Fitzgerald family and attend the wake:

> I had to sit down and think for a couple of days afterwards, ask myself: *Are you prepared to face this? It's quite likely that you yourself will be killed in time. Are you really prepared to do this?* ... I had this kind of discussion with myself. I faced death quite calmly and coolly and decided, well if death is to come, there it is and I'm going to do what I believe to be right, and that is to continue.[84]

In the immediate aftermath of the ambush, however, MacBride had other things on his mind: namely, the rescue of Seán Dolan from Mercer's hospital. Taken there after his leg had been blown off outside College Street station, the story presented to the hospital staff was that he had been knocked over by a tram. Mercer's hospital was considered unfriendly to the IRA, and when Dolan was examined prior to surgery to fully amputate the leg, the matron 'found the splinter of a bomb ... she rang up Dublin Castle and a charwoman overheard her conversation'.[85] The charwoman was the mother of Tom Carass, officer in B Company, and she immediately told her son. Carass, MacBride and three others soon arrived at the hospital:

82 MacBride, *That Day's Struggle*, p. 27.
83 'Seán MacBride Remembers'.
84 MacBride, *That Day's Struggle*, p. 28; Coogan, *Michael Collins*, p. 143.
85 BMH, WS 626, John Donnelly Witness Statement.

When we walked into the hospital, the matron picked up the phone immedi-ately. I remember Tom Carass pushed her right back with one hand and with the other hand ripped the telephone clean off the wall ... Having found Dolan in his bed, another big man lifted him up. For some reason there were spikes sticking out from the stump of the leg. It may have been for draining purposes. Anyway we lifted him up and carried him to the car.[86]

Dolan was taken to the house of Mrs Darrell Figgis, where he was nursed back to health.[87] The ambush over, the IRA had to take stock of what had occurred. Two Auxiliaries had been killed, and three wounded. But three civilians lay dead, numerous others injured, and they had provoked 'widespread terror in the district'.[88] Two of their own men had been killed, two seriously wounded, and two taken prisoner. The judgement of Mark Sturgis, a Dublin Castle official – 'on balance, a victory for us' – seems appropriate.[89]

The Making of a Staff Officer

MacBride's position in the IRA is difficult to determine. Having joining B Company as a rank-and-filer, it appears that he received some special treatment from his peers. Coming from exotic Paris via London, and settling in comfortable Stephen's Green, meant that his place on the social spectrum was entirely different to that of his B Company comrades, who were mostly from the working-class area around Great Brunswick Street. Much of the social cachet that MacBride enjoyed within the republican movement was, of course, entirely down to his parents' fame; Todd Andrews noted that '[as] well as the prestige attached to [MacBride] as the son of Major MacBride, so vengefully executed in 1916, much of the glamour of his mother, Maud Gonne, had rubbed off on him.'[90] It was not surprising, therefore, that MacBride was eager to push himself forward into a position of responsibility within his IRA company. Looking back, he was clear on his value to the company:

> I used to direct these ambushes. This was my squad. I was pretty well in complete control of this Active Service Unit. It grew, rather than was formed. I think some of the officers in the company were rather glad that it had been formed, for they could take a lot of the credit for the Activities of 'B' Company, 3rd Battalion. They could mark up quite a respectable number of ambushes, which could not have been marked up otherwise.[91]

MacBride's eagerness to emphasise his military importance may indicate the precariousness of his position. For all his illustrious family connections, MacBride was an outsider, in Ireland, in Dublin, and in B Company. His emphasis that the B Company Active Service Unit (ASU) 'grew, rather than was formed', indicates

86 MacBride, *That Day's Struggle*, p. 30.
87 MacBride also recounted this story to Dorothy Macardle. See Dorothy Macardle, *The Irish Republic* (Dublin: The Irish Press, 1958, first published, 1937), p. 426.
88 *Irish Independent*, 15 March 1921.
89 Sturgis, *The Last Days of Dublin Castle*, p. 142.
90 Andrews, *Dublin made me*, p. 236.
91 MacBride, *That Day's Struggle*, p. 29.

that he was not part of the official ASU of the Dublin Brigade. Acting rather on his own initiative, he took increasing risks, possibly in an attempt to prove his mettle to his IRA comrades. His well-turned-out appearance and modulated, accented voice proved an effective disguise, allowing him to pose as a journalist in order to gain information from the police, a dangerous strategy considering that he had narrowly escaped arrest at the beginning of March. But such risks, along with definite advances in the Mount Street area of Dublin – the area in which MacBride claimed his 'squad' operated – paid dividends by the early summer of 1921.[92] With chronic manpower shortages due to the Crown forces' successful identification and internment of many officers of the Dublin Brigade, MacBride rose to the rank of Second Lieutenant, under Peadar O'Meara and Seán O'Keeffe, although he is not listed as such in the IRA's semi-official record of the war.[93] Whether through foolhardiness, fortuitousness or bravery, MacBride had joined a relatively active company and had participated in a number of important ambushes. His record was such that he soon came to the attention of GHQ and Michael Collins.

Much of Collins's strength within the republican movement was attributable to his building of personal networks; he cultivated a certain camp-following, a group of fiercely loyal men who formed the core of the post-Treaty Free State Army. Collins's band were either cronies from West Cork, Squad members with a visceral, almost feudal sense of fealty, or men like MacBride, barely out of boyhood and subjected to the full force of his magnetic personality. When he summoned MacBride, the younger man succumbed to the flattery and accepted a transfer into GHQ as a staff officer. MacBride's first appointment was to visit counties Wicklow, Wexford and Carlow and attempt to ginger up the IRA activities there. This appears to have been part of a wider scheme to utilise university students in the Dublin Brigade, at a loose end now that term had ended. The three Leinster counties with whose reinvigoration MacBride was tasked were particularly weak. As late as the beginning of 1921, police in all three counties were reporting relatively quiescent areas: 'Compared with other counties [Carlow] has been comparatively quiet ... the measures which are being taken to frustrate the efforts of the IRA seem to be inspiring more confidence amongst the more loyal elements of the people'; [in Wexford] there has been no attack on police or military during the month and no intimidation reported'; '[Wicklow] was generally in a peaceable state. There was but little activity among the Sinn Féiners.'[94]

Having visited all three counties, MacBride focused his attention on Wicklow. It was a logical choice: the Kavanagh brothers who formed the core of the East Wicklow Brigade had been friendly with the Fitzgeralds of Great Brunswick Street,

92   UCDA, Richard Mulcahy Papers, P7A18, Patrol Report of B Company, 3rd Battalion, 23 May 1921.
93   UCDA, Richard Mulcahy Papers, P7A23, Officers of B Company, 3rd Battalion, [n. d.] August 1921; See lists of Dublin officers in *With the IRA in the Fight for Freedom*, p. 19; Ormonde Winter, *Winter's Tale: An Autobiography* (London: Richards Press, 1955), pp. 329–30.
94   CO904/144, Inspector General's Monthly Confidential Reports, January and February 1921 [microfilm, Queen's University Belfast]. See also R. Roche, 'Events in Wexford – 1920', *Capuchin Annual* 37 (1970), pp. 574–5; M. Kavanagh, 'Events in Wicklow, 1920', *Capuchin Annual* 37 (1970), p. 589–93; and W. Nolan, 'Events in Carlow, 1920–21', *Capuchin Annual* 37 (1970), pp. 583–4.

and Maud Gonne's cottage at Glenmalure was a useful base from which to direct operations. But by the time MacBride went down to Wicklow, hostilities had begun to wind down. In May and June of 1921, there was a varying but unmistakeable degree of exhaustion to the IRA campaign, and the long summer days and short nights offered no prospect of respite to the weary flying columns. The passage of the Government of Ireland Act in 1920 and the inauguration of the northern parliament had increased the pressure on the republican leadership to respond to the peace feelers of moderates within Dublin Castle and agree to some sort of compromise solution approximating Dominion Status. The alternative was facing a renewed and much more stringent British military campaign, the planning stages of which had begun by the spring of 1921. That such an extreme shift of policy was considered had a dual effect: it shocked the British Cabinet into opting for a negotiated truce, and it reinforced IRA determination to push on before the expected reinforcements arrived. Keith Jeffery's comment that, ultimately, 'both the British government and the Irish republicans were materially influenced by the sombre prospect of a final military "push"' appears accurate.[95] MacBride, and presumably other lowly figures within GHQ, was certainly aware that a truce was on the cards. His instructions in Wicklow centred around that point: 'The IRA leadership wanted to see this other part of the country which had been dormant suddenly flaring up ... This would accelerate the pressure on the British and make them realise that there was no area in the country which hadn't an active IRA unit.'[96]

MacBride did, however, encounter a certain degree of reluctance among local Volunteers, remembering that '[the] last thing any of them wanted was activity in their area. It was alright if it was Cork, Tipperary or Dublin but let ye leave Wicklow alone.'[97] He did his best, however, bringing down Jack Hunter from his old B Company and mobilising a flying column consisting of the entire Brigade staff. This was a pattern which had had some success elsewhere: bring the entire brigade staff into an ASU or flying column, train them extensively in engaging the enemy, and run some operations before dispersing the men back into their original formations. It was hoped that, on return to original battalions and companies, the men would reproduce what they had learned on a larger scale.[98] By embroiling the Wicklow men in violent confrontations with police and military, MacBride also planned to override any reluctance to bring the struggle to a hitherto peaceful area: 'I circumvented all [their objections] by putting them out with some of my tough guys in the one operation. After that I had them: there was no going back.'[99]

The planned engagements were largely to take the form of attacks on RIC barracks; these, however, did not go as anticipated. Whether through inadequate preparations or intelligence deficiencies, when MacBride and his 'column' arrived outside Avoca barracks, they discovered, to their chagrin, that there was nobody

95 Keith Jeffery, *Field Marshal Sir Henry Wilson: A Political Soldier* (Oxford: Oxford University Press, 2006), pp. 272–3.
96 MacBride, *That Day's Struggle*, p. 38.
97 MacBride quoted in *An Phoblacht – Republican News*, 21 January 1988
98 See Augusteijn, *From Public Defiance to Guerrilla Warfare*, pp. 130–1 for this scheme in the Wexford context.
99 MacBride quoted in *An Phoblacht – Republican News*, 21 January 1988

within. This was a repetition of earlier disappointed efforts to ambush military convoys near Glenealy; having carefully laid mines and dug trenches, the convoy never showed.[100] Police reports from Wicklow in the early summer of 1921 show a small increase in anti-state activity. Thirty-nine outrages were reported in June, although the county inspector was careful to emphasise that the attack on Tinahely RIC barracks – which may have been the work of MacBride's column – was 'rather half-hearted in nature'. Other 'outrages' were rather more mundane in character; that the Wicklow inspector saw fit to include in the list of outrages the theft of a constable's bicycle outside Talbotstown church indicates the relative levity of the conflict even at so late a stage.[101]

The murders of two policemen in early July may have been attributable to MacBride's column; the county inspector certainly indicated in no uncertain terms that 'there were other signs of attempts to stir up trouble in this County which up to that period had been comparatively free from very serious outrage'.[102] One final operation was to attack Rathdrum barracks, which lay close to a large British military camp at Avondale. Before the IRA could attack the barracks, however, they ran into a patrol of policemen, fired hurriedly on them, and quickly made their escape across the Wicklow hills. A prearranged motor car never showed, and the column had to make their way by foot across the mountains to Glenmalure, where MacBride had stored the heavy weaponry. The Crown forces, however, were aware of the MacBride household – decidedly a rebel stronghold in their eyes – and filled the valley with lorries, raiding Ballinagoneen House at Glenmalure and seizing all the equipment.[103] The column made instead for the friendly Glendalough Hotel where, recovering from a badly sprained ankle, MacBride learned that a truce had been declared.

While the general population was jubilant, reactions among the IRA to the truce were varied. Ernie O'Malley's response was bewilderment and confusion: 'What did it mean? and why had senior officers no other information than a bald message?' Charles Dalton thought 'maybe it was a joke, or a trap to catch us off our guard'.[104] MacBride was, by his own account 'furious … I felt the Truce was absolutely unnecessary at the time, and we should have carried on for another few months, and that then we would have been in a stronger position to argue.'[105] MacBride made immediately for Dublin, travelling by bicycle, sidecar and train to make a personal protest to his supervisors. His interview with Bob Price, Director of Organisation, was instructive, revealing the confused thinking at a high level within the republican movement:

100 MacBride, *That Day's Struggle*, p. 38.
101 CO904/150, Weekly Summary of Outrages (Wicklow), 12 June 1921 [microfilm, Queen's University Belfast].
102 CO904/116, Inspector General Monthly Confidential Report, Wicklow, July 1921 [microfilm, Queen's University Belfast].
103 MacBride, *That Day's Struggle*, pp. 37–9; MacBride White and Jeffares (eds.), *The Gonne-Yeats Letters*, Maud Gonne MacBride to W. B. Yeats, 24 August [1921], pp. 426–7.
104 O'Malley, *On Another Man's Wound*, p. 336; Dalton, *With the Dublin Brigade*, p. 173. See *Irish Times*, 12 and 14 July 1921 for reception of the Truce in Dublin and Galway; and especially *Irish Independent*, 13 July 1921.
105 'Seán MacBride Remembers'.

But he said 'Ah well there it is; they have decided on these negotiations. Don't take this too much to heart. This will give us a pause, a breathing space during which we can reorganise and restructure some of the units which were not active' ... He tried to reassure me quite a lot that I needn't worry, that Collins would never agree to this ... unless it was to provide the breathing space so as to win right on to the end with no question of compromise.[106]

Whether Price believed this or not is unclear, but to give such assurances to a young hothead like MacBride was dangerous. If substantial numbers of Volunteers believed that the truce was merely an opportunity to regroup, rearm and reorganise, whatever settlement came back from London would be inadequate. The die was cast early for the entrenched positions of 1922.

106 MacBride, *That Day's Struggle*, p. 40.

4

Rising through the Ranks:
1921–1926

Although the truce of 1921 seemed, on the surface, a simple moment of victory, as the months advanced it brought an increasing sense of confusion and uncertainty. MacBride's claim, typical of the attitude of some local commandants, that 'we could have got much better terms by continuing for another couple of months' was mirrored by British security forces in Ireland, who maintained that 'if the Government had stuck it out for another fortnight, [the rebels] would have been glad to surrender'.[1] As the wider Irish public greeted the truce with jubilation and celebratory bonfires, the republican leadership focused their energies on an extensive training and recruitment programme across the country, a policy which had the added attraction of occupying their more extreme members. But although the popular reaction to the truce was overwhelming, the cessation presented the IRA with two related problems: one linked to the indiscipline that stemmed from the arrogance of a perceived victory, the other related to the influx of new recruits or 'trucers', as they were derisorily tagged by seasoned veterans.

In an attempt to deal with these problems, officer training camps were established all over the country, in order to impose some level of central control on what had often been a series of semi-autonomous local struggles. Such training camps were serious affairs; a surviving record of one in Tipperary includes classes on musketry and bayonet use, theory of rifle fire, fighting at close quarters, the use of hand grenades, rifle cleaning, and report writing.[2] MacBride was assigned to a similar training camp in Glenasmole, on the border between Dublin and Wicklow, where he had been sent before the truce to 'ginger up' local IRA activities. A surviving progress report from 'Staff Captain MacBride' indicates the amount of ground still to be made up in IRA structures in Wicklow: 'In some [Wicklow companies] there were neither Adjutant, Quartermaster nor Intelligence Officer. Up to now there has been no intelligence service at all in the Battalion, so I appointed a Battalion Intelligence Officer and insisted that Intelligence Officers should be appointed in each Company.'[3] The camp was successful, attracting 150

1 Quoted in Paul McMahon, 'British intelligence and the Anglo-Irish truce, July–December 1921', *Irish Historical Studies*, vol. xxxv, no. 140 (November 2007), p. 526; Seán MacBride, *That Day's Struggle: A Memoir, 1904–1951* ed. Caitriona Lawlor (Dublin: Currach Press, 2005), p. 40.
2 University College Dublin Archives [UCDA], Richard Mulcahy Papers, P7/A/17(14).
3 UCDA, Richard Mulcahy Papers, P7/A/23(90), Seán MacBride to Director of Training, 23 August 1921.

men for the weekend sessions, and retaining about a third of these for the entire week.[4] MacBride's focus was the map-reading classes, but he also participated in the customary send-off for trainee officers:

> two nights before the last day ... we would spread rumours throughout the camp that the truce had broken down and that hostilities might resume very quickly ... We would then provide them with detailed instructions as to what they might do if they were attacked ... Then on the second last night the alarm was sounded at three in the morning. Myself and a few others would run down the Glen na Smol valley and start firing a few shots in the air. This was taken to be an attack. The results were interesting. Quite a large number ceased to obey orders, running off in all directions.[5]

The exercise provided some much needed respite to the harried camp organisers, but it boded ill for the prospects of the IRA should negotiations for an agreed settlement with the British break down. With the prospect of the full force of the British army taking the lead role in renewed hostilities, much work needed to be done to turn the Trucileers into a fighting force. Related to this was the increased emphasis placed on the importation of arms, of even greater importance since the demands of the spring 1921 campaign had reduced supplies to near catastrophic levels. GHQ's focus on training camps, improving discipline and extending arms supplies, however, sent a dangerous message to the more militaristic members of the IRA, intimating that the truce was merely a brief pause to prepare for a longer, more thorough assault against the British forces in Ireland. Such an impression made the prospects of an agreed compromise ominously unstable.

Gunrunning

Whereas the IRA fixation with weaponry had always imbued arms importation with a potently symbolic meaning, the severe shortage of both arms and ammunition as the organisation faced into the truce made the issue a concrete imperative. An internal GHQ memorandum from early in the truce urged that '[the truce] be utilised to the fullest possible extent for developing the Munitions supply. There should be no question of Vacation or Half-time work on the part of anybody engaged in this department.'[6] Germany was the primary target of the IRA in the search for arms, and republican attempts to secure arms deals featured a cast of characters almost as idiosyncratic as the political upheavals shaking the infant Weimar Republic. Early IRA representatives in Germany included the mysterious John Dowling and Jewish Dubliner Robert Briscoe, who used his extensive business contacts throughout the country to arrange deals; while personalities on the German side included members of the paramilitary *Freikorps* and the fledgling Nazi party.[7] Weaponry of all kinds fell under the control of Liam Mellows, Director

4 UCDA, Richard Mulcahy Papers, P7/A/23(90); Bureau of Military History [BMH], WS 340, Witness Statement of Oscar Traynor.
5 MacBride, *That Day's Struggle*, p. 41.
6 UCDA, Mulcahy Papers, P7/A/24, GHQ Memorandum, July 1921.
7 Andreas Roth, 'Gunrunning from Germany to Ireland in the early 1920s', *The Irish Sword*, vol. xxii, no. 88 (2000), pp. 290–320; Robert Briscoe, *For the Life of me* (London: Longmans, 1958), pp. 77ff.

of Purchases, who oversaw the related departments of Chemicals – headed by James O'Donovan – and Munitions – run by Seán Russell.[8] Mellows immediately attempted to regulate and improve a hitherto haphazard system, launching an investigation into Dowling's activities and sending MacBride to Germany to report on progress of the arms deals. During the summer of 1921, MacBride made a number of journeys to Europe to liaise with Briscoe and provide progress reports to Mellows. One arms expedition was under the guise of a family holiday in Bavaria to visit the new opera house in Munich and hear Wagner – a journey planned by Maud Gonne to lift Iseult's spirits after the death of her baby Dolores in July.

Significantly, all of the personnel who featured in the importation of arms from Germany opposed the eventual Treaty agreed in London. Mellows, Russell, O'Donovan, MacBride and Briscoe were among the most adamant opposition to any agreed compromise with the British state. Having expended such time and energy on the importation of arms, in the face of assurances from the IRA leadership that such arms were necessary for the resumption of hostilities against the British forces, their apparent intransigence is cast in a new light.

With the Treaty Delegation

While the IRA were focusing on retraining and rearming, the political leaders of the republican movement had to confront the realities of a negotiated compromise, with well-established peace feelers having developed into agreement to hold a full-scale conference to determine the future of the newly divided island. Once a date had been agreed for the commencement of the conference, attention turned in Dublin to the makeup of the Irish delegation. De Valera's decision to remain behind during the negotiations has been much commented upon and attracted significant attention at the time; in later years, MacBride joined in the criticisms, noting that while he did not hold de Valera responsible for the civil war, he did

> blame him for not having participated in the treaty negotiations ... From my experience later on as Minister for External Affairs I certainly would not have allowed any delegation of officials to go to negotiate even a minor trade or other agreement with the British or any other country, without being in daily contact with them, finding out exactly what was happening from day to day[...][9]

The rationale for de Valera's course of action did, on the surface, make sense. As well as attempting to bring the recalcitrant Cathal Brugha and Austin Stack around to the intellectually sophisticated notion of external association, by staying in Dublin and insisting that any final decision be taken by the Cabinet there, the Irish leader was attempting to protect the delegation from the intensity of British pressure. The makeup of the delegation – Arthur Griffith, Michael Collins, Robert Barton, George Gavan Duffy, Eamon Duggan – was, from de Valera's perspective, a coalition of all the disparate elements in the Sinn Féin movement, from hardline republicans to soft 'dual monarchists', with each wing adequately balancing the

8   C. Desmond Greaves, *Liam Mellows and the Irish Revolution* (London: Laurence & Wishart, 1971), p. 223.
9   MacBride, *That Day's Struggle*, pp. 72–73.

other. But it was perhaps this very feature which necessitated de Valera's presence; presiding over an even more divided cabinet, Lloyd George markedly headed the British delegation himself and, as Alvin Jackson has noted, was able to turn the same divisions into an effective bargaining tool.[10]

After the selection of the delegation, preparations quickly began for the negotiations in London. As well as the customary secretarial staff, Collins brought a personal retinue with him, mostly IRB colleagues with whom he replicated the boisterous atmosphere of their Dublin haunts. MacBride was selected as part of this entourage, with special responsibility for bringing the delegation's despatches over and back from London via the mailboat in Holyhead. This was intended to keep the Cabinet in Dublin fully aware of the progress of the negotiations but, in practice, never really bridged the communication divide. MacBride's observation that the delegation should have returned to Dublin every weekend to consult with the other Cabinet members and that the failure to do so caused 'a complete loss of contact and loss of touch between the members of the cabinet at home ... and the delegation itself' is an interesting proposition. If this had been the established routine, with regular opportunities for the exchange of views and discussion of strategy in person, as opposed to the limited scope of written communication, the final Cabinet meeting before the Treaty was signed, on 3 December, might not have been such a fraught affair.[11]

Accommodation for the Irish delegation was secured at two fashionable locations in London, 22 Hans Place and 15 Cadogan Gardens, after extensive reconnaissance work by two Collins associates, Joseph McGrath and Dan McCarthy; two residences immediately signified two distinct camps within the delegation and their associated staff.[12] This division was acknowledged across the delegation as between the 'military' house and the 'politicians'; the latter term had gained currency during the previous years' hostilities and carried a definite derogatory charge, prefiguring the venomous public discourse which would follow the Treaty split.[13] MacBride's inclusion in Collins's personal staff was surprising: still a teenager, he was by some considerable distance the junior of the other men; and he was not a member of the IRB. Furthermore, his somewhat haughty demeanour and cultivated European sophistication was far removed from the rough-and-tumble, emphatically rural, attitudes of the other residents of Cadogan Gardens. Although there was an even larger age gap between MacBride and the remainder of the Irish delegation at Hans Place, socially he was much more at home there. He frequently played bridge with members of the household, and joined in the more restrained afternoon tea served there, for which he received much ribbing from the 'military' house. MacBride's later recollection that he was 'the only person who visited from one house to the other and was on friendly terms with

10 Alvin Jackson, *Ireland, 1798–1998* (Oxford: Blackwell Publishers, 1999), p. 259.
11 MacBride, *That Day's Struggle*, pp. 72–3; 'Seán MacBride Remembers', RTÉ, originally broadcast 1989; John M. Curran, *The Birth of the Irish Free State, 1921–1923* (Alabama: University of Alabama Press, 1981, first published 1980), pp. 116–18.
12 BMH, WS 722, Witness Statement of Dan McCarthy; MacBride, *That Day's Struggle*, p. 45; Kathleen Napoli-McKenna, 'In London with the Treaty delegation: personal recollections', *Capuchin Annual*, 38 (1971), pp. 317–21.
13 MacBride, *That Day's Struggle*, p. 45.

people in both houses' offers a sobering glimpse into the cleavages which were already present within the movement.[14]

'Now we have to face our diehards'[15]

In Dublin when the Treaty was signed, MacBride was absent for the extreme tension of its final stages: the divisions among the Irish delegates finally voiced, the miscalculation of Griffith in unilaterally signing a commitment on Ulster revealed, and the threat of 'immediate and terrible war within three days' forcing the delegates to abandon their original instructions and sign without reference to Dublin. News of the signature of the Anglo-Irish Treaty and its terms caused consternation within the ranks of the republican movement. Celia Shaw, a student at University College Dublin and contemporary of MacBride's, recorded in her diary the reaction of the student circles: 'no-one knows what to think. There is an oath, though subtly worded ... not a bonfire, not a flag, not a hurrah. We go down in the evening again to see the same old crowd. Opinion pretty much divided, Michael Rynne, Sarsfield Hogan for, Seán MacBride, Eddy Lennon against.'[16] Opinion for or against the Treaty was by and large quickly formed; MacBride was no exception, identifying himself as strongly anti-Treatyite within days. MacBride's hierarchy of reasons for opposition ran along common republican lines: conviction that better terms had been available, opposition primarily to the hated oath of allegiance, and a secondary antipathy to the partition of Ireland.[17] After the delegation had returned to Ireland and faced their Cabinet colleagues – Cosgrave proving the unforeseen deciding vote swinging the decision in favour of the agreement – it was announced that the Treaty would be debated in Dáil Éireann on 14 December.

Although the reverberations of choosing sides were widely felt, the divisions within the IRA were the most serious outcome of the Treaty split. Nominally a national army, the IRA was more than that; in at least the same measure as any other republican institution, it was a political body, intensely concerned with Ireland's political future. But the IRA was a body very much of its own making, with little if any control exercised by GHQ over provincial units, still less by the civil republican authorities. Although attempts had been made to formally organise the IRA along conventional military lines, the system of divisionalisation actually served to entrench the autonomy of regional commanders and strengthen their local power bases. But for most within the IRA, positioning oneself on either side of the Treaty divide was not a straightforward political choice; friendships and enmities influenced the taking of sides, and for the most part 'it all depended what crowd you got into'.[18]

---

14   'Sean MacBride Remembers'. See also John Bowman, '"*Entre nous*": some notes by Erskine Childers on the making of the Anglo-Irish Treaty, 1921', in P. Fox (ed.), *Treasures of the Library, Trinity College Dublin* (Dublin: Royal Irish Academy, 1986), pp. 222–9, for a further insight into the divisions among the Irish delegation.

15   Liam Tobin to David Neligan, quoted in Kenneth Griffith and Timothy O'Grady, *Curious Journey: An Oral History of Ireland's Unfinished Revolution* (London: Hutchinson, 1982), p. 259.

16   National Library of Ireland [NLI], Celia Shaw Diary, MS 23,409, 7 December 1921.

17   MacBride, *That Day's Struggle*, p. 55.

18   Seán Harling quoted in Griffith and O'Grady, *Curious Journey*, p. 285.

MacBride's opposition to the Treaty fell outside these parameters, however. In rejecting any form of compromise, he was alone among Collins's retinue in London. Moreover, the Collins circle in IRA GHQ – Liam Tobin and Tom Cullen especially – had been to a large extent MacBride's closest colleagues within the revolutionary movement: never quite at home within his company of the Dublin Brigade, the dazzling orbit of Collins had provided MacBride with a sense of belonging that he had otherwise struggled to find. MacBride's rejection of the terms brought back by Collins from London thus represented a decisive break with the colleagues he had come to consider as friends. Thereafter, as he brusquely noted in his memoir, he was 'more or less bereft of personal friends in the movement'.[19] MacBride was also isolated, initially at least, at home: Maud Gonne was at first supportive of the limited measure of independence provided by the Treaty. In this she was possibly influenced by her old association with Griffith; those with personal memories of the long struggle for Home Rule were arguably more readily convinced that the Treaty represented a significant advance in what had been a fifty-year campaign for some measure of autonomy. Within the MacBride household, therefore, something of a rift occurred, although the bitterness which characterised other familial breaches was absent. Mother and son 'agreed to disagree. We ceased to exchange views very much – political views.'[20]

'Gone was the old chivalry and esprit de corps'[21]

While the MacBrides managed to accommodate this difference of opinion, rapid polarisation led to entrenched bitterness across the nationalist movement. MacBride attended the public and private debates on the Treaty; in retrospect, he considered the speech of Mary MacSwiney the most impressive of the ninety-five or so contributions during the course of the debate. Her fiery defence of 'the living Republic' ended with a declaration that the Republican government would not be destroyed by 'the Wizard of Wales'.[22] For MacBride this speech 'made an impression of deep logic and integrity'; to a more jaundiced observer, MacSwiney 'contributed nothing but bitterness and hatred and malignancy'.[23] Overall, MacBride seems to have borne the bitterness of the dispute with equanimity; not for him the agonies of Liam Deasy, who remembered that 'we had to listen to men who a few short months before were fighting as comrades side by side, now engaging in bitter recriminations, rancour, invective, charges and counter charges'.[24] That partition was not the subject of sustained attention during the debates did not escape MacBride's notice, although his underlining of the issue in his memoir may be more indicative of his later adoption of the issue as his *idée*

19 MacBride, *That Day's Struggle*, p. 55.
20 MacBride, *That Day's Struggle*, p. 56. See also Ronan Sheehan, 'Interview with Seán MacBride', *The Crane Bag*, vol. 2, no. 1 (1978), pp. 302–3.
21 Liam Deasy, *Brother Against Brother* (Dublin: Mercier Press, 1982), p 32.
22 *Dáil Éireann Debates*, vol. 3 col. 126, 21 December 1921.
23 MacBride, *That Day's Struggle*, p. 59; P. S. O'Hegarty, *The Victory of Sinn Féin: How it Won it and How it Used it* (Dublin: University College Dublin Press, 1998, first published 1924), p. 77.
24 Deasy, *Brother Against Brother*, p 32.

fixe rather than representative of his opinion at the time. On 7 January 1922, after fifteen days' debate and argument, a vote was recorded on the Treaty: 64 in favour, 57 against. Although the majority in Dáil Éireann was a mere seven votes, as the *Irish Times* noted, the narrow victory reflected 'the will of at least nine-tenths of the Irish people'; the IRB-dominated nomination of candidates for the 1921 election had ensured that the Dáil's political outlook was much more extreme than that of the movement at large, or society as a whole.[25] But the real crux of the issue lay with the IRA: whether loyalty to the majoritarianism of the Dáil or the purity of the Republic would prevail was increasingly becoming crucial in determining the success of the compromise settlement.

During this period, MacBride was more preoccupied with political than with army affairs, perhaps indicative of his relative isolation within the IRA. In the immediate aftermath of the Treaty vote, MacBride moved closer to de Valera, whose swift denunciation of the compromise terms he approved of, and was diverted by the upcoming Irish Race Convention in Paris. Claiming, as MacBride does in his memoir, that his task was 'to finalise plans' for the Convention – a claim faithfully reproduced by Elizabeth Keane – is grossly to overstate the significance of what was a minor administrative role.[26] Originally planned to demonstrate the unity of the Irish people across the world, by January 1922, political divisions on the Treaty conspired to make the Convention a political irrelevance, degenerating into in-fighting and backbiting. MacBride was largely too preoccupied with administrative duties to attend the public functions and official sessions associated with the Convention; arranging lunches and dinners for de Valera's group, he worried constantly about bills for republican extravagance. It was, however, a useful exercise for the young MacBride, bringing him to the attention of important figures within the new republican movement. Whereas previously he had associated almost exclusively with the Collins entourage, the Race Convention marked the beginning stage in the establishment of a new identity.

'One would like to draw a curtain over all the subsequent shillying and shallying'[27]

Arriving back from Paris at the beginning of February 1922, MacBride returned to a political and military vacuum. In the first of a series of delaying tactics, the newly formed Provisional Government of the Irish Free State, headed by Collins, decided to postpone formal elections to a new parliament, effectively depriving the Irish public of an early opportunity to register popular opinion of the Treaty. This decision, arising from an agreed compromise with the de Valera camp, afforded breathing space on both sides of the political divide: republicans could focus on reorganising their rump of a fragmented party-political machine, while

25   *Irish Times*, 9 January 1922; O'Hegarty, *The Victory of Sinn Féin*, pp. 53–5.
26   MacBride, *That Day's Struggle*, p. 60; Elizabeth Keane, *Seán MacBride: A Life* (Dublin: Gill & Macmillan, 2007), p. 42. For more detail on the Convention, see Gerard Keown, 'The Irish Race Conference, 1922, reconsidered', *Irish Historical Studies*, vol. xxxii, no. 127 (May 2001), pp. 365–76.
27   Seán O'Faoláin, *De Valera* (Harmondsworth: Penguin, 1939), p. 10.

the Provisional Government concentrated on coordinating the British military withdrawal and building the machinery of government.[28]

It was, however, primarily an attempt by Collins and Mulcahy to buy time to win back the support of anti-Treaty elements of the IRA. This should not imply that this group was by any means united or uniform in their attitudes. There was much variation among IRA members opposed to the Treaty. Collins, Mulcahy and Eoin O'Duffy, the new Chief of Staff, attempted to bridge the divide between extremists and moderates, but their eagerness to convince estranged former comrades that acceptance of the Treaty did not equate with the abandonment of republican ideals meant that the gross insubordination of officers refusing to adhere to parliamentary authority and normal military discipline was enormously indulged. All three, Mulcahy in particular, had worked hard to implement a degree of professionalism into the IRA; that they were willing to fatally undermine this by cosseting republican egos for much of the first half of 1922 is indicative of the desperation with which Collins, above all, approached the project of reunification. This project became the rationale for key elements of the Treatyite strategy and manifested itself in three crucial areas during the months of drift up to June 1922: the framing of a republican-tinged constitution, the provision of covert assistance to the northern IRA in the deteriorating security situation north of the border, and the reluctance of the Provisional Government to face down the extremist challenge presented by a series of extraordinary manoeuvres by the anti-Treaty IRA during the spring and early summer of 1922.

In March, a proscribed Army Convention went ahead in the Mansion House; repudiating the authority of the Minister of Defence, an executive of sixteen was appointed, amid even more fractures and disagreements.[29] In the press, both the Convention and the extremist anti-Treaty IRA were associated primarily with Rory O'Connor, former Director of Engineering in IRA GHQ. Although O'Connor was not elected to any special position of power within the new executive, his infamous press conference of 22 March, when he blithely declared that he had not understood the Treaty and appeared unconcerned by the portrayal of the IRA as a military dictatorship, made him the identifiable face of extremism.[30] To Field-Marshal Sir Henry Wilson, he was 'O'Rory O'Gory O'Connor'; to the *Round Table* correspondent he was the emblem of the zealotry of the IRA: 'The Republic is [O'Connor's] religion and compromise is sin. If the people are in heresy, they must be converted, by force if necessary.'[31] It was around O'Connor that MacBride would construct the lasting comradeships of his Civil War experience; along with Ernie O'Malley, Liam Mellows and Peadar O'Donnell, O'Connor and his coterie

---

28 Michael Laffan, *The Resurrection of Ireland: The Sinn Féin Party, 1916–1923* (Cambridge: Cambridge University Press, 2005, first published 1999), pp. 372–3; John M. Regan, 'Michael Collins, General Commanding-in-Chief, as a historiographical problem', *History*, vol. 92, no. 307 (June 2007), p. 323.

29 NLI, Florence O'Donoghue Papers, MS 31,425.

30 *Irish Times*, 23 March 1922; C. S. Andrews, *Dublin made me: An Autobiography* (Dublin: Lilliput Press, 2001, first published 1979), p. 233.

31 *Irish Times*, 28 April 1922; 'Ireland at the crossroads', *Round Table*, vol. xii, no. 47 (June 1922), p. 519.

provided the 18-year-old MacBride with a sense of soldierly unity which he had lost when he broke with the Collins camp.

After the March Convention, it should have been clear to Collins and Mulcahy that the course of mediation they had been striving towards had disappeared; by then, even the previously moderate Liam Lynch was writing to his brother that 'we have started to put an end to the Free State and general disgraceful compromise and we mean now to see it through'.[32] Another decisive stage was passed in April 1922, with the Irregular (as the anti-Treaty IRA was dubbed by the Free State) occupation of a number of important buildings across Dublin: the most significant of these was the Four Courts. It was an incongruous location for a rebel fortress: amid the neoclassical flourishes of James Gandon's great dome, sandbags were piled to form barricades and legal tomes stacked against windows. MacBride was appointed assistant director of organisation to Ernie O'Malley: their work consisted mainly of statistical surveys of the strength of the anti-Treaty IRA units across the country.

It was not all work, however; O'Malley and MacBride made regular jaunts down Grafton Street to take coffee in Mitchells café and meet college girls. That the two could nonchalantly incorporate morning coffee and romantic assignations into their daily routine is indicative of the light-heartedness that still prevailed among sections of the republican movement: to Andrews, it was clear that MacBride and O'Malley 'at that time were [not] very serious'.[33] Equally, that two well-known Irregulars could blithely stroll down one of Dublin's busiest thoroughfares without molestation by either the newly formed Civic Guard or the burgeoning Free State Army, reflects the reluctance on the part of the Provisional Government to resort to force in nullifying the extremist challenge to its authority. As well as enjoying the glamorous side of republican extremism, MacBride was also engaged in 'mysterious journeys': the continuation of his gunrunning activities from Germany. This was undertaken, as before, in conjunction with Bob Briscoe, at the request of Collins and with the blessing of the Irregular executive.

The cooperation of the opposing wings of the IRA in this area was the result of an important impulse within the republican movement mitigating against civil war. While there was a hard-core of extremist republicans – clustered around O'Connor and Mellows – who appeared unperturbed by the prospect of violent confrontation with their estranged former comrades, there remained a significant cross-section of republican opinion for whom such a course was to be avoided at all costs. As late as April 1922, Harry Boland, Collins's erstwhile confidant and latterly an anti-Treatyite, wrote to Joseph McGarrity of Clan na Gael: 'Do not be afraid of the Civil War bogey. There will be no civil war in Ireland. There may be a few isolated episodes until things settle down.'[34] But at the time of Boland's letter, civil war of a sort already existed in a part of Ireland: the rapid escalation of sectarian violence north of the border provided an avenue for reunification of the splintered republican forces in the south, and one which unity-minded elements were keen

32   NLI, Liam Lynch Papers, MS 36,251, Liam Lynch to Thomas Lynch, 31 March 1922.
33   Todd Andrews recorded in 1970, broadcast on 'What If?', RTÉ Radio 1, 17 February 2008.
34   NLI, Joseph McGarrity Papers, MS 33,365, Harry Boland to Joseph McGarrity, 20 April 1922.

to exploit.[35] The joint IRA offensive of April 1922 was the short-term result.[36]

From MacBride's evidence, Collins had long envisaged that the northern question would restore the unity of the IRA, aiming as early as July 1921 that MacBride's continued importation of arms would principally supply the north.[37] Supplying the northern IRA with the necessary weaponry to defend the beleaguered nationalist minority, particularly in Belfast, was an issue on which both wings of their southern counterparts could effectively cooperate. As well as the imported guns, cooperation centred around the exchange of arms: the Free State Army's new supply of British guns was exchanged for anti-Treaty weapons, to avoid the discovery of British serial numbers in engagements north of the border. This exchange of weapons – to MacBride's eyes 'in substantial amounts, in lorry-loads' – formed the backdrop to a renewed, if unsuccessful, attempt to forge unity.

Further Divisions

MacBride, however, was nothing more than an interested bystander to many of these events. As well as occupying a junior position within the staff of the anti-Treaty IRA, he was absent for lengthy periods during the early summer of 1922, arranging arms deals on the continent. He returned, in the wake of failed negotiations towards army unity, to an anti-Treaty executive divided among itself. Events had accelerated rapidly in the days preceding his return: the much vaunted Collins–de Valera pact had evidently been repudiated by Collins during a speech in Cork; the much awaited Constitution had been published – to the dismay of republicans – and the much heralded election to secure a democratic mandate in favour of the Treaty held on 16 June. Having returned to Dublin early on the morning of 18 June, MacBride was thrust into the preparations for the Convention summoned as a showdown between the moderation-minded Lynch camp and the extremist faction within the Four Courts.

Organisation of the Convention devolved to O'Malley, as director of organisation: he, MacBride and Andrews spent the morning in Parnell Square inspecting the credentials of delegates to the Convention. As Andrews bluntly put it, '[t]hey were all rigged.'[38] The intransigents in the Four Courts intended that the Convention should definitively reject Lynch's proposals for conciliation, but an alternate proposal by Tom Barry to declare war on the British within seventy-two hours produced an unlikely result. MacBride maintained, both in the immediate aftermath of the Convention and in writings and interviews towards the end of his life, that Barry's proposal was

35 Alan Parkinson, *Belfast's Unholy War: The Troubles of the 1920s* (Dublin: Four Courts Press, 2004); Robert Lynch, 'The people's protectors? The Irish Republican Army and the "Belfast Pogrom", 1920–1922', *Journal of British Studies*, vol. 47, no. 2 (2008), pp. 375–91.
36 See Robert Lynch, 'Donegal and the joint-IRA offensive, May–November 1922', *Irish Historical Studies*, vol. xxxv, no. 138 (November 2006), pp. 184–99; and Michael Hopkinson, *Green against Green* (Dublin: Gill & Macmillan, 2004, first published 1988), pp. 83–6.
37 'Seán MacBride Remembers'.
38 UCDA, Ernie O'Malley Papers, P17/6/088, Todd Andrews interview.

very foolish ... it was neither the time nor the place for it. in fact, such a proposal meant putting the onus of declaring war on Great Britain on a body of men who had been selected by the various units of the Army, to select an Executive which was to appoint a Chief of Staff and to direct the policy of the Army until a Republican Government was formed ... As a policy the substance of his motion was quite right, but by putting it forward at a Convention without consulting anybody, as he did, was putting those who supported that policy in a very awkward position.[39]

Lengthy speeches followed Barry's intervention – prompting MacBride's observation that 'speech-making undoubtedly seems to be one of our National failings' – but the final vote on the proposal was highly contested.[40] The final result was a narrow defeat for the Barry proposal, by 118 votes to 103; the most telling consequence of the vote was the refusal of the O'Connor camp to abide by the decision of the majority. Staging a walk-out of the Convention and a retreat to the Four Courts, O'Connor, Mellows and McKelvey sent MacBride back into the chamber to retrieve Mellows's hat and announce their withdrawal. MacBride bounded back into the Convention and 'shout[ed] in his queer French-accented voice, swinging over his head his .45 Colt automatic at the end of a lanyard, "All who are in favour of the Republic follow me to the Four Courts"': in the silence that followed, his footsteps echoed like gunshots.[41]

The split had incurred a further split: the anti-Treaty executive, established to guide the army away from the contagion of compromise, was now hopelessly divided. Returning to the Four Courts, the doors were locked behind the militants, excluding the Lynch faction; this action, representing a break with the militarily and politically weighty 1st Southern Brigade, was an important moment. For Todd Andrews, commenting bitterly in retrospect, it demonstrated 'the intransigence, the *jusqu'auboutissme* that was largely consisted of MacBride, McKelvey, Mellows and O'Malley'; similarly, Peadar O'Donnell later castigated the Irregular leadership – of which he was a part – as 'a very pathetic executive, an absolutely bankrupt executive. All it did was oppose the Treaty – it had no policy of its own'.[42] Two days later, the situation further deteriorated when Field Marshal Sir Henry Wilson was assassinated on his doorstep in London. Much historiographical attention has centred on the question of Collins's involvement in the murder.[43] Opinion at the time, however, centred not on Collins but on the Four Courts garrison; the

---

39 National Archives of Ireland [NAI], D/T S1233, Extract from notes made by Seán MacBride on the final Army Convention. See also MacBride, *That Day's Struggle*, p. 64.

40 NAI, D/T S1233, Extract from notes made by Seán MacBride.

41 Andrews, *Dublin made me*, p. 242; NAI, D/T S1233, Extract from notes made by Seán MacBride

42 Todd Andrews recorded in 1970, broadcast on 'What If?', RTÉ Radio 1, 17 February 2008; Jackson, *Ireland*, p. 269; Fintan O'Toole, 'A portrait of Peadar O'Donnell as an old soldier', *Magill* (February 1983), p. 26.

43 Wilson's biographer has concurred with Peter Hart's assessment that 'there was no solid evidence to support a conspiracy theory linking Michael Collins or anyone else to the murder'. Keith Jeffery, *Field Marshall Sir Henry Wilson: A Political Soldier* (Oxford: Oxford University Press, 2006) p. 284; Peter Hart, *The IRA at War, 1916–1923* (Oxford: Oxford University Press, 2005, first published 2003), p. 219.

British Cabinet concluded that 'it was intolerable that Mr Rory O'Connor should be permitted to remain with his followers in open rebellion in the heart of Dublin in possession of the Courts of Justice, acting as a centre of murder organisation and propaganda'.[44] Secret orders were delivered to General Macready, commander of the remaining British garrison in Ireland, to attack the Four Courts; Macready delayed their execution, arguing perceptively that a British attack on the Four Courts would rally support to the republican side. The anti-Treaty republicans came agonisingly close, therefore, to reaching their goal – the resumption of hostilities against British forces.

But the O'Connor faction further raised the domestic stakes by insisting on the propagation of the ill-advised Belfast boycott; in addition to extracting money from a number of businesses, on 26 June a republican party commandeered cars from Ferguson's Garage in Dublin. The Provisional Government had decided that such activities would not be tolerated and accordingly arrested the party's leader, Leo Henderson. In retaliation, O'Malley and a party of fourteen men, including MacBride, arrested J. J. 'Ginger' O'Connell, a close ally of Collins and the assistant Chief of Staff of the Army.[45] The following morning, Collins asked the British forces for the loan of artillery. Interpretations of the immediate cause of the civil war have centred around the amount of pressure the British Government brought to bear on the Provisional Government in the wake of the Wilson assassination. But such a case can easily be overstated: there was a growing determination within the Provisional Government – centred around Griffith, O'Higgins and Blythe – to face down the gunmen. More crucial, moreover, was the grimly coalescing realisation by Collins and Mulcahy that their policy of conciliation had failed. This, together with the Provisional Government's knowledge that the anti-Treaty executive had undergone a further split, was arguably the key factor in determining the timing of a move against the Four Courts garrison; the kidnapping of O'Connell merely the pretext. The second split, therefore, was the critical moment, one participant later arguing bitterly that 'it was for that reason … that the Free State decided it was safe to attack the Four Courts. They had no belief that the Dublin Brigade would fight. And they felt if they cleaned up the Four Courts, that would be the end.'[46]

'The cloud we had seen coming opened its floodgates to deluge our country in blood'[47]

The attack on the Four Courts finally came on the night of 27 June, after the Provisional Government's ultimatum to surrender expired. At 4.07 am on 28 June, the first shells from the borrowed 18 lb British field gun were fired.[48] Although

---

44 National Archives London [NAL], CAB/23/39, Cabinet conclusions of 22 June 1922. See also Kevin Matthews, *Fatal Influence: The Impact of Ireland on British Politics, 1920–1925* (Dublin: University College Dublin Press, 2004), pp. 81–3.

45 NLI, Fred Johnson Papers, MS 27,609A, Thomas Johnson to Fred Johnson, 5 July 1922.

46 Todd Andrews recorded in 1970, broadcast on 'What If?', RTÉ Radio 1, 17 February 2008.

47 BMH, WS 544, Witness Statement of Joseph O'Connor.

48 NAL, CAB/24/137, Report by the General Officer Commanding on the situation in Ireland for week ending 1 July 1922.

word had begun to filter through of the impending attack on the evening of 27 June, the republican garrison had been unable to adequately prepare to resist the attack, lacking arms and ammunition. More seriously, the Irregulars failed to secure key outposts surrounding the Four Courts necessary for the defence of the building: this deficiency was attributable to the leadership's decision that they would countenance no actions which could be interpreted as having fired the first shots in the fast onrushing Civil War. This mindset also dictated that the Dublin Brigade of the Irregular IRA, who would have been ideally placed to undertake such auxiliary operations, were not mobilised in time to occupy positions ahead of the Free State assault.

These decisions, which effectively paralysed the Irregular resistance, were further exacerbated by widespread confusion over the command structure within the Four Courts. Paddy O'Brien, officer in charge of the Four Courts garrison, was chary of exerting authority over the Irregular executive; similarly, Ernie O'Malley, whom O'Brien appointed at the head of the GHQ section, was reluctant to issue orders to McKelvey and Mellows.[49] All of these flaws in the Irregular defence of their positions came as a consequence of the primary, catastrophic, decision: to stand and fight in the Four Courts itself. As ruefully recalled by one anti-Treaty IRA member, '[t]he [Four Courts] garrison if they came out could have beaten anything surrounding them ... the best men of the IRA were in there and then were locked up for the rest of the civil war.'[50]

The spectacle of landmark buildings within the capital seized by rebels carried, of course, unmistakeable resonances of Easter week. Self-consciously referencing the stance of the Easter rebels, an Irregular executive statement in the first day of the assault captured the evocation of the spirit of 1916: 'Gallant soldiers of the Irish Republic, stand vigorously firm in its defence and worthily uphold their noblest traditions. The sacred spirit of the illustrious dead are with us in the great struggle.'[51] But as had been displayed six years previously, the isolated occupation of the Four Courts was completely unsuited for combat against a better equipped adversary. That the leadership of the Irregulars had not grasped that the success of the preceding years' struggle against the British lay in small-scale ambushes, not set-piece engagements, boded ill for the military prospects of their campaign. The siege of the Four Courts is curiously absent from MacBride's recorded reminiscences of the Civil War. Yet, the 1916 parallels carried an intensely personal charge: trapped inside the dome of the Four Courts along with the other members of GHQ, as the shells rained down, MacBride was for the first time able to access a shared experience with his father, Major John MacBride.[52] The presence in the Four Courts of Frs Albert and Dominic, two of the Capuchin friars who attended the Easter

49   NLI, MS 33063, Account by Commandant Simon Donnelly of attack on Four Courts, written 1923; Ernie O'Malley, *The Singing Flame* (Dublin: Anvil Books, 1979), pp. 91–3; Hopkinson, *Green against Green*, pp. 121–2.

50   Paddy Morrisey, quoted in Tom Garvin, *1922: The Birth of Irish Democracy* (Dublin: Gill & Macmillan, 2005, first published, 1996), p. 33.

51   Army Executive Statement, *Poblacht na hÉireann War News*, 29 June 1922. This parallel is curiously not drawn in a recent cultural history of the 1916 rising: Clair Wills, *Dublin 1916: The Siege of the GPO* (London: Profile Books, 2009).

52   MacBride, *That Day's Struggle*, p. 65.

rebels in the GPO and the executed leaders in Kilmainham, drew the analogy even more starkly; the final dénouement, as the Irregulars surrendered and marched in fours down the quays, to await imprisonment or worse in Mountjoy, also carried striking echoes of the surrender of the Jacob's Factory garrison in 1916.

The defence of the building had gone poorly from the start, stymied by the handicaps detailed above. Further difficulties were created by the apparent reluctance of the Irregulars to engage the Free State army: Nevil Macready reported to the British Cabinet that 'very few of the houses on the opposite side of the Street to those occupied by the republicans show marks of bullets'.[53] Although the borrowed British artillery was slow to find its range, by the second day of the siege shells were falling with terrible accuracy on the dome of the building, and by midnight on 29 June Free State troops had succeeded in retaking parts of the building. The following day, two huge explosions in the Four Courts shook windows across Dublin: flames from repeated shelling spread into the munitions section, housed in the Public Record Office adjacent to the Four Courts, destroying countless and priceless historical documents. The disdain shown by the Irregulars for the plain people of Ireland's present was matched by their criminal destruction of the records of Ireland's past.[54]

The spread of the fire throughout the Four Courts complex brought events to a rapid conclusion; while the Irregular leadership – including MacBride – argued the rights and wrongs of surrender with Fr Albert and each other, a communication arrived from Oscar Traynor, commander of the anti-Treaty Dublin Brigade forces: 'If the Republic is to be saved your surrender is a necessity. As Senior Officer outside I take it that I am entitled to order you to make a move which places me in a better military position.' After much discussion, the senior officers made the decision to capitulate.[55] MacBride marched in the first company of the garrison, alongside O'Connor, O'Malley and Mellows, as the garrison surrendered to Free State forces at 4 p.m. The Irregulars, numbering some 150 men, were taken to Jameson's distillery and thence to Mountjoy jail. The active phase of MacBride's participation in the Civil War had ended, along with that of the majority of the anti-Treaty officers in the IRA. The theatre of operations now shifted for MacBride to the prison war, and experiences which would dominate his Civil War memories.

Prison Life

Comprising most of the Irregular army executive and the most vehement and militant opponents of the Treaty, it is not surprising that this first group of prisoners commenced a violent campaign of non-cooperation with prison governors. There

53 MacBride, *That Day's Struggle*, p. 65.
54 Caitríona Crowe has described the destruction of the Public Record Office as 'an unparalleled act of cultural vandalism' in RTÉ Radio's, 'What If?', broadcast 17 February 2008. See also S. C. Radcliff, 'The destruction of the Public Record Office in Dublin', *Historical Research*, vol. 2, no. 4 (June 1924), pp. 8–9.
55 Cormac O'Malley and Anne Dolan (eds.), *No Surrender Here!: The Civil War Papers of Ernie O'Malley, 1922–1924* (Dublin: Lilliput Press, 2007), Oscar Traynor to Ernie O'Malley, 30 June 1922, p. 31; NLI, MS 33,063, Account by Commandant Simon Donnelly of attack on Four Courts.

was, thus, an overtly confrontational aspect to MacBride's Mountjoy existence: conflict with both temporal and spiritual authorities became a defining feature of the Civil War prisons. Underlying this bellicosity, however, was an intense spirit of comradeship; the intimacy of prison conditions forged friendships which lasted throughout the Civil War and into the post-independent era. For MacBride in particular, who had always struggled to integrate himself fully into the republican movement, the importance of the prison experience should not be underestimated. The initial campaign was centred on securing prisoner-of-war status, and struck a violent note from the beginning. After the republican prisoners arrived at Mountjoy, political status was demanded; this being denied, the prisoners refused to enter their cells in D-Wing. As a consequence, they were forced 'to lie on the grass all night with machine guns trained on them' Subsequently, after forcible removal to the cells, the prisoners began destroying D-Wing: 'We broke out of our cells yesterday at 5.15, got no exercise and rotten food. All windows broken. Hole 5 by 2 between each cell. All doors now open and the locks smashed. We are running the wing ourselves in every way.'[56]

There was another manifestation of this rejection of prison discipline: prisoners in D-Wing were able to peer out of their cell windows to the gathered crowds beneath, communicating with loved ones and making a mockery of the prison authorities' decision to forbid visits. On 14 July, an order was given to the prisoners to desist signalling and shouting to the crowds gathered outside; the warning ignored, prison officers opened fire on the cell wings, slightly injuring two prisoners, although it appears that 'most of the shots were deliberately wide'.[57] While inside Mountjoy, such altercations were accepted as part of the travails of prison life, outside, the noise of the firing caused consternation. Maud Gonne arrived in the evening, frantic with worry. She had not seen her son for some months: he had been in the Four Courts since April and abroad immediately prior to the June Convention, while she – in keeping with her initial support for the Treaty – had travelled at the request of Arthur Griffith to Paris to help with publicity for the Provisional Government. Returning to Dublin to find her son a prisoner and bullets whizzing down the wings of Mountjoy, she immediately travelled to government buildings to appeal to Griffith, her old friend: 'Mr Griffith refused to see her, but sent word that he was "quite aware of the situation" and added that "the shooting took place at the orders of the Governor and he took full responsibility".'[58]

The firing had its intended chastening effect, and the prisoners agreed to move into C-Wing. Although they further defied prison discipline by blocking their cell doors so they could not be locked, the prisoners eventually settled down into a relatively quiescent relationship with the authorities. Despite sporadic problems

56 Rory O'Connor to 'Joe', 2 July 1922, quoted in *Poblacht na hÉireann War News*, 4 July 1922; Liam Mellows despatch, 30 June 1922, quoted in *Poblacht na hÉireann War News*, 2 July 1922.

57 *Freeman's Journal*, 15 July 1922; Peadar O'Donnell quoted in Uinseann MacEoin, *Survivors: The Story of Ireland's Struggle as Told Through Some of her Outstanding Living People Recalling Events from the Days of Davitt, Through James Connolly, Brugha, Collins, Liam Mellows, and Rory O'Connor to the Present Time* (Dublin: Argenta Publications, 1980), p. 26.

58 *Poblacht na hÉireann War News*, 17 July 1922; Anna MacBride White and A. Norman Jeffares (eds.), *Always Your Friend: The Gonne–Yeats Letters, 1893–1938* (London: Hutchinson, 1992), p. 429.

with the prison diet – 'putrid meat' was allegedly supplied to the prisoners in August – and notwithstanding Frank Gallagher's horror at the conditions when arriving in October 1922, life inside Mountjoy was not too bad in the summer and autumn of 1922.[59] The prisoners had relative freedom of movement within the wings, and a series of lectures, classes and discussion groups were established to pass the time. MacBride shared a cell with Rory O'Connor, later describing their relationship as that of 'uncle and nephew', regarding the Dubliner as an old man although he was barely 38: 'His hair was turning grey, he wasn't very robust and he had a bad cough.'[60] O'Connor's unhealthily saturnine appearance – described by O'Malley as 'a Byzantine portrait' – reflected a deeper internal solemnity: while Liam Mellows and Dick Barrett engaged in some of the lighter moments of prison life, O'Connor remained a brooding presence, preferring to concentrate on continuing battles with the authorities.[61] For MacBride, however, he remained his closest friend inside Mountjoy, a regular opponent in chess and a confidant and interlocutor on matters of republican politics.

Conspiracy Theories

As the Civil War progressed into the 'Munster Republic', the prisoners inside Mountjoy were but helpless observers. This did not mean, however, that they viewed events with equanimity; every advance and every reversal was discussed at length, theories formulated, and conspiracies suspected. MacBride was particularly susceptible to this latter, especially prone to discerning the malign influence of the British Secret Services in most catastrophes which befell Irish nationalism – and himself – through the twentieth century. Possibly the most elaborate of the conspiracy theories formulated by MacBride was forged in Mountjoy and centred on Michael Collins.[62] MacBride's theory, rooted in discussions in Mountjoy with O'Connor, had a lengthy gestation, and was originally revealed in an interview with Tim Pat Coogan in the *Irish Press* in 1982.[63] The Treatyite government were commonly presented as dictators in the republican underground press, but MacBride's arguments were slightly more complex. Collins's resignation from the Provisional Government on 12 July 1922 to become Commander-in-Chief of the Army and his subsequent formation of a War Council comprising himself, Richard Mulcahy and Eoin O'Duffy was, according to MacBride, reflective of 'a very deep split within the Provisional Government' and designed 'to oust Cosgrave, Blythe *et*

---

59   *Poblacht na hÉireann War News*, 10 August 1922. Frank Gallagher recorded his disgust in his diary: 'Cell filthy, place filthy. Floor near top seething mass of stanching water and what seemed sewerage. Continual feeling of retching.' NLI, Frank Gallagher Papers, MS 18356, Prison Diary, 26 October 1922. For more on Gallagher, see Graham Walker, '"The Irish Dr Goebbels": Frank Gallagher and Irish republican propaganda', *Journal of Contemporary History* vol. 7 (1992), pp. 149–65.
60   *Irish Times*, 16 October 1985.
61   Andrews, *Dublin made me*, p. 238; O'Malley, *The Singing Flame*, p. 120; Peadar O'Donnell, *The Gates flew Open* (London: Jonathan Cape, 1929), pp. 29–30.
62   Regan, 'Michael Collins, General Commanding-in-Chief as a historiographical problem'; Peter Hart, *Mick: The Real Michael Collins* (London: Macmillan, 2005).
63   *Irish Press*, 16 and 18 October 1982; 'Seán MacBride Remembers.'

al and negotiate directly with the IRA and end the Civil War'.[64] MacBride further alleged that Collins's assassination was at the behest of the British Secret Service, after Collins had unmasked one of their longest serving Irish spies: Tim Healy. A mysterious Collins diary entry for 4 August reading 'Markham – Thorpe – Healy' was held as evidence that Collins's special Dublin Castle investigator Thomas Markham, tasked with profiling government officials, had unmasked Healy as the mysterious Thorpe, betrayer of the Invincibles of 1882.[65] The convergence of this discovery, coupled with Collins's unilateral moves towards ending the Civil War, was – according to MacBride – the compelling reason behind his assassination. Such theories have been categorically rubbished by Collins's most recent biographer, but more important for our purposes here is the insight they afford into the inner workings of MacBride's mind: conspiratorial, suspicious and instinctively Anglophobic.

Word of Collins's death was largely greeted with dismay inside Mountjoy, where prisoners knelt to say the Rosary. The 'Götterdämmerung' of falling national figures on both sides – Cathal Brugha and Harry Boland along with Arthur Griffith and Michael Collins – evidenced the immense cost of the Civil War. Even *Poblacht na hÉireann War News*, the underground republican daily, struck a sorrowful note: 'we acknowledge his bravery though we know the cause that he has died to support is not worthy of the sacrifice of even one life'.[66] But although the great casualties on both sides may have been roughly equal, the balance of success in the Civil War was heavily on the Free State side by the autumn of 1922: successful National Army incursions by sea and land into the heart of Munster had brought much of that province under control, and the elaborate and lengthy communications of the Irregular executive appear nothing more than a paper war. More seriously, while the death of Collins was clearly a major blow to the nascent Free State, it also had grave consequences for the Irregular forces. Rory O'Connor might have sneered at W. T. Cosgrave as 'one who can be easily scared to clear out', but the new Cabinet laid down a mark with the Special Powers Act, which imposed the penalty of death for possession of weapons, and special statutory instruments to regulate the operation of military courts martial.[67]

But draconian powers meant nothing unless the government were prepared to use them: on 17 November the first official executions took place – five unknown republican prisoners – paving the way for the execution of Erskine Childers on 24 November. The Irregular response attempted to match this raising of the stakes, issuing a general order to kill supporters of the Provisional Government. In *Poblacht na hÉireann War News*, the catalogue of names of TDs who had voted for the extraordinary measures read chillingly like a death list:

64 'Seán MacBride Remembers.'
65 Gerard O'Brien, *Irish Governments and the Guardianship of Historical Records, 1922–1972* (Dublin: Four Courts Press, 2004), pp. 25–6.
66 *Poblacht na hÉireann War News*, 30 August 1922.
67 O'Malley and Dolan (eds.), *No Surrender Here!*, Rory O'Connor to Ernie O'Malley, 12 September 1922, p. 175; Eunan O'Halpin, *Defending Ireland: The Irish State and its Enemies since 1922* (Oxford: Oxford University Press, 1999), pp. 27–8.

There is only one means by which the nation can cleanse itself – the casting out and just punishment of these and all other Irishmen who make their country a byword through a cowardly subservience to the English enemy ... it is our work and the work of every brave Republican to see that both the repentance and the retribution for this crime will be complete.[68]

But these orders were only acted upon once, with catastrophic results: on 7 December TDs Seán Hales and Pádraic Ó Máille were shot on Ormond Quay in Dublin. Ó Máille survived; Hales, who had actually abstained from the key vote, died. That evening, a tense cabinet agreed to the request of senior army officers – conveyed by Mulcahy – that four high ranking republican prisoners be executed in reprisal.

'Iron has entered the soul of Ireland'[69]

The events of the night of 7 December marked MacBride indelibly, and formed the core of his Civil War memories throughout the later years.[70] In the preceding weeks, tensions had begun to rise in Mountjoy as nerves were frayed hearing of the previous month's executions; rumours circulated that prisoners were to be transported overseas, to the British territories of St Helena or the Seychelle Islands. But although the news of the first executions brought an ominous note into the prison, life on C-Wing continued as normal. On 7 December, while Rory O'Connor carved chessmen, Dick Barrett attended a lecture on 'Women in Industry – Equal Pay for Equal Work' and Joe McKelvey finished *The Gadfly*, an Italian revolutionary novel doing the rounds in C-Wing, memorable for a particularly gruesome execution scene. For MacBride, that evening passed normally: he and O'Connor played chess, and settled down to bed early, joking about the transportation plans and chatting about an escape tunnel which was expected to reach the exercise yard any day.

Early in the morning, Prison Governor Paudeen O'Keefe arrived in the cell, asking both men politely to get up, dress and pack their things. Some moments later, MacBride's 'heart skipped a beat' as O'Keefe told him he was not required after all. O'Connor divided his belongings, leaving the chessmen to a young prisoner named Kelly and attempting to leave his money with MacBride. In republican lore, there was a horrible symbolism to the gold and silver coins in O'Connor's pockets, held to have been used the previous October at the wedding of Kevin O'Higgins, for whom O'Connor had been best man and who had been the last minister to agree to the executions. MacBride, unwilling to accept the finality of his cellmate's departure, insisted that O'Connor would need the money on the Seychelles and sewed the coins into the belt of his trousers. Peering out

---

68 *Poblacht na hÉireann War News*, 25 November 1922.

69 Seán O'Faoláin, *The Life-story of Eamon de Valera* (Dublin: Talbot Press, 1933), p. 99.

70 Sixty years later, MacBride and O'Donnell visited the cast of Ulick O'Connor's *Executions* to speak about their memories of the executions. Irish Times, 16 October 1985; Ulick O'Connor and Richard Ingrams (eds.), *A Cavalier Irishman: The Diaries of Ulick O'Connor, 1970–1981* (London: John Murray Ltd, 2001), 15 October 1985, p. 171; Ulick O'Connor, *Executions* (Dingle: Brandon Press, 1992).

on the landing as O'Connor departed, MacBride shook hands with Mellows and McKelvey, the latter with 'a Santa Clause sack of old books upon his back' and listened as Dick Barrett sang 'The Hills of Donegal' going down the stairs.[71] The selection of the four men has often been ascribed to their representing the four provinces of Ireland; more pertinently, perhaps, all four were members of the IRB. Three – O'Connor, McKelvey and Mellows – had been prominent members of the Irregular army executive, and Dick Barrett had often spoken cryptically about Collins's plans to operate 'a dark hand' to assassinate undesirables. For republicans, the four were shot because they knew too much.[72]

The execution, however, was delayed as the prison chaplain attempted to persuade the men to sign a form renouncing their actions so they could receive absolution and the last sacraments, a course denigrated by republicans as a particularly odious form of spiritual blackmail. As the other prisoners filed out to Mass – it was a holyday, the Feast of the Immaculate Conception – MacBride heard 'shots near the front of the prison. A volley; another volley then a number of isolated shots.'[73] Later that day, Frank Gallagher recorded the scene in the chapel when the chaplain announced the sacrifice of the Mass 'for four of your comrades who went before their God this morning': 'An awful silence, then a whispering ghostly and intense, then silence again ... I couldn't think, my head seemed swollen and throbbing ... The enormity of what had happened was too great to be understood.'[74]

MacBride's immediate response was anger, confronting Canon McMahon in the sacristy, and engaging in a blazing row about the Church's position vis-à-vis the Civil War. So carried away were the pair that MacBride left the prison and walked down the avenue of Mountjoy outside the main prison gate, arguing away. Still in a state of 'mental aberration', MacBride returned to the prison, knocked on the gate and was admitted by equally shocked prison guards.[75] The atmosphere in the prison was deeply gloomy, lyrically recalled by Peadar O'Donnell: 'The wing that day was a grave: we were a wordless, soulless movement of lives suddenly empty.'[76] Brutal as the executions were, they served as a notable deterrent to the republican policy of assassination: no further TDs were targeted, and the demoralisation in republican ranks was notable.[77] Prison life immediately became a more fraught affair: the enmity between prisoners and guards was increased, and whereas previously Mountjoy had seemed a reasonably pleasant place to wait out the end of hostilities, escape now became a matter of urgency.

71 UCDA, O'Malley Papers, P17/b/87; 'Seán MacBride Remembers'; MacBride, *That Day's Struggle*, pp. 66–7.
72 Jackson, *Ireland*, p. 271; Greaves, *Liam Mellows and the Irish Revolution*, p. 385; O'Donnell, *The Gates Flew Open*, p. 31.
73 MacBride quoted in MacEoin, *Survivors*, p. 119.
74 NLI, Frank Gallagher Papers, MS 18356, Prison Diary, 8 December 1922.
75 MacBride, *That Day's Struggle*, pp. 68–9; 'Seán MacBride Remembers'.
76 O'Donnell, *The Gates Flew Open*, p. 86.
77 Sean Etchingham, anti-Treaty TD from Wexford, was 'stunned to semi-paralysis by the horror of the deed', while to Ernie O'Malley, recovering in Portobello Barracks after a shoot-out with Free State soldiers, it was as 'if I had again been wounded, the same swift disappearance of my innards, an icy chill where they had been, and a trembling in my legs'. John J. Burns Library, Boston College, Molly Flannery Woods Papers, Box 1 Folder 4, Seán Etchingham to Molly Woods, 10 December 1922; O'Malley, *The Singing Flame*, p. 197.

With the gloom of Mountjoy permeating every day, MacBride may well have been relieved to be transferred to Newbridge camp, along with the rest of C-Wing, on 9 January 1923. A large-scale operation, the prisoners were handcuffed together on lorries to Kingsbridge Station and thence transported by train to Newbridge.[78] The atmosphere in Newbridge camp was drastically different to the suffocating psychological intimacy of Mountjoy. Removal from Mountjoy prison to an internment camp also implied distance from the danger of execution; as one republican commented, 'All that we had to do in Newbridge was to put in time.'[79] On the intelligence staff of the camp council, MacBride's daily tasks included the monitoring of escape plans. With so many groups and factions, multiple tunnels soon became a problem, but MacBride was more focused on his own personal escape, which was foiled when his concealed position on a camp lorry was discovered and he was transported back to Mountjoy.

Outside the prisons, the military mismatch of the Civil War was becoming painfully clear, compounded by the disappearance of most of the experienced Irregular commanders from the field. After the death of the puritanically militant Liam Lynch in April 1923, the more pragmatic Frank Aiken became Chief of Staff, and immediately began drawing up plans for a cessation of hostilities. On 24 May, a 'cease fire – dump arms' order was promulgated, followed immediately by de Valera's more lyrical salutation to the 'Soldiers of the Republic – Legion of the Rearguard'. Despite the ceasefire, Free State prisons and internment camps remained overflowing with captured Irregulars. MacBride was part of an elaborate and highly secret tunnel plot in Mountjoy: the prisoners first broke into the roof of the prison, fashioned a ladder down a defunct chimney down to the basement, and began constructing a tunnel there.[80]

The tunnel was eventually stymied by the republican hunger strike of October 1923. The decision to commence the strike ultimately came from within the prisons, and was uncontrolled and inefficiently organised from the beginning. The decision to strike had been strongly resisted by the tunnellers; because the tunnel had been constructed under conditions of extreme secrecy, most of the prisoners were unaware of its existence. According to MacBride, the tunnel group 'did its best to head off the hunger strike' but ultimately had to give way. After the decision to strike in Mountjoy, the hunger strike spread across the other prisons and internment camps, with the invitation from the Irregular executive to support the strikers in Mountjoy widely interpreted as pressure to join in. In Mountjoy, a kindly prison doctor ordered the heating to be turned on for the prisoners: when nothing worked, investigations were made up in the attics and the complex tunnel paraphernalia was discovered.[81] MacBride was among the suspected ringleaders rounded up for transport to Kilmainham Gaol; all were suffering the effects of five days without food and depressed at the prospect of a prolonged hunger strike.

78   O'Malley and Dolan (eds.), *No Surrender Here!*, Ernie O'Malley to Liam Lynch, 10 January 1923, p. 348; MacBride, *That Day's Struggle*, pp. 74–5.
79   Neil Gillespie quoted in MacEoin, *Survivors*, p. 164.
80   'Seán MacBride Remembers'; MacBride, *That Day's Struggle*, pp. 78–81.
81   'Seán MacBride Remembers'.

Early on the morning of 20 October, the prisoners were woken and roughly loaded – in their pyjamas – onto lorries for transportation: midway through the journey, MacBride's lorry became detached from the convoy, prompting the guards to leave the prisoners to discuss directions with the driver. Rather reluctantly, MacBride and Michael Price made a dash for freedom, 'rather cursing having to do it. I didn't feel at all well, [and] I felt I was probably going to get shot or beaten up ... but automatically when you saw the option of escaping you escaped'.[82] The two made for the home of Maureen Buckley, an acquaintance from student days, in Cabra: swimming the canal, they heard gunfire but sauntered nonchalantly past a Dublin corporation official, affecting to be returning from a dance. Having encountered two sympathetic soldiers – who pretended the escapees had attacked them – the two finally made it to Buckleys where, MacBride having been asked to prove his identity by speaking French, they were admitted.[83]

Freedom

It was freedom of sorts after sixteen months of captivity, but highly circumscribed. MacBride spent much of the subsequent months in the west of Ireland travelling secretly with Michael Carolan, Director of Intelligence of the IRA, attempting to conceal his conspicuous French accent by adopting plummy English tones.[84] Although the Irregular IRA had conceded defeat, its leadership was adamant that surrender was only a temporary measure:

> [the press] are quite wrong if they think they have heard the last of the IRA and the Irish Republic. Although we have dumped our arms we have not surrendered and there are several thousand men, women and boys in Ireland yet who believe it their duty to free their country and to see that ... their dead comrades have not died in vain.[85]

But morale was catastrophically low: the hunger strike, devoid of central direction, had ended disastrously with the unedifying spectacle of starving prisoners stampeding to grasp food while a few diehards continued to hold out: one, Denis Barry of Cork, died after thirty-four days. The Civil War had reaped a bitter harvest: along with the seventy-seven executed republican prisoners, the conflict crippled the Free State economy from the off and institutionalised a residual bitterness in every aspect of public life. More seriously, because no political or military terms had been agreed, the anti-Treaty IRA were never reconciled to the reality of the new state. Stalemate had been reached, not reconciliation.[86]

MacBride was intimately involved in the process of restructuring the shattered remnants of the anti-Treaty IRA through the early months of 1924, retaining the rank of staff-commandant, to which he had been appointed in the heat of the Four

82 'Seán MacBride Remembers'.
83 MacBride, *That Day's Struggle*, pp. 82–4; *Irish Times*, 23 October 1923.
84 *Irish Times*, 24 September 1974.
85 NLI, Florence O'Donoghue Papers, MS 31,242, Frank Aiken to ?F, 6 July 1923.
86 Tom Garvin, 'The aftermath of the Civil War', *The Irish Sword*, vol. xx, no. 82 (1997), pp. 387–95.

Courts attack. In April 1924, he was sent by the Army Council on an exhaustive investigation into the IRA north of the border, which, since the debacle of the joint IRA offensive, had abstained from participation in the Civil War. MacBride's report reveals his first recorded reflections on the northern question; glimpses of nuance and insight are present, but stifled by the blunt force of republican dogma. Identifying two key reasons for northern support of the Treaty – anticipation of a favourable and speedy decision of the Boundary Commission and hoping for a united southern administration to advocate on their behalf – and recognising the propaganda benefits of a northern agitation, MacBride recommended that the IRA 'make a big push to strengthen and fortify our Organisation in the Northern Counties'. Displaying a glimmer of understanding of the northern question, MacBride underlined that:

> Before being able to do anything there, it is essential to secure some under-standing of the Northern point of view: to them the struggle is not so much one of Republic versus Free State as a struggle for their own existence and any appeal made to them should be made with that in view.

But the solipsism of the republican mentality returned: '[the northerners] need to be made understand that their own situation depends solely on the situation in the Twenty-Six Counties'.[87] MacBride's recommendations were, evidently, taken seriously: regional reports preserved in the Moss Twomey Papers reveal wholesale changes in structure and staff in the northern brigades, with satisfactory results.[88] In the autumn of 1924, indicative both of his growing stock within the Irregulars and the dearth of senior figures, MacBride was appointed Director of Finance and attempted to regulate chaotic army accounts.[89]

Possibly stemming from his familiarity with the northern IRA, he also partici-pated in one of the more curious episodes in the history of the post-Civil War IRA: the attempted rescue of republican internees from Larne prison camp in December 1924. Like their southern brethren, the northern internees were fixated by tunnels, and on a grand scale: they intended tunnelling all the way from the prison camp to the sea shore. Accordingly, IRA GHQ approved a sea rescue and appointed MacBride to lead the mission: under his direction a hand-picked team sourced a boat, made it seaworthy and crewed it themselves. Great store had been placed on the concealment of both the mission and the identities of the crew: the boat was accordingly christened the *St George* while MacBride adopted the persona of Lt John Swift of Southampton, supposedly the nephew of a Royal Navy admiral. But although their true identities remained secret, almost every other aspect of the mission failed dismally. The prisoners' tunnel was discovered, the mission was aborted, and on the return journey to Southampton – where the *St George* was to be docked until the next such assignment – the boat ran aground during a terrible storm. 'John Swift' and his crew were rescued by the Newcastle coastguard

87   UCDA, Moss Twomey Papers, P69/145 (310–11), 'Re Northern Situation', Seán MacBride to Chief of Staff, Adjutant General, Director of Intelligence, Director of Publicity, 15 April 1924.
88   UCDA, Moss Twomey Papers, P69/180 (25–8).
89   UCDA, Moss Twomey Papers, P69/145 (68). See also MacBride, *That Day's Struggle*, pp. 95–6.

and were entertained over the New Year period in the officers' mess of Ballykinlar barracks, nonchalantly raising their glasses to the King's health.[90] Although the rescue mission would have scored a dramatic propaganda coup, it proved to be unnecessary; on Christmas Eve all the republican internees were released. For MacBride, the adventure inaugurated a love of sailing, which remained with him for the rest of his life, although he preferred the relatively calmer waters of Ireland's inland waterways.[91]

Roman Holiday

While the IRA was focused on rebuilding its shattered forces, political life in Ireland carried on. The election results of 1923 demonstrated clearly that the functioning of the new state was no longer in question: as de Valera wrote resign-edly to Joseph McGarrity in April 1925, 'The elections have given [the Free State] a stability which promises to last for some time.'[92] The Sinn Féin leader was convinced of the necessity to engage in the political process, essentially moving towards a policy of 'working the institutions' of the Treaty settlement to arrive at a outcome more palatable to republican opinion. In the summer of 1925, MacBride travelled with de Valera to Europe, acting as interpreter and secretary. Anxious to secure theological approval for entering Dáil Éireann, de Valera's journey was to colloque with two key advisers, Archbishop Daniel Mannix of Melbourne and Monsignor John Hagan of the Irish College in Rome. The pair travelled to Italy via London and Paris – MacBride on one of his many false passports, de Valera assuming the identity and clerical garb of Fr Patrick Walshe of Blackrock College.[93] When the discussions eventually took place in the Irish College in Rome, Hagan argued strongly in favour of entering parliament, declaring the oath of allegiance 'a mere empty formality.'[94] The similarities between Hagan's words and de Valera's eventual justification of the oath as an 'empty formula' is striking. However, MacBride's opinion that it was during these meetings that 'the whole plan of campaign for the future policy of Fianna Fáil and the dismantling of the Treaty was drawn up' overstates the case.[95] De Valera's record as an intransigent republican during the Civil War is best understood as a catastrophic aberration in

90   The full story of the *St George* can be found in Michael MacEvilly, 'Seán MacBride and the republican motor-launch *St George*', *The Irish Sword*, vol. xvi (1984–1986), pp. 49–57; MacBride, *That Day's Struggle*, pp. 97–9; and Tony Woods's recollections in MacEoin, *Survivors*, pp. 326–8.

91   In the 1930s, MacBride purchased the first of many boats, the *Lady Di*, and sailed her on the Shannon and on the Grand Canal in Dublin, to the great suspicion of Special Branch. Seán MacBride, 'The Lordly Shannon', in *A Message to the Irish People* (Cork: Mercier Press, 1985), pp. 7–11.

92   NLI, Joseph McGarrity Papers, MS 33,364, Eamon de Valera to Joseph McGarrity, 30 April 1925.

93   MacBride, *That Day's Struggle*, pp. 86–7.

94   Hagan memorandum on meeting, quoted in Dermot Keogh, 'Mannix, de Valera and Irish nationalism' in John O'Brien and Pauric Travers (eds.), *The Irish Emigrant Experience in Australia* (Dublin: Poolbeg, 1991), p. 28.

95   MacBride review of Dermot Keogh's *The Vatican, the Bishops and Irish Politics, 1919–39* in the *Irish Press*, 18 October 1982.

an essentially moderate, democratic political career. Moreover, MacBride's privileging of the role of the Church in establishing Fianna Fáil – characteristically, he believed that the Vatican had scripted Hagan's and Mannix's arguments – excludes the importance of key figures around de Valera already leaning towards participation. In the evenings after the meetings, wandering through the Roman streets and visiting historical and religious sites, MacBride attempted to argue the republican case with de Valera, to little avail.

Given his knowledge of the significant development within de Valera's political position, MacBride could not have been surprised when simmering tensions within the republican movement came to a head at the 1925 Army Convention, held on 14 and 15 November. Aiken was rapidly being viewed as the weak link in the IRA's maintenance of an autonomous position, and ahead of the Convention a formal request was made by a number of senior IRA members that the Chief of Staff clarify the army's position regarding Dáil entry. Aiken's confirmation that informal discussions had taken place among Sinn Féin TDs led, in Peadar O'Donnell's words, to 'an outburst of pain and passion'. A resolution proposed by O'Donnell – that the army 'sever its connection with [the ghostly Second] Dáil and act under an independent executive' – allowed the IRA to purge dangerous politicians from their ranks, resituating itself as a purely military organisation.[96] Aiken was unrepentant, writing to the Army Council on 18 November: 'It is, I maintain, an honourable policy to use the powers which the Free State and Six County governments possess in order to achieve the independence of our country, provided we don't have to admit their legitimacy by any oath or declaration whatsoever and that we maintain openly that our object is to establish a lawful government for the Republic.'[97] Despite the subsequent formation of Fianna Fáil, the scattered republican family remained largely bound together under the Cosgrave regime; but once Fianna Fáil took power and the expected Republic did not immediately materialise, the events of the 1925 Army Convention assumed greater significance, with MacBride and Aiken engaging in a public spat in 1933 over disputed interpretations of the latter's actions eight years previously.[98] In siding with the republican rump in 1925, MacBride remained at the centre of a new, militant grouping at the heart of the IRA: figures like Moss Twomey, Peadar O'Donnell and Mick Price would form the nucleus of the new-look IRA and remain his closest associates for the next decade.

MacBride's activities for the remainder of 1925 are difficult to trace, possibly owing to his concentration on affairs of the heart: in January 1926, on MacBride's twenty-second birthday, he married Catalina Bulfin. 'Kid' Bulfin, as she was known, was the daughter of William Bulfin, a well-known travel writer and journalist.[99]

96 Peadar O'Donnell, *There will be Another Day* (Dublin: Dolmen Press, 1963), pp. 35–6; UCDA, Ernest Blythe Papers, P24/165(3–5), 'Report of General Army Convention, November 1925'; Richard English, *Radicals and the Republic: Socialist Republicanism in the Irish Free State* (Oxford: Clarendon Press, 1994), pp. 66–70. See also M. L. R. Smith, *Fighting for Ireland? The Military Strategy of the Irish Republican Movement* (London: Routledge, 1997), pp. 59–60.
97 UCDA, Frank Aiken Papers, P104/1320, Aiken to Chairman of the Army Council, 18 November 1925.
98 *Irish Press*, 11–22 November 1933.
99 William Bulfin's most famous work is *Rambles in Eirinn* (Dublin: Gill & Son, 1907).

Although her brother Eamon – a St Enda's boy, favourite of Pearse and Easter Rising veteran – had refused to participate in the Civil War, Kid had continued her work as secretary to Austin Stack and later worked in the Four Courts, where she first encountered 18-year-old MacBride. Imprisoned in Kilmainham after the surrender of the Four Courts, Kid was held alongside Iseult Stuart and Maud Gonne, making a favourable impression on the MacBride women which subsequent years did nothing to dispel. In the post-Civil War years, Kid was part of a cohort of fashionable, sophisticated republican women around whom republican men like MacBride buzzed. Like MacBride, Kid shared a foreign background – she had been born in Buenos Aires, but returned to County Offaly in her early childhood – and her sophisticated, worldly manner marked her out from her contemporary Irishwomen. Todd Andrews remembered Kid as 'a typical woman of the Twenties, elegant, smoking cigarettes through a very long holder, short-skirted and not sparing décolletage'.[100] Their marriage, in University Church on Stephen's Green, was intensely clandestine: the wedding party was arranged for the previous evening while the ceremony itself took place at six o'clock in the morning to avoid the attention of Special Branch. MacBride almost missed the wedding when his chauffeur, Tony Woods, failed to collect him that morning, believing news of the marriage to be merely the latest in a series of pranks between the two men: undeterred, MacBride hitched a lift with Tom Daly, his best man, and arrived 45 minutes late at University Church. The ceremony complete, the newly-weds travelled on honeymoon to France, where they would remain for the remainder of the year. It was, for them at least, a happy ending to the upheavals of the revolutionary years.

100   C. S. Andrews, *Man of no Property* (Dublin: Mercier Press, 1982), p. 35.

5

'The Driving Force of the Army':[1]
1926–1932

By 1926, the consolidation of the Free State was no longer in question. Militarily, the Civil War had been well won by the Treatyite forces and the republicans resoundingly defeated. More pertinently, whereas the elections of 1923 had provided a fillip to republican morale, the rapid disintegration of Sinn Féin's electoral machinery in the years after 1924 underscored a corresponding collapse in the basis of that party's appeal to a general public that was slowly responding to the state-building efforts of the Free State government. With state institutions up and running, and daily life functioning with a large degree of normality, republican adherence to the mantras of abstentionism and armed opposition to the Free State appeared more illusory than ever, particularly in the wake of the formation of Fianna Fáil. The ability of Fianna Fáil to successfully fuse latent republican sentiment and popular discontent with an awesomely powerful political machine left both Cumann na nGaedheal and the IRA enormously unprepared for the runaway success of de Valera's new party.

Arguably, neither Cumann na nGaedheal nor the IRA ever recovered from the twin defeats visited on them by Fianna Fáil in the 1930s, and in failing to adapt to the changed political context of the Free State, the republican movement essentially condemned itself to political irrelevance. MacBride was a key figure in the playing-out of that process in the years before the first Fianna Fáil administration in 1932, and soon became a recognisable public figure and a frequent speaker at republican events and street meetings. It is important, however, not to dismiss all IRA initiatives and actions during the late 1920s and early 1930s as unimportant; aside from its ostensible role as the controlling armed wing of the Fianna Fáil party, the republican movement also reflected wider political trends, both European and imperial. Disputes within the IRA as to the proper place of these trends in directing the organisation's activities would become a recurrent feature of the new-look IRA and form an integral part of MacBride's personal and political relationships over the subsequent decade.

---

1 National Archives of Ireland [NAI], JUS2007/56/187, Kevin O'Higgins murder files, handwritten Justice report dated 21 July 1927.

Paris

In the aftermath of their marriage in January 1926, MacBride and his new wife Catalina departed to Paris. There, they rented a flat close to his boyhood home of Passy and MacBride secured employment as a journalist on the *International Herald Tribune*. It was an opportune time to leave Ireland; as Richard English has underlined, the early years of the Free State offered a chilly environment for republicans.[2] As the post-war boom turned into a post-war slump, unemployment was rife: in republican lore, this stringent atmosphere had a disproportionate impact on republican communities. Certainly, as MacBride noted, the oath of allegiance was not merely a parliamentary appendage: applied to all candidates for state employment, it had the intended effect of excluding republicans from the Garda Síochána, the National Army and the civil service along with other public sector jobs.[3] Post-war shortages also contributed towards the renewal of emigration, which revived with a vengeance after the wartime suspension: one republican remembered that '[p]eople were emigrating in droves. The best of Republicans were going. The very people that Ireland needed.'[4] Perhaps the most significant long-term result of this republican 'mini-diaspora' was, as MacBride perceptively pointed out, their final destination: the United States's open welcome to European immigrants meant that the Irish-American community in the 1920s received an injection of radical republicanism which was still a factor fifty years later, when organisations such as NORAID (Northern Aid) successfully tapped this latent militancy to support the Provisional IRA's violent campaign.[5]

This, then, was the context for MacBride's departure in January 1926: as well as the immediate danger of being picked up by Free State authorities – he was still officially on the run after his escape from prison in October 1923 – prospects for employment were decidedly grim. Although Elizabeth Keane has recently endorsed Seán MacEntee's assessment that MacBride's position from 1926 to 1929 is 'somewhat obscure', ascribing this 'vagueness' to his marriage, Parisian life did not necessarily mean a complete distancing from republican activities.[6] MacBride remained a key contact for the IRA on the continent during this period. Many of his activities were undertaken in conjunction with the IRA leadership in Britain, and centred on republican attempts to liaise with Soviet agents to make common cause against their perceived shared enemy.[7] IRA agents in Britain supplied the

2 Seán MacBride, *That Day's Struggle: A Memoir, 1904–1951* ed. Caitriona Lawlor (Dublin: Currach Press, 2005), pp. 100, 105; Richard English, *Armed Struggle: The History of the IRA* (London: Pan, 2004, first published 2003), p. 45.
3 'Seán MacBride Remembers', RTÉ, originally broadcast 1989.
4 John Joe Sheehy quoted in Uinseann MacEoin, *Survivors: The Story of Ireland's Struggle as Told through some of her Outstanding living People, Recalling Events from the Days of Davitt, through James Connolly, Brugha, Collins, Liam Mellows, and Rory O'Connor, to the Present Time* (Dublin: Argenta Publications, 1980), p. 360.
5 'Seán MacBride Remembers'.
6 Elizabeth Keane, *Seán MacBride: A Life* (Dublin: Gill & Macmillan, 2007), p. 47; University College Dublin Archives [UCDA], Seán MacEntee Papers, P67/539, Synopsis of political history of Seán MacBride SC, Roebuck House.
7 Thomas Mahon and James Gillogly, *Decoding the IRA* (Cork: Mercier Press, 2008); Emmett O'Connor, *Reds and the green: Ireland, Russia and the Communist Internationals, 1919–1943*

Soviets with military intelligence and espionage material in return for promised financial and arms aid; placed as he was in the politically and culturally vibrant Paris of the mid-1920s, MacBride was ideally situated to act as a conduit between the two groups.

Throughout 1926, MacBride met regularly with IRA links in Britain, and passed on to Soviet agents details of the Royal Navy's advanced sonar detection system. He was also responsible for sending at least one thousand rounds of '.45 ammunition' along with assorted political papers to Art O'Connor of Sinn Féin.[8] Despite his covert activities, MacBride managed to stay on the right side of the French authorities, cultivating links with Colonel Lacassi of French military intelligence. Lacassi kept MacBride abreast of British attempts to interpret his mail and of a further attempt to secure his extradition, which merely heightened MacBride's already unhealthy obsession with the British secret services. The MacBride flat in rue de l'Annonciation was also a refuge for republican travellers, such as Ernie O'Malley, in his peripatetic stage after release from prison.

Return to Active Service

The Paris sojourn was coming to an end, however: expecting their first child, Kid had already returned to Dublin for her *accouchement* by the time MacBride received a telegram from Andy Cooney asking him to resume full-time IRA duties in Ireland. The immediate pretext for this request was the arrest of a number of IRA GHQ officers following a series of raids on police barracks across the country, an ominously coordinated attack resulting in the murder of two Gardaí. Public outrage, on all sides, followed: the government's successful introduction of a Public Safety Act had to be suspended following revelations of police ill-treatment of republican prisoners in Waterford, while the IRA were immediately the subject of intense police attention.[9] MacBride therefore returned to an atmosphere of heightened political tensions coupled with a period of important personal developments; an IRA comrade wrote rather plaintively, 'we are going to have a difficult time here. The Army, as a whole, was not prepared for the operation and there will be much local dissension ... A young daughter [was born] to Sean and Kid [MacBride] and we can't celebrate the event.'[10]

MacBride's public occupation, once he returned to Ireland, was manager of Roebuck Jam Factory, a cottage industry established by Maud Gonne in the aftermath of the Civil War to provide employment for republicans. The factory was housed in the grounds of Roebuck House, which Maud Gonne had purchased

(Dublin: University College Dublin Press, 2004), p. 112.

8 Various communiqués deciphered in Mahon and Gillogly, *Decoding the IRA*, pp. 56, 63 and 84. See also NAI, D/T S5864B, Anti-State activities, Report on the activities of unlawful and dangerous associations in Saorstát Éireann, August 1931.

9 UCDA, Desmond FitzGerald Papers, P80/853, Documents for agenda of meeting of Executive Council, n.d; Seosamh Ó Longaigh, *Emergency Law in Independent Ireland, 1925–1948* (Dublin: Four Courts Press, 2006), pp. 75–6.

10 Andy Cooney to [?Seán Russell], 25 November 1926, deciphered in Mahon and Gillogly, *Decoding the IRA*, pp. 107–8. Anna MacBride was born on 24 November 1926; a son, Tiernan, was born in 1927.

with Charlotte Despard, a fellow republican activist of advanced years and privileged English background, and offered 'pure jam'.[11] Maud Gonne's ability to financially subsidise her son, although her fortune had been diminished by the wartime collapse of the French stock exchange, was an important in enabling MacBride to concentrate on full-time republican activities in the decade following the Civil War. With his mother providing a house and income for his young family, he was freed from the customary obligations of husband and father.

But the Free State to which MacBride returned had not merely been shaken by a resurgence of IRA violence: of far greater import had been the foundation in May 1926 of a new republican party under the leadership of de Valera. This further fracturing of the movement – most of the best political brains departed to Fianna Fáil – would ultimately prove the decisive political moment of twentieth-century republicanism: once de Valera had extricated himself from the straitjacket of the republic, his new party combined his republican mystique with an intense localism to develop arguably the purest party-political machine in modern Europe.[12] MacBride, of course, was absent for the moment of the division; whether he might have joined Fianna Fáil had he been in Ireland is a moot point. His admiration of de Valera and later political engagement might point to a different path had he been present to be swayed by political and personal pressures. In one sense, MacBride remained outside the Fianna Fáil tent peering enviously in; but there was an obstinacy to him and the remainder of the IRA in the 1920s. As Peadar O'Donnell ruefully commented, 'When de Valera founded Fianna Fáil, all that was really progressive in the anti-Treaty forces went with him. What was left was rigid IRB types. Anything that wasn't physical force was politics, and politics was disapproved of.'[13]

Nonetheless, in the immediate aftermath of the foundation of Fianna Fáil, and with the 1927 general election looming, there did appear a possibility for a united republican front. The leadership of the IRA – MacBride among them – recognised the need for some sort of political engagement and above all the need to protect the wider movement from another bitter split. This imperative lay behind MacBride's first public engagement after his return from France, at the republican commemorations at Easter 1927. Addressing a gathering at Glasnevin Cemetery, he urged unity: 'Let us leave petty difference behind and unite to be ready to give the final push when the time comes ... This is the only way we can pay a suitable tribute to our dead comrades.'[14] But the IRA leadership's attempts to forge a common purpose between the three republican organisations – Fianna Fáil, Sinn Féin and the IRA – foundered on the new party's reluctance to bind itself into the kind of ideological quagmire from which it had so recently emerged. The IRA's proposals for republican unity were humiliatingly rejected by Fianna Fáil: these principally comprised an agreed panel of election candidates; a repudiation of the

11 Advertisement for Roebuck Jams, *An Phoblacht*, 20 March 1927.
12 Richard Dunphy, *The Making of Fianna Fáil Power in Ireland 1923–1948* (Oxford: Clarendon Press, 1995), pp. 71–4.
13 Peadar O'Donnell quoted in Fintan O'Toole, 'A portrait of Peadar O'Donnell as an old soldier', *Magill* (February 1983), p. 27.
14 *An Phoblacht*, 29 April 1927.

recently concluded Ultimate Financial Agreement between the Free State and the British Government; a rejection of partition; and a pledge to refuse the oath of allegiance.[15] The one area which did see Fianna Fáil-IRA cooperation – much to the latter's detriment – was the land annuities campaign, which had just begun to gather speed in the early months of 1927. Spearheaded by O'Donnell, but merely tolerated by the remainder of the IRA leadership – MacBride displayed no interest in this agitation – the land annuities were a potentially explosive issue for popular mobilisation; Fianna Fáil were quick to spot and exploit this potential for massive electoral gain.[16]

'Mr O'Higgins played a big part in the revolution against the Irish Republic, and revolutions have a habit of swallowing those that make them'[17]

Fianna Fáil's journey towards the Free State might have continued to advance incrementally were it not for the assassination of Kevin O'Higgins on 10 July 1927. The radical change this murder wrought in both the fabric and the course of Irish political life has been much commented upon: part of the emergency legislation introduced in the aftermath of the murder was an Electoral Amendment Bill requiring all election candidates to pledge to take the oath of allegiance, a cunning step designed to box Fianna Fáil into a corner but which ultimately resulted in expediting the party's full participation in the institutions of the state and their rise to power five years later.[18] Although the historian James Hogan recorded a sense of 'general jubilation' in Cork when the news came, the murder of O'Higgins (who was shot down while walking alone to Mass from his house on Booterstown Avenue), was a profound shock to the whole political establishment. Attempts to identify his killers and bring them to justice dominated police proceedings for the remainder of the year.[19] Despite the IRA Army Council's repudiation of responsibility for the act, a general round-up of IRA members in Dublin followed immediately, although most of the senior members appeared to have gone into hiding, and MacBride was instantly identified as one of the chief suspects.[20] By the end of

15 Army Council Statement, printed in *An Phoblacht*, 3 June 1927; Richard English, *Radicals and the Republic: Socialist Republicanism in the Irish Free State, 1926–1937* (Oxford: Clarendon Press, 1994), pp. 102–3; Brian Hanley, *The IRA, 1926–1936* (Dublin: Four Courts Press, 2002), pp. 115–17.
16 T. M. O'Neill, 'Handing away the trump card? Peadar O'Donnell, Fianna Fáil and the non-payment of land annuities campaign, 1926–32', *New Hibernia Review*, vol. 12, no. 1 (spring 2008), pp. 19–40. The classic account of the campaign is in O'Donnell's *There will be another Day* (Dublin: Dolmen Press, 1963).
17 *An Phoblacht*, 15 July 1927.
18 John M. Regan, *The Irish Counter-revolution, 1921–1936* (Dublin: Gill & Macmillan, 2001, first published 1999), pp. 272–6; Paul Bew, *Ireland: The Politics of Enmity, 1789–2006* (Oxford: Oxford University Press, 2008), p. 450.
19 James Hogan, 'Memoir, 1913–1937', in Donncha Ó Corráin (ed.), *James Hogan: Revolutionary, Historian and Political Scientist* (Dublin: Four Courts Press, 2001), p. 201.
20 The IRA members arrested on 11 July 1927 included Frank Kerin, George Plunkett, Mick Fitzpatrick, Kevin O'Carroll, Joseph Reynolds, and Aubrey and Henry Hunt. The homes of the following republicans were searched – all, apart from O'Malley, GHQ members – Seán

the month, Gardaí were receiving reports from their northern counterparts that 'it is generally stated in Dublin that the murder was committed by Ernest O'Malley and two men named MacBride and Price'.[21]

In fact, as publicly revealed in 1985, O'Higgins's murderers were Archie Doyle, Bill Gannon and Timothy Coughlan – none of whom featured among the thirty-five official suspects – all IRA members but not, seemingly, sanctioned by GHQ; apparently coming upon O'Higgins by chance en route to a football match, the men fired opportunistically.[22] MacBride always professed ignorance as to the identity of the assassins, admitting in 1972 that

> To this day I don't even know exactly who did it or why it was done. There were various conflicting theories. One was that he might have been assassinated by some dissidents in the Army. O'Higgins was a strict disciplinarian and he was worried by the state of indiscipline in the Army at the time. Another theory was that he was killed by some IRA people who had grudges against him.[23]

But while the police investigation continued, the government introduced emergency legislation to counter what they believed to be a renewed threat from the IRA. The Public Safety Act, initially designed to stand for five years, gave the government powers of expulsion and suppression, clarified what constituted an illegal organisation, established special courts, and extended powers of detention at the discretion of a Garda superintendant, a district judge and a minister of government. It was, claimed W. T. Cosgrave, 'the minimum that any government entrusted with the responsibility of maintaining the State or preserving the public peace or security could ask for'.[24]

The legislation came into effect on 11 August; thirteen days later MacBride was arrested at Roebuck House and verbally charged with the murder of the minister by Superintendent Peter Ennis. MacBride, however, apparently had a cast-iron alibi: he had been out of the country on jam factory business – he later maintained to have read of the murder in a Brussels café – and cited Major Bryan Cooper, a Cumann na nGaedheal TD, as verification, claiming to have spoken to the deputy on the mail boat to Holyhead.[25] There were, however, a number of problems with this alibi. MacBride was unable to produce his passport as evidence, probably owing to the fact that he used a false one; his wife refused to swear that she had

---

Russell, Seán MacBride, Moss Twomey, Ernie O'Malley, Mick Price, Peadar O'Donnell,and Jack Plunkett. None of the men were at home. NAI, JUS2007/56/187, Murder of Kevin O'Higgins; *Irish Independent*, 11 July 1927.

21 NAI, D/J 2007/56/188, RUC Inspector General to Garda Commissioner, 30 July 1927.

22 Harry White and Uinseann MacEoin, *Harry* (Dublin: Argenta Publications, 1985), p. 106 n. 1.

23 National Library of Ireland [NLI], Seán O'Mahony Papers, MS 44,110(1), MacBride interview in *The Word*, December 1972.

24 *Dáil Éireann Debates*, vol. 20 col. 842, 26 July 1927; Bill Kissane, 'Defending democracy? The legislative response to political extremism in the Irish Free State, 1922–39', *Irish Historical Studies*, vol. xxxiv, no. 134 (November 2004), p. 158.

25 NLI, Hanna Sheehy Skeffington Papers, MS 41,177(29), details of Seán MacBride's arrest, 1927; MacBride, *That Day's Struggle*, pp. 106–7. MacBride's account of his movements corresponds with a military intelligence report sent to the Department of Justice on 11 July 1927 that 'Seán MacBride was until a fortnight ago to be seen in William St every day ... but has not been seen since.' NAI, JUS 2007/56/188, D. Bryan to D. Neligan, 11 July 1927.

not seen him in between the dates he claimed to be away; and Cooper's corroboration was far from straightforward:

> Major Cooper does not know McBride personally and cannot say whether the latter travelled on the boat with him. The Major has a recollection of someone speaking to him as the mail-boat entered the harbour at Holyhead but so far as he can recollect, the person was ... a middle-aged stout-built person. This description does not coincide with that of MacBride.[26]

Identity parades held on 25 and 31 August before five witnesses failed to secure a positive identification of MacBride as one of O'Higgins's murderers; undeterred, the authorities altered the charge to one of conspiracy to murder.

On 25 August, the provisions of the Public Safety Act were activated for the first time as MacBride was brought before the Dublin District Court, the first in a series of legal manoeuvres which saw MacBride arrested and charged on a variety of offences under both new and older legislation. Finally, on 6 September Justice Hanna in the High Court ruled definitively – albeit 'with great hesitation' – that the Act could be successfully implemented in MacBride's case.[27] The police were certain of MacBride's complicity in the crime: as Neligan confided in James Hogan:

> They were satisfied MacBride had gone out of his way to make an alibi for himself, or at least to show that he was not in Dublin at the time of his crime, and from his behaviour they did not doubt that he knew of the impending crime and was therefore likely to have connived in it or planned it.[28]

An Phoblacht was defiant, proclaiming MacBride's innocence and declaring that 'no case in recent years has fluttered the legal profession to such a degree ... Seán MacBride's case revealed the perniciousness of the Public Safety Act in a way that shocked even those who were out-and-out supporters of the Imperialists'.[29] But while the political parties prepared for the second general election of the year – Fianna Fáil underlining their republican credentials by citing the MacBride case in election advertisements – MacBride was lodged in Mountjoy, 'locked in a tiny cell, twenty-two hours out of twenty-four, deprived of everything – not even allowed a pencil or notebook for study, while his business is being ruined by his enforced absence'.[30] On 9 September, Gardaí made a further application to detain MacBride by ministerial order; Richard Mulcahy signed the committal order on 13 September, and MacBride remained in prison until 24 October.

Various attempts were undertaken by both the MacBride family and the republican community to secure his release. Maud Gonne enlisted the assistance of W. B. Yeats, now a Free State senator, appealing for her son's release on sentimental grounds owing to the imminent death of his old nursemaid Josephine Pillon, who had come over from France a decade previously. It was a shameless attempt at

26 NAI, D/J 2008/56/187, Garda report dated 1 September 1927.
27 Irish Law Reports, [1928] IR 451; *Irish Independent*, 7 September 1927.
28 Hogan, 'Memoir', pp. 201–2.
29 *An Phoblacht*, 10 September 1927.
30 *Irish Independent*, 9 September 1927; NLI, Hanna Sheehy Skeffington Papers, MS 41,177(29), details of Seán MacBride's arrest, 1927.

emotional manipulation, but it had the desired effect on Yeats, who made fruitless representations to Cosgrave on the MacBrides' behalf. The senator was, however, unsure as to MacBride's guilt, confiding in a friend:

> His family are not anxious it seems – think it a mistake or an electioneering move – but I am. Indeed it is something of a night-mare ... He was & probably is a friendly simple lad but has been subject to a stream of terrible suggestion and may not have been able to resist. All ones [sic] ordinary world think him devoted to making jam & quite harmless but there are others who have a different story and it is impossible to sift out the truth.[31]

Similarly, Kid MacBride's uncle Frank Bulfin, a former Cumann na nGaedheal TD, made representations but to no avail. Attempts from within the governmental party having failed, in October 1927 Fianna Fáil took up the baton. In Dáil Éireann Paddy Ruttledge declared that '[no] offence has been proved against [MacBride] and no offence dare be proved against him, except the offence of trying to serve Ireland according to his lights, as his father tried to serve Ireland before him.'[32] More pertinently, another Fianna Fáil deputy wrote to Kid MacBride proposing that her husband's case be used to apply for a writ of habeas corpus, thereby retesting the validity of the Public Safety Act. Before a resolution on the best course of action could be taken – tellingly, Kid MacBride passed the decision to Moss Twomey and the IRA – MacBride was suddenly released on the order of Mulcahy.

MacBride never stood trial for conspiracy to murder, nor for any other charges relating to the O'Higgins assassination. Debating the issue after MacBride's release, Colonel Maurice Moore castigated the tortuous legal proceedings as 'a record of perverted ingenuity and a determination to get the man into prison'; on balance the belief of the authorities that he was somehow involved in the planning of the crime appears unfounded.[33] The stigma of the O'Higgins charge remained with MacBride: at the entry of the first inter-party government to Dáil Éireann in 1948, Thomas F. O'Higgins, brother of the slain minister, walked alongside MacBride. Fianna Fáil deputies shouted across the chamber: 'Fine company you are keeping, Dr O'Higgins!'[34] In sum, the investigation into the murder of O'Higgins was mishandled from the beginning, officers fixated from an early stage in pinning the crime on a conveniently high profile IRA leader rather than apprehending the true culprits through basic police work. The O'Higgins case was the first in a series of high profile political murder cases over the subsequent decade that would remain unsolved, and the files of the investigation bear

31 John Kelly (general ed.), *The Collected Letters of W. B. Yeats*, W. B. Yeats to Olivia Shakespear, 7 September [1927], at www.nlx.com/titles/titleh17.htm, accessed 4 May 2009; Anna MacBride White and A. Norman Jeffares (eds.), *Always your Friend: the Gonne–Yeats Letters, 1893–1938* (London: Hutchinson, 1992), pp. 432–44.
32 *Dáil Éireann Debates*, vol. 21, col. 80, 12 October 1927.
33 UCDA, Moss Twomey Papers, P69/60(6–9); *Seanad Éireann Debates*, vol. 10, col. 31, 16 November 1927.
34 Leon Ó Broin, *Just like Yesterday: An Autobiography* (Dublin: Gill & Macmillan, 1986), p. 88. O'Higgins then allegedly asked Seán MacEoin, Minister for Justice, if it was possible to prosecute another minister for murder. I am grateful to Paul Bew for this reference.

witness to the chaotic and amateurish approach of the Gardaí; an unnamed Justice official commented pointedly that 'it would be most dangerous to allow the official records as to the murder to be ever published: they are full of innuendo, conjecture, [and] conclusions based on hearsay.'[35]

MacBride and Anti-imperialism

The murder of O'Higgins has traditionally been interpreted as the last rumblings of the Civil War – a particularly poisonous example of the hatred still fermenting in Irish political life. But the IRA leadership's pointed disavowal of responsibility for the crime indicates a rejection of the older tactics of assassination and guerrilla warfare, which had served a previous incarnation so well. This was, of course, in many ways a frank recognition of the political realities of the Irish situation and the impossibility of forcing an armed insurrection along the lines of the 1919–21 struggle; but the move away from traditionally violent tactics also highlights the currency of 'revolutionary' thinking within sections of the leadership. The Army Council's statement to a 1928 Clan na Gael meeting illustrates this tendency: 'In addition to the aim of recruiting and maintaining an effective military force, we are simultaneously encouraging the growth and spread of revolutionary principles and action with a view to producing among the civilian population a revolutionary feeling and atmosphere which would be favourable to military action.'[36]

A diversity of impulses lay behind this shift and it is important, as English has underlined, to recognise that the old-style physical force philosophy remained the fundamental existential basis for the IRA.[37] James McHugh has perceptively identified 'a striking variety of social outlooks' operative within the IRA in the late 1920s ranging from, on the right wing, traditional apolitical (or anti-political) militarists, Catholic conservatives, pragmatic conservatives and, on the left, anti-capitalist, pro-labour and pro-communist sentiment.[38] While dedicated socialist republicans such as Peadar O'Donnell, Frank Ryan and Mick Price believed fervently in the inherent value of revolution as a vehicle for social and political justice, for pragmatists and militarists within the army leadership, revolution was viable only in so far as it allowed the IRA to seize power and achieve its primarily political objectives. Whereas most of the IRA leadership are easily classified on that spectrum, MacBride has tended to pose a problem of interpretation. Certainly, he maintained good relationships on both wings of the movement: Peadar O'Donnell and his wife Lile were close friends of MacBride and Kid, while Moss Twomey – often viewed as an old-style Fenian – had also been fond of MacBride since their first meeting in Mallow in 1922. Twomey's assessment of MacBride, that 'he was equally adept at politics or soldiering when it suited him', indicates the pragmatism with which MacBride approached the fluctuations in political orientation within the IRA.[39]

---

35 NAI, JUS 2008/56/187, Handwritten and undated report on Justice-headed paper.
36 Quoted in English, *Radicals and the Republic*, p. 110.
37 English, *Radicals and the Republic*, pp. 112–17.
38 J. P. McHugh, 'Voices of the rearguard: a study of *An Phoblacht*: Irish republican thought in the post-revolutionary era, 1923–1937' (UCD, MA thesis, 1983), p. 260.
39 Uinseann MacEoin, *The IRA in the Twilight Years, 1923–1948* (Dublin: Argenta Press, 1997),

Such ruthless pragmatism can, of course, easily elide into careerism and opportunism: charges of inconsistency and hypocrisy were later levelled, with some justification, at MacBride by enemies both inside and outside the IRA.

Anti-imperialist agitation became the main focus of IRA activity during the late 1920s, and was the perfect medium to reconcile socialist and militarist outlooks. For the majority of the republican community, anti-imperialism simply equated anti-English sentiment; for socialist republicans, anti-imperialism was a deeply held conviction with an intensely valuable international element. The internationalisation of anti-imperialist organisations in Ireland was, in the main, achieved through republican participation in the League Against Imperialism, a loose umbrella group of Comintern origin, which provided a forum for communication and collaboration for anti-colonial and nationalist movements in Europe and the British Empire. Although in 1980 MacBride dismissed the League as 'one of these high-sounding organisations that we felt we had to support in pre-Hitler days', in the late 1920s, he was a leading figure in the Irish branch, and served as secretary for a lengthy period. In 1928 he presided over the first mass meeting of the Anti-Imperialist League in the Mansion House with Arthur Cook, late of the General Strike, as the main speaker. Introducing Cook, MacBride declared that '[i]mperialism was rampant from one end of the country to the other' and called for a revolution to overthrow imperialist tendencies.[40] In August 1929, MacBride and Peadar O'Donnell were the Irish representatives at the Second World Congress of the League Against Imperialism, held in Frankfurt: there, MacBride introduced a resolution calling on the organised workers of Britain 'to force the British Labour Government to withdraw the threat of war against Ireland and to allow Ireland freely to organise her own life in accordance with her working-class ideals'.[41]

'Working-class ideals' may have been a far cry from MacBride's privileged background – and his personal *hauteur* belied a preference for more rarefied pursuits – but in the late 1920s, as the post-war slump turned into a worldwide economic depression, appeals to workers' solidarity and anti-imperialist struggles were more attractive (and relevant) than the old catch-cries of republican tradition. While the meetings of the League Against Imperialism attracted attendances in the thousands, the more simplistically republican meetings failed to capture the public imagination: MacBride's address at a Dublin commemoration of the 1922 executions in December 1928 was to an audience of fewer than 100 people in O'Connell Street.[42]

Whereas the League Against Imperialism attempted to inject an internationalist dimension into the often narrowly conceived Irish republican vision, the most politically significant of anti-imperialist activities centred on anti-Poppy Day demonstrations, a tense and uncomfortable day in the Dublin calendar since

p. 843. See also Brian Hanley, 'Moss Twomey, radicalism and the IRA: a reassessment', *Saothar*, vol. 26 (2001), pp. 53–60.

40 *Irish Times*, 5 October 1928.

41 *Irish Independent*, 5 August 1929.

42 NAI, D/T S5864A, Anti-State activities, April 1929–October 1931; Kate O'Malley, *Ireland, India and Empire: Indo-Irish Radical Connections, 1919–64* (Manchester: Manchester University Press, 2008), p. 32; *Irish Times*, 10 December 1928.

1919. Although sporadic violence attended Armistice ceremonies through much of the 1920s, 1928 was, as Fearghal McGarry has commented, 'the highpoint of the republican campaign'.[43] As well as running battles on the streets between poppy wearers, Trinity College students and republicans, the IRA Dublin Brigade smashed windows of businesses displaying the Union Jack and, in a strikingly ambitious move, bombed a number of royal statues across Dublin.[44] Such violence had, it seemed, the desired effect – the number of Union Jacks on display fell dramatically – but republicans continued to use Armistice Day protests and demonstrations as a means of rallying public opinion and boosting morale. It was also a useful exercise to placate those of a more militarist outlook, giving the Dublin brigade some form of meaningful activity.[45]

In the years of the Cosgrave administration, Armistice Day was the occasion for widespread republican and anti-Free State cooperation, with republican and Fianna Fáil leaders sharing platforms. MacBride acted in conjunction with Fianna Fáil organisers in arranging a large public turnout for demonstrations in 1930, for instance: the resultant meeting had an audience of some 4,000 who heard speeches from MacBride, Mick Fitzpatrick and Eamon de Valera.[46] Violence ensued after this meeting also, as a Garda report indicates:

> a section of the crowd ... became disorderly and attacked a uniformed Garda in the vicinity of the Savoy Cinema. They also attacked individuals who were wearing poppies ... as they were getting entirely out of hand and there being one uniformed Garda in the vicinity at the time, D/Os Goggins and McAree who were on the scene, deemed it advisable to discharge a number of shots in the air, five in all, for the purpose of dispensing the crowd.[47]

However, once Fianna Fáil were elected to government, much of the impetus faded away from the Poppy Day protests; with the wider mass of republican opinion supporting the government, the anti-Free State rationale of the demonstrations was weaker than in previous years. Republicans attempted to maintain this momentum, switching the focus of anti-imperialist activities to a British Boycott – a visceral corollary to the Economic War – which centred on ill-advised hijacking of Cadbury's lorries in Dublin and the boycott of Bass ale. MacBride was strongly behind this campaign, calling on the government in 1932 to 'place an embargo on English goods and confiscate English business interests', arguing that 'if there was to be any poverty or hardship, it should be inflicted on England's supporters'.[48]

43 Fearghal McGarry, '"Too damned tolerant": republicans and imperialism in the Irish Free State', in Fearghal McGarry (ed.), *Republicanism in Modern Ireland* (Dublin: University College Dublin Press, 2003), p. 66.
44 NAI, JUS2008/117/887; Yvonne Whelan, 'The construction and destruction of a colonial landscape: monuments to British monarchs in Dublin before and after independence', *Journal of Historical Geography*, vol. 28, no. 4 (2002), pp. 522–4.
45 Hanley, *The IRA*, pp. 72–3.
46 NAI, JUS 8/682, Anti-imperialists, 1928–1933, copy of letter addressed to Mr Seán MacBride from Mr. Seán Lemass and Mr Gerald Boland, and Garda report dated 11 November 1930.
47 NAI, JUS 8/682, Anti-imperialists, 1928–1933, Garda report from Superintendent Ennis, dated 12 November 1930.
48 *Irish Independent*, 11 November 1932; NAI, D/T S5864A, Anti-State activities April 1929–

Raids and Arrests

While both MacBride and his mother continued to immerse themselves in a variety of republican and anti-imperialist organisations, MacBride's continued association with the IRA – he maintained his position on the Army Council, switching from Director of Intelligence to Adjutant-General – made him and his home the focus of constant police attention. A series of raids took place in Roebuck House throughout 1928 and 1929, partly ascribable to MacBride's residence there and partly to the activities of Maud Gonne. Roebuck House was something of an 'open house' for activists of a various political persuasions, and it was this feature as much as anything else which attracted the attention of the authorities:

> The house is a refuge for persons evading arrest and suspicious characters of every description. On occasions of raids there, a number of girls have been found sleeping in the various rooms ... Several young men also sleep in the house but owing to their antagonistic attitude towards the Police they would not disclose any particulars of themselves.

The number of residents was such that the authorities appeared to suspect the house was being used as a house of ill-repute: 'On one occasion girls sleeping in the house got out of bed in a totally nude state and smoked cigarettes unconcernedly while officers were in the room ... one of the officers found in a number of rooms rubber preventatives used by females.'[49] The disdain of the searching officers for the lifestyle they observed in Roebuck was, however, wholly reciprocated: Maud Gonne wrote disgustedly to a friend that:

> Yesterday morning I was awoken by a man in a trenchcoat and clutching a gun crawling under my bed. It was one of General O'Duffy's CID raiding for 'felons'. There were 20 of them in the house, as illconditioned and unmannerly crowd of ruffians as anyone could see. God help any of the poor boys who fall into their clutches.[50]

MacBride was never at home for any of these raids; the police generally encountered only the MacBride women – Maud Gonne, Kid MacBride and, from time to time, Iseult Stuart, on one of her sporadic periods of respite from her difficult marriage. The principal casualty of the raids was the elderly and frail Charlotte Despard, whose removal to hospital after a fall in October 1928 was disrupted by yet another police visit, an incident the subject of a parliamentary question.[51]

The Roebuck raids came in the context of heightened tension between the police and the IRA. Although the organisation had shifted focus slightly towards a broader anti-imperialist outlook in the aftermath of the O'Higgins assassination, hostilities continued through 1928, including the attempted murders of both the

October 1931, 'Outrages and activities by members of irregular organisation since 1/1/1931'.

49   NAI, JUS 2007/56/081, Search of Roebuck House 1928–29, Report of Superintendent Ennis to Secretary of Department of Justice, 29 October 1928.

50   NLI, Patricia Lynch and R. M. Fox Papers, MS 40,327(9), Maud Gonne MacBride to Patricia Lynch, 2 December [1928].

51   NAI, JUS 2007/56/081, Search of Roebuck House 1928–29, Garda report of search for firearms, 25 October 1928; *Dáil Éireann Debates*, vol. 26, col. 1128, 31 October 1928.

chief warder at Mountjoy and an IRA informer. Signalling their determination to face down the republican threat, the Gardaí instigated a policy of continual harassment of leading republicans, repeated raids on their homes and frequent, if short-lived, arrests. Significantly, however, none of these arrests were made under the Public Safety Act, which was permitted to lapse at the end of 1928. Without the security of special courts, the prospects of securing convictions for political crimes receded dramatically, a feature underlined by the collapse of Frank Ryan's treason trial in March 1929.[52] Predating the expiry of the act, however, was the appearance of the mysterious 'Ghosts' correspondence, a series of threatening letters addressed to jurors and witnesses in republican trials, apparently instigated by Sighle Humphries. This step, however, did not have the approval of the IRA proper, the Adjutant-General reprimanding Humphries for her unilateral action:

> We are opposed to the making of anything in the nature of futile threats ... I am directed to say that the Staff resent very strongly the independent action you have seen fit to take. I am further instructed to say that in future your organisation is not to take any action in matters in which volunteers are involved until the measures you propose are submitted to and receive the sanction of this Headquarters.[53]

The Ghosts campaign – authorised or not by the IRA – took a violent turn at the beginning of 1929, with the attempted murder of a jury foreman and the murder of a prosecution witness in two separate trials. MacBride's first trial under the auspices of the Irish Free State would therefore take place in a period of extreme tension.

MacBride was arrested on 13 January 1929 in a loft in Pallas, Co. Offaly, with six other men. His purpose there was unclear: documents discovered indicated general IRA business, whereas later intelligence suggested that a court martial was in process.[54] It was certain, however, that illicit republican activities of some kind were underway, and the authorities might well have been heartened by the apparently strong case they could build against a leading republican who had long proved slippery. MacBride and his fellow prisoners awaited trial under the Treasonable Offences Act for six long months in Mountjoy: as was becoming customary in an atmosphere of widespread jury intimidation, the trial was shifted to the Central Criminal Court. An attempt to obtain an absolute habeas corpus order, with the representation of the much admired Joseph O'Connor, failed in April 1929, and the prisoners had no choice but to sit it out. It was a difficult experience: MacBride befriended a Limerick man who had murdered a German foreman on the Shannon electrification scheme and was awaiting execution. He was hanged on 25 April, another case which strengthened MacBride's belief in

---

52 Fearghal McGarry, *Frank Ryan* (Dundalk: Historical Association of Ireland, 2002), p. 20.

53 UCDA, Moss Twomey Papers, P69/67(4), Adjutant-General to Honorary Secretary, Cumann na mBan, 30 November 1927; MacEoin, *Survivors*, pp. 348–9. It is likely that MacBride was the Adjutant-General who wrote to Humphries, although it is unclear at what point in the late 1920s he took over that role from Jim Killeen.

54 NAI, D/T S 5864A, Anti-state activities April 1929–October 1931; UCDA, Seán MacEntee Papers, P67/550, Notes on IRA activities, 1941–47.

the evils of capital punishment, although his apparent willingness to sit on court-martial proceedings and hold a leadership position in an organisation which routinely executed informers might be considered to damage somewhat his moral precepts on the issue.[55] While MacBride was mentally robust enough to shrug off the strains of imprisonment and execution, the stress soon told on one of his fellow IRA prisoners. Nicholas Egan, the local O/C in Offaly who had been arrested along with MacBride, was under observation owing to a history of mental illness in his family; soon he began to 'show signs of early melancholy' and 'told one of the chaplains who was trying to induce him to go to confession that he would like to go to confession to Seán MacBride'.[56]

MacBride valiantly attempted to obtain release; in addition to the unusual step of launching a legal challenge to the validity of his detention, he also wrote personally to the Secretary of the Department of Justice asking for seven days' parole in which to carry out an audit of Roebuck Jam, of which he was the titular managing director:

> I am making this request very earnestly in the hope that you will grant it as it really is essential to the existence of the business. I am very anxious to do anything possible to avert the closing down of the factory, owing to the hardship it would impose on those employed there. Needless to say, I am quite prepared not to make use of my absence on parole for any other purpose other than those stated herein and not to do or discuss anything which you might possibly consider objectionable – I mean this in the widest sense.[57]

MacBride's appeal failed, however, and he was obliged to await his trial on 4 June in the Central Criminal Court. Although prisoners neither recognised the court nor had legal representation, MacBride produced a bravura performance, cross-examining Garda witnesses with gusto. The state's case was fatally undermined by the fact that the arresting Gardaí were under suspension for allegedly mistreating prisoners:

> McBride [sic]: Are you suspended at present? – Yes.
> For assaulting prisoners in custody? – I am not charged with assault.
> What are you suspended for? – Being one of the party.
> That did it? – Yes ...
> How is it that you have not been charged in due course of the law when suspected of having committed a criminal offence? Why are you not standing in the dock instead of us? Are you not ashamed of giving evidence here? – No reply.[58]

MacBride further punctured the prosecution case by pointing out that the charge – of belonging to an illegal military organisation called Óglaigh na hÉireann –

---

55 MacBride, *That Day's Struggle*, pp. 108–09; *Irish Times*, 26 April 1929. MacBride erroneously dated his encounter with Cox to his imprisonment on suspicion of the O'Higgins murder in 1928.

56 NAI, D/T S 5864A, Anti-state activities April 1929–October 1931, report dated 24 June 1929.

57 NAI, D/T S 5864A, Anti-state activities April 1929–October 1931, Seán MacBride to Secretary, Department of Justice, 20 April 1929. MacBride's legal challenge was in contravention of IRA General Order 24, which forbade members from recognising Free State courts. See Hanley, *The IRA*, pp. 37–8.

58 *Irish Times*, 5 June 1929, transcript of trial proceedings.

was unsustainable: 'He [MacBride] produced a book which he said was an Act of the Free State Parliament, and which contained the words, "This force shall be known as Óglaigh na hÉireann."' The state was hoist on its own nomenclature; the jury found all six men not guilty. It was a formidable victory. Whether the verdict was entirely attributable to MacBride's forensic legal skills is, however, open to question. Although, at the time, Fianna Fáil deputies made great play of the apparent injustice of MacBride's lengthy period on remand only to be acquitted, Fianna Fáil in government took a different view of the case: Gerald Boland declared in Dáil Éireann in 1946 that 'both the judge and the jury were threatened' during the 1929 case.[59]

Justice had become ugly in the Irish Free State: the question of jury intimidation was a central feature of the political landscape, while allegations of Garda brutality were widespread in republican circles. Although parts of the country were relatively peaceable, there remained a hard core of IRA activity: Clare, Kerry and Dublin, where Eoin O'Duffy described the leaders, including MacBride, as

> still a nasty problem. They give their whole time and a great deal of energy to the fostering and cultivation of this dangerous secret society, travel about the country in motor cars, keep various units in touch, distribute war equipment and training instructions, and generally help to maintain the organization by the commission of acts of violence and intimidation at intervals.[60]

Anxious to preserve the judicial system from yet more political corrosion, the government passed the Juries Protection Act, which kept the names of jurors from the public record and allowed for majority rather than unanimous verdicts.[61] It was a measure which failed to have the desired effect, and cases of jury intimidation continued to rise. That it coincided with the appearance of Comhairle na Poblachta – another umbrella republican organisation – did not go unnoticed.[62] MacBride's activities in Offaly in January 1929 may have been connected with this new organisation, which was formally approved at the General Army Convention the same month: it was essentially a compromise, a middle ground between left-wing republicans who were urging for the adoption of a more frankly socialist programme – this would follow in 1931 – and the traditional wing of the movement who were suspicious of anything with communistic overtones.

Equally importantly, Comhairle na Poblachta provided the IRA, which had been caught in a fatal drift since Fianna Fáil successfully swallowed the oath without choking its republican support base, with a more meaningful political engagement with Irish public life. The organisation, which combined IRA, Sinn

---

59   *Dáil Éireann Debates*, vol. 30, col. 1045, 30 June 1929; *Dáil Éireann Debates*, vol. 101, col. 1127, 29 May 1946. This echoes material in the MacEntee papers: owing to the intimidation of jurors [MacBride] was acquitted at Central Criminal Court on charge of taking part in an unlawful organisation'. UCDA, Seán MacEntee Papers, P67/550, Notes on IRA activities, 1941–47.

60   UCDA, Ernest Blythe Papers, P24/477, Report on organisations inimical to the State, 5 July 1929.

61   Ó Longaigh, *Emergency Law in Independent Ireland*, pp. 95–8; Fearghal McGarry, *Eoin O'Duffy: A Self-made Hero* (Oxford: Oxford University Press, 2005), pp. 180–2.

62   F. S. L. Lyons, *Ireland since the Famine* (Suffolk: Fontana Press, 1982, first published 1971), p. 502.

Féin and Cumann na mBan members, aimed to 'rally the earnest people of Ireland in a virile, forward movement for complete independence' and to 'co-ordinate and direct the efforts of Republicans who lose direction'.[63] However, perhaps because Comhairle na Poblachta thus represented compromise on all sides, the organisation never really left the ground, despite a Garda assessment that it was composed of 'the most virulent and active extremists in the country' – MacBride and Maud Gonne amongst them.[64] A public meeting on 3 November failed to attract any significant public support; soon the organisation – which had never really been more than a pressure group – was abandoned. The next IRA political venture would be a departure on two fronts, signalling a final break with the increasingly irrelevant Sinn Féin party and the apparent, if short-lived, ascendency of leftist tendencies.

Return to Violence

By the early 1930s, MacBride had become one of the leading figures within the republican movement, overcoming obstacles of accent and youth to rise to a key position on the Army Council. As Adjutant-General, he was constantly in contact with local IRA units, and was accurately described in a Justice memorandum as 'the principal travelling organiser of the IRA'.[65] Within the IRA, he was viewed as an effective and thorough administrator, if a little stand-offish. Perhaps coloured by later events – especially the formation of Cumann Poblachta na hÉireann – many IRA members remembered him as torn between politics and soldiering: 'MacBride in my opinion, while he too had a great record, did not know where he was going. He was half into arms on one hand and half into politics on the other.'[66] High rank, however, also brought attention of the unwanted kind: as well as the incessant police raids on Roebuck House, there was something of a public humiliation in November 1930, when relatives of Alfred Lawless, the scion of a 'respectable family' who was charged with chaining a Garda to a lamppost, castigated MacBride for 'sheltering behind foolish young men like [Lawless]'. The affair, commented Garda intelligence, 'was bound to have an adverse effect on the morale of the Irregulars'.[67]

While, publicly, republican activities in 1930 were dominated by anti-Imperialist agitation, behind the scenes an intense ideological debate was taking place. The failure of Comhairle na Poblachta to effect any change in republican fortunes, coupled with growing social and economic unrest as the Great Depression made

63 *Meath Chronicle*, 12 January 1929; 'Ireland: events in the Free State', *Round Table*, vol. xix, no. 74 (March 1929), p. 386.

64 NAI, D/T S 5864A, Anti-state activities April 1929–October 1931,

65 NAI, D/T S 5864B, Anti-state activities, Department of Justice report on the present position, n. d.

66 Dan Keating, quoted in MacEoin, *The IRA in the Twilight Years*, p. 621. See also Bob Bradshaw's comments, p. 428; and Walter Mitchell's description of MacBride as 'an intelligent and able man' in MacEoin, *Survivors*, p. 390.

67 NAI, D/T S 5864A, Anti-State activities April 1929–October 1931, Report of successful investigation into armed outrage on policemen, dated 8 November 1930; *Irish Times*, 29 October and 1 November 1930.

itself felt, strengthened the hand of left-leaning republicans who had long argued for the need for the IRA realign itself along socialist lines. Similarly, the runaway success of Fianna Fáil sucked much of the vibrancy from IRA organisation on the ground, underlining the need for a meaningful political engagement. Although the original Saor Éire proposals had been defeated at the 1929 General Army Convention, the transformed political situation through 1930 necessitated a rethink; testing the ground, Moss Twomey published the draft constitution in *An Phoblacht* in late November. As Richard English has underlined, the constitution was heavily Pearsean in inspiration, a point echoed by MacBride in describing the eventual policies adopted as 'modelled to a certain extent on the programme of the First Dáil'.[68] Despite some criticism, the reaction was broadly positive, and in February 1931 the General Army Convention endorsed the Saor Éire proposals: as Garda intelligence reported: 'The general tone of the delegates was for action; they complained that demoralisation was setting on because of inactivity.'[69] Inactivity, however, did not last long.

Ahead of the Convention, the Dublin IRA had executed Patrick Carroll, a Garda informer: he had been shot twice and his head blown off by a bomb. In March 1931, in a decision also authorised by the Army Council, Garda Superintendent John Curtin was shot dead outside his home in Tipperary, after he instituted proceedings against local IRA members for illegal drilling.[70] This blow to the operation of justice in the Free State was followed by a third murder, in July 1931, of John Ryan, a witness in the Curtin case. A frank government report in August of 1931 admitted that in Tipperary and Kerry people 'were afraid to be seen talking to the police. The policy of an unarmed force, one of the Saorstát's proudest and most legitimate boasts, is being made impossible.'[71] The first months of 1931 also saw IRA numbers swell to over 4,000 – a jump from the previous year's figure of 1,833. Such an increase, coupled with more frequent drilling and other public displays of strength, created an acute sense of crisis within police and government.

The growing alarm was given a focal point in June 1931 when the government proscribed, at very late notice, the annual republican commemoration at the grave of Wolfe Tone in Bodenstown. The highlight of the republican calendar, the 'pilgrimage' to Bodenstown was an important public event, attracting representative organisations from across the republican spectrum. Pointedly, in 1931 Fianna Fáil still attended the broader republican event; the joint parade seemed to the Cabinet an ominous display of strength by a rival government and a rival army, 'as if the authorised Defence Forces of the State and the IRA were merely rival bodies equally entitled to parade in public'.[72] MacBride, as Acting Secretary to the

---

68 MacBride, *That Day's Struggle*, p. 114; English, *Radicals and the Republic*, pp. 124–5. See also Jonathan Hammill, 'Saor Éire and the IRA: an exercise in deception?', *Saothar*, vol. 20 (1995), pp. 56–7.

69 UCDA, Desmond FitzGerald Papers, P80/856(16), Copy of confidential report by Eoin O'Duffy for period 1/1/1931 to 31/5/1931, dated 26 June 1931.

70 NAI, D/T S 5864A, Anti-State activities, April 1929–October 1931, Outrages and activities by members of irregular organisation since 1 January 1931; *Dáil Éireann Debates*, vol. 40, col. 33, 14 October 1931.

71 NAI, D/T S 5864B, Anti-State activities, Department of Justice report, August 1931.

72 NAI, D/T S 5864B, Anti-State activities, Department of Justice report, August 1931.

Organising Committee, was informed on the morning of the commemoration, Sunday 21 June, that the Minister for Defence had issued a written order cancelling the customary special trains to Sallins. The previous evening, Seán Russell and Michael Price, both of whom had been scheduled to address the gathering, were arrested under the Treasonable Offences Act.[73] It was a significant move, a response to the increasingly frantic Garda Commissioner declarations that 'the IRA was on the verge of open insurrection and the police close to breaking-point'.[74]

Equally significant, however was the defiance of the government ban by both the IRA and Fianna Fáil. Despite the eleventh-hour cancellation of special trains, MacBride and the organising committee arranged to hire a fleet of buses; augmented by 'every vehicle that could move, taxed or untaxed' and dedicated cyclists from all over republican Ireland, the assembly site was thronged.[75] Although the commemoration was broadly peaceable, the presence of Irish Army soldiers in full battledress and a sizeable contingent of Gardaí heightened tensions. A government direction that military commands were forbidden threatened to spill over into violence; MacBride, at the head of the Dublin Brigade, questioned the senior Garda officer, 'How are we to move them without issuing orders?' With the intervention of a priest, however, the parade proceeded without incident into the graveyard, where MacBride and O'Donnell jointly deposited the republican wreath and O'Donnell delivered a fiery speech, concluding that 'in the final phase we must be prepared to meet force with force'.[76]

'Gained over to the Communist movement': MacBride and Saor Éire[77]

The successful defiance of the Bodenstown ban galvanised the move to embrace the Saor Éire proposals. Although the project was very much the brainchild of Peadar O'Donnell and David Fitzgerald, MacBride seems to have been assigned to complete most of the organisational duties on the ground, particularly in the tinder-box atmosphere of republican Kerry; his straight-faced assertion that he was prepared to 'go the whole hog for the Worker's [sic] Republic' is some measure of his public commitment to the Saor Éire project.[78] In July, MacBride travelled to Kerry: his plan was to work his way back to Dublin, organising branches along the way. He had an instant entry into the intensely familial nature of Kerry republicanism via the Daly family – Tom Daly had acted as MacBride's best man for his wedding five years earlier, while Charlie Daly had been one of the Irregulars' most venerated martyrs after his execution at Drumboe Castle, County Donegal in March 1923. MacBride was, apparently, popular in Kerry: May Dálaigh, sister of Tom and Charlie, later commented that MacBride 'had the greatest sense

73 *Dáil Éireann Debates*, vol. 39, col. 950, 24 June 1931.
74 McGarry, *Eoin O'Duffy*, p. 183.
75 O'Donnell, *There will be another Day*, p. 125.
76 *Irish Times*, 22 June 1931; *Southern Star*, 27 June 1931; NAI, D/T S9472, Summary of events from January 1931 to March 1932.
77 NAI, D/T S5864B, Anti-State activities.
78 *An Phoblacht*, 14 February 1931; James Hogan, *Could Ireland become Communist? The Facts of the Case* (Dublin: Cahill, 1935), pp. 98–107.

of humour of any of them'.[79] Throughout the summer of 1931, MacBride was engaged in a forceful confrontation with Kerry Gardaí, cementing the realisation of the authorities that the present legislation and judicial system was unable to cope with the threat posed by an apparently resurgent IRA.

On 19 July, MacBride was arrested outside Listowel; coincidentally, Roebuck House had again been raided the previous night.[80] Stopped by Gardaí near Coolard crossroads in the company of six local men, MacBride told the detectives he was merely out for a walk, prompting the sarcastic reply: 'Isn't it far you came for your walk.' Although the Gardaí did not detain him, the discovery of up to 200 men nearby in military formation pointed to illegal activity of some kind. Later that evening, MacBride was arrested on a charge of illegal drilling; crucially, in his suitcase were documents relating to Saor Éire. Despite perceptive intelligence on the state of the IRA in the first half of the year and an accurate report of the General Army Convention of February, MacBride's arrest was the first occasion when the authorities had obtained concrete evidence on the nature of the new organisation. The discovery of what 'appeared to mark the definite union of communism in this state' provoked considerable alarm.[81]

Even more worrying was the manner with which MacBride again swatted away Free State attempts to arraign him for illegal activities.[82] When MacBride and his six fellow prisoners appeared before Justice Johnson of the Listowel District Court, the atmosphere was tense: a unit of Irish Army soldiers, newly deployed from Limerick, occupied the packed courtroom until MacBride queried their presence in what was ostensibly a civil court. The court appearance ought to have been a routine step in returning the men for trial, but MacBride again took the initiative, arguing both on his own and his fellow prisoners' behalf that their presence in Coolard was for a commemorative ceremony only. On MacBride's application, the judge retired to consider the case and on return directed that the men were 'too far away from the drilling party to be deemed guilty of the charge' and declined to return MacBride and three of his fellow prisoners for trial.[83]

It was another resounding defeat for the forces of the state, as the Chief Superintendent for Kerry wrote despairingly:

> The interrogation of the so-called IRA men or any of their type, with the existing law, is a farce and a mere waste of time. They absolutely refuse to give any account of their movements; they laugh with impunity at the Gardaí, knowing the latter are powerless, nevertheless they must be allowed to depart unmolested. Juries acquit them. Judges and Justices give most ridiculous decisions in their favour on mere technicalities and I fear the Guards must soon weaken in their resolve if they are not supported.[84]

79 MacEoin, *Survivors*, p. 368.
80 New York Public Library [NYPL], International Committee for Political Prisoners Records, Maud Gonne MacBride to Roger Baldwin, 24 July 1931, Reel 7.
81 NAI, D/T 5864B, Anti-State activities, 'Events in Kerry', n. d. [1931].
82 This episode is omitted from Keane's *Seán MacBride*.
83 NAI, D/T 5864B, Anti-State activities, 'Events in Kerry', n. d. [1931]; *Irish Independent*, 21 July 1931; *Irish Times*, 20 July 1931; MacBride, *That Day's Struggle*, pp. 114–15.
84 NAI, D/T 5864B, Anti-State activities, 'Events in Kerry', n. d. [1931]. See also McGarry, *Eoin O'Duffy*, pp. 183–4 for the Garda Commissioner's arguments in the same vein.

The confrontation with the Kerry authorities was not over, however: in September 1931 MacBride returned to the area, giving an oration – and a Saor Éire party political speech – at the unveiling of a republican monument in Ballyduff:

> Today I have good news for you. Within the last two months there has been a resurgence and a national re-awakening of the spirit of Freedom. It is a re-awakening that is not be stopped or stifled. The Free State Government realise that this national resurgence exists and are preparing new Coercion and Public Safety Bills and a new reign of terror has been launched to frighten and terrorise us. I think I can speak for us all when I tell them that we will be quite prepared to meet all those Coercion Acts.[85]

If returning to organise in Kerry at all was a bold move, MacBride's next step was positively brazen. In an interview with the *Irish Press*, the recently established Fianna Fáil organ, MacBride alleged constant harassment from Gardaí, even claiming that a prominent Garda Superintendent had warned him to leave the county, as his life was in 'immediate danger'. The *Press* took his case further, editorialising the next day that: 'Everywhere [MacBride] goes in Kerry, it is alleged, he is followed by two motor cars, full of detectives. There is no suggestion that these detectives follow him for his protection, but it is evident that he could hardly be murdered without their connivance.'[86] MacBride was accurate in forecasting new and stringent emergency legislation. In the aftermath of his initial arrest in July 1931, the Cabinet ordered the drafting of a new bill with the necessary powers to meet the deteriorating security situation and the newly discovered 'Bolshevik' threat. The government also sent an extensive dossier, known as the 'red book' to the Catholic hierarchy: 'We are confronted with a completely new situation. Doctrines are being taught and practised which were never before countenanced amongst us and I feel that the influence of the Church alone will be able to prevail in the struggle against them.'[87]

While the leaders of Church and State reflected, Saor Éire pressed ahead, holding a national congress on 26–7 September in Dublin. After addresses from Fitzgerald in his capacity as national secretary and Seán Hayes as chairman, MacBride read the constitution to the assembly of 120 delegates. The objects of Saor Éire were

- to achieve an independent revolutionary leadership of the working class and working farmers towards the overthrow of British imperialism and its ally, Irish capitalism;
- to organise and consolidate the Republic of Ireland on the basis of the possession and administration by the workers and working farmers, of the land, instruments of production, distribution and exchange;
- to restore and foster the Irish language and culture.

85 *Irish Press*, 14 September 1931.
86 *Irish Press*, 18–19 September 1931. The newspaper painted a lurid picture of Garda indiscipline in north Kerry, where 'a feeling of tense uneasiness is said to prevail ... [and] parties of detectives armed with rifles and revolvers scour the countryside in cars night after night'.
87 NAI, D/T S5864B, Anti-state activities, W. T. Cosgrave to Joseph Cardinal McRory, 10 September 1931; Fergal Davis, *The History and Development of the Special Criminal Court, 1922–2005* (Dublin: Four Courts Press, 2007), pp. 42–6.

In recommending the draft constitution to the delegates, MacBride 'hoped it was going to be the one that united economic and social questions with the national one' and expressed his desire for a 'Republican Ireland which would be controlled by the working class people'.[88] Quite where this would leave a man of privilege such as him was left unanswered. The congress represented Saor Éire's open entry into the political arena; in doing so, however, it guaranteed its own demise.

There were a number of fundamental flaws to the organisation from the very beginning. While Brian Hanley has modified traditional interpretations of Moss Twomey as an unthinking old-style Fenian, the tepid attitude of important sections of the IRA leadership towards the initiative stymied any chance of real acceptance by the organisation at large.[89] A further problem was the attempt to graft the new organisation whole-scale onto the skeleton of the old, regardless of potential clashes of opinion and personnel. This move deprived Saor Éire of any independent identity and facilitated the crackdown by the authorities. But the real issue was systemic: traditional Irish republicanism – to which most IRA members subscribed – was, in sum, incompatible with socialist republican thought; therein lay the core reason for the failure of Saor Éire.[90]

MacBride's commitment to the Saor Éire project is difficult to ascertain. Much of his public pronouncements on the initiative seemed in tune with solid socialist thinking, but his advocacy of Saor Éire is at odds with his attitude towards socialist initiatives for the rest of his career within the republican movement. In later years, MacBride was decidedly sceptical about the value of Saor Éire, describing the leftist turn within the IRA as 'somewhat impractical'. He was also jokingly bitter about his confrontations with the authorities at this time, commenting that 'while Saor Éire was to a large extent Peadar O'Donnell's child I was the one who went off to organise it and finally ended up in jail on account of Saor Éire. I was the only victim of Saor Éire at that time.'[91] More fundamentally, however, MacBride was burned by the failure of Saor Éire, rightly concluding that a socialist programme held no appeal for the Irish public, working farmers or not. While MacBride's subsequent rejection of socialist thinking attracted brickbats from colleagues inside the IRA and criticism from historians, such actions represent a political awareness without ideological constriction, a feature lacking in some of his more contemporarily admired IRA comrades.

Saor Éire was undoubtedly a mistake, the extent of which became clear the following month with the introduction of a constitutional amendment known as Article 2A and the issuing of a condemnatory pastoral from the Irish bishops. The pastoral referred specifically to Saor Éire and the IRA as 'sinful and irreligious', declaring that 'no Catholic can lawfully be a part of them'. In Dáil Éireann, Cosgrave characterised 'the new patriotism based on Muscovite teaching with a sugar-coating of Irish extremism' and declared his government's intention to use

---

88 *Irish Times*, 28 September 1931; *Irish Independent*, 28 September 1931.
89 Hanley, *The IRA*, p. 179.
90 Richard English, 'Socialist republicanism in independent Ireland, 1922–49', in Mike Cronin and John Regan (eds.), *Ireland: The Politics of Independence, 1922–49* (London: Macmillan, 2000), p. 89.
91 MacBride, *That Day's Struggle*, p. 114.

the new legislation to proscribe the IRA, Saor Éire, the Irish Friends of Soviet Russia, the Irish Communist Party, and other such affiliations.[92] Fianna Fáil opposed the proposed constitutional amendment, arguing that the existing law was sufficient to deal with any existent threat. De Valera and Fianna Fáil played a clever hand during the Saor Éire episode, voicing enough opposition to ensure the continued support of militant republicans and maintaining a slightly radical socio-economic position while avoiding the contamination of Bolshevik tendencies. Crucially, although the party had voted against the resultant legislation, Article 2A was not repealed the following year and formed the bedrock of the Fianna Fáil government's eventual confrontation of the IRA threat.

The End of the Coercionist Regime?

Whereas stringent governmental measures were not unexpected, confirming in republican eyes the craven nature of the Free State government, the IRA recognised the danger of the pastoral. *An Phoblacht* outlined the traditionally compartmentalised republican attitude to episcopal pronouncements, declaring that: 'The Hierarchy is not the Church. In former situations, similar to this, our people were intelligent enough to distinguish between the politics of the Bishops and the true teachings of the Catholic Church.'[93] MacBride, as Adjutant-General, sent a reassuring communiqué to IRA units, condemning the pastoral letter as

> inspired by the desire to rescue the Free State Gov from its difficulties, political and economic and to attempt to check the organising of the people against Imperialism and the chronic conditions arising out of it. Again, as in 1922 the Hierarchy are lending their sanction to brutal and repressive measures against Republicans. They are taking advantage of the religious feelings and scruples of our people, to promote certain interests and political opinions which they hold.

He urged, however, for a certain cooling of tempers, warning against 'any violence or sporadic outbursts'.[94] This was a deliberate move on the part of the Army Council: the activation of the Military Tribunal, provided under Article 2A, was imminent, and the IRA wished to avoid mass imprisonment of their members and the loss of momentum ahead of an election year. The term of the Cosgrave government did not expire until October 1932, so it was entirely possible that a long twelve months would elapse, under harsh security legislation, before the country went to the polls. The economic climate altered the timing of the election, however: with the Cabinet 'at their wit's end in financial matters' and the prospect of a harsh budget in April, the government decided to cut its losses, pinning their electoral hopes on a ten-year record of effective government and a campaign built around the red scare.

92 *Irish Times*, 19 October 1931; *Dáil Éireann Debates*, vol. 40, col. 37, 14 October 1931; Dermot Keogh, *The Vatican, the Bishops and Irish Politics, 1919–39* (Cambridge: Cambridge University Press, 1986), pp. 180–1.
93 *An Phoblacht*, 24 October 1931.
94 NAI, D/T S5864C, Adjutant-General IRA to Commanders of Independent Units, 27 October 1931.

The Dáil was dissolved on 29 January, but the IRA had already issued instructions to its members. On 12 January a communication was issued, suspending General Order 28 which forbade voting in Free State elections: 'Volunteers and supporters are recommended to vote against the candidates of the Cumann na nGaedheal party ... [r]ealising the natural urge to end the rule of a party which has been responsible for so much national disaster and economic distress.'[95] It was a pragmatic decision, recognising the strength of feeling against the government and its attendant security apparatus. For MacBride the position was simple: a Fianna Fáil government was the best way of 'ending the systematic harassment of republicans by the police'.[96] During the election campaign, the Fianna Fáil electoral machine swung into action, its case strengthened by the government's ill-advised suppression of the *Irish Press* and prosecution of editor Frank Gallagher. An added boost was the additional support provided by IRA Volunteers, especially in the Dublin district, in the mundane election work of canvassing, postering, ferrying voters to the polls and voting themselves: as Paddy Browne, a Curragh internee during the Emergency ruefully recalled, 'in 1932 ... I voted forty-six times for Fianna Fáil.'[97] The election results were the cue for mass republican celebrations, as Fianna Fáil's seventy-two seats enabled them to form a minority government with the support of the Labour Party. The peaceable transition of power was the final testament to the democratic solidity of the Free State. Although the newly formed Army Comrades Association would be the initial target of subversive fears, even before de Valera had formed a government a perceptive observer identified the real threat to Fianna Fáil stability: 'Your trouble is going to be with the IRA. They will want to do as they please and if you allow them you will, before a year, have two governments.'[98] The IRA did not realise it, but de Valera and Fianna Fáil would prove more formidable opponents than any they had yet encountered.

---

95 Adjutant-General to Commanders of Independent Units, 12 January 1932, reproduced in Hanley, *The IRA*, pp. 210–11.
96 MacBride, *That Day's Struggle*, p. 120.
97 Pat Browne quoted in MacEoin, *The IRA in the Twilight Years*, p. 740.
98 NYPL, William Maloney Collection, Box 7 Irish Historical Papers 104–8, Patrick McCartan to Seán T. O'Kelly, 20 February 1932.

6

'The Guiding Influence of the Mass of the People should be the IRA':[1]
1932–1937

Although the first handover of power in the Irish Free State ultimately proved commendably peaceable, the weeks between the publication of the election results and the formation of the new government were a period of extreme tension within the political and military structures of the state. What lay behind this tension was the shadow of the IRA, who were widely perceived to be merely awaiting an opportunity to stage a coup. W. B. Yeats reported the rumours swirling around Dublin streets:

> One hears such comments on political events as 'when those Church of Ireland gunmen, the Gilmours [sic], get out of jail everything will start popping' or will 'De Velera [sic] have the nerve to suppress Shawn Gonne before he shoots the town up', and I remember Shawn Gonne so like the Christ child that O Delany (Maud Gonnes [sic] old retainer) said her prayers to a rosary made out of his shed buttons.[2]

This perception of de Valera being unwilling or unable to control IRA militancy reinforced the tendency to view the Fianna Fáil victory as a prelude to a fully fledged Bolshevik-inspired IRA takeover. Indeed, elements within the IRA viewed the situation in similar terms, the pseudonymic 'Grangegorman' writing smugly in August 1932 that 'Cosgrave's rule is as dead as the Tsar's, and Kerensky is in power.'[3]

Fianna Fáil and the IRA

The secret negotiations between Fianna Fáil and the IRA, initiated by the former immediately after election day, appeared to confirm this belief. On 19 February, Frank Aiken wrote to Moss Twomey, IRA Chief of Staff, urging that the two organisations 'be fused at once', pre-empting Patrick McCartan's advocacy of a 'working agreement – one which should not be put into writing'.[4] The proposed fusion was

---

1 MacBride as quoted in University College Dublin Archives [UCDA], Seán MacEntee Papers, P67/626, Minutes of General Army Convention of the IRA, 17 March 1934.
2 John Kelly (general ed.), *The Collected Letters of W. B. Yeats*, W. B. Yeats to Augusta Gregory, 22 February [1932], at www.nlx.com/titles/titleh7.htm (accessed 4 May 2009).
3 *An Phoblacht*, 20 August 1932.
4 UCDA, Frank Aiken Papers, P104/1322(1), Frank Aiken to Moss Twomey, 19 February 1932;

predicated upon the IRA's acceptance of the ceasefire proposals of 1923, where the army would submit to a government prepared to defend republican principles. But it was not a true fusion of forces that Aiken sought; rather, it was the entire subjugation of the IRA to Fianna Fáil and their 'effective neutralisation' as a force within Irish politics.[5] The IRA Army Council were awake to this danger, and after a series of meetings between Aiken, Twomey, MacBride and Seán Russell, delivered a formal refusal, indicating that the basis of any agreement had to be the Army constitution which superseded the 1923 proposals. MacBride, moreover, was hostile to Aiken's offer of high rank in the Irish Army in return for the union of the IRA and Fianna Fáil forces, describing his reaction as 'highly indignant: I told him to get out. There was a complete divergence between me and Aiken and Fianna Fáil, from the start.'[6] Aiken and MacBride certainly rubbed each other the wrong way; less clear, however, is MacBride's attitude towards Fianna Fáil. Some of his republican comrades certainly suspected that he was 'soft' on the question of cooperation between the two bodies, and these suspicions contributed to the hostility MacBride later attracted from both left- and right-wing factions of the IRA.

The first Fianna Fáil attempt at engineering union between the two republican forces having failed, the initiative was shelved as the business of government began. Although the feared purge of Treatyite supporters from state employment did not materialise – save for a number of politically sensitive appointments – the new administration did make one significant gesture towards the republican constituency. On 9 March, the day the new government took office, its first decision was recorded in the Cabinet minutes: the release from Arbour Hill and Mountjoy of twenty republican prisoners. The releases on 13 March were the occasion of mass republican celebration, with the newly liberated prisoners welcomed at a large rally on College Green. To an estimated crowd of 30,000 and amid euphoric celebrations, MacBride, in his guise of 'Secretary of the Republican Prisoners' Reception Committee' – one of the many officious bodies which permitted the IRA Army Council to control republican events – MacBride sounded a note of caution:

> We must remember amidst our rejoicing that, while the day of coercion has passed for a time, the task we have set ourselves to achieve has not yet been achieved. We still have that task in front of us ... We can assure the people of Ireland that the Irish Republican Army will advance until this success is achieved; until the Irish Republic has been established here.[7]

New York Public Library [NYPL], Willam Maloney Collection, Box 7 Irish Historical Papers 104–8, Patrick McCartan to S. T. O'Kelly, 20 February 1932.

5 UCDA, Frank Aiken Papers, P104/1322(1–2), Frank Aiken to Moss Twomey, 19 February 1932; Brian Hanley, *The IRA, 1926–1936* (Dublin: Four Courts Press, 2002), pp. 126–7.

6 UCDA, Frank Aiken Papers, P104/1322(8), Secretary to Army Council, IRA to Frank Aiken, 25 February 1932; MacBride quoted in Uinseann MacEoin, *Survivors: The Story of Ireland's Struggle as Told through some of her Outstanding Living People recalling Events from the Days of Davitt, through James Connolly, Brugha, Collins, Liam Mellows, and Rory O'Connor to the Present Time* (Dublin: Argenta Publications, 1980), pp. 122–3.

7 *Irish Press*, 14 March 1932; National Archives of Ireland [NAI], JUS 8/698, Procession and public meeting held in Dublin, 13 March 1932, Garda Report of same date.

Although the assembled crowd and parading battalions of IRA members were not observed to have been carrying arms, this show of strength did cause some anxiety to the authorities. Frank Ryan, one of the recently released prisoners, bullishly concluded his speech by declaring that there would be only one army – the IRA. Two days previously, a document had been circulated to the new Cabinet warning that IRA reservists had been called onto active duty, that recruiting activities were to be intensified, and that the possibility of IRA members carrying arms at the upcoming meeting and the long spring and summer of republican events was relatively strong.[8]

Despite the failure of the unity attempt, for most of 1932, the mutual understanding between the IRA and Fianna Fáil meant that neither was willing to pressurise the other. Notwithstanding de Valera's declaration in Dáil Éireann that his party stood for 'one Government and one Army', government policy focused primarily on steps which would appeal to the republican constituency: through the first months of the new administration, the abolition of the oath of allegiance, the retention of the land annuities and the beginning of the economic war between Britain and Ireland dominated political life.[9] In an important interview to foreign journalists on St Patrick's Day 1932, de Valera signalled that the existence of the IRA would be tolerated until the oath was abolished, provided that the organisation did not engage in illegal activities. He further implied that he believed the abolition of the oath would reconcile the IRA to the state. In what was presented in some sections of the press as a reciprocal gesture, MacBride, speaking on behalf of the IRA, indicated that the organisation did not envisage political action at the present time.[10] Both parties, however, fundamentally underestimated the other. In viewing Fianna Fáil as a stalking horse for the transformation of the Irish state into an Irish Republic, the IRA failed to grasp that the battle for republican hearts and minds had been completely transformed. As de Valera set about fashioning the state after his own image, a significant section of the republican constituency was essentially satisfied by the slow but steady progress, further diminishing the toleration for violence.[11] Sections of the IRA leadership – MacBride amongst them for much of the 1930s – displayed every sign of subscribing to the Bolshevik parallel; this complacency condemned the organisation to a policy of drifting along on Fianna Fáil's coattails, without offering anything resembling a viable republican alternative. Similarly, however, de Valera himself was guilty of misjudging the depth of IRA commitment to militancy. Solipsism ran right across the republican spectrum, and de Valera's exclusivist political outlook – constructed around his self-image as leader of the Irish republican tradition – prevented him from fully grasping the nature of militant republican opposition to the Free State, just as it had obscured the validity of the civic nationalism espoused by Cumann na nGaedheal.

8 NAI JUS 8/698, Department of Justice memorandum circulated to members of the Executive Council, 11 March 1932.
9 *Dáil Éireann Debates*, vol. 41 col. 146, 15 March 1932; Deirdre McMahon, *Republicans and imperialists: Anglo-Irish relations in the 1930s* (London: Yale University Press, 1984), pp. 38–71.
10 *Irish Independent*, 17 March 1932; *Manchester Guardian*, 18 March 1932.
11 Ronan Fanning, '"The rule of order": Eamon de Valera and the IRA, 1923–40', in J. P. O'Carroll and John A. Murphy (eds.), *De Valera and his Times* (Cork: Cork University Press, 1983), pp. 160–72.

Notwithstanding this mutual confusion, the internecine nature of republican politics meant that close contact between Fianna Fáil and the IRA existed at every level: Fianna Fáil cabinet members appointed local IRA men as their ministerial drivers, and prominent IRA members were regular attendees of Fianna Fáil funerals. This position reflected the confused nature of IRA policy vis-à-vis their republican rivals; MacBride was at the centre of this confusion, attracting notice for his appointment, arranged by Fianna Fáil insider Frank Gallagher, as a sub-editor on the *Irish Press*-controlled *Evening Telegraph*:

> I understand that there is a good deal of comment on the fact that Seán MacBride is now on the staff of the Evening [Telegraph]. Have you any knowledge of any such comments being made by Volunteers and Republicans ... if there is any dissatisfaction, it will have to be explained to the Brigade and also our attitude in regard to such positions.[12]

Personal circumstance dictated the need for the job – the recent sale of Roebuck Jam Company meant that MacBride had not even a nominal income – but although MacBride eventually resigned his post in sympathy with striking Dublin newsboys, his perceived proximity to the Fianna Fáil establishment raised some hackles within the IRA. These suspicions were heightened when MacBride participated in another round of negotiations designed to unite the IRA and Fianna Fáil in the summer of 1932.

The initial approach came from Tom Barry, who had remained in the IRA but opposed anything resembling a 'social programme'; during meetings with de Valera and Aiken, the Fianna Fáil men revealed a plan to incorporate the IRA into a new Volunteer Reserve, to be attached to the Irish Army. This proposal appealed to Barry, who predicted that the new force could be used against the British forces in Northern Ireland and looked forward eagerly 'to the possibility of armed conflict developing'. The same month, Barry met with members of the IRA Army Council – Twomey, MacBride and George Gilmore – and proposed that IRA officers should provide the organising muscle for the new Reserve force, which could then 'be used politically to force any government to declare the Republic'.[13] There was merit in Barry's argument: by remaining outside the political structures since the end of the Civil War, the IRA had condemned itself to a position of increasing political irrelevance, particularly once Fianna Fáil had successfully marshalled republican sentiment in a vociferously anti-Treaty but essentially constitutional direction. The transformation of republican politics since the advent of the Fianna Fáil government required a similarly transformative attitude on the part of the militant republican movement; that the Army Council was unable to adjust to the new dispensation reflects what Henry Patterson has termed 'the political hollowness' of the movement.[14] At a further meeting with Aiken and Barry, the IRA

---

12 UCDA, Moss Twomey Papers, P69/155(73), letter to O/C Dublin Brigade, 6 June 1932; Mark O'Brien, *De Valera, Fianna Fáil and the* Irish Press (Dublin: Irish Academic Press, 2001), p. 51.
13 UCDA, Moss Twomey Papers, P69/42(54–7).
14 Henry Patterson, *The Politics of Illusion: Republicanism and Socialism in Modern Ireland* (London: Hutchinson, 1989), p. 54.

representatives repeated their customary arguments for a conference of national organisations and labour bodies – with the IRA as the controlling force – as the best way forward towards the Republic. They did, however, make one extraordinary intervention: '[the] situation is best met by political agreement ... a military force, even if formed, everybody consenting, is not enough, the essential need is agitation and organisation of people throughout the Twenty-Six Counties.'[15] This astonishing statement from the leadership of a self-styled army – a tacit admission of its inadequacy – ought to have been the prelude to a graceful exit or at least a formal disavowal of violence; instead, its significance appears to have passed unnoticed.

In the aftermath of this meeting, the IRA leadership ought to have been disabused of any notions of riding the Fianna Fáil tiger to victory. Twomey at least appears to have had some clarity on the issue, writing to a colleague in August of that year: 'Make no mistake about it: Fianna Fáil's ideas as to how the British threat should be fought and ours do not coincide.' Yet simultaneously, over a period of some eighteen months, MacBride was engaged in a series of meetings with de Valera, in what became the only formal leadership contact between the IRA and Fianna Fáil. Although the meetings were intended to deal with on-going practical issues, they degenerated into a reiteration of stalemates. Clearly, MacBride had been chosen to represent the IRA at the meetings with de Valera owing to their previous associations of the mid-1920s; their friendly relations did not, however, make the Fianna Fáil leader any better disposed towards the IRA. MacBride's account of these meetings, contained in an October 1933 letter to Joseph McGarrity, reveals something of the frustration he felt in confronting the immoveable de Valera:

> The same arguments, practically word for word, were reiterated at each interview. Briefly these were: that recognition of majority rule was essential. That once the Oath was removed there could be no objection to a recognition of majority rule and to recognising the Free State Parliament as a legitimate body upon which rested the function of leading the people. That even if we did not recognise majority rule as right per se we should recognise it as a rule of order and progress.[16]

MacBride attempted to counter de Valera's majoritarian arguments, sharply pointing out that majoritarianism was only morally enforceable 'in a free country', holding no obligation in one 'which was not free and was not even a single unity, under the control of one majority'. Moreover, de Valera's advocacy of majority rule was particularly redundant in light of his famous statement in 1922 that 'the majority had no right to do wrong'. De Valera's fundamental position was that the IRA ought to disband itself, and his refusal to budge from this stance afforded MacBride a glimpse into the experiences of others who had attempted to engage de Valera in a rational political debate:

---

15 UCDA, Moss Twomey Papers, P69/42(54–7), C/S to O/C Cork Brigade, 19 July 1932.
16 National Library of Ireland [NLI], Joseph McGarrity Papers, MS 17,456, Seán MacBride to Joseph McGarrity, 19 October 1933.

He is a very hard person to argue with and he spent a tremendous amount of time reiterating his position and justifying his actions on 1921–22–23 and 27 and I found it extremely hard to get him to consider anything but his own point of view ... [his] personality [is] strong and being conscious of this he plays upon it, with the result that I found our protracted interviews of little practical value. He always tried to put me in the position of having to be blunt and of even having to hurt his personality, before taking cognisance of our own point of view. He would then put his integrity and his judgement as against my argument.[17]

It was a perceptive appraisal of de Valera's negotiation tactics; MacBride was unable to bring the same acuity to bear on the position of the IRA. Still clinging to the idea of a national conference of national forces – in MacBride's formulation 'a united front in the economic crisis' – the Army Council were attempting the replicate the circumstances surrounding the conscription crisis of 1918 and benefit from the creation of a pan-nationalist front to ferment a revolutionary situation. This strategy perfectly underscored the primary problem with the IRA at large and MacBride in particular: a failure to adapt to changing circumstances and to mature politically. In seeking to reproduce and emulate the success of their predecessors of 1919 to 1921, the new IRA condemned themselves to political irrelevance.

'All the time trying to pressure Fianna Fáil along republican lines, but failing, slowly failing'[18]

While MacBride's meetings with de Valera were continuing – the final one coming sometime in the autumn of 1933 – the IRA were still searching for a meaningful role within the new dispensation. A brief effort to revive the anti-imperialist activities of the previous decade resulted in the 'Boycott British' campaign, clearly an IRA attempt to build on the Anglophobia of the Economic War; primarily targeting Bass ale, the campaign was roundly condemned as a 'damn foolacting business', with paltry results.[19] A snap election was called in January 1933, raising again the question of IRA support for Fianna Fáil in the upcoming ballot. Although the de Valera-MacBride talks were still ongoing, the Fianna Fáil determination to find a role for the IRA within its party structures ought to have made it clear that the party would not long countenance a rival army unreconciled to the state. Furthermore, the failure of the IRA to mobilise republican opinion behind the bulk of their activities over the course of 1932 was an ominous sign of difficulties which might lie ahead. George Gilmore was certainly aware of the problems posed by Fianna Fáil hegemony:

I believe that practically all the Republican and anti-FS feeling in the country is hopelessly pro-Dev and that FF are going to hold the field for a long time to come, and I do not think anything we could have done for the past 6 months

17 National Library of Ireland [NLI], Joseph McGarrity Papers, MS 17,456, Seán MacBride to Joseph McGarrity, 19 October 1933.
18 MacBride quoted in MacEoin, *Survivors*, p. 123.
19 De Valera quoted in Seán Cronin, *The McGarrity Papers* (Tralee: Anvil Books, 1972), p. 156.

would have altered that ... the fact is that I am completely fed up and pessimistic about everything past, present and future.[20]

Although there were more widespread reservations as to Fianna Fail's commitment to republican principles, an extraordinary IRA convention ahead of the election recommended that 'the Fianna Fáil government should be assisted into office again'.[21] The decision to continue to support Fianna Fáil – who increased their share of first preference votes to 47.9% and came one seat short of an overall majority – and the wider question of the overall direction of the army was beginning to pose serious difficulties for the army leadership. Widespread violence had attended the election campaign, with clashes between the IRA and the Army Comrades Association a regular feature of electoral meetings. Despite the IRA's fixation with their newfound enemies, another, sterner adversary would soon appear: what MacBride termed 'the honeymoon period' with Fianna Fáil had come to an end.[22]

Divisions Crystallise

Ahead of the 1933 General Army Convention the divisions within the IRA were coming into sharp focus. The failure of the Saor Éire initiative of 1931 to energise the Irish public had not dented the hopes of socialist republicans to build a truly revolutionary Irish Republic. If anything, the success of Fianna Fáil mobilising the public along lines which socialist republicans had in the past advocated – non-payment of the land annuities, a more statist approach to industrial development, and pledges to assist the working farmers and working class – served to strengthen the belief that the Irish people were becoming slowly radicalised. Peadar O'Donnell, Frank Ryan and George Gilmore were particularly active proponents of this line, and had moved towards arguing in favour of a pan-radicalist front. Ranged against this opinion, however, were traditionalist militant republicans on the one hand – principally represented by Seán Russell and Tom Barry – and those of a more pragmatic mindset, primarily Moss Twomey and Seán MacBride. The support of these latter two for the Saor Éire project had proved crucial in securing Army Council approval for the initiative, as we have seen; but the extreme reaction from both Church and State and, it must be said, the palpable disinterest displayed by the Irish public in such an overtly socialist enterprise militated against any similarly explicit forays into left-wing politics.

A marked demonstration of the divisions which the socialist orientation was causing in IRA ranks came with the Gralton affair in early 1933. James Gralton, a Leitrim-born communist recently returned to his native county from the United States, was the focus of a clerically inspired witch-hunt, culminating in a deportation order served on him by the de Valera government in February 1933. Although the IRA leadership was, broadly speaking, supportive of Gralton, local IRA units were opposed to his radicalism and opposed any IRA attempts to intervene

20   UCDA, Moss Twomey Papers, P69/53(368), George Gilmore to Chairman Army Council, 16 September 1932.
21   *An Phoblacht*, 14 January 1933.
22   MacBride quoted in MacEoin, *Survivors*, p. 123.

or organise on Gralton's behalf.[23] During the convention, therefore, the Army Council had the difficult task of negotiating a path between the socialist views of a significant section of the leadership, the outspokenly militant cohort also within the Army Council, and the hostility to radicalism emanating from the rank and file. For Twomey and MacBride, it was a difficult task.

MacBride appears to have taken the principal role in steering the discussions within the convention, and was at the centre of much heated debate. The question of the IRA's attitude to Fianna Fáil and to the Treatyite regime more generally received much attention. MacBride raised heckles in giving a bald assessment of Fianna Fáil's position vis-à-vis the army, noting that the *Irish Press* had begun a campaign against the possession of arms by private citizens – the IRA and the Blueshirts – and that once conditions of entry to the Free State Parliament were removed, republicans would come under increasing pressure to adjust their attitude to that institution.[24] This statement, on the surface a reasonable assessment of the difficulties which might lie ahead, provoked a storm of righteous protest, evidently tapping into latent fears within the movement that MacBride's commitment to the overall IRA project had been somewhat diminished by his recent lengthy (and private) meetings with de Valera. An earlier off-the-cuff remark by MacBride that 'if the Governor-General and the Oath were removed ... the position would be very difficult' was seized upon by socialist republicans fearful of any move towards accommodation with Fianna Fáil. Responding to MacBride, Frank Ryan warned against compromising core IRA beliefs: 'If we do not stand by the programme we have stood for for years, we should become a left wing of Fianna Fáil.' Peadar O'Donnell asked pointedly, 'What happens if the Governor-General goes?'; despite MacBride's reassurances that '[u]ntil the Republic for thirty-two counties is established, my attitude remains unchanged', a note of distrust remained. George Gilmore later inflated MacBride's comment to an argument in favour of political activity on the part of the IRA, a charge repeated by supporters of Seán Russell in the disfiguring split in the army in 1938.[25]

The most contentious issue raised at the convention was a motion prohibiting IRA members from joining other political organisations, a move which, if passed, would have serious implications for the leftist wing within the leadership, most of whom held overlapping membership in a variety of radical groups. MacBride made a lengthy speech supporting the motion, arguing that 'the very existence of the Army depended on the fate of this resolution'. He continued:

> The question is 'to whom do you give your allegiance?' Do you recommend that this organisation has power over life and death – if so, it must have your allegiance and this organisation alone must have it ... We had to expel many Volunteers who gave their allegiance to Fianna Fáil – this may also apply to members joining other political org[anisations]. What will be the position of a Volunteer who is in a communist party and becomes a candidate for election and sits in parliament? This question must be settled here.

23   Brian Hanley, 'Moss Twomey, radicalism and the IRA, 1931–33: a reassessment', *Saothar*, vol. 26, (2001), pp. 55–6.
24   UCDA, Moss Twomey Papers, P69/187 (91), Notes of General Army Convention, 1933.
25   UCDA, Moss Twomey Papers, P69/187(92–3), Notes of General Army Convention, 1933; Gilmore quoted in MacEoin, *Survivors*, p. 398.

Despite the entreaties of Gilmore and others – 'if we pass this resolution we will be drifting into a military clique' – the motion passed. Coupled with the defeat of O'Donnell and Gilmore's resolution calling for the establishment of a pan-radical front, the convention signalled that the flirtation with socialism had come to an end for the organisation as a whole.[26] Further evidence of this parting of the ways, ideologically speaking, can be found in the IRA's Governmental Programme, approved at the 1933 convention but not circulated until the following year. MacBride described the programme as a 'constitution to put in force when we take over the country'. The arrogance implicit in such an attitude infuriated historian and contemporary observer James Hogan, who wondered 'whether the IRA is conscious of the denial of democracy implied in proclaiming in advance a Constitution without any stipulation as to its being submitted to the people'.[27] Guaranteeing the right to private property and securing the position of private enterprise alongside promises of social justice and a welfarist state, the 1933 programme was more than a dilution of the socialism of Saor Éire: it was a deletion.

It was the IRA Chief of Staff who signalled clearly the move away from radicalism, stating bluntly at the Bodenstown commemoration in July 1933 that 'I emphatically and officially declare on behalf of the IRA that these charges [of irreligion] are deliberate falsehoods ... The policy of the IRA is not Communism, as could easily be proved, nor are we in alliance with the Communist movement.'[28] But whereas Twomey has largely escaped censure for steering the IRA away from socialism, MacBride drew opprobrium from socialist republicans as 'the theoretician of the IRA as it moved towards the right'.[29] Such criticism is, however, a little harsh. MacBride was an active proponent of the Saor Éire strategy, taking on much of the organisational duties of the initiative and suffering close attention from the authorities as a result. That the organisation failed miserably to ignite popular opinion, even within the IRA at a rank-and-file level, indicated the difficulties inherent in a leadership attempting to impose an ideology on an unwilling public. If further evidence was required of the temperature of Irish public opinion towards anything with a 'red' smear, the sacking of Connolly House, headquarters of the Communist Party of Ireland, by a mob incited by inflammatory Lenten sermons was a stark example.[30] This event and the Gralton affair bookended the IRA Convention, underlining the near impossibility of successfully implementing a socialist programme in a rabidly anti-socialist Free State.

Despite Moss Twomey's cheerful assertion that 'the air has been cleared of a lot of things which were causing a lot of friction for the [Army] Council, especially

26 UCDA, Moss Twomey Papers, P69/187(105), Notes of General Army Convention, 1933; Richard English, 'Socialism and republican schism in Ireland: the emergence of the Republican Congress in 1934', *Irish Historical Studies*, vol. xxvii, no. 105 (May 1990), p. 51.

27 James Hogan, *Could Ireland become Communist? The Facts of the Case* (Dublin: Cahill & Co., 1935), p. 1. See also Richard English, *Radicals and the Republic: Socialist Republicanism in the Irish Free State* (Oxford: Clarendon Press, 1994), p. 182; Patterson, *The Politics of Illusion*, p. 55; J. P. McHugh, 'Voices of the rearguard: a study of *An Phoblacht*: Irish republican thought in the post-revolutionary era, 1923–1937' (UCD, MA thesis, 1983), p. 126.

28 *Meath Chronicle*, 24 June 1933.

29 George Gilmore, *The Republican Congress 1934* (Dublin: Dóchas Co-op. Society Ltd, n.d.), p. 25.

30 *Irish Press*, 28 and 30 March 1933; English, *Radicals and the Republic*, pp. 177–8.

about Saor Éire and political activities generally', cleavages which had been held at bay since 1925 were beginning to form a chasm.[31] Much of these divisions centred around the political orientation and radicalism of the IRA, but personal animosities also coloured political allegiances. Arrested attempting to defend Connolly House, the defence of Charles Gilmore – one of three Gilmore brothers – was that the IRA had authorised his armed presence.[32] Officially, it had: Gilmore's older brother and commanding officer, Harry, had sanctioned the defence. But ahead of Gilmore's trial, MacBride – in one of his last actions as Adjutant-General before taking up the post of Director of Intelligence – wrote to the press repudiating this claim: 'Charles Gilmore had not permission from the Army Authorities to be in possession of arms last night (Wednesday), nor had he any orders to be in Gt. Strand St.' This provoked a disgusted response from Geoffrey Coulter, a former assistant editor of *An Phoblacht* and member of the left-leaning section of the IRA:

> The cowardly, treacherous and despicable behaviour of your Adjutant-General is enough to make a dog vomit. If Charlie Gilmore committed an act of indiscipline – which his OC denies – the proper court of action was to court-martial him, not to act as Crown Witness for imperialism to facilitate courts which the A/G affects not to recognise in the jailing of a republican who has done quite exceptional work and made quite exceptional sacrifices in the Republican cause.[33]

Having earned the enmity of the Gilmores – popular figures within the left wing of the movement – MacBride also fell out with Frank Ryan around this time. As a corollary to the step away from socialist republicanism, the Army Council re-exerted control over *An Phoblacht*, which had been a platform for radical ideas during the past seven years. When the editorship passed to Frank Ryan from Peadar O'Donnell, this social radicalism continued, to the point where it was coming into open conflict with army policy. Ryan, a volatile character, and Hanna Sheehy Skeffington, the assistant editor, bitterly resented the Army Council attempt to dictate editorial policy, Sheehy Skeffington writing sharply to Twomey: 'It would be lamentable if your organisation were to be swung to the right, becoming a Bulmer Hobson-MacNeill wing of Fianna Fáil.'[34] After the convention, these tensions came to a head: MacBride, 'under great pressure ... [and] under very great personal inconvenience', was appointed by the Army Council to act as editor in chief over Ryan. It amounted, as Peadar O'Donnell bluntly put it, to muzzling. Although Ryan had already tendered his resignation, he left immediately along with Sheehy Skeffington; Dónal O'Donoghue eventually took over as editor; and

---

31 UCDA, Moss Twomey Papers, P69/185(48), Moss Twomey to Connie Neenan, 21 March 1933. Neenan was, after McGarrity, the IRA's chief contact in Clan-na-Gael in the United States. A Civil War veteran, he had joined the republican exodus to the United States in the mid-1920s.

32 *Irish Times*, 31 March 1933.

33 *Irish Independent*, 31 March 1933; UCDA, Moss Twomey Papers, P69/53(238–9), Geoffrey Coulter to Chief of Staff, 3 April 1933.

34 UCDA, Moss Twomey Papers, P69/53 (167ff), Hanna Sheehy Skeffington to Moss Twomey, n.d.

for MacBride, another personal relationship had been sundered.[35] The lines along which the split of the following year would be drawn were coming sharply into focus.

'A raison d'être to the IRA': The Blueshirts[36]

Amidst this factionalism, the growth of the Blueshirt organisation presented a momentary diversion, briefly offering the army a focal point for unity. Instead, the leadership struggled to control its rank and file, as the violent clashes which had attended the 1933 election campaign increased in intensity throughout 1933 and 1934. The enmity between the Blueshirts and the republicans was fierce; as Cumann na mBan's Sighle Humphries bluntly put it, 'We hated them like the Devil hates holy water.'[37] There were a number of contributory factors to this deep-running hatred: the obvious Civil War bitterness and the disproportionately harsh effects of the economic war on middle and large farmers, as well as longer traditions of agrarian and electoral violence and locally based faction fighting. Indeed, the 'violence as pastime' aspect to the clashes which disfigured the Free State's political landscape during this period should not be underestimated, along with equally well established traditions of electoral violence. Recently released archival material in the National Archives in Dublin offers a stark picture of the brutality which passed for political activism in the southern state during this period, hinting at much more widespread violence and civic disorder than previously understood.

Although de Valera moved to face down the Blueshirt threat by banning a proposed commemoration march to Government Buildings in August 1933, the violence continued unabated. Large-scale riots and violent disruption of National Guard meetings were regular occurrences, with particularly vicious attacks taking place in Tralee, Kilkenny and Drogheda. But the violence was a grass-roots phenomenon within the IRA, with local leaders making the running against the wishes of the Army Council. Although IRA leaders who would later form the Republican Congress saw in the Blueshirts a fascist target around which to rally leftist opinion, non-socialists within the army leadership sought to minimise IRA involvement in any violent incidents. On 16 October, a captured IRA document confirmed to the government that the Army Council had counselled against violence, forbidding the carrying of weapons apart from training exercises, and prohibiting any acts of violence against individuals, any intimidation or threats against individuals, any holding-up of individuals, any raiding of homes, or any 'organised interference with political meetings, by units or Volunteers'. The communiqué spelled out clearly the Army Council's position on the Blueshirt question:

> Volunteers have recently taken certain indisciplined unauthorised actions which are doing incalculable injury to the prestige of the Army and are, in fact,

---

35 UCDA, Moss Twomey Papers, P69/53/170, Moss Twomey to Hanna Sheehy-Skeffington, 31.3.1933; p. 313; Peadar O'Donnell quoted in English, *Radicals and the Republic*, p. 182.

36 Gerald Boland quoted in 'Gerry Boland's story, part 4', *Irish Times*, 11 October 1968.

37 Sighle Humphries quoted in MacEoin, *Survivors*, p. 350.

bringing it into contempt. These indisciplined and pointless actions cannot fail to create in the minds of the people the idea that our organisation is without, or despises, leadership and control – a fatal idea to get abroad.[38]

From the leadership's perspective the position was clear: IRA involvement in destabilising street fighting and public disorder would force the government to move against their organisation, an accurate analysis. But it was a difficult rationale to sell to grass-roots republicans. Reflecting the reluctance of the leadership to really grapple with the issue, MacBride made few public pronouncements on the Blueshirts: a sole address to an anti-Imperialist meeting in June 1934 constitutes the only public record of his opinion. There, his remarks focused on the result of the Blueshirt threat:

> Mr Seán McBride [sic] said that General O'Duffy had been helpful to the Fianna Fáil Government because he had served to distract the attention of the people from the real issue in Irish politics. He [MacBride] did not consider that the Blueshirts were a menace to Republicanism in Ireland, because the workers had made it very clear that they would not have Fascism.[39]

Despite the best efforts of the IRA leadership to studiously ignore the Blueshirts, however, they could not disregard the legal and political manoeuvres used by the de Valera government to confront and nullify them; these measures were swiftly brought to bear on the IRA themselves.

Recruitment, the Volunteer Reserve and the Broy Harriers

The prohibition of the Blueshirt march in August 1933 was made under Article 2A, the hated legal mechanism enacted by the Cosgrave government to deal with the IRA and Saor Éire in 1931. Suspended but not rescinded by de Valera in 1932, it was revived the following year to proscribe the planned march; the prohibition of both the National Guard and the Young Ireland Association swiftly followed. Significantly, the Military Tribunal was revived in 1934 to try a variety of offences; although a mere handful of IRA members were convicted by the Tribunal in 1934 compared to over 300 Blueshirt members, it set an important precedent in de Valera's Ireland. But in 1934 the possibility of such legal machinery being used to target the IRA on a wider scale appeared remote. Part of de Valera's strategy to wean the IRA away from violence were the constitutional adjustments to the Anglo-Irish Treaty – particularly the abolition of the Oath of Allegiance and the debasement of the office of Governor-General ahead of its deletion – but an equally important component in this direction was the enactment of a new Military Services Pensions Bill in 1934 to provide for republicans who had opposed the Treaty. The

38 NAI, JUS 2008/117/140, Communiqué from Chief of Staff, IRA, 16 October 1933. For more on the IRA's attitude to the Blueshirts, see Mike Cronin, 'The Blueshirts in the Irish Free State, 1932–1935: the nature of socialist republican opposition and governmental opposition', in Tim Kirr and Anthony McElligot, *Opposing Fascism: Community, Authority and Resistance in Europe* (Cambridge: Cambridge University Press, 2004, first printed 1999), pp. 80–96.

39 *Irish Times*, 4 June 1934.

IRA Army Council denounced the Pensions Bill, urging members not to 'allow yourselves to be weakened in your allegiance by a bribe.'[40] As MacBride remembered, his position on the pensions question was straightforward: 'I refused to take a pension because I had not done anything believing that there might be financial benefits accruing from it.'[41] Although the Act did not include any requirement to desist from current IRA activities, the army rightly identified it as a measure not merely to provide recompense for the many anti-Treatyites who had been unjustly excluded from the original 1924 Act, but as a means of drawing present-day IRA members into the Fianna Fáil net. To a certain extent, it worked; as one veteran republican bitterly recalled, '[people] were bought and stayed bought; people were de Valera-ites when they should have been Republicans'.[42]

Two other measures enacted by the Fianna Fáil government aimed at a similar result: the Volunteer Reserve and the new Special Branch of the Gardaí, popularly known as the Broy Harriers. Both aimed at enticing past or present members of the IRA into the forces of the state. As shown, the Volunteer Reserve had long been part of the Fianna Fáil governmental programme, and had formed part of the negotiations with the IRA immediately after the party took office. With IRA representatives having declined formal integration of their organisation into the new force, Fianna Fáil pressed ahead, beginning the drafting of the necessary legislation in late 1933. Although government ministers were at pains to insist that the primary function of the new force would be to strengthen the Free State's defensive capabilities, the IRA suspected a more insidious intention. Tom Barry's warning that 'this will sweep the unattached youth into [the Free State Government's] ranks' was precisely correct; Seán Lemass had already stated privately that the function of the new reserve force was 'the provision of an opportunity of military training in a manner beneficial to the State, to young men to whom military manoeuvres are an attraction and who if they do not get the association they desire in an official organisation may be induced to seek it in illegal organisations'.[43] The *Round Table* noted perceptively that 'it is clearly Mr de Valera's intention to weaken the IRA by providing past and present leading lights with lucrative employment'; the appointment of anti-Treaty IRA veterans as recruitment officers meant that the IRA were now in direct competition with Fianna Fáil for new blood.[44]

A number of countering strategies were attempted, centring around a recruiting drive: Garda intelligence in October 1933 reported that

> as a set-off to the Government Volunteer Reserve, Battalion O/Cs have been instructed to enrol all the veterans possible of the pre-Truce IRA in a reserve force of the IRA, with the object of getting control over such persons, and to

40 *Irish Independent*, 3 October 1934.
41 Seán MacBride, *That Day's Struggle: A Memoir, 1904–1951*, ed. Caitriona Lawlor (Dublin: Curragh Press, 2005), p. 95.
42 Dan Gleeson quoted in MacEoin, *Survivors*, p. 275.
43 UCDA, Moss Twomey Papers, P69/52 (53); Lemass quoted in Lar Joye, '"Aiken's slugs": the reserve of the Irish Army under Fianna Fáil', in J. Augusteijn (ed.), *Ireland in the 1930s: New Perspectives* (Dublin: Four Courts Press, 1999), p. 145. See also Brian Hanley, 'The Volunteer Reserve and the IRA', *The Irish Sword*, vol. xxi, no. 83 (1998), pp. 93–8.
44 'The Irish Free State – *Quo vadis?*', *Round Table*, vol. xxiv, no. 94 (March 1934), p. 374.

prevent them as members of the IRA from joining the Government Volunteer Reserve.

Certainly, the period 1933–1934 represented the peak in membership of the IRA, rising to a figure of approximately 13,000.[45] Simultaneously, speakers at republican events increased calls for enlistment. Seán Russell, in March 1933 'called on young men not to become members of the new force, but to join the Republican Army, drill, arm and equip, and be ready to strike for freedom when the opportunity arrived'; while MacBride in July 1933 quoted Patrick Pearse to a large republican gathering: 'The Irish Republicans declare that they have the right to assert the freedom of Ireland by force of arms if necessary ... we should remember Pearse's words, "It is not sufficient to say I believe, you must also say I serve."'[46] The Broy Harriers focused their recruitment efforts at the same group of IRA veterans, and were specifically created to tackle the Blueshirt menace. But whereas the Blueshirts were an almost comically transparent organisation, easily identifiable, the IRA were more opaque; a new force of police drawn from the same gene pool, intensely familiar with the republican milieu, were in a much more powerful position to effectively target the IRA when the final break eventually came. The real importance of both the new organisations, however, was to signal increasingly frosty relations between the IRA and Fianna Fáil.

From the government's perspective, the IRA remained stubbornly opposed to the state despite Fianna Fáil's success in 'republicanising' Irish society, political culture and public life, and de Valera was losing patience: 'We desire unity, but desires will get us nowhere unless we can get some accepted basis for determining what the national policy shall be and where leadership shall lie. What is the use of talking any more with people who are too stupid or too pig-headed to see this.'[47] The republican leadership, too, were becoming increasingly critical of Fianna Fáil policy. MacBride delivered a stinging rebuke to the government during the anti-Poppy Day protests of 1933, one of the most popular days on the republican calendar: 'the present attitude of the Fianna Fáil leaders was daily justifying every act of the Cosgrave government when in power. Mr Cosgrave said he was taking the Treaty as a stepping-stone, and Fianna Fáil was now telling [us] the same thing.'[48] This was a favourite theme of IRA speakers from the mid-1930s, and it was one which Fianna Fáil representatives found difficult to refute. The republican movement clung proudly to its record of constancy, and delighted in highlighting the inconsistencies and hypocrisies of the government party.

The republican movement moved towards open conflict with Fianna Fáil in the Northern Ireland general election of November 1933. MacBride gave a bald assess-

---

45 NAI, JUS 2008/117/48, Garda Report dated 11 November 1933. The strength of the IRA, it should be noted, paled in comparison with the of the Blueshirts, which at its peak numbered some 47,000. Mike Cronin, *The Blueshirts and Irish Politics* (Dublin: Four Courts Press, 1997), p. 115, table 5.1.

46 NAI, JUS 2008/117/48, Garda Report dated 6 November 1933; 'The Irish Free State', *Round Table*, vol. xxiii, no. 91 (June 1933), p. 644; *Meath Chronicle*, 8 July 1933.

47 Eamon de Valera to Joseph McGarrity, 31 January 1934, quoted in Cronin, *The McGarrity Papers*.

48 *Irish Press*, 11 November 1933.

ment of the options open to the electorate: 'Six-County Republicans want the issue in these elections to be a clear cut choice between Republicanism and Imperialism – between national unity and independence and Imperialism and subjugation.'[49] But the republican campaign did not go well. In a mark of the definite divisions between the IRA and Fianna Fáil, Eamon de Valera stood and was elected as an abstentionist nationalist candidate in the constituency of South Down, a nationalist heartland that the republican candidate might have been expected to carry. Cahir Healy, rising leader of the Nationalist Party, launched a stinging attack on the IRA campaign, which had led to increased tensions in Belfast: 'The six-county Nationalists welcomed the co-operation of their friends across the border, but the IRA odds-and-ends, who drifted across the border now, represented nobody but themselves and were merely preparing for a greater offensive later in the Free State if they succeeded in the North-East.'[50] De Valera's thinking in opposing the republican candidate was simple: Fianna Fáil, in purporting to be the true voice of Irish republicanism, could not allow a rival organisation to represent republicanism north of the border. Quite what MacBride and the IRA hoped to achieve is more puzzling. The contradictory nature of presenting candidates for election in Northern Ireland while continuing to rule out – and rapidly approaching a split on the issue – any question of organising politically in the Free State is striking. For MacBride, his close involvement in the northern elections campaign is a further indication that his opposition to the revival of Saor Éire was on ideological grounds – he no longer believed that socialist platforms would appeal to the Irish people – rather than an expression of apoliticism.

'Anything that was not the gun, was politics'[51]

By 1934, tensions within the republican movement had come to a head, the frustrations arising from the failure to eat into Fianna Fáil support underscored the ideological cleavage which was beginning to paralyse the movement. Although Twomey and MacBride, both pragmatists, had tried their hand at socialist initiatives, the disappointment of Saor Éire meant that they were resistant to efforts to push the IRA once more to the left. Conversely, the leftist grouping inside the movement were intensely dissatisfied by the reluctance of the Army Council to commit the IRA to officially combating the Blueshirts. With street clashes increasing daily, and the discourse of political culture in Ireland becoming more extreme, the group around O'Donnell, Ryan and Gilmore considered the moment ideal to launch a broad-fronted movement to radicalise the Irish public:

49 *Sunday Independent*, 12 November 1933. MacBride, along with Moss Twomey, Mrs Austin Stack, the O'Rahilly and Mr Alex Lynn formed a fund-raising committee for the republican candidates.
50 *Irish Times*, 27 November 1933; Brian M. Walker (ed.), *Parliamentary Election Results in Ireland, 1918–92: Irish Elections to Parliaments and Parliamentary Assemblies at Westminster, Belfast, Dublin, Strasbourg* (Dublin: Royal Irish Academy, 1992), pp. 52–3. One republican candidate, Patrick McLogan, was elected in South Armagh, although Patrick Thornbury polled well against the veteran Joseph Devlin in Belfast Central.
51 Peadar O'Donnell, *Monkeys in the Superstructure: Reminiscences of Peadar O'Donnell* (Galway: Salmon Publishing, 1986), p. 18.

'a Congress of the Ireland of the poor, so easily mobilisable if the IRA organisation and tradition could be brought to bear on the task'.[52] A confrontation over the future role of the army was imminent.

The 1934 General Army Convention, held over 17 and 18 March in Dublin saw these simmering tensions bubble over in a series of destructive arguments with MacBride at the centre, an important episode in his IRA career which Keane's biography fails to mention. The eventual secessionists had planned a confrontation, quietly canvassing delegates and hoping to win over enough support to carry a carefully worded resolution calling for a congress of republican opinion.[53] Events did not go as planned, however, when Michael Price – not known for his radical views – attempted to tie the IRA to the full implementation of its 1933 Governmental Programme, thereby removing the possibility of cooperating with a suitably republican (although perhaps not a socially radical) government. MacBride was blunt in his opposition to such a move, while claiming to hold fast to the economic policies of the 1933 programme. As English has pointed out, what seemed like a casuistic quibble went to the heart of the IRA's commitment to social radicalism, exposing the hollowness beneath.[54] But to overly criticise MacBride for opposing Price's resolution obscures the extent to which the 1933 Governmental Programme was in essence a compromise document, a mid-point between the extremism of the Saor Éire ideologues and the traditionalists within the movement.

Since it was drawn up, the hostility of the Irish public to anything carrying the smear of communism had been firmly demonstrated. Retreat from radicalism, while it drew the lasting disdain of leftist republicans, appeared to be politically expedient. Price withdrew from the convention in disgust, leaving the floor to a further challenge to army policy. O'Donnell and Gilmore proposed 'a Republican Congress which will restate the Republican standard and confront the imperialists with a solid form of nationalist masses pledged to the achievement of the Republic of Ireland and to the revolutionary struggle in solid association with the IRA'.[55] This last clause was important: for O'Donnell, Gilmore and Ryan, the IRA remained at the heart of the republican struggle. What they saw unfolding before them was 'a situation crying out for action' in which the IRA should take a lead. As the radical Frank Edwards remarked: 'You can't keep people, potential revolutionaries, going for ever on a diet of hustings, commemorations, flags, banners and Bodenstowns.'[56]

Again, however, MacBride was at the heart of opposition to the resolution, nailing his anti-constitutionalist credentials to the mast:

52 George Gilmore, *The Irish Republican Congress* (Cork: Cork Workers' Club, 1974, first published 1935), p. 14.

53 Dónal Ó Drisceoil, *Peadar O'Donnell* (Cork: Cork University Press, 2001), p. 83.

54 UCDA, Seán MacEntee Papers, P67/525, Minutes of General Army Convention of the IRA, 17 March 1934; English, *Radicals and the Republic*, pp. 185–7.

55 UCDA, Seán MacEntee Papers, P67/525, Minutes of General Army Convention of the IRA, 17 March 1934.

56 Gilmore, *The Irish Republican Congress*, p. 15; Frank Edwards quoted in MacEoin, *Survivors*, p. 7.

Fianna Fáil captured the leadership of the nationalist elements in the country. They are now stepping away from any pretence they had of the establishment of the Republic. The people who have supported them are now leaving Fianna Fáil disappointed. Fianna Fáil are now losing that leadership. There is some need for gaining the leadership of these people. My objection to any form of organisation is this, that as soon as you form any kind of organisation you will be called upon to contest elections & work within constitutionalism. At first it may not but ultimately it will.

Citing the popular acceptance of the Treaty, MacBride declared: 'I have very little faith in the mass of the constitutional Republicans nor in the opinion of the mass of the people.'[57] In a subsequent meeting with the Cumann na mBan leadership, whom the IRA were anxious to keep onside during the split, MacBride enunciated his opposition to Congress more clearly:

Asked, for his reason for opposing the Congress Sean MacBride stated that personally he was opposed to them because:
1. It would not be under the control of the Army and would be at the mercy of those composing it.
2. Those so far composing it did not make it clear that they did not intend going into Leanster [sic] House.
3. The proper place to decided on the policy to be adopted by Volunteers was at the Convention.
4. Many of those who would compose the Congress would be those who disapproved [sic] with Fianna Fáil on some side issue, but who were not revolutionists.

He concluded that, 'all constitutional parties gained first gained support by the extremeness of their views, but subsequently they all followed the same road'.[58] Tellingly, the majority of delegates at the convention voted in favour of the Congress resolution, but the army executive votes were enough to defeat it. The Congress leaders – Gilmore, O'Donnell and Ryan – left the convention floor and the IRA ahead of their formal court martial and dismissal the following month. The secessionists formally constituted the Republican Congress in Athlone on 7–8 April 1934, drawing support from dissatisfied IRA members – particularly among the Dublin Brigade – a significant section of Cumann na mBan, trade unionists, and the Communist Party of Ireland.[59] The Army Council's statement on the split was not especially hostile, noting in language echoing MacBride above that 'inevitably [Republican Congress] will follow the road which has been travelled by

57 UCDA, Seán MacEntee Papers, P67/525, Minutes of General Army Convention of the IRA, 17 March 1934.
58 UCDA, Sighle Humphries Papers, P106/1153(3), Meeting of Cumann na mBan Executive with Army Representatives, 18 April 1934.
59 Dónal Ó Drisceoil, '"The Irregular and Bolshie situation": republicanism and communism, 1921–36', in Fearghal McGarry (ed.), *Republicanism in Modern Ireland* (Dublin: UCD Press, 2003), pp. 53–4. For personal recollections of the Republican Congress, see George Gilmore, *The Irish Republican Congress* (Cork: Cork Workers' Club, 1974, first published 1935); George Gilmore, *The Republican Congress 1934* (Dublin: Dóchas Co-op. Society Ltd, n.d.); Peadar Byrne, *Memories of the Republican Congress* (London: Connolly Association, n.d.); Nora Connolly-O'Brien, *We Shall Rise Again* (London: Mosquito Press, 1981).

other constitutional parties which, though setting out with good intentions, will end in failure.'[60] The secessionists were not so magnanimous, however, their new journal *Republican Congress* launching a fusillade of criticism at the IRA leadership, week by week.

Perhaps with these words ringing in their ears, the IRA leadership proceeded to the Bodenstown commemoration of 1934. Republican Congress, as Henry Patterson has underlined, were uncommonly proud of their reaching out to Protestant workers in Northern Ireland: in the wake of the Outdoor Relief Riots of 1932, somewhat unrealistic hopes had arisen of a union of purpose between workers artificially divided along confessional lines.[61] It was, therefore, with great pride that the Congress included two Northern Protestant groupings among their parade as they attempted to participate in the main republican commemoration. The IRA leadership ordered that two unauthorised banners carried by the Northern Protestant grouping – bearing such dangerous slogans as 'James Connolly Club Belfast; United Irishmen 1934; Connolly's Message Our Ideal' and 'Wolfe Tone Commemoration 1934; Shankill Road, Belfast Branch; Break the Connection with Capitalism' – within the Congress contingent be furled. When the Northern groups refused, the Tipperary Brigade of the IRA attacked them and destroyed the banners. In protest, the Republican Congress withdrew from the procession at the gates to the churchyard and held a rival meeting in the assembly field. O'Donnell declared that 'the mask had been torn from hypocrisy that day', continuing:

> What had happened would, he thought, bring thousands more to their banner because the young men would see the reaction and the hypocrisy which had been displayed in the attack. The IRA leadership was afraid of the Congress and they had used as their tools that day poor, deluded workers from the Midlands ... The shame of it was that the son of Major MacBride, Moss Twomey and Mick Fitzpatrick should have driven good Tipperary lads to attack the banner of Belfast republicans.[62]

The Bodenstown commemoration of 1934, along with similar incidents the subsequent year, formed part of a larger Republican Congress critique of the alleged anti-radical nature of the Army Council, one in which MacBride featured prominently. The question of control of such set-piece republican events raised ideological tensions even higher.[63]

Shortly after this fracas, a disturbing document reached Garda intelligence. In a letter to all independent units, Twomey ordered that 'within at least twelve months the Army be trained, equipped and fit to take the field', calling for 'a smooth and efficient military machine'. Earlier in the summer, the strength of the IRA had been estimated at 6,000, after the defections to Republican Congress. The Garda commissioner's response to this threat was extremely interesting. Conceding that the document was 'rather alarming' in so far as it appeared to

60   *Irish Independent*, 11 April 1934.
61   Patterson, *The Politics of Illusion*, p. 65.
62   *Irish Press*, 18 June 1934; NAI, JUS8/310, 1934 Bodenstown Report, 18 June 1934.
63   UCDA, Sighle Humphries Papers, P106/3815–3834, *Republican Congress*, no. 8 (23 June 1934).

threaten an attempted coup, the commissioner was dismissive of any real danger posed by the IRA:

> This general instruction is nothing more than an attempt to put some spectacular objective before the rank and file of the organisation in a desperate endeavour to stem the disorganisation and disintegration that threatened its very existence ... the circular need give no cause for alarm whatsoever. It is thought that the orthodox IRA will never be a serious menace to the Government as at present constituted.

Instead, the commissioner considered the Republican Congress a much more subversive body: 'The more this organisation's efforts are thwarted by the existence of the orthodox IRA the better. If the latter ceased to exist there would be much more recruitment to the Congress with the inevitable social consequences.'[64] This letter may represent another strand in government thinking which delayed a final crackdown on the IRA during the mid-1930s: the IRA was apparently considered a bulwark against social disorder. It was a curious position for a government to take, pledged to uphold the rule of order: the toleration of a self-avowed revolutionary army outside the structures of the state in order to prevent radicalisation. Such forbearance may have been ascribed to the Army Council's general avoidance of violence since Fianna Fáil came to power, including a valiant attempt to prohibit IRA members from clashing with the Blueshirts; when, in 1935, the organisation returned with force to the gun, toleration ended. In the interim, Republican Congress self-imploded amid another secession of almost half its original members, greeted in some quarters with hilarity: 'Students of Irish political news will soon require a pocket political dictionary in order to follow the names and aims of our various parties.'[65] Just as the IRA had represented a safeguard against socialist extremism to the government, Republican Congress had, to a certain extent, insulated the IRA from the scrutiny of the authorities. Once that threat had disappeared, the IRA would be harried and harassed as never before.

In Search of a Purpose: Land and Labour Disputes, 1935

Through the early months of 1935, the IRA were drifting. Aside from constantly preparing members for a military uprising – the prospect of which retreated further as numbers shrank – much of its drive and purpose had been sapped by the defection of the Republican Congress. In an attempt to find a rallying point, the leadership sanctioned intervention in land and labour issues in late 1934 and early in 1935. The most notorious of these was the More O'Ferrall affair in Edgeworthstown, County Longford, in which the IRA sought to utilise an old-fashioned agrarian dispute to bolster its support among small farmers, recently drawn wholesale towards Fianna Fáil. The affair also reveals a glimpse into the plight of the farming community as the disastrous effect of the economic

---

64   NAI, JUS 2008/117/740, Intercepted letter from Chief of Staff, dated 31 August 1934, and Garda Commission to Secretary for Justice, 29 September 1934.
65   'The Irish Free State: the split in the opposition', *Round Table*, vol. xxv, no. 97 (December 1934), p. 161.

war on agricultural trade made itself felt; attempting to secure a 50 per cent reduction in rents, the local tenants' association approached the IRA for assistance after an earlier approach to Fianna Fáil TD James Victory had failed.

From November 1934, it is clear that Gardaí were closely observing events on the Saunderson estate, as IRA involvement threatened to transform a peaceful rent dispute into something far more sinister, focused on the local agent, Gerald More O'Ferrall. MacBride was due to attend a tenants' meeting on 2 December. Unable to attend, he sent Michael Kelly in his place, who told the meeting, 'If the Guards use rifles and revolvers, you must also use rifles and revolvers, and that bough of the tree convenient to More O'Ferralls and 6 feet of rope might be necessary.'[66] Whether such sentiments were sanctioned by the IRA leadership is unclear; what is certain, however, is that on the night of 9 February, IRA members burst in on the More O'Ferrall house as the family were dining. In the altercation which followed, both the agent and his son, 27-year-old Richard More O'Ferrall, were shot, the latter succumbing to his injuries on 20 February. The murder provoked outrage, strengthening opposition and press calls for the government to proscribe the IRA. De Valera's response, a week after the murder, was that

> Any action that may be necessary for the maintenance of public order will be taken in regard to the Irish Republican Army and other military or semi-military organisations, but it is not the opinion of the Executive Council that the necessity has arisen for the course suggested in the question.[67]

But although the government still hesitated to definitively move against the IRA, a further blow was dealt to the organisation by the Catholic bishops' Lenten pastorals. Alarmed by what it viewed as the rise of communistic influence in the Republican Congress, Catholic bishops across Ireland condemned the IRA along with their former comrades.[68] The next move of the Army Council was to prove disastrous.

On 2 March 1935, Dublin tramway and bus workers went on strike, after a bus driver was dismissed for dangerous driving. As the city struggled to cope with the paralysis of its public transport system, the government placed Free State Army lorries on the streets to alleviate distress. On 22 March the Army Council issued a statement condemning the use of the Free State Army for strike-breaking purposes, offering 'to assist in mobilising the maximum support for the Dublin transport workers', and proposing a meeting of representatives of the IRA and

---

66 In the aftermath of the murder, a Garda report urged that 'it ought seriously be considered whether some effort should not be made to discover whether control of affairs was not taken over by GHQ of [the IRA]'. NAI, JUS2008/117/924, More O'Ferrall case; Hanley, *The IRA*, pp. 58–9.

67 Frank Columb, *The Shooting of More O'Ferrall* (Cambridge: Evod Academic Publishing Co., 1997); *Dáil Éireann Debates*, vol. 55, col. 1, 27 February 1935. Although four men were eventually tried for the outrage, the first jury failed to reach a verdict and the second found them not guilty, having returned to his legal studies, assisted with Joseph O'Connor QC with the preparation for the case. MacBride, *That Day's Struggle*, p. 125.

68 *Irish Times*, 4 March 1935. For more on the 1935 pastorals and the Edwards affair, see Patrick Murray, *Oracles of God: The Roman Catholic Church and Irish Politics, 1922–37* (Dublin: UCD Press, 2000), pp. 337–45.

those of the Strike Committee.[69] The same evening, three Gardaí were fired upon in apparently coordinated attacks in Dublin. Garda intelligence indicated that the strike committee had agreed a meeting with the IRA and that the latter planned to intervene as 'a militant body, attack and set fire to military lorries.[70] Finally, the government acted. In a large-scale roundup of almost fifty Dublin republicans on 26 March, Roebuck House was among the first to be visited: MacBride, however, was not at home, avoiding arrest along with Moss Twomey, Seán Russell, Frank Ryan and George Plunkett.[71] For the first time since Fianna Fáil came to power, the IRA leadership went on the run.

They regrouped on 28 March to issue a lengthy statement severely critical of the government, and by the beginning of April whispers were reaching Garda ears of a planned insurrection at Easter, scheduled to coincide with de Valera's unveiling of Oliver Sheppard's Cúchulainn statue in the General Post Office (GPO). Although the Garda commissioner considered it unlikely that the IRA would engage in open conflict with the state, he feared a stunt of some kind. Accordingly, military protection was placed on all public and government buildings on Easter weekend, armed Garda patrols were increased, and stand-to parties readied. They need not have worried: despite Twomey's passionate denunciation of the 'time-servers, the sycophants and those who had once served the Republic', the republican ceremonies were a flop, with very poor attendances and heckling from the Dublin public. MacBride had a similarly doleful time in Mayo, where he addressed a republican gathering in the pouring rain and was paddled across the River Moy in rowing boat before catching a lift in a lorry to Sligo.[72] The glamour of the revolutionary lifestyle was fading fast.

As the summer of 1935 approached, the government still had not definitively moved against the IRA. Although some of the March arrestees were prosecuted by the Military Tribunal, most were released without charge and the fugitive leadership permitted to return unmolested to their homes. In Dáil Éireann, de Valera issued a final warning, stating clearly that 'there must be order'; the writing was clearly on the wall for the IRA, but it staggered on, pinning its hopes on 'hope, enthusiasm and militancy ... to improve our organisation, efficacy and fighting spirit'.[73] MacBride was chief organiser and speaker at the 1935 Bodenstown commemoration; the records of his organisational attempts speak not merely of the massive logistical demands of staging such an event, but also of the decrease in republican sentiment across the country. Whereas the previous year had attracted some 17,000, now the excuses poured in. In Laois, republican bodies claimed the 'flu; in

---

69 *Irish Press*, 25 March 1935.

70 *Weekly Irish Times*, 30 March 1935; NAI, JUS8/405, Tramway Employees Strike, Garda Report dated 25 March 1935.

71 NAI, JUS 2008/117/953, Arrest of IRA members and Republican Congress under Article 2A of the Constitution, 1935.

72 NAI, JUS 2008/117/743, IRA Celebrations, Easter Week 1935.

73 NAI, JUS 2008/117/488, IRA Intercepted Documents, 1935, Chief of Staff to Independent Units, 6 May 1935; Maurice Moynihan, *Speeches and Statements by Eamon de Valera, 1917–1973* (Dublin: Gill & Macmillan, 1980), p. 264. See also Bill Kissane, 'Defending democracy? The legislative response to political extremism in the Irish Free State, 1922–39', *Irish Historical Studies*, vol. xxxiv, no. 134 (November 2004), pp. 167–8.

Dundalk, 'disorganisation'; in Charleville, worries about 'getting Mass' prevented attendance; and in Sligo the reason was straightforward: 'We are hard-hit in money matters.'[74]

Delivering the oration, MacBride claimed to speak 'on behalf of the youth of Ireland, that is pledged to Tone's sacrifice, that is armed, and that is prepared to make sacrifices in order to secure this objective'; his speech stuck to conventional militant lines, emphasising the hypocrisy of Fianna Fáil cant of republican unity and condemning the iniquity of partition.[75] Being afforded the prestigious position of delivering the oration ought to have been one of the high points of MacBride's republican career; instead, the occasion was marred by a poor turnout and a repeat of the clashes with the Republican Congress contingent. On 29 June, Ryan and Gilmore wrote a letter to the press condemning MacBride's attempt to exclude the Republican Congress banner and noting that he was the principal opponent to the formation of that body:

> Would it not be better for Seán MacBride to be a bit ashamed of himself for attempting to force a gang-war between Republicans? ... MacBride and the other Republicans leaders are degrading the splendid idealism of Republican youth, and making themselves obnoxious by a Brass Hat play-acting which we had hoped was eradicated long ago.[76]

MacBride's response is not recorded.

But the IRA were alive to the threat posed by the Republican Congress rump who continued sniping in their journal, calling the IRA 'a caste' who sought to maintain power 'by Hitlerite methods'. The Army Council were also aware of plans by Gilmore and Ryan to launch a renewed call for republican unity.[77] In what was to the Republican Congress a brazen volte-face, the IRA Extraordinary Convention of September 1935 approved the formation of an auxiliary organisation which would organise politically.[78] MacBride was the publicist for the IRA plans, writing to the press to announce the creation of 'a separatist organisation' in the 'near future':

> It might be necessary to put forward candidates at elections who would be pledged to the Republic. Steps were being taken to devise the best means of doing these things. Anything done in that direction must be based on the non-recognition of the institutions imposed on this country. As soon as plans were definitely made, people would be asked to rally once more to the standard of the Republic as in 1918. But this time they must build on more solid foundations. They must undo the conquest not only in name but in practice.[79]

---

74 UCDA, Sighle Humphries Papers, P106/2102, 2113.
75 *Nenagh Guardian*, 29 June 1935; *Irish Times*, 24 June 1935.
76 *Irish Independent*, 29 June 1935.
77 This was made, with the support of the maverick Fianna Fáil TD Dan Breen, in September 1935. NAI, JUS 2008/11//740, Republican Unity Call, Wynn's Hotel, 22 September 1935; UCDA, Sighle Humphries Papers, P106/3815–3834, *Republican Congress*, 16 November 1935.
78 NAI, JUS 2008/117/740, Reports of Óglaigh na hÉireann conventions, August–September 1935.
79 *Irish Press*, 24 and 28 September 1935.

MacBride later claimed that he was not involved in this new political organisation – 'I stayed out of it' – but the records show that he was intimately involved in arguing for its creation, the drafting of its constitution and manifesto, and publicly organising on its behalf.[80] The constitution of Cumann Poblachta na hÉireann was a fairly pedestrian reassertion of what were held to be traditional republican values, some of them bearing the imprint of MacBride's thinking: England was held to be the root of all of Ireland's ills, and civil servants were marked out as a particularly malevolent force within the Irish political system. Some mild gestures were made in the direction of social justice and Gaelic ideals were espoused in suitably vague terms. The new party also officially committed itself to abstentionism.[81]

The manifesto and the new organisation were officially launched on 8 March 1936; the founding members included MacBride – Secretary of the Provisional National Council – and Twomey, Patrick McLogan MP, Dónal O'Donoghue, the O'Rahilly and representatives of Cumann na mBan. MacBride began an energetic campaign to raise the profile of the new party, becoming a frequent correspondent in the letter columns of the Irish press, and travelling the country on organisational duties. Proving willing to stomach almost anything in his quest to publicise his new party, at a public debate in April 1936, MacBride managed to straight-facedly second a motion proposed by Frank Pakenham acclaiming de Valera as, 'not only the greatest living Irishman but the greatest living statesman', having spent the previous hour denouncing the Fianna Fáil government and having closed his speech pledging to 'repudiate ... de Valera or any other leader who accepted something less than complete freedom'.[82] Attempting, in Cork, to explain to an audience mostly comprised of IRA members the rationale for organising politically at that stage, MacBride's reasoning was rather garbled:

> The reason the IRA did not contest the last two elections was that they would leave Fianna Fáil get into power and expose its policy to the Republicans of Ireland. That was why the Republicans supported Fianna Fáil in the 1932 elections and when [they] got into power they said their majority in the Dáil was not large enough to declare a Republic. Republicans once again realised that this was a plea which would appear plausible to the public and so once again they left Fianna Fáil win the last election. Since then Fianna Fáil showed that it was ready to accept something less than freedom.[83]

This confused reading of recent political history helps to explain the failure of Cumann Poblachta na hÉireann to make any impression on the electoral landscape. In the June 1936 local elections, none of the candidates, including Maud Gonne,

80 MacBride quoted in MacEoin, *Survivors*, p. 123.
81 UCDA, Eithne Coyle O'Donnell Papers, P61/10, Cumann Poblachta na hÉireann: Manifesto, Constitution and Rules for Organisation. See also Richard English, '"Paying no heed to public clamour": Irish republican solipsism in the 1930s', *Irish Historical Studies*, vol. xxviii, no. 112 (1993), pp. 427–30; and Eithne MacDermott, *Clann na Poblachta* (Cork: Cork University Press, 1998), pp. 9–10 for further discussion on the constitution of Cumann Poblachta na hÉireann.
82 *Sunday Independent*, 5 April 1936; *Irish Times*, 6 April 1936.
83 NAI, JUS 2008/117/846, Cumann Poblachta na hÉireann, Clipping from *Cork Examiner*, 27 April 1936.

won more than 700 votes, out of an average poll of 27,588. The candidate in the Wexford by-election in August performed equally dismally, despite his many GAA connections, winning a mere 2.8 per cent of the first-preference vote. His name was Stephen Hayes, who four years later was at the centre of the near collapse of the IRA amid suspicion, recrimination, and alleged treachery.[84] MacBride's enthusiasm for Cumann Poblachta na hÉireann, only a year after he had vehemently opposed socialist republican attempts to create an auxiliary political organisation, did much to strengthen opinion of him as insincere, opportunist and duplicitous. Although his professed lack of faith in the 'mass of the people' boded ill for his subsequent reinvention as a democratic politician, his opposition to Republican Congress appeared in retrospect driven more by ideological disagreement with the potential for an explicitly socialist organisation to mobilise the Irish people than by opposition to the principle of political organisation *tout court*.

'Assassination rather than armed revolt is now the real danger'[85]

By this stage, the game was almost up for the IRA. Shortly after its launch in March 1936, the IRA committed one of the most reviled murders in its catalogue of horror, that of Vice-Admiral Boyle Somerville, a 72-year-old retired British naval officer living quietly in his home village of Castletownshend, County Cork. His alleged crime was to assist youths from the Cork and Kerry districts who had come to him seeking advice and references for entry into the British navy, a traditional occupation for young men in the locality. Shot in the chest as he answered the door late in the evening, a crude placard was pinned to his corpse: 'This English Agent sent 53 Irishmen into the British Army in the last seven weeks.'[86] There was a long tradition of anti-recruiting activities within the republican movement, and as recently as 1934 MacBride had declared from a republican platform that, 'I do know that the British Army is recruiting here in Ireland, and paying as much as five shillings per head for recruits. And, what is more, they are using the Civic Guards to check up on intending recruits.'[87] This background rhetoric, along with a high degree of militancy in the Cork IRA – partly resulting from the popularity of the Blueshirts in that district – had led local Volunteers to push for action. The Somerville murderers may have over-interpreted their brief, but it appears certain that GHQ, in the person of Tom Barry, gave the order to 'get him [Somerville]'.[88] A month after the Castletownshend murder, John Egan was executed by the IRA in Dungarvan, shot dead in the middle of the street.

The long delayed government crackdown began instantly: large-scale arrests ensued in Cork and Dublin in the wake of the Egan murder. On 18 June the IRA

---

84 *Irish Times*, 2 July 1936; Walker, *Parliamentary Election Results in Ireland, 1918–92*, p. 143.
85 'Mr de Valera's dilemmas', *Round Table*, vol. xxv, no. 99 (June 1935), p. 557.
86 NAI, JUS 2008/117/866, Somerville murder, Garda Report dated 24 March 1936.
87 *Irish Times*, 6 June 1934.
88 Richard English, *Armed Struggle: The History of the IRA* (London: Pan, 2004, first published 2003), p. 52. Although much Garda suspicion centred on the Barry circle, no one was ever convicted of the murder. The identities of the murderers were revealed as Tadhg Lynch, Angela Lynch and Joe Collins in Joseph O'Neill's compelling family memoir, *Blood-dark Track: A Family History* (London: Granta Books, 2001).

was formally declared an illegal organisation under Article 2A, and the impending Bodenstown commemorations banned. Gerald Boland, Minister for Justice, declared his intention to 'smash [the IRA] just as effectively as we have smashed [the Blueshirts]'.[89] Moss Twomey, arrested the previous month, was sentenced on 19 June to three years for membership of an illegal organisation; amid the chaos, MacBride was appointed Chief of Staff on an interim basis. He later described his appointment as 'more or less by accident' but, in truth, it was a position he had been working towards for almost twenty years. By the time the top job was finally attained, the IRA was in turmoil, haemorrhaging members and facing severe strain with the onset of Fianna Fáil security measures. MacBride attempted to put a brave face on matters, writing to Joseph McGarrity that the situation was 'rather good':

> The Free State Gov have clarified the position and have now taken exactly the same stand as their predecessors. While nationally this is regrettable, it clears the decks as far as we are concerned. We have steadily tried to avoid pushing de Valera into the position occupied by Cosgrave but apparently he was bent on occupying that position.[90]

To his depleted Volunteers, MacBride urged unity in the face of oppression and 'a campaign of coercion and terrorism against the Irish Republican Army ... The present attack on our organisation will be again defeated and the Army will again emerge triumphantly.'[91]

MacBride's tenure of the Chief of Staff position was exceedingly brief and fraught with tension; his prickly personality and elevated manner were not best suited to a position of leadership. The bulk of his difficulties were with Seán Russell, Quartermaster-General, who had been on the IRA executive since the days of Collins. A puritanical militant, Russell had viewed the IRA's flirtations with socialism and politics with equal disdain, quietly building his own support base within the organisation for a return to traditional militant values. MacBride and Russell had clashed frequently as colleagues on the Army Council, and when the punctilious MacBride tried to insist on proper records, Russell's non-cooperation infuriated him. Matters reached crisis point in the summer of 1936 when Russell, having travelled without IRA permission to the United States to confer with McGarrity, committed the Army Council to enter into negotiations as part of a peace mission to bring together de Valera, Craigavon and the IRA.[92] This was the mistake MacBride had been waiting for, and he acted swiftly to court-martial Russell on a variety of offences, with the support of Tom Barry and Dónal O'Donoghue. Russell was found guilty of indiscipline, usurping Army authority and failing to furnish accounts.[93] But it was a short-lived victory: MacBride's open

89 *Dáil Éireann Debates*, vol. 62, col. 2617, 17 June 1936.
90 NLI, Joseph McGarrity Papers, MS 33,364(1), Seán MacBride to Joseph McGarrity, 24 June 1936.
91 NAI, JUS 2008/117/721, IRA Correspondence, 'Order of the Day', issued by Chief of Staff, 30 June 1936.
92 Cronin, *The McGarrity Papers*, pp. 162–3; *Irish Independent*, 8 December 1936.
93 NLI, IRA Papers, Court martial of General Seán Russell, MS 43,133(1–3).

pursuit of Russell had earned him enemies within the IRA, and his position of Chief of Staff was not renewed at the next army convention. He was replaced by Tom Barry, then by Mick Fitzpatrick. After ten years of Moss Twomey's direction, the IRA was floundering through a series of short-lived, tension-ridden leaderships.

The enactment of the 1937 Constitution provided a useful end-point for MacBride in later years, claiming that after the document received a popular mandate in July 1937 'the whole position in the country was radically altered'.[94] While he had certainly been moving in the direction of political engagement – as evidenced by the enthusiasm directed towards Cumann Poblachta na hÉireann – for MacBride it was not so much the constitution but a range of converging factors which led him to officially resign from the IRA the following year. His spell as Chief of Staff had been disastrous, characterised by personal disagreements and enmities and a complete failure to provide the IRA with anything resembling leadership, direction or innovation. The organisation itself was in a desperate state, almost unrecognisable from the high point of 1932. MacBride had also resumed his legal studies and the lure of the Irish bar, with all the prestige and social position it could offer, made the reality of the IRA appear even more grubby.

Finally, at the 1938 convention, Russell made a remarkable comeback, his personal retinue buoyed by his assurances of taking the fight to England. His appointment as Chief of Staff signalled the end for a host of old-timers: MacBride resigned, along with Tom Barry, Mick Fitzpatrick, Dónal O'Donoghue, Tomás Malone, Con Lehane and Tadhg Lynch.[95] For MacBride, in particular, continuing in the IRA under Russell's leadership was impossible, but it must have been something of a wrench. The IRA had been the centre of his personal, political and social world from the age of 16; literally, it was all he had known. Facing the coming years, as war approached, a new identity would have to be forged.

94 MacBride, *That Day's Struggle*, p. 123.
95 John Joe Sheehy quoted in MacEoin, *Survivors*, p. 361.

7

Becoming Legitimate?
1938–1940

At the beginning of 1939, MacBride was at a crossroads. The disfiguring fallout of the feud with Seán Russell, a feud in which MacBride was significantly invested, had led to the departure of most of the IRA 'old guard' during the heated 1938 Army Convention.[1] MacBride had officially ended his active membership of the IRA, the organisation through which he had defined his personal and political sense of self for two decades. In many respects, it was an opportune time to sever links with the IRA which, under Russell's stewardship, had embarked on a dangerous new strategy designed to satisfy the militants who had long grown impatient with 'political' intrigues. The first step in this programme was the transfer in December 1938 of legitimate republican authority from the ghostly remnants of the Second Dáil to the Army Council of the IRA. This was closely followed, on 12 January 1939, by an ultimatum addressed to the British Foreign Secretary, Lord Halifax, demanding 'the withdrawal of all British armed forces stationed in Ireland.[2] When the deadline passed – apparently to the general disinterest of the British authorities – the scheme known as 'S-Plan' (or Sabotage Plan) was implemented.

This was the brainchild of James O'Donovan, the former Director of Chemicals for the IRA, now an engineer for the Electricity Supply Board and married to Monty Barry. Scathingly described by Todd Andrews as 'the most foolish and irresponsible act which bedevilled Anglo-Irish relations in my lifetime',[3] the 'S-Plan' has often been viewed as a bungling, blundering stopgap between the lethal efficiency of both the Fenian dynamitards of the 1880s and the Provisional IRA terrorism of the 1970s and 1980s, both movements which targeted civilian life in Britain.[4] More recent scholarship, however, has emphasised the sophistication of the original scope of 'S-Plan', which was conceived by O'Donovan as a blueprint for the effective paralysis of English public utilities and transport infrastructure.[5]

---

1 Richard English, *Radicals and the Republic: Socialist Republicanism in the Irish Free State, 1925–1937* (Oxford: Clarendon Press, 1994), pp. 257–8.
2 *Irish Times*, 4 February 1939.
3 C. S. Andrews, *Man of No Property: An Autobiography* (Dublin: Mercier Press, 1982), p. 316.
4 See, for instance, Eunan O'Halpin's analysis in *Defending Ireland: The Irish State and its Enemies since 1922* (Oxford: Oxford University Press, 1999), pp. 148–9; and M. L. R. Smith, *Fighting for Ireland? The Military Strategy of the Irish Republican Movement* (London: Routledge, 1995), pp. 62–3.
5 For different perspectives, see Gary McGladdery, *The Provisional IRA in England: The Bombing*

On 16 January, the planned operations were set in motion; explosions at seven major power stations across England signalled the beginning of the bombing campaign. Some aspects of the 'S-Plan' have an uncomfortable contemporary resonance, particularly the planting of bombs by the IRA in London underground stations and on London buses. But judged by the very terms of the 'S-Plan', the campaign went wrong from the beginning: despite O'Donovan's insistence that civilians not be targeted, in Manchester a bomb designed to paralyse the gas and electricity supply instead killed 27-year-old Albert Ross.[6] Equally, despite initial gaps in intelligence, the British authorities moved, arresting many of the key figures and seizing a number of documents which laid bare the scope of the 'S-Plan' within a short period of time. Further explosions occurred through the spring and summer of 1939, although these marked a progressive tendency towards softer targets in public settings instead of a serious attempt to cripple state infrastructure; this trend produced the bloodshed in Coventry on 25 August, when a bomb in the city centre killed five people and injured dozens more.

Although the inept execution of 'S-Plan' coupled with an effective crackdown by the British authorities made the military success of the IRA campaign improbable, of far greater import was the challenge posed to the authority of the Irish state. In assuming the title 'Government of the Irish Republic', the IRA was explicitly defying the legitimacy of the Fianna Fáil government. Furthermore, the 'right to declare war in the name of our people' was, for de Valera, a usurpation of the sovereignty of the Irish people, at last given democratic expression in the Fianna Fáil administration.[7] Concerned above all with maintaining internal security, de Valera moved swiftly to enact legislation to face down the IRA threat. After a difficult passage through the Oireachtais, exacerbated by the protests of a number of public bodies outside Parliament, the Offences Against the State Act (1939) became law on 14 June 1939: it contained a series of prohibitions against unlawful organisations, unlawful military exercises, and secret societies within the police or army, while providing for internment and special criminal courts without juries. This Act, along with the Emergency Powers Act later that year, would provide the basis for de Valera's crackdown on the IRA throughout the war years, and formed the legal framework within which MacBride, as a barrister, pursued the most important of his cases.

But the Offences Against the State Act did not operate in a vacuum. Throughout its enactment, the debates inside Dáil Éireann were punctuated by the continuing violence of the IRA's bombing campaign in England. Despite an awareness at senior governmental level that the bombing campaign was a 'terrorist plot', the failure of the Irish authorities to provide meaningful security cooperation with their British counterparts is a mark of the solipsism that became an increasing

---

Campaign, 1973–1997 (Dublin: Irish Academic Press, 2006), pp. 29–45; Paul McMahon, British Spies and Irish Rebels: British Intelligence and Ireland, 1916–1945 (Woodbridge: Boydell & Brewer, 2008), pp. 262–75; John Maguire, IRA Internments and the Irish Government: Subversives and the State, 1939–1962 (Dublin: Irish Academic Press, 2008), pp. 21–5.

6 The Times, 17 January 1939.
7 Dáil Éireann Debates, vol. 74, col. 1306, 2 March 1939.

feature of wartime politics.[8] No reality existed outside the Irish reality, and no threat was serious enough to warrant action if it were not an internal threat to the security of the state. This mindset made it entirely rational for de Valera to ignore, delay and deny British requests for intelligence on IRA members while proscribing the organisation under the new legislation on 23 June 1939.

'On legal affairs or when speaking to a brief he had genius'[9]

When MacBride ended his official involvement with the IRA, he was already 'a member of one of the best clubs in the world'.[10] His admission to the Bar on 1 November 1937 marked five years since graduation from King's Inns, and it was almost seventeen years since he had first begun his legal studies at UCD.[11] His examination record was above average, and he received second-class honours in the Senior Continuous Course and final examination in May 1937. Among a class that included Noel Hartnett and Vivion de Valera – both prize-winning students – it was MacBride to whom the *Irish Independent* drew attention, noting that he was 'a well-known Republican and a son of Madame MacBride'.[12] By the time MacBride entered the Law Library, the institution had recovered its equilibrium after the upheavals of the revolutionary period; the eight years of exile in Dublin Castle after the Civil War destruction of the Four Courts had ended in 1931, and the reconstructed buildings were an appropriate physical symbol of the restored authority of the new state.

MacBride's first appearance as a barrister was before Justice Reddin at Lucan District Court on 16 December 1937.[13] Although he soon carved out a more than adequate living in civil and criminal cases, he was never completely at ease on the circuit. But the company of colleagues, and the respectability the Bar afforded, became increasingly important to MacBride. As a barrister, he could occupy the place in Dublin society to which he had always felt entitled but from which he had always been excluded. He operated well inside the Law Library: his 'particularly soothing manner' of speech, as recalled by Todd Andrews, combined with 'his urbanity and courteousness towards his colleagues in a case, as well as his adversaries' helped to foster widespread acceptance of MacBride within the Four

8   National Archives of Ireland [NAI], D/T, S11534A, IRA Activities in Ireland, 1939–1950, Memorandum on the policy of the Government with regard to Offences against the State, p. 4.
9   *Irish Times*, 6 April 1968, 'Peadar O'Donnell – a portrait in depth – part 6', O'Donnell on MacBride.
10   Eugene Sheehy, *May it Please the Court* (Dublin: Fallon Books, 1951), p. 50.
11   J. Clancy, M. Connolly and K. Ferguson, 'Alphabetical index to barristers' memorials, 1868–1968', in Kenneth Ferguson (ed.) *King's Inns Barristers, 1868–2004* (Dublin: The Honourable Society of King's Inns in association with the Irish Legal History Society, 2005), p. 234; *Irish Times*, 2 November 1937.
12   *Irish Independent*, 28 May 1937. Despite their family politics and MacBride being 'on the run' for part of his exams, he and Vivion de Valera established friendly relations during their studies. Seán MacBride, *That Day's Struggle: A Memoir, 1904–1951*, ed. Caitriona Lawlor (Dublin: Currach Press, 2005), p. 124.
13   *Irish Times*, 17 December 1937.

Courts, whatever his previous associations had been.[14] Evidence of MacBride's growing legitimacy within the Irish establishment can be detected by his attendance at a number of social functions throughout 1938: a reception at the French legation, the changing of the garrison at Spike Island in July, where he stood alongside Fianna Fáil establishment figures and representatives of the Irish Army, and the Solicitors' Bar Association annual dinner.[15]

Despite this newfound respectability, the older associations were difficult to truly shake off. Although MacBride had distanced himself from the more traditional republican demonstrations – taking no part, for example, in the Bodenstown commemorations in 1937 and 1938 – he was part of a welcoming committee 'of fifty men of the Irish Republican Army' at Kingsbridge Station, to greet Moss Twomey and ten other prisoners released from the Curragh on 14 December 1937, two days before his first appearance as barrister in Lucan District Court.[16] This double existence can be seen as establishing a pattern to MacBride's career for the subsequent nine years: moving away but not completely detaching himself from the IRA on the one hand, and being drawn towards the alluring, constitutional, surroundings of the Law Library on the other. His position as the republican movement's standing counsel was established relatively early in his legal career, with his appearance at the inquest into the death of Peter McCarthy, an IRA volunteer who had been shot dead in Clanbrassil Street by off-duty Gardaí using an unregistered weapon in June 1937, an ugly portent of the explosive violence that would become a recurrent feature of IRA-Gardaí relations during the war years. MacBride was plain in his charge to the jury:

> There was no doubt that McCarthy was shot by a policeman. The police, he said, were empowered to carry arms for special purposes only, and, in these days of dictatorships a grave responsibility rested on the jury to see that the police force of this country were going to be kept under control in dealing with the powers which they had.[17]

The jury declined to indict the policemen and Peter McCarthy was soon forgotten, but a newly confrontational note had been struck. In his representation of IRA members before the courts, often charged with the murder of Gardaí, a new note of hostility was injected into MacBride's dealings with the State, and especially the Fianna Fáil establishment.

While MacBride was concentrating on his professional career, the government was pressing ahead with action against the IRA. Seán Russell's defiant intransigence from his highly publicised American tour and the continuing explosions in English cities over the summer of 1939, formed the immediate backdrop to the

---

14 Andrews, *Man of no Property*, p. 192; 'Seán MacBride: an appreciation', *Irish Law Times*, vol. 16, no. 1 (January 1988), p. 42.

15 *Irish Independent*, 11 February 1938; *Irish Times*, 12 July 1938, 28 November 1938.

16 *Irish Times*, 15 December 1937.

17 It was unclear whether Garda Brocklebank, who shot McCarthy, was in fact on duty at the time. Equally, the weapon used was an old RIC revolver which had never been licensed to Brocklebank. *Irish Press*, 22 July 1938; *Irish Times*, 23 July 1938; Uinseann MacEoin, *The IRA in the Twilight Years: 1923–1948* (Dublin: Argenta Press, 1997), p. 393.

crackdown on the IRA in August 1939, as war came ever closer.[18] This crackdown – the logical consequence of the new legislation, which had been almost a year in gestation – was essentially the activation of a series of important provisions of the Offences Against the State Act, namely the establishment of the Special Criminal Court and the powers of internment. With most of the republicans who appeared before the courts refusing legal representation, in keeping with IRA policy, the prison population soon began swelling.

Irish Neutrality

Speaking in Dáil Éireann after the German invasion of Poland, de Valera was clear on the policy to be adopted by the government and on the difficulties which lay ahead: 'it was the aim of Government policy, in case of a European war, to keep this country, if at all possible, out of it'.[19] The Irish government's decision to remain neutral received an almost universal welcome. Even the London *Times* was in favour, writing approvingly that 'Éire's neutrality is the best possible policy that Mr de Valera's government could have adopted.'[20] In Ireland itself the mood was partly one of relief that the country was determined to remain out of the war, and partly one of panicky preparations for the anticipated privations to come. In October 1939, Eduard Hempel, the German Minister in Dublin, sent an assessment of the mood of the country to the Foreign Office in Berlin, underlining that the policy of neutrality had 'the support of the great majority of the Irish people, despite the undermining elements of certain pro-English circles. It has visibly strengthened Irish national self-consciousness.'[21] The hint at barely concealed divisions within Irish society on the question of wartime allegiances was an important factor in the government's decision to opt for neutrality.[22]

MacBride's reaction to the outbreak of war is unrecorded, but something of his ideological alignment may be gleaned from an address he gave at the Republican Students' Club of University College Dublin, Trinity College Dublin and the Royal College of Surgeons on 10 March 1938. In his paper 'Ireland and the Next War', MacBride stated that 'thinking Republicans' – a category in which he evidently included himself – were 'perturbed' by the prospect of Irish people being on England's side. The detail of his paper indicated the level of his ideological sympathies with Germany:

> A properly organised Ireland could be a very serious menace to England. Modern development had increased Ireland's capacity to injure Britain in a war: Germany was roughly 600 miles away, Italy only 900, and with modern craft

18   *New York Times*, 9 June 1939; NAI, J8/802, Seán Russell file, Irish envoy in United States to Secretary of External Affairs, 1 June 1939.
19   *Dáil Éireann Debates*, vol. 77, col. 3, 2 September 1939.
20   *The Times*, 9 September 1938.
21   *Documents on German Foreign Policy, 1918–1945: Series D, Vol. VIII: The War Years* (London: Her Majesty's Stationery Office, 1954), Hempel telegram to Foreign Office, Berlin, 8 October 1939, p. 242.
22   O'Halpin, *Defending Ireland*, pp. 151–3; John A. Murphy, 'Irish neutrality in historical perspective' in Brian Girvin and Geoffrey Roberts (eds.), *Ireland and the Second World War: Politics, Society and Remembrance* (Dublin: Four Courts Press, 2000), pp. 12–13.

these countries were within easy reach, which solved the difficulty of obtaining arms from both these countries should they engage in a war with Britain. Refuelling bases in Ireland for aircraft and submarines would enable a powerful air force to cripple England's air force, and England could also be dealt a crippling blow in the matter of food supply.[23]

MacBride's argument – crucially formulated *before* the return of the Treaty ports – envisages Ireland throwing in her lot with the emerging Axis powers. It is essentially an inversion of contemporary perceptions of the role that Ireland – or, more to the point, her bases – might play in a European war; instead of the three Treaty ports being used for British refuelling purposes, they would form the basis of a hostile encirclement of the United Kingdom. The consequences of such a move for North–South relations are left untouched, however – a further indication of MacBride's blinkered approach to the Northern question.

MacBride and Germany

MacBride's willingness to consider alliance with Germany was a long-standing aspect of his thinking, and may have had its origins in his experiences in procuring German weapons for the IRA during the Truce. But the Germany he had known in 1921 was very different now, under the darkening shadows of Hitler's regime. Knowledge of the darker sides of Nazism was certainly current among Ireland's political elite; as early as 1933 Dan Binchy, professor of Celtic Studies and former Irish representative in Berlin, had published a biting portrait of Hitler and his rise to power, emphasising the centrality of anti-Semitism to the Nazi ideology.[24] Moreover, Irish newspapers, particularly the *Irish Times*, did not flinch from reporting the violence directed against Jewish communities by the Nazi state, and by the advent of *Kristallnacht* in November 1938, ignorance was impossible.

Certainly, in the MacBride extended family discussions on the fate of the Jews in Germany were taking place. Kathleen Lynn, the Dublin paediatrician, confided to her diary her shock at Iseult Stuart's 'very anti-Semitic reaction' to news of Jewish persecution; Francis Stuart, Iseult's husband wrote a series of letters to the Irish press in December 1938 urging a rethink of Irish plans to aid Jewish refugees: 'suffering foreigners', he argued, would have to wait their turn behind the more deserving Irish.[25] Equally distasteful were the writings of Maud Gonne MacBride in this period, which explicitly linked Jewish money and influence to British malfeasance in Ireland and elsewhere.[26] As well as long-standing links with a number of republican organisations, the MacBride family also were in close

23 *Irish Times*, 11 March 1938.
24 Dan Binchy, 'Adolf Hitler', *Studies*, vol. xxii (March 1933), p. 47. See also Michael Kennedy, 'Our men in Berlin: some thoughts on Irish diplomats in Germany, 1929–39', *Irish Studies in International Affairs*, vol. 10 (1999), pp. 53–70.
25 Library of Royal College of Physicians of Ireland, Kathleen Lynn Diaries, 16 November 1938; *Irish Times*, 13 December 1938.
26 A particularly memorable example is an article entitled 'Ireland, Fascism and Communism', originally published in James O'Donovan's *Ireland Today* on 3 March 1938, reproduced in Karen Steele, *Maud Gonne's Irish Nationalist Writings: 1895–1946* (Dublin: Irish Academic Press, 2004), pp. 238–9.

contact with members of the Nazi German community in Ireland in the pre-war years, and it was the combination of these associations which posed so serious a threat to Irish security during the Emergency.

The German community was centred around the *Auslandsorganisation*, an ex-pat association for Nazi Party members, whose affiliates included high ranking officials in Irish public life, particularly Dr Adolf Mahr, Director of the National Museum and Colonel Fritz Brase, head of the Irish Army School of Music. Another key figure in this group, Helmut Clissmann, a former student at Trinity College Dublin, was an Irish-based representative of the German Academic Exchange Service. By the mid-1930s, however, this organisation had been wholly subsumed into the Nazi regime and became 'an organ for Nazi propaganda and penetration in foreign countries'.[27] In Ireland, it was building on a rich tradition of German scholars of Celtic Studies and linguistics with long-established links with the academic community. However, the new emphasis on intelligence gathering within the Nazi system soon cast a different light on previously innocent activities. Clissmann spent two stretches at Trinity College, working as an exchange lecturer in German from 1933 to 1934 and from 1936 to 1937, and led a number of expeditions into the Irish countryside. Jupp Hoven, also on an academic exchange programme, travelled extensively in the Glens of Antrim, supposedly to conduct anthropological research, but his activities immediately attracted the suspicions of the Royal Ulster Constabulary (RUC).[28] Apart from gathering topographical information – which might form the basis of military preparations for a future invasion – pre-war German activities in Ireland were largely directed towards the establishment of links with the republican community.

The history of German-IRA contacts has attracted some scholarly attention in the years since the war.[29] Whereas MacBride's official distance from the IRA from 1938 onwards removed him from the mainstream of German-IRA contacts, he was at the heart of its origin. This appears to have been in early 1936, when MacBride held the post of Director of Intelligence and it was during this period that the German-IRA link was initiated. Furthermore, Tom Barry later admitted to his old comrade Florence O'Donoghue – then working for G2, Irish Military Intelligence – that MacBride had arranged for his 1937 visit to Germany, accompanied by Jupp Hoven.[30] MacBride was a close associate of both Clissmann and Hoven; Colonel Dan Bryan, then head of G2, wrote to External Affairs at the close of war:

27 Eunan O'Halpin (ed.), *MI5 and Ireland, 1939–1945: The Official History* (Dublin: Irish Academic Press, 2003), p. 39.

28 *Irish Times*, 25 January 1936; O'Halpin (ed.), *MI5 and Ireland*, pp. 39–40.

29 Enno Stephan was the first academic to mine this rich seam in *Spies in Ireland* (translated from the German by A. Davidson) (London: Macdonald Press, 1963). See also Carole Carter, *The Shamrock and the Swastika: German Espionage in Ireland in World War II* (Palo Alto, California: Pacific Books, 1977); Mark Hull, *Irish Secrets: German Espionage in Ireland, 1939–1945* (Dublin: Irish Academic Press, 2003).

30 Irish Military Archives, Cathal Brugha Barracks, Dublin [IMA], G2/X/0093, Record of conversation between O'Donoghue and Barry, June 1940. This visit resulted in Nazi subvention of the S-plan bombing campaign via Clan-na-Gael.

There is information, although not of a conclusive nature, to indicate that when he was Director of Intelligence for the IRA he was largely responsible for their contacts with the Germans. This is confirmed by the fact that MacBride was evidently associated with and knew Von Tevenar, the Chief of Fifth Column German activities in Celtic countries and also with Hoven and Clissman [sic] who were directly concerned with German activities in Ireland.[31]

The motivation behind the IRA's collaboration with Nazi German agencies was not, however, monolithic. For those of a purely militaristic bent, like Seán Russell, the German link was merely a means to obtain weapons and money to further the ultimate aim of complete Irish independence; no consideration was given to what the consequences of alliance with a fascist country might be. Reflexive Anglophobia was a determining factor in deciding the allegiances of many within Irish society more generally but such impulsive responses could break dangerous ground. Mechanical reactions against Ireland's 'traditional enemy' overlapped with ideological convictions not dissimilar to the Nazi programme. Thus for Tom Barry, as for others, traditional opposition to Britain sat easily alongside his public fulminations against 'the Jew-owned Bank of England'.[32] Yet there were dissenting voices within the IRA, notably from the leftist wing which had returned from the Spanish Civil War. Peadar O'Donnell was prominent in leading a number of protests against Hitler in the years preceding the outbreak of war; one, memorably, attracted violent counter-demonstrations from off-duty members of the St Vincent de Paul society determined to break up the 'communist' meeting. Equally, George Gilmore, who predicted the response war would bring within republican society, was another vehemently anti-fascist republican. In the summer of 1940, as Britain stood alone and Irish sentiment grew pragmatically pro-German, Gilmore and O'Donnell produced a memorandum arguing against IRA flirtations with Nazi Germany. Placing the responsibility for fomenting the Nazi link firmly at the feet of 'that section of the Blueshirts which accepted direction from international Fascism', the authors argued strongly in favour of preserving neutrality:

> The question for everybody with any responsibility to the republican movement is how best to co-operate with the people to organise for neutrality as they were organised to beat off conscription ... The IRA have gone through a very unfortunate period. Their control was quite unequal to the task of leadership ... But for all its mistakes the IRA are not a fifth column seeking invasion by any foreign power.[33]

MacBride, however, was not among this group of intellectually coherent dissenters. In the development of the IRA's relationship with Nazi Germany, he saw an opportunity for personal advancement which he was unable to resist. His involvement in the collusion with Nazi agencies which had begun in 1936 continued, to the

---

31 NAI, DFA A/72 Francis Stuart File, D. Bryan to F. H. Boland, 17 August 1945.
32 *Irish Times*, 29 March 1937.
33 National Archives, London [NAL], DO 130/86, 'Invasion! If the British come back? If the Germans land? If both come – what then? A republican answer by Peadar O'Donnell and George Gilmore', n. d. [1940].

point that G2 estimated that he 'was working for the Germans even more than for the IRA'.[34]

However, the extent to which MacBride embraced Nazi anti-Semitism is unclear. Dónal Ó Drisceoil has argued convincingly that there was 'widespread or latent anti-Semitism at all levels of Irish society and politics during this period',[35] and MacBride had certainly been exposed to anti-Semitic modes of thought in his private affairs. His mother's long-standing anti-Semitism, a hangover from her association with Boulangist factions in nineteenth-century France, remained with her throughout her life, and led her to become an active consumer of Nazi propaganda in the late 1930s. This was primarily through the *Deutsche Pfichte Bund* or German Truth Society, whose Irish agent Oscar Pfaus had also operated successfully as a spy in Ireland, travelling to Dublin in February 1939 to meet with Russell, O'Donovan and others. Pfaus corresponded with Maud Gonne after his return to Hamburg, writing tantalisingly that 'most of the British propaganda which is flooding Eire is coming from British Jewish sources in Belfast'.[36] She replied immediately, asking him eagerly for evidence of this and noting further that 'the Jews have bought a great deal too much land in and around Dublin [and] I think no foreigner should be allowed to buy land'.[37] Such discourse evidently had rubbed off on her daughter; as noted by Kathleen Lynn, Iseult was vehemently anti-Semitic in her thought. Francis Stuart, Iseult's husband from whom she was later estranged, claimed in 1987 that she was the real Nazi in the family: 'Funnily enough, I was the one who went to Germany but my wife was the far more convinced.'[38] Yet despite the recorded views of his family, only one instance exists linking MacBride to anti-Semitism, and it is far from conclusive.

Its origins lie in a dispute between John Hamilton and Stephen Carroll Held in 1939. Held was a Dublin businessman, the stepson of a German national who had established a successful sheet-metal business in Ireland at the turn of the century. In 1938, he became associated with John Hamilton, an ex-serviceman who was down on his luck, but their friendship soon turned sour. The following year, Hamilton sued Held in the Dublin High Court for theft of patented documents relating to an anti-crash device for aircraft, which Hamilton had allegedly invented. The case was dismissed, but Hamilton had already approached the British authorities with even more fantastical allegations. During the course of an interview with Scotland Yard, Hamilton alleged that Held had boasted to him of his association with the IRA and his role as a conduit between that organisation and the German government. In addition to these activities, Hamilton also stated that Held had told him of a secret anti-Jewish group in Dublin called 'the Invincibles', which brought together

34 IMA, G2/1722, Summary of German activities.
35 Dónal Ó Drisceoil, 'Jews and other undesirables: anti-Semitism in neutral Ireland during the Second World War' in Ethel Crowley and Jim Mac Laughlin (eds.), *Under the Belly of the Tiger: Class, Race, Identity and Culture in the Global Ireland* (Dublin: Irish Reporter Publications, 1997), p. 71.
36 IMA, G2/2278, Oscar Pfaus to Maud Gonne MacBride, 17 July 1939.
37 IMA, G2/2278, Maud Gonne MacBride to Oscar Pfaus, 20 July 1939.
38 Francis Stuart interview with Richard English, Dublin, 24 February 1987. I am grateful to Richard English for providing me with a transcript of this interview.

Nazis, former members of the IRA, and members of the Irish Communist Party to drive Jewish business interests out of the country. Included among the list of alleged members of the 'Invincibles' were Seán MacBride, Simon Donnelly, Con Lehane, Seán Russell, George Gilmore and Peadar O'Donnell.[39]

The later pro-German activities of Russell, MacBride, Lehane and Donnelly might at first indicate a degree of accuracy to the report, but the inclusion of O'Donnell and Gilmore entirely discredit Hamilton's allegations. Both deeply anti-fascist and vehemently opposed to Hitler's regime, the likelihood of their membership of such an organisation – the name of which also seems improbable – is dubious. Hamilton's contentions were dismissed: Liam Archer, then head of G2, reported to MI5 that '[Hamilton] is regarded by police as a "plausible scoundrel and an inveterate liar"' and emphasised that 'the Held family were not known to have any contacts with the German colony here and have the reputation of being law-abiding and respectable'.[40] However, when Held was unmasked as a German agent in May 1940, Hamilton's allegations had to be revisited. In his subsequent reinterview by MI5, Hamilton gamely embroidered his tales, but could give no concrete details on Held's connections with German agencies.[41] Nor was any further evidence discovered on the 1938 Invincibles.

Of much greater import in historical terms was MacBride's friendship with Eduard Hempel at the German Legation in Dublin. Sympathetic treatments of the German minister have insisted that as a career diplomat, who only joined the National Socialist Party in 1938 when it was made compulsory, he was somehow distinct from the ideology of the state he represented.[42] Certainly Hempel was well regarded in Irish government circles, cultivating a particularly close relationship with Joseph Walshe, Secretary of External Affairs, who was known to the Hempel children as 'Uncle Joe'.[43] Hempel's telegrams to the Foreign Office in Berlin urged absolute caution in establishing any sort of arrangement with the IRA: 'in my opinion complete restraint continues to be advisable for us ... the IRA is hardly strong enough for action with promise of success or involving appreciable damage to England and is also probably lacking a leader of any stature'.[44] But as the American representative in Dublin, David Gray, underlined in his post-war memoir, in 1937 when Hempel was appointed, 'No German at that time was getting a diplomatic job who was out of line.'[45] Hempel's decidedly undiplomatic

39 NAL, KV2/1449, C. Liddel to V. Vivian, 29 September 1940; KV2/1450, Note on Stephen Carroll Held case, n. d.

40 IMA, G2/H/39, L. Archer to C. Liddell, 26 October 1939; NAL, DO130/1, File on German Minister in Dublin, Memorandum by Chief Constable, Scotland Yard, n. d.

41 NAL, KV2/1440, Note of interview with John Hamilton, Central Police Station, Coventry, 26 June 1940.

42 Dermot Keogh, *Jews in Twentieth-century Ireland* (Cork: Cork University Press, 1998), p. 153. See also J. P. Duggan, *Herr Hempel at the German Legation in Dublin, 1937–1945* (Dublin: Irish Academic Press, 2003), pp. 26–7.

43 David Gray, 'Behind the green door', chapter VII, unpublished memoir. I am grateful to Professor Paul Bew for providing me with a copy of this manuscript.

44 *Documents on German Foreign Policy, 1918–1945: Series D, vol. VIII*, Hempel telegram to Foreign Office, Berlin, 14 November 1939.

45 Gray, 'Behind the green door', chapter IV.

activities, however, lay in the future; in the pre-war period Hempel concentrated on establishing cordial relations with the Irish establishment and with the republican movement.

Key in this latter relationship was his friendship with the extended MacBride family. In many respects the MacBrides were the closest friends the Hempels possessed in Ireland; the files of G2 reveal a constant stream of visits from the German Legation to Roebuck House and Laragh Castle, home of Francis and Iseult Stuart, as well as the exchange of gifts at Easter and Christmas.[46] Such was Dr Hempel's familiarity with the layout of Roebuck [a large complex with numerous outbuildings and substantial gardens], that by 1941 he was casually entering the side door, normally reserved for family members. More seriously, when her grandson Ian Stuart remarked, on seeing Hempel, 'that is the man for my Grannie's letters', the Irish authorities grew suspicious that the German minister was carrying letters for Maud Gonne, enabling her to evade the eye of the censor, which as a matter of policy opened all the post issuing from Roebuck House.[47] But even before the outbreak of war, this relationship was a matter of concern to the Irish and British authorities. In August 1939 a secret report from a source inside the German Legation reported negotiations between Hempel, MacBride and Francis Stuart: 'Recently Dr HEMPEL has been in touch with Francis Stuart, the Irish author, and his brother-in-law MacBride. He is discussing with them a scheme for organising an Irish legion which would fight on the side of Germany against Great Britain.'[48] This was most likely connected with Stuart's planned return to Germany in the autumn of 1939. Earlier that year, Iseult had approached Helmut Clissmann to arrange a German lecture tour for Stuart under the auspices of the German Academic Exchange Service. The tour went well, and Stuart returned to Ireland in July 1939 to await a formal appointment as a visiting lecturer at the University of Berlin.

Stuart's departure was delayed by bureaucratic red tape, and by the time the appointment was confirmed, war had begun. Travelling to Germany was, there-fore, a more politically loaded gesture than previously. Before Stuart travelled to Berlin in January 1940, MacBride drove him to a meeting with James O'Donovan at his home in County Dublin; there Stephen Hayes, the newly appointed Chief of Staff in Russell's absence gave Stuart a message to deliver to the *Abwehr* in Berlin. Stuart made his way to Berlin and delivered his message. Soon his teaching duties were augmented by writing and broadcasting propaganda material to Ireland on the Nazi radio station, *Irland-Redaktion*, a political stance which reverberated through the remainder of his literary career.[49] At home, the triangular relation-ship between the MacBrides, the Stuarts and the Hempels continued. MacBride's trusted position as a former member of the IRA grew ever more important as the republican movement and the Irish government moved towards open conflict.

46 IMA, G2/0214.
47 IMA, G2/2278, report dated 26 July 1941.
48 NAL, KV3/120, Information received from the Czechoslovak chargé d'affaires, 5 August 1939.
49 For a thoughtful discussion of these reverberations, see Colm Tóibín, 'Issues of truth and invention', *London Review of Books*, 4 January 2001, and Brendan Barrington (ed.), *The Wartime Broadcasts of Francis Stuart: 1942–1944* (Dublin: Irish Academic Press, 2000).

'The martyr complex in Irish politics was something to be avoided like the plague'[50]

The gradual tensions which had been building between the two parties since the bombing campaign in England immediately took on a much graver aspect once war had begun. Central to this worsening relationship was the government's enactment of stern emergency legislation to deal with the exigencies of war. The Emergency Powers Bill was rushed through the Dáil, expanding the powers already available to the government under the Offences Against the State Act to include extended powers of search and arrest for Gardaí and important changes in the functioning of the courts, inquests and juries. In a significant move, de Valera replaced Paddy Ruttledge as Minister for Justice with Gerald Boland. The latter was a steely IRA veteran whose loyalty to de Valera combined with personal experience of the steps needed to tackle subversion to create an immovable object in the face of increasing IRA violence inside neutral Ireland. Boland's first action as Minister was to draw up a list of names scheduled for arrest under the Offences Against the State Act; by the end of September 1939 Boland told the Dáil that 93 suspects had been arrested, with 67 held at Arbour Hill prison and a further 15 awaiting trial before the Special Criminal Court.[51]

In an attempt to force concessions from the government, a group of republican prisoners commenced a hunger strike, most prominent among them being Patrick McGrath, a veteran of the Easter Rising and War of Independence who still carried a British bullet lodged in his chest. The prospect of de Valera 'allowing' such an eminent former comrade to die prompted a large outpouring of emotion within republican circles and a *crise de conscience* within the government. Public expression of this disquiet was, however, severely hampered by the strict censorship regime: the first the Irish public learned of the hunger strike of McGrath and his comrades was a terse government statement that 'arrest and detention ... are the only means available for the maintenance of public order and security ... the State authorities [cannot] be deprived of these means by the power of the hunger-strike'.[52] Privately, though, the government was receiving a flood of letters and resolutions appealing for the release of McGrath. Appeals came from the wide spectrum of nationalist opinion and largely focused on McGrath's history within the independence struggle. Margaret Pearse wrote memorably of asking her executed brothers to intercede on behalf of McGrath: 'for Ireland's sake I don't hesitate to say that more tragedy will ensue if Paddy dies now. I am asking mother & Pat & Willie to pray for you & your Ministers & for Paddy.'[53]

Among the IRA and their supporters, the mystique of de Valera was palling somewhat: Kathleen Lynn noted the disillusion felt within republicanism at de Valera's apparent betrayal – '[e]veryone seems horrified with Dev. He's no longer

50 John Cudahy to Sec. of State, 29 December 1939, quoted by Aengus Nolan, *Joseph Walshe: Irish Foreign Policy 1922–1946* (Cork: Mercier Press, 2008), p. 144.
51 *Dáil Éireann Debates*, vol. 77, col. 247, 27 September 1939.
52 *Irish Press*, 1 November 1939.
53 NAI, D/T, S11515, Hunger Strikes, Nancy O'Rahilly to Eamon de Valera, 15 November [1939], Margaret Pearse to Eamon de Valera, 15 November 1939.

people's hero'[54] – while the spectacle of republican women raucously inter-
rupting de Valera's address to the Society of St Vincent de Paul at the Mansion
House indicated the depth of feeling McGrath's impending death provoked.[55] The
Taoiseach's strongly worded speech to the Dáil was fatally undermined when,
on 15 November McGrath and the two other hunger strikers were released from
Mountjoy to Jervis Street Hospital; this was compounded on 7 December when
the State entered a *nolle prosequi* on all charges pending against McGrath under
the Offences Against the State Act.[56] Boland later maintained that McGrath was
released for health reasons – he had been seriously wounded during the War of
Independence – but the overriding impression was that de Valera's mettle had
been tested, and had been found wanting. The impact of McGrath's release was,
moreover, drastically reinforced by the beginning of MacBride's arguments before
the High Court in what became known as the habeas corpus case.

A Legal Triumph

MacBride had remained out of the public eye during the McGrath hunger strike
crisis; Eduard Hempel's telegram to Berlin to the effect that 'sensible adherents of
the radical nationalist movement, correctly sizing up the situation and the danger,
are opposed to coming out into the open at the present time' can be interpreted as
referring directly to MacBride's position.[57] But the day after McGrath was released
from Mountjoy, MacBride revealed at least part of his hand: in representing
IRA members over the course of the Emergency, MacBride was in a position
to continue working for the republican movement without placing himself in
personal jeopardy. On 17 December 1939 MacBride appeared for Seamus Burke, a
Mayo IRA man who had been arrested under the Offences Against the State Act
in September of that year and held in Arbour Hill. MacBride made an application
for an order of habeas corpus against the governor of Arbour Hill, contending that
the Offences Against the State Act was in breach of the Constitution. MacBride
argued forcefully before Justice Gavan Duffy that 'the issues raised in this case
are of tremendous importance. They raise the question of whether the Executive
or a Department of State has the right arbitrarily to deprive a citizen of his liberty
without charge or trial.'[58] MacBride's argument centred around the provision in
the Act which stated that 'whenever a Minister of State is satisfied that any particular person is engaged in activities calculated to prejudice the preservation of the
peace, order, or security of the State, such Minister may by warrant under his hand
order the arrest and detention of such person under this section.' This was held
to be in direct conflict with Article 40 of the Constitution, which provided that 'no
person shall be deprived of his personal liberty save in accordance with the law'.[59]

54 Library of Royal College of Physicians, Dublin, Kathleen Lynn Diaries, 10 November 1939.
55 *Irish Press*, 15 November 1939.
56 *Irish Times*, 16 November and 8 December 1939.
57 *Documents on German Foreign Policy, 1918–1945: Series D, vol. VIII*, Hempel telegram to
    Foreign Office, Berlin, 14 November 1939.
58 MacBride before Gavan Duffy J., quoted in *Irish Times*, 18 November 1939.
59 Offences Against the State Act (1939), Section 55, available at www.irishstatutebook.ie/1939/en/
    act/pub/0013/index.html (accessed 10 November 2009); *Bunreacht na hÉireann*, Article 40.4.1.

MacBride's reasoning was succinct: 'If a Minister, without hearing evidence, sitting in his office, can by a mere stroke of his pen deprive a citizen of his liberty for an indefinite and unlimited period of time, then that Article of the Constitution ceases to count.'[60] After a week's adjournment, the court reconvened before *two* judges of the High Court, Gavan Duffy and O'Byrne. Burke's legal team successfully argued that the applicant had the right to submit his application to a judge of his choosing and to one judge of the High Court alone. This was duly granted, and MacBride subsequently applied to Gavan Duffy at his private residence for an order of habeas corpus against Lennon and the Attorney General. Gavan Duffy granted the request and the case began in earnest on 28 November.

The selection of George Gavan Duffy was crucial to the outcome of the case, and in arguing for the right to apply to Gavan Duffy alone, MacBride had made a calculated judgement that paid off. Outside the legal establishment, Gavan Duffy was, of course, known personally to MacBride: in what must have seemed a lifetime ago, they had played bridge together at Hans Place in London on off-days during the Treaty negotiations.[61] In presenting his arguments before the court on 28 November, MacBride contended that if the clause of the Offences Against the State Act permitting internment was upheld by the court, a doomsday scenario could unfold:

> if this Act is valid, would not an Act enabling an unscrupulous Government to deprive citizens of their electoral rights also be valid?; would it not be possible for an unscrupulous Government under this Act to arrest TDs and Senators at a time of crisis when one or two votes might possibly mean a change of Government?[62]

On 1 December Gavan Duffy delivered his judgement, one which had enormous implications for government policy against the subversive threat. Gavan Duffy crucially upheld MacBride's argument that when a minister satisfied himself that a person was engaging in activities prejudicial to the security of the state, he was exercising judicial functions; this indicated an important distinction from the relevant clause of the previous Public Safety Act, which merely stipulated that a minister should be of the opinion that such activities were being engaged in. Memorably, Gavan Duffy denied right of appeal to the Supreme Court:

> The Constitution, with its most impressive Preamble, is the Charter of the Irish People and I will not whittle it away. The right to personal liberty and the other principles which we are accustomed to summarise as the rule of law were most deliberately enshrined in a national Constitution ... and the power to intern on suspicion or without trial is fundamentally inconsistent with the rule of law.[63]

It was a landmark moment in Irish legal history, the first case to test the new constitution. As Gerard Hogan has demonstrated, Gavan Duffy's judgement came

---

60 MacBride before Gavan Duffy J., quoted in *Irish Times*, 18 November 1939.
61 MacBride, *That Day's Struggle*, pp. 45–7.
62 *Irish Times*, 29 November 1939.
63 Irish Law Reports, [1940] IR 470. This prohibition was confirmed on appeal to the High Court on 15 December 1939.

as a surprise to the government, not least in view of his input in the framing of the 1937 constitution, when Gavan Duffy had expressed concern that the proposed constitution did not contain impediments to internment without trial.[64] As well as being a blow to the government, the judgement was a momentous victory for MacBride and the republican movement, and represented a massive boost of confidence after what had seemed like inescapably repressive legislation. MacBride himself was aware of the huge propaganda boon presented by the ruling, writing to fellow republican and UCD academic Roger McHugh that 'win or lose [the proposed appeal] I think that Gavan Duffy's judgement will survive in the mind of the people'.[65] It would, however, prove a false dawn.

'Our Pearl Harbour'

Burke was duly released shortly after judgement had been delivered; and as expected, a further fifty-four prisoners were also released on foot of Gavan Duffy's judgement. It was a cause for celebration within republican circles and immense credit was given to MacBride: 'After Seán MacBride's masterly treatment of Burke's case proving illegal detention Burke was released and now all the prisoners are out and Con Lehane is taking action against the Government and Mountjoy for wrongful detention. It is well to show them there is a limit to their aggression.'[66] Amid apparent government uncertainty on how best to repair the legislative gap wrought by the Burke judgement, the IRA sought to press home the advantage. On the evening of 23 December, the Magazine Fort in Phoenix Park, the principal ammunition store for the Irish Army, was raided by the IRA whose well prepared party arrived with lorries ready to transport the yield. Over one million rounds of ammunition were taken along with a negligible amount of weaponry. Described by Dan Bryan as 'our Pearl Harbour', the raid was, as Richard English has pointed out, as much a retaliatory strike against the government for the harsh measures of the previous six months as an ominous mark of the dangers a tight-knit, well financed organisation could pose in wartime. At the time, the shock caused by the raid among the government and the wider public was immense; as John Cudahy commented, 'No one knew whether it was merely a "stunt" ... or whether the attack was preliminary to some more serious action.'[67]

Even more disquietingly, the raid revealed systemic failures in the conduct of the Irish Army and alarming reluctance on the part of the Magazine Fort soldiers to put up anything even remotely resembling resistance; as T. F. O'Higgins scornfully underlined, the soldiers meekly submitted 'without as much as a blackthorn

---

64 Gerard Hogan, 'The Supreme Court and the reference of the Offences Against the State (Amendment) Bill 1940', *The Irish Jurist*, vol. xxxv (2000), p. 51.
65 National Library of Ireland [NLI], Roger McHugh Papers, MS 31756(5), Seán MacBride to Roger McHugh, 6 December 1939.
66 Library of Royal College of Physicians of Ireland, Kathleen Lynn Diaries, 2 December 1939.
67 Richard English, *Armed Struggle: A History of the IRA* (London: Pan, 2003), p. 54; United States National Archives and Records Administration, College Park, Maryland [NARA], MF1231, Roll 9, Political Affairs, John Cudahy to Secretary of State, Despatch no. 313, 10 January 1940.

being used'.[68] If this was how the Irish Army reacted to a few IRA men with pistols, the prospect of successfully repelling any serious military invasion was negligible. Among the long list of chronic security lapses were an inadequate defence guard for the Fort and a number of unfilled posts, the sentry's complete deviation from orders relating to the opening of inner and outer gates – which had apparently been a long-standing error never corrected – and a widespread laxity in the approach to the defence of the Fort.[69] Colonel Niall Harrington's investigation into the circumstances of the raid revealed that this slackness of the approach had been identified as early as 1937, when plans had been drawn up but abandoned to conduct a similar raid. Moreover, a number of army personnel were discovered to have given information and sold arms to the IRA from 1937 to 1939.[70] The Magazine Fort raid, apart from making a laughing stock of the Irish Army, who were tremendously humiliated, revealed the existence of IRA sympathisers inside the army, a highly dangerous situation in time of war, and cast the IRA's potential as a fifth column in a grave light.

In pulling off this audacious coup, the IRA had, in fact, shown their hand too early and in doing so ensured public opposition, with a flood of information to the authorities resulting in more ammunition being recovered than was originally stolen. More than anything, the raid pushed the government to react strongly to what had been a growing sense of crisis since the release of the hunger-strikers and the habeas corpus judgement: the need for new emergency legislation to replace the sections of the 1939 Offences Against the State Act which had been struck down took on a new urgency. Despite the reservations of the opposition, the required amendments to both the Emergency Powers Act and the Offences Against the State Act were swiftly passed. The prohibition on interning Irish-born citizens in the original of the former was removed, and in both acts, the opinion of a minister was enough to secure the arrest without warrant and internment of any individual. In one stroke, MacBride's habeas corpus victory was null and void: no impediment to the internment of members of the IRA remained. This was confirmed by de Valera's deliberate referral of the new Offences Against the State Act to the Supreme Court, with the explicit warning that 'if the Legislature and the judiciary are going to be at loggerheads ... we shall have to change that situation'. The Supreme Court duly complied, albeit by a narrow majority, and the Act was duly signed into law on 9 February 1940.[71] But by that point, another crisis had arisen, as the IRA and MacBride switched their focus from points of constitutional law to the old certainties: murder, death sentences and protests.

68 *Dáil Éireann Debates*, vol. 78, col. 1415, 3 January 1940.

69 This is revealed in Colonel Niall Harrington's report into the circumstances of the raid. See NLI, Niall Harrington Papers, MS 40,632 and MS 40,633.

70 NLI, Niall Harrington Papers, MS 40, 633(3) Third Statement of Private Kieran Downey. See also Seán MacEntee's copy of the inquiry into the raid. University College Dublin Archives [UCDA], MacEntee Papers, P67/531.

71 *Dáil Éireann Debates*, vol. 78, col. 1353, 3 January 1940; *Irish Times*, 10 February 1940; Hogan, 'The Supreme Court and the reference of the Offences Against the State (Amendment) Bill 1940'.

The Coventry Bombers

On 14 December 1939, just before attention had been diverted by the habeas corpus case, the Coventry bombers, Peter Barnes and James McCormack, were sentenced to death.[72] As the date of execution approached, and cases at the Court of Criminal Appeal and House of Lords failed, a committee was established at the Mansion House to coordinate efforts towards a reprieve.[73] This committee drove the public protests surrounding the death sentences, which included a number of public bodies passing resolutions in favour of reprieve. The reaction within republican circles was to be expected; more surprising was the response of the Irish authorities. Widespread coverage of the agitation for reprieve was allowed, even encouraged, in the press. The Censor explicitly justified this position as 'stopping matter which, in our judgement, was likely to militate against a reprieve while allowing all reports calculated to influence a decision favourable to the prisoners'.[74] The government was evidently sensitive to an attack on its republican flank, and used the death sentences as a way of reclaiming some of the ground they might appear to have lost after the previous year's moves against the IRA.

With this in mind, the government itself moved to explicitly take control of the reprieve movement, making representations for clemency to the British government via John Dulanty, High Commissioner in London, and to Sir John Maffey. The American representative in Dublin was dismayed by the Irish government's apparent hypocrisy on the issue: 'I find it difficult to reconcile this point of view that foreign governments may not place IRA members in "deterrent confinement" whereas the Irish Government maintains that it can arrest its own citizens on suspicion and hold them indefinitely without trial.'[75] What Cudahy failed to understand, however, was that precisely because it was a foreign government moving against Irish republicans, the Irish government was compelled to act. Anything short of that would have been perceived as weakness on the national question and presented the possibility of being outflanked. The public protests and the governmental representations failed; Barnes and McCormack were hanged on 8 February. In these executions, as Richard English has underlined, can be seen the most important legacy of the bombing campaign and a dangerous signpost for the future: the reiteration of 'the capacity for popular mobilisation in Ireland on behalf of those punished for republican activities – activities which would not in themselves have elicited popular support'.[76] The recurrence of this tendency,

---

72   *The Times*, 15 December 1939. A full account of the trial and subsequent appeals may be found in L. Fairfield (ed.), *The Trial of Peter Barnes and Others (The IRA Coventry Explosions of 1939)* (London: William Hodge, 1952).

73   NLI, Roger McHugh Papers, MS 25,620, Minute Book of Mansion House Committee for Reprieve of Barnes and McCormick. The committee included Maud Gonne MacBride, Roger McHugh, Dr Patrick McCartan, Peadar O'Donnell, Hanna Sheehy Skeffington, Andy Cooney and Con Lehane. MacBride was a curious absentee, perhaps preoccupied with the defence of Tomás MacCurtain (see below).

74   UCDA, Frank Aiken Papers, P104/3467(1), Report of censor for February 1940.

75   NAL, DO 130/9, Maffey to Machtig, 31 January 1940; NARA, MF1231, Roll 9, Political Affairs, J. Cudahy to Secretary of State, Despatch no. 308, 13 February 1940.

76   English, *Radicals and the Republic*, p. 259.

although at times stifled, would form a central part of the IRA's and MacBride's appeal to the Irish public over the subsequent years.

The Barnes and McCormack executions are best understood as a postscript to 1939, a coda to the bombing campaign. It had been a busy year for MacBride; he had secured his first major legal victory, and had transitioned into a new role within the republican movement. But 1939 was also for him a year of funerals. On 28 January W. B. Yeats died in the South of France; his death, however, did not overly affect MacBride. Elizabeth Keane's contention that Yeats had been a 'surrogate father' to MacBride and to Iseult is both a gross overstatement of the position that the poet held in MacBride's life and a highly reductionist description of the emotional complexity which governed Iseult's relationship with Yeats. Maud Gonne's moving account of the last meeting between the two in August 1938 should not obscure the distance between the two families in the preceding decades; the militancy of the MacBrides' political beliefs had driven an almost insurmountable wedge between them, and visits were rare.[77] Essentially, Yeats remained for MacBride a remote, pompous figure with whom he had once flown some kites on a Normandy beach and lived with for a summer in Galway. None of the MacBride family attended the memorial service for Yeats in Dublin on 6 February: the prohibition against Catholics attending Protestant services keeping them, along with many others, away.[78] But in 1948. MacBride, as Minister for External Affairs, represented the Irish government at the reinterral of Yeats's remains, according to his wishes, at Drumcliffe in County Sligo, and was given three of the poet's manuscript books by George Yeats, characteristically sensitive to the right gesture.[79]

Other old friends had also passed away in 1939. The greatest shock was the death of Tom Daly, who had been best man at MacBride's wedding to Kid Bulfin in 1926. The funeral of Daly, a former member of the Kerry No. 2 Brigade of the IRA and veteran of the ambush at Castlemaine in 1921, attracted a large attendance; as well as representatives of the government, his old comrades formed a guard of honour, which included MacBride, Moss Twomey, Con Lehane, Andy Cooney and Dónal O'Donoghue. Daly's coffin was wrapped in the same tricolour which had covered his brother Charlie, executed in Donegal during the Civil War, linking the uncertainties and fragmentation of the republican present to the assured unity of the republican past.[80]

On 10 November 1939 Charlotte Despard died aged 95, following a fall on a blacked-out staircase in her home in Whitehead, County Antrim. Since her fragile health had been adversely affected by constant raids on Roebuck House in the early 1930s, she had moved away from the MacBrides, perhaps also indicative of a growing political distance between her own staunch communism and

77 Elizabeth Keane, *Seán MacBride: A Life* (Dublin: Gill and Macmillan, 2007), p. 61; Maud Gonne MacBride, 'Yeats and Ireland', in Stephen Gwynn (ed.), *Scattering Branches: Tributes to the Memory of W.B. Yeats* (London: Macmillan, 1940), pp. 24–5.

78 *Irish Times*, 7 February 1939.

79 NAI, 411/3/16 I, Return of Remains of W. B. Yeats; R. F. Foster, *W. B. Yeats: A Life: 2: The Arch-poet, 1915–1939* (Oxford: Oxford University Press, 2003), p. 657.

80 *Irish Press*, 24 August 1939.

Maud Gonne's ambivalence towards fascism. Her final years in the North were a sad catalogue of financial bungling, deceitful servants and, finally, squalid bankruptcy.[81] Her funeral in Dublin was, however, exactly what she would have wanted, in which the MacBrides played a prominent part. Seán MacBride was a pall-bearer, along with Peadar O'Donnell, Roddy Connolly, Michael Price and others, and Maud Gonne, distraught, delivered an emotional oration for her friend – 'a white flame in defence of prisoners and the oppressed' – albeit marred by a typically overblown description of Madame Despard's sheltering of Belfast refugee children 'shot like rabbits by Orange snipers on the way to school'.[82]

After the failure of the reprieve movement for Barnes and McCormack, the IRA sought to build on any republican sympathies which might have resurfaced among the Irish public after the executions. A gilt-edged opportunity presented itself in February 1940, when a group of republican prisoners embarked on a mass hunger strike in Mountjoy, demanding that two fellow prisoners should be transferred to military custody. Among their number was Tomás MacCurtain, only son of the murdered Lord Mayor of Cork, who had been arrested for the murder of a Garda during a scuffle in Cork city, and Jack Plunkett, brother of Easter martyr Joseph Mary Plunkett. This was potentially extremely serious for the government: two of the hunger strikers this time round were relatives of republican martyrs with privileged access to the vagaries of nationalist psychology. While the prisoners attempted to raise the stakes by staging violent protests inside Mountjoy and friends and supporters outside attempted to mobilise public opinion as had been done so successfully in the past, the powerful censorship regime clamped down like a vice on all attempts to publicise the hunger strike. De Valera and his ministers stood firm. In refusing to capitulate on this issue – and undoubtedly the capitulation to the McGrath hunger strike the previous November was uppermost in the mind of the authorities – the government nullified this most potent of weapons in the Irish republican armoury. The final stages of this *danse macabre* were reached on 16 and 19 April, when Tony D'Arcy and Jack McNeela – a nephew of Fianna Fáil veteran TD Michael Kilroy – succumbed on the fifty-first and fifty-fourth day respectively of refusing food. There were unreported IRA demonstrations in the streets of Dublin; David Gray watched one, 'impressive ... sinister ... very grim, a dedication not to love of country but to hate of the established order'.[83]

The strike ended not without controversy; amid clerical intervention, disputed orders sent in from the IRA, and well meaning republican women, the strikers apparently believed that Boland had given an assurance that their demands would be met. This was brought to the public's attention during the inquest into the death of McNeela, where MacBride represented the family of the deceased. Calling a number of witnesses, including Úna Stack and a Fr O'Hare who had both been self-appointed intermediaries, MacBride had a particularly heated exchange with Gerald Boland, who he placed 'in the dock as far as the Irish nation is concerned':

81   Margaret Mulvihill, *Charlotte Despard: A Biography* (London: Pandora, 1989), pp. 187–93.
82   *Irish Press*, 13 November 1939.
83   Gray, 'Behind the green door', chapter V.

I put it to you that you come here when you are personally indicted and charged as being responsible for the deaths of two men? – I do my duty as Minister for Justice and see that people who break the law are dealt with.

Responding to Boland's barb about MacBride's 'party', the latter answered loftily:

I am here as counsel. I am not attached to any organisation, and if I speak with some heat it is in the sake of humanity and tolerance and to try and put an end to the intolerance which your Government has shown in this matter.[84]

It was a bruising encounter for the normally unflappable Boland, who later described it as 'one of the worst experiences I have ever had'.[85] The jury's riders, that political prisoners should not be subjected to criminal status and that O'Hare should have been granted access to Mountjoy earlier in order to persuade the hunger strikers to desist, were perceived as a republican victory. As a signal that the IRA was not unduly disheartened by the deaths of McNeela and D'Arcy, on 25 April an attempt was made to blow up the Special Branch section of Dublin Castle, injuring two Gardaí. This attack was followed by a 'raging gun battle' on Merrion Square on 7 May: an attempt to seize British diplomatic mail was prevented by two Gardaí, who bravely repelled the IRA gunmen although grievously wounded. In an important public intervention, de Valera addressed the nation on radio and issued a sombre warning:

The policy of patience has failed and is over ... a deadly conspiracy exists which does not hesitate to call the people's representatives 'the enemy' and to declare war on the Government which the community has freely elected ... if the present law is not sufficient, it will be strengthened; and in the last resort, if no other law will suffice, then the Government will invoke the ultimate law – the safety of the people.[86]

But events were moving rapidly. While the next stage of the German conquest of Europe began on 10 May with the invasion of the Low Countries, a week previously, a Nazi agent had parachuted into Ireland, with a mission directed towards the IRA. The MacBride family became embroiled with this spy, with near catastrophic results.

Crisis for the MacBrides

When his parachute came down in a field in County Meath, Hermann Goertz was a 50-year-old Great War veteran and had already been convicted of espionage in Kent in 1936, after a highly publicised trial.[87] Given that his name and photograph was already known to the British authorities, this might have been thought

---

84 *Irish Independent*, 23 April 1940.
85 Robert Fisk, *In Time of War: Ireland, Ulster and the Price of Neutrality, 1939–1945* (London: Deutsch, 1983), p. 345.
86 NAI, J8/792, Mine explosion at Detective Branch Headquarters, Dublin Castle; Conor Brady, *Guardians of the Peace* (Dublin: Gill AND Macmillan, 1974), p. 236; Maurice Moynihan (ed.), *Speeches and statements by Eamon de Valera, 1917–1973* (Dublin: Gill & Macmillan, 1980), p. 433.
87 *The Times*, 6 March 1936; *Manchester Guardian*, 6 March 1936; *Irish Times*, 7 March 1936.

to exclude him from future missions within the British 'sphere of influence'; his selection nonetheless is an indication of the unprofessional, even amateurish, nature of the *Abwehr* approach to Ireland. While in Berlin preparing for his mission, Goertz contacted Francis Stuart. Although both men later played down the significance of their acquaintance, neither willing to mention Stuart's links to the IRA, Stuart gave Goertz the address of his wife in Laragh Castle. Armed with this address and at least $26,000, Goertz flew to Ireland on 4 May 1940. His immediate instructions were focused on Northern Ireland: to direct IRA activities there against British naval installations, with the corollary of encouraging the IRA to reach some form of reconciliation with the Irish government.[88] Although Goertz later evidently adopted a quasi-messianic attitude to the latter of these goals – he believed his destiny was to reunite the warring IRA, which had torn itself asunder over the Hayes confession – it made perfect military sense for the Germans to encourage a *rapprochement* between de Valera and the IRA, in an attempt to further isolate Britain in preparation for an expected invasion. More particularly, MacBride's actions in the summer of 1940 can only be properly understood in the light of Goertz's mission.

On 9 May 1940, after a disastrous parachute drop, Goertz reached the door of Laragh Castle. He had landed in County Meath – although he had aimed for Tyrone – and had been obliged, after hiding his parachute, to make his way to Wicklow on foot. The 80-mile trek was completed by a series of night-time marches, punctuated by a near fatal swim across the Boyne, whereby the invisible ink secreted in his shoulder pads was destroyed, and enquiries for directions made at Poulaphouca Garda station, where, evidently, a bedraggled man wearing German war badges, riding boots and a beret – Goertz having by this stage abandoned his Luftwaffe greatcoat – asking the way to Laragh in a thick German accent failed to raise suspicions. He appeared, exhausted, at Iseult Stuart's door on 9 May, where he apparently received a warm welcome.[89] The Inspector General of the RUC, a generally reliable source of information on republican activities in Ireland during the Emergency, wrote to MI5 that Mrs Stuart 'received [Goertz] with open arms, owing to his first of all being a German spy, and secondly, on account of his fellowship with her husband'.[90]

Having put the exhausted spy to bed, Iseult informed Roebuck House; Maud Gonne and Helena Molony immediately came down to Laragh, much to MacBride's disgust, who was heard to mutter angrily that 'this is Helena Molony's doing'.[91] MacBride's anger was understandable: Goertz's arrival at Laragh threatened to shatter MacBride's carefully constructed public persona, which had been predicated on remaining firmly within the sphere of legitimate activities. While Molony looked after the spy and the children, Iseult and Maud purchased new clothes for

88 *Irish Times*, Hermann Goertz, 'Mission to Ireland – I', 25 August 1947; Hull, *Irish Secrets*, p. 86.

89 NAL, KV2/13122, Goertz Document of December 1944; see also *Irish Times*, Hermann Goertz, 'Mission to Ireland – III', 29 August 1947.

90 NAL, KV2/1321, Inspector General of the RUC to C. Liddell, 12 January 1942.

91 A. Norman Jeffares, Anna MacBride White and Christina Bridgewater (eds.), *Letters to W. B. Yeats & Ezra Pound from Iseult Gonne: A Girl that knew all Dante Once* (Basingstoke: Palgrave, 2004), pp. 151–2.

Goertz at Switzer's in Dublin – a crucial error. James O'Donovan arrived shortly afterwards to take Goertz to his home in Shankill, and from there he was soon shifted to a number of other safe houses, where he had a series of meetings with the IRA leadership.

On 22 May, Gardaí raided the home of Stephen Held, where the presence of a suspicious stranger had been noted. Goertz escaped arrest by jumping over the wall of a neighbouring garden, but all his belongings were seized: uniform, medals, coded messages, a large sum of money and Goertz's new clothes. In the pocket of his new overcoat was a receipt from Switzer's, which the authorities soon traced back to Iseult Stuart. When this was collated with the earlier information received on Held – John Hamilton's allegations had to be thoroughly reassessed – new suspicion fell on the MacBrides. Local Gardaí arrived to search Laragh Castle on 23 May, opportunely missing the gun and further stash of dollars which Goertz had left behind;[92] the next day, detectives from Dublin arrived and arrested Iseult Stuart. Brought before the Special Criminal Court at Collins Barracks on 25 May, she was charged under Section 47 of the Offences Against the State Act with assisting a person unknown to escape apprehension and with refusing to give information relating to the offence committed by another person.[93]

On 28 May, the authorities moved against MacBride, in a step indubitably linked to Iseult's arrest. He was arrested and brought to the Bridewell, where documents from Stephen Hayes, Chief of Staff of the IRA, were found on his person. These related to an attempt to broker a deal between the IRA and the government. Such were the powers available to the Minister for Justice at the time, mere possession of these documents would have been sufficient to secure MacBride's internment. But the government evidently satisfied itself with obtaining a promise from MacBride to behave himself. At two am, he signed a declaration:

> I, Sean MacBride, do solemnly and sincerely promise as follows, that is to say, that I shall not engage in or encourage any acts prejudicial to the peace, order, or security of the State and in particular that I shall not (a) Have any unlawful dealings or unlawful communications with any member of the organisation commonly referred to as the IRA (b) Assist or encourage the agents or armed forces of any other state to enter this State, or to operate within it or to obtain information save so far as the same may be done in an open, peaceful and lawful manner.[94]

The latter part of the declaration relates not merely to the arrival of Goertz, but also to the deteriorating external security situation. From the middle of May 1940, as the Germans swept through the Benelux countries and on into France, British military intelligence feared that Ireland was the target of an imminent German invasion. It was therefore feared that the unknown agent was tasked with coordinating IRA cooperation with German forces within Ireland, an impression reinforced by the

---

92 As recalled by Kay Stuart Bridgewater in Jeffares, MacBride White and Bridgewater (eds.), *Letters to W. B. Yeats & Ezra Pound from Iseult Gonne*, p. 152.

93 *Irish Times*, 27 May 1940; 1 June 1940.

94 UCDA, MacEntee Papers, P67/542(34), Text of declaration of Seán McBride [*sic*] in 1940, arrested 2 am, 28 May 1940.

discovery of Plan Kathleen, a crude IRA-authored document which envisaged the arrival of 50,000 Nazi troops.[95] Given his half-sister's involvement with Goertz, who remained at large and unidentified, the Irish authorities evidently believed that MacBride could be a central figure in this scenario.

The reason the authorities did not intern MacBride may be linked to the acquittal of Iseult Stuart of all charges in July 1940, after she had been refused bail and held in Mountjoy for six weeks to await trial. Stephen Held had been charged with five offences relating to the harbouring of Goertz, who remained at large; Held was found guilty of three of these charges after an open trial, and sentenced to five years penal servitude.[96] Conversely, Iseult Stuart's trial was held in camera, at the request of the Attorney-General, and on 2 July she was acquitted of all charges. The discrepancy in the treatment of Iseult Stuart and Stephen Held is notable; whereas he was subjected to the full rigour of the law – a public trial and stiff sentence – she was afforded significant leniency. Whereas David Gray speculated that her acquittal was to 'muzzle her formidable brother', it is possible that at the time of her trial, shortly after the fall of France when Nazi supremacy in Europe appeared impregnable, the Irish authorities calculated that it would not be politic to convict the wife of one of the most prominent Irish citizens in Berlin, moreover, one who was apparently integrating himself well into the Nazi regime.[97] The same consideration could arguably have applied to MacBride; equally, the internment of a high profile member of the Bar would inevitably have drawn protests from his colleagues in the Law Library, who might have been induced to put the weight of their collective legal expertise into his representation.

Normality Returns

MacBride soon put the upheavals of May behind him and returned to his customary activity of representing IRA prisoners, a service for which he never billed the movement. While de Valera was wrestling with the British offer of Irish unity in return for the use of the ports, more legislation was being drawn up to deal with the renewed gravity of the IRA threat. The Emergency Powers Amendment (No. 2) Act provided for the establishment of military courts to try civilians – that is, members of the IRA – which could only pass a sentence of death on those convicted, from which there would be no appeal.[98] This was intended to deal with the IRA's 'technique of duplicity which is part of a deliberate and well thought out plan to use the institutions of the State for the purposes of destroying it'. These included the following:

> The intimidation of jurors and witnesses, which is carried to the length of murder, is accompanied by loud voiced demands for the abolition of the Special Criminal Court and the restoration of trial by jury; and men who 'refuse to recognise the Court' when put on trial, hasten to recognise and avail of all their

95 Brian Girvin, *The Emergency: Neutral Ireland, 1939–1945* (London: Macmillan, 2006), pp. 101–4.
96 *Irish Times*, 27 May 1940; 1 June 1940; *Irish Independent*, 27 June 1940.
97 Gray, 'Behind a green door', chapter X.
98 *Dáil Éireann Debates*, vol. 80, col. 1739, 19 June 1940.

rights of appeal under the laws they have sought to subvert, when once they have been convicted, and will stop at nothing to try and evade the penalties they have incurred.[99]

This undated passage may have been referring directly to the case of Tomás MacCurtain, who after surviving a 55-day hunger strike, was finally brought before the Special Criminal Court on 11 June 1940, refusing either representation or to recognise the Court. MacCurtain was sentenced to death by hanging, to be carried out on 5 July, and immediately a campaign swung into action, prompted by memories of his martyred father. A mass of letters, telegrams and resolutions urging for reprieve descended on the government. One submission presented a twist on the customary appeals for clemency based on illustrious parentage, writing that MacCurtain merited reprieve on the grounds of 'only hysterical and unbalanced advice available from early childhood; unbalanced by female relatives' adulation; ghouls glorified the tragedy of his father's death until the boy became mentally elated; complete absence of balanced male control and advice; heredity: proved insanity on both sides; and the misfortune of his birth'.[100]

MacBride agitated on MacCurtain's behalf, although he had not yet been officially engaged as his counsel. With Albert Wood, he sent a detailed memorandum to the Cabinet urging a reprieve on legal grounds which included the failure of the Gardaí to produce a warrant for MacCurtain's arrest, emphasised the confusion of the struggle which had resulted in the fatal shot, and the effect of the murder of MacCurtain senior by policemen in 1920, a 'a fact which, in our opinion, have subconsciously operated in the mind of the accused in the course of the fatal struggle'.[101] Although Maurice Moynihan later maintained that there was unanimity within the government that the murderers of Gardaí would face the ultimate penalty, inside the Cabinet there was evident unease in some quarters at the prospect of executing the son of an old, venerated comrade. Seán T. O'Kelly was the most susceptible to feelings of guilt and, with MacBride, hatched a plan to overturn the sentence:

> Seán T. O'Kelly sent for me and said, 'Look they've turned down, by a majority in the cabinet, the granting of a reprieve to Tomás MacCurtain. But I think that if you could, some way or another, succeed in postponing the execution ... I will be able to swing things back in favour of a reprieve.'[102]

MacBride feigned detachment until the last possible moment, made a twelfth-hour habeas corpus application to Gavan Duffy in the High Court which, as he calculated, was refused, and immediately lodged an appeal in the Supreme

99 NAI, D/T, S11534A, IRA Activities in Ireland, 1939–1950, Memorandum on the policy of the government with regard to Offences Against the State, p. 1.

100 NAI, D/T, S11974, Thomas MacCurtain, Peadar O Dálaigh to Eamon de Valera, 14 June 1940. Other individuals who appealed for clemency included Owen Sheehy Skeffington, Rosamond Jacob and Eoin O'Duffy.

101 NAI, D/T, S11974, Considerations submitted by Albert Wood KC and Seán MacBride BL, 18 June 1940.

102 MacBride, *That Day's Struggle*, p. 127; Seosamh Ó Longaigh, 'Emergency law in action, 1939–1945', in Dermot Keogh and Mervyn O'Driscoll (eds.), *Ireland in World War Two: Diplomacy and Survival* (Cork: Mercier Press, 2004), p. 65.

Court.[103] The Supreme Court was unable to convene that evening, owing to Justice Murnaghan's absence walking his dog, and the execution was duly postponed. The Cabinet commuted his sentence to life imprisonment on 10 July. It was another victory for MacBride, although it perhaps owed more to disquiet within government circles than to the quality of his legal arguments.

But at this point, MacBride must have been satisfied with his lot. The regime with which he had secretly allied himself was sweeping all before it in Europe; after the fall of France, Britain stood perilously alone against Nazi Germany. While some sympathy might have stirred for his childhood home, the establishment of the Vichy regime can be viewed as a partial triumph of the old Boulangist faction with whom the MacBrides had always identified. Although the IRA was operating within the strictest of security regimes, it was not yet quelled, and appeared to be biding its time, waiting for the anticipated German invasion. MacBride was doing the same. The following years would see the apex and subsequent collapse of those dreams.

---

103 G. M. Goulding, *George Gavan Duffy: A Legal Biography* (Dublin: Irish Academic Press, 1982), p. 131.

8

'Standing Counsel to the Illegal Organisation' 1940–1942

By July 1940, with MacBride's successful securing of a reprieve for Tomás MacCurtain, he had manoeuvred himself into a potentially powerful position. With both eyes firmly fixed on the emerging 'New Order' in Nazi-dominated Europe, he had skilfully cultivated links with German representatives in Dublin, both official and unofficial, while remaining ostensibly on the right side of the law at all times. His reputation in Irish public life was growing; and David Gray, the American representative in Ireland from March 1940, remembered him as 'the brilliant, unsmiling, young Dublin barrister who was defiantly defending such members of the IRA as the de Valera police had taken into custody',[1] As well as the MacCurtain reprieve, he had been associated with a number of legal successes, most importantly, the habeas corpus ruling of 1939 and the stipulations of the jury in the inquest into the death of Jack McNeela in April 1940. These cases had cemented his position as the legal representative of the republican movement and the subsequent years of the Emergency would flesh out Seán MacEntee's later charge that MacBride was 'virtually Standing Counsel to the illegal organisation'.[2]

The 'illegal organisation' – the sacred name of the IRA was rarely used by government ministers to describe these national apostates – had also reason to feel optimistic by the summer of 1940. Long-standing secret contact with the intelligence agencies of Nazi Germany appeared to be bearing fruit; if the calibre of German spies parachuted into Ireland may have raised some eyebrows, the seemingly unstoppable march of the German army across Europe was reassuring. Britain stood alone against Nazi hegemony in Europe, and in the monochrome political vision of the republican leadership, there was no doubt as to the proper position of the IRA: 'What is England doing? Fighting the Nazis. Then up the Swastika! Against England. Heil Hitler!'[3]

---

1 David Gray, 'Behind the green door', unpublished memoir, chapter X.
2 University College Dublin Archives [UCDA], Seán MacEntee Papers, P67/373 (4), Text of speech at Clonmel, n. d. [October 1947]
3 Jim Phelan, *Churchill can Unite Ireland* (London: Victor Gollancz, 1940), p. 53.

Public and Government Opinion in Ireland

The level of pro-German feeling within Irish society has been the subject of some historiographical attention in recent years. Measuring this tendency, however, remains difficult. Eamon de Valera's blunt assertion in July 1940 that 'the people were pro-German' conflicts with the assurances of John Maffey, United Kingdom representative in Dublin, to the Dominion Office in London that 'Eire today is 90 per cent pro-Ally.'[4] As Paul McMahon has demonstrated, Maffey's despatches to the Dominions Office are best understood as an attempt to cool tempers in London and counter increasingly alarmist reports from British intelligence services, obsessed by the threat of a German fifth column in Ireland ready to spring into action with the IRA and launch a *coup d'état* prior to a German invasion.[5]

But if Maffey was anxious that wiser counsels should prevail, other indications point to a deeply ambivalent streak within Irish society. Whereas the overall attitude of the 'plain people of Ireland' throughout the war is to be found in J. J. Horgan's oft-quoted encounter with a West Cork farmer – 'We would like to see the English nearly bate'[6] – by the summer of 1940, the apparent likelihood of a Nazi victory produced 'considerable defeatist pro-German sentiment in Dublin aside from Republican Army. If enemy struck before Fifth Column is jailed conditions would be very serious.'[7] This defeatist sentiment was also to be found within the highest level of government; Eduard Hempel, the German minister in Dublin, reported to Berlin in July 1940 that, 'From various indications in talks with Walshe and Boland I assume that the Irish Government may be placing hope in future German interest in the maintenance and completion of an entirely independent Irish state.'[8] While the politics of defeatism or, more accurately, the dictates of *realpolitick*, drove the Irish government to seek an accommodation with what it perceived to be the likely victors in the war, wider Irish sentiment had a more complex makeup. The position of the farmer from West Cork might have been the attitude of a large section within Irish society, but there were other, conflicting, currents. Much pro-German sentiment was, of course, dictated by the sort of reflexive Anglophobia which had long been a corrosive streak in Irish psychology, neatly encapsulated by Seán O'Faoláin's comment in 1939 that 'the curse of nationalist opinion in Ireland [is that] it automatically looks to see what Great Britain is doing in any given situation, and without a thought it does the opposite',[9]

4   National Archives London [NAL], DO130/12, John Maffey to Cecil Parkinson, 24 April 1940; De Valera quoted in Brian Girvin, 'The republicanisation of Irish society, 1932–1948', in Jacqueline R. Hill (ed.), *A new History of Ireland, vol. VII: Ireland, 1921–1984* (Oxford: Oxford University Press, 2003), p. 151.

5   Paul McMahon, *British Spies and Irish Rebels: British Intelligence and Ireland, 1916–1945* (Woodbridge: Boydell & Brewer, 2008), pp. 302–3.

6   Gray, 'Behind a green door', chapter IX.

7   United States National Archives and Records Administration, College Park, Maryland [NARA], MF1231, Roll 9, Political Affairs, David Gray to Secretary of State, 29 May 1940.

8   *Documents on German Foreign Policy Series D (1937–1945), Volume X, The War Years, June 23– August 31 1940* (London: Her Majesty's Stationery Office, 1957), Eduard Hempel to Foreign Office, Berlin, 31 July 1940, p. 110. Joseph Walshe and Fred Boland were, respectively, Secretary and Assistant Secretary in the Department of External Affairs.

9   Seán O'Faolain, *De Valera* (Harmondsworth: Penguin, 1939), p. 176.

But there was a darker side to pro-Nazi sentiment in Ireland, as the work of R. M. Douglas has demonstrated. Through the first half of 1940, a number of pro-German organisations mushroomed into existence, combining admiration for the Nazi New Order with ultra-Catholic anti-Semitism and a Gaelicist outlook.[10] These groups, and wider pro-German sentiment, took on a much more serious aspect once Irish government circles began to believe that a German invasion was looming. The escalating sense of trepidation in Dublin was exacerbated by the first in a series of British warnings about the likelihood of invasion, when on 1 June 1940 F. H. Boland received a letter from the United Kingdom legation stating that 'there were a growing number of indications that such an invasion is not only seriously planned and prepared with the help of the IRA, but is imminent'.[11] This warning evidently was on de Valera's mind when David Gray visited him on 6 June:

> He went to the map of Donegal Bay, where Lough Esk extends north of the border, 50 miles to the north-east, the head of Lough Swilly. 'If I were the Germans', he said, 'I would land at these points and proclaim myself a liberator. If they should do that, what I could do, I do not know.'[12]

De Valera's unease at the potential of an invading German army to manipulate the Irish nationalist sentiment he himself had so successfully harnessed for the previous decade underscores the delicate balance the government had to maintain between preserving the nationalist pieties of independent Ireland while remaining aware where precisely the real guarantors of Irish sovereignty and universal liberty lay. This finely wrought equilibrium was shaken towards the end of June 1940, when Dominions Secretary Malcolm MacDonald presented a British memorandum proposing a declaration in favour of Irish unity in return for Irish entry into the war and the immediate opening of the Treaty ports to the British navy and airforce. De Valera rejected the British offer, distrustful of the bona fides of this declaration and mindful that during a previous world war another Irish nationalist leader had been politically destroyed by the failure of previous British governments to keep to their promises. Crucially, though, de Valera was unwilling to ally himself to what appeared to be the defeated side in a conflict drawing to a close.[13] But, the following month the worst fears of the Irish government appeared about to be realised: a German submarine bound for Ireland departed from Wilhelmshaven.

---

10 R. M. Douglas, 'The pro-Axis underground in Ireland, 1939–1942', *Historical Journal*, vol. 4,9 no. 4 (2006), pp. 1155–83; Fearghal McGarry, *Eoin O'Duffy: A Self-made Hero* (Oxford: Oxford University Press, 2005), pp. 326–30. See also R. M. Douglas, *Architects of the Resurrection: Ailtirí na hAiséirghe and the Fascist 'New Order' in Ireland, 1942–1958* (Manchester: Manchester University Press, 2009).

11 National Archives of Ireland [NAI], DFA A/3, M. E. Antrobus to Fred Boland, 1 June 1940.

12 Gray, 'Behind the green door', chapter 8.

13 Brian Girvin, *The Emergency: Neutral Ireland, 1939–45* (London: Macmillan, 2006), pp. 110–24; John Bowman, *De Valera and the Ulster Question, 1917–1973* (Oxford: Clarendon Press, 1982), p. 235.

Operation Dove

The mission of U-65 – Operation Dove – was to deposit two passengers off the Irish coast, the latest in a series of German agents to land in Ireland; Herman Goertz remained at large since the discovery of his spy cache at the home of Stephen Held in May 1940. But the latest mission carried not German nationals unfamiliar with the politics of subversive Ireland, but two figures who, potentially, could provide a focal point around which the increasingly fractured republican movement could rally: Seán Russell and Frank Ryan. Russell's ill-advised publicity campaign in the United States had led to his arrest. Released on bail, he travelled secretly to Genoa and on to Berlin where he embarked on a course of instruction in the art of Nazi sabotage.[14] Ryan's personal odyssey towards Nazi Germany is more morbidly compelling. His fervent socialist principles rendered him perhaps the best known Irish advocate of the Republican government in Spain, and he became the highest ranked Irish officer in the International Brigade, rising to the rank of major by early 1938. Following a disastrous engagement at Calaceite, Ryan had been captured by the Francoists, held prisoner at San Pedro and sentenced to death following court martial in June 1938.[15] Thanks to German intervention, Ryan was allowed to escape from prison in July 1940, travelling via Paris to Berlin, and into the heart of Russell's conspiracy with the Nazis.

The status of the IRA was the subject of considerable uncertainty and much inaccuracy outside Ireland. In Germany, Russell, who had been absent from Ireland since April 1939, played up the stature of the organisation. Helmut Clissman later recalled that Russell 'made an excellent impression in Berlin; he was a munitions man and he knew what he was about. We thought then that the IRA was a fairly coherent organisation and had no inkling that anything was wrong with it.'[16] The Nazis were not the only observers to over-estimate the strength and influence of the IRA: in September 1940 British intelligence predicted that a German attack on Ireland would be supported by the IRA, 'the nucleus of which is believed to consist of some 2,000 to 3,000 men, all well armed'.[17] When the two Irishmen met in Berlin on 4 August, Ryan agreed to accompany Russell in the U-boat sailing for Ireland on 8 August. The mission, however, was abandoned on 14 August following the death of Russell on board; the submarine was merely a hundred miles off the coast of Galway, but Ryan, who apparently had no idea of the details of Russell's mission instructed the submarine captain to return to Germany, after burying Russell's body at sea.[18]

14 Mark Hull, *Irish Secrets: German Espionage in Ireland, 1939–1945* (Dublin: Irish Academic Press, 2003), pp. 107–34

15 Fearghal McGarry, *Frank Ryan* (Dundalk: Dundalgan Press, 2002), pp. 44–57; Fearghal McGarry, *Irish Politics and the Spanish Civil War* (Cork: Cork University Press, 1999), pp. 226–7.

16 Robert Fisk, *In Time of War: Ireland, Ulster and the Price of Neutrality, 1939–1945* (Dublin: Gill & Macmillan, 1983), p. 342.

17 Quoted by Eunan O'Halpin, 'British intelligence, republicans and the IRA's German links', in Fearghal McGarry (ed.), *Republicanism in Modern Ireland* (Dublin: University College Dublin Press, 2003), p. 118.

18 NAI, J8/802, Seán Russell file, Memorandum by Fred Boland on meeting with Mrs Helmut

The Irish authorities were unaware of the planned submarine mission, still less of the fate of its passengers. Irish Military Intelligence (G2) remained ignorant of Russell's whereabouts, and a stream of inaccurate intelligence reports continued to flood into G2 throughout 1940 and 1941, placing Russell, variously, in Berlin with Joseph McGarrity, in Connemara, parachuting into County Kildare, and living in Dublin.[19] In subversive circles, however, knowledge of Russell's death was current from October 1940. This was traced directly to MacBride, who informed Moss Twomey (who, like MacBride, was no longer officially a member of the IRA, but whose O'Connell Street newsagent's shop served as a talking shop for various shades of republican opinion), that Russell had been dead since August.[20] MacBride refused to reveal the source of his information, but circumstances point to Francis Stuart, MacBride's brother-in-law, who was by then well settled into his own Berlin interlude.[21]

Stuart became an associate of Ryan after the latter's return to Berlin; there is much variety, however, in Stuart's representation of their relationship, from a flattering portrayal in the immediate post-war period to more negative accounts in the later years of his life.[22] Stuart's own role in the abortive Russell-Ryan mission is also suspicious: immediately after the war an unidentified Northern Irishman reported that he had met Stuart in Germany, who had 'further indicated to him that if Russell and Ryan's submarine mission had been a success, he, Stuart, was later to follow them with a cargo of arms'.[23] According to Francis Stuart, Frank Ryan was in no doubt of the privileged position he would hold in the event of a German conquest of Europe:

> I remember once walking down to the university where I was teaching, he accompanied me, and shortly before we parted he said: 'You know, Frank ... if Germany wins the war I'll be a member of the next government.' And, to some extent, it seemed to me some sort of veiled threat.[24]

MacBride must have believed he was in a similar position to Ryan: he was a trusted adviser to the German legation and close confidant of the German minister; his national 'record' was such that, like nationalist demagogues in Croatia and Romania, he could theoretically appeal to the Irish people as a leader; and he

Clissman, 6 June 1946. Mrs Clissman's version of events on board the submarine was received from Frank Ryan after his return to Germany.

19 NAI, J8/802 Seán Russell file, P. Carroll, Ard Cheannphort Gardaí Síochána to Secretary for Justice, 19 February 1941.

20 NAL, DO121/86, Cable from German Legation to Foreign Office Berlin, 25 June 1942.

21 Although most of the post arriving into and issuing from Laragh Castle was examined by G2, Francis and Iseult Stuart evidently managed to correspond through an American conduit: Mrs H. R. Vera McWilliams of Shreveport, Los Angeles. It may have been via this method that MacBride learned of Russell's death. NAI, DFA, A/12 IRA Activities, Irish-German-American notes, n. d.

22 Contrast Francis Stuart, 'Frank Ryan in Germany', parts I and II, The Bell, vol. xvi, nos 2 and 3 (November and December 1950) with Kevin Kiely's recent version that 'they remained wary and suspicious of each other.' Francis Stuart: Artist and Outcast (Dublin: Liffey Press, 1007), p. 139.

23 NAI, DFA A/72, Francis Stuart file, Dan Bryan to Fred Boland, 18 August 1945.

24 Francis Stuart interview with Richard English, Dublin, 24 February 1987.

had never been in any doubt of his rightful place within Irish politics. Russell's death, and with it the dramatic decline in the likelihood of a German invasion, thus represented a massive dent in MacBride's ambition to become a gauleiter, as Gerry Boland bluntly put it.[25]

Shootout on Rathgar Road

Around the time of Russell's death, however, MacBride was immersed in another legal and political crisis: the trial and execution of Patrick McGrath, who had successfully secured release from Arbour Hill by hunger strike the previous November. McGrath had been arrested, along with Thomas Harte, on 16 August at 98 Rathgar Road, an IRA training department; Detective Officer John Hyland was killed and two other officers injured during the raid.[26] McGrath's willing-ness to resort to arms was, apparently, driven by the shooting the previous month of Volunteer Micksey Conway: McGrath remarked to Kit Quearney that '[Special Branch] have the gloves off now ... they need expect no mercy from me.'[27] The venom between the IRA and the forces of the State was further compounded by the death of John Joe Kavanagh, shot dead by Special Branch while tunnelling into Cork Jail in an apparent attempt to 'escape' prisoners inside. Such instances, and rumours that 'detectives have orders to shoot at sight', certainly contributed to pre-existing tensions; that the IRA were increasingly resembling *desperados* in their viciousness indicates the raised stakes in the unofficial blood feud with Special Branch, which had been simmering since 1938.[28]

The government response was deceptively swift: although it appeared that the establishment of the Special Military Court was an instantaneous reaction, the work of Seosamh Ó Longaigh has demonstrated that this development was part of an ongoing government initiative to toughen up its policy vis-à-vis the subver-sive threat.[29] The Military Court was free to impose only one penalty on convic-tion – the death sentence – and no appeal was permitted. Moreover, the Military Court was responsible for the prosecution of a much wider range of offences than previously, from possession of firearms and acts of sabotage to membership of an unlawful organisation. Sentences were to be carried out within twenty-four hours, thereby avoiding the prospect of destabilising public protests. Speaking in Dáil Éireann in 1946, Gerry Boland spoke plainly of the Military Court's design: 'This court has been described outside as a terror court. I have no objection to its so being described. That is exactly what it was. It was a terror court – a court set up to meet terror in a drastic and summary manner.'[30]

The Military Court was convened for the first time on the evening of 16 August under the Emergency Powers (No. 41) Order. The next day McGrath and Harte

25   *Dáil Éireann Debates*, vol. 101, col. 1128, 29 May 1946.
26   NAI, D/T, S12048A, Garda Metropolitan Report, 20 August 1940.
27   Christy Quearney quoted in Uinseann MacEoin, *The IRA in the Twilight Years, 1923–1948* (Dublin: Argenta Press, 1997), p. 777.
28   Library of Royal College of Physicians, Kathleen Lynn Diaries, 22 August 1940.
29   Seosamh Ó Longaigh, *Emergency Law in Independent Ireland, 1922–1948* (Dublin: Four Courts Press, 2006), pp. 246–59.
30   *Dáil Éireann Debates*, vol. 101, col. 1116, 29 May 1946.

were charged before it and, the following week, convicted and sentenced to death by firing squad. It was at this point that, having previously refused legal representation in keeping with what appears to have been a fluctuating IRA policy, they engaged MacBride to appeal on their behalf – notwithstanding the prohibition against appeal in the terms of the Emergency Powers (Amendment) No. 2 Act. MacBride attempted to repeat the pattern that had proved successful in previous cases by appealing directly to Justice Gavan Duffy in his home for a habeas corpus order. This, however, failed: Gavan Duffy, working off the basis of the Emergency Powers Act and not the Offences Against the State Act, declined to grant an absolute habeas corpus order, commenting that 'in view of the public importance of the emergency legislation it was, perhaps, regrettable that the objections taken by counsel should happen to be of a rather technical character'.[31]

This was a thinly veiled criticism of MacBride's professional approach to the case and to his argumentation, much of which was subsequently reproduced before the Supreme Court. MacBride's arguments were highly technical, focusing on the validity of the entire Emergency Powers Act, the procedural steps taken by the President to sign the bill into law, and the existence of the war footing inside Ireland. MacBride also raised the question of the suitability of a Military Court to try civilians, a somewhat hypocritical claim for the legal representative of a self-styled army, some of whose members had recently hunger striked to death for the right to be held in military custody. But the hypocrisy ran both ways: that the state should deny military status to IRA prisoners and internees but insist on the right to try them summarily before military courts comprised of army officers and held in military barracks indicates the convoluted logic inherent in the state's response to the subversive threat during the war years. An argument which appeared to have more currency, however, was MacBride's contention that 'whatever law or orders the appellants had been tried under had been non-existent at the time of their address'. This was compounded by the failure of the government to lay the same law or orders either before the Oireachtas or before the public by the time of McGrath and Harte's trial. At any other time, such an omission would almost certainly have ensured the quashing of the sentence handed down, but the Supreme Court judgement, like Gavan Duffy's in the High Court, was robust, unanimously dismissing all of MacBride's arguments without hearing counsel for the State.[32]

The domestic political climate was such that it was popularly recognised that a failure to apply the ultimate penalty to McGrath and Harte was tantamount to an admission on the part of the government of their unsuitability to govern. MacBride's reliance on complex legal technicalities to argue McGrath and Harte's case was a likely consequence of the popular reaction against the murder, and a realisation that the facts of the case appeared clear-cut. In the run-up to the executions, the customary clamour was raised in favour of clemency, although not as

31 *Irish Independent*, 27 August 1940.
32 *Irish Times*, 3 September 1940; Irish Law Reports, [1941] IR 77. See also Fergal Davis, *The History and Development of the Special Criminal Court, 1922–2005* (Dublin: Four Courts Press, 2007), pp. 86–7.

vociferously as with the case of MacCurtain.[33] There was a qualitative difference to the appeals for clemency this time, however. Instead of merely petitioning for mercy for the condemned men, fuller proposals were delivered to the government detailing the basis on which a truce with the IRA might be agreed. On 5 September 1940, the eve of the McGrath and Harte executions, MacBride called on de Valera, presenting terms for a truce:

> The IRA to cease drilling, carrying arms, manufacturing arms or explosives, transporting arms or explosives into the six counties, to cease the publication of War News in the twenty-six counties and to cease broadcasting from the twenty-six counties. The campaign in England to be called off.

In return, the government would 'instruct police to suspend all activities against IRA, to suspend sentences against IRA in prison and to gradually release prisoners'. In a covering letter, MacBride wrote that formal guarantees would be forthcoming to secure the IRA's agreement, adding that 'it would be superfluous for me to emphasise the beneficial results of some such agreement upon the national position'.[34] De Valera declined to reply, and the truce initiative failed. The government had no real incentive to agree to the proposal. It finally had the legal machinery in place to effectively deal with the IRA threat, and any agreement with the IRA would place it in an almost impossible political position vis-à-vis the opposition. The question of trust was, moreover, paramount, and any residual trust which had existed between the Fianna Fáil government and the estranged members of the republican family had been blown away by the discovery of the IRA's collusion with Goertz.

MacBride's attempt to broker a truce having failed, McGrath and Harte's sentences stood. The government's yielding to McGrath the previous November had counted against the veteran this time round; by reimmersing himself within the violent republican milieu, McGrath had effectively squandered any lingering goodwill within the government. De Valera was particularly pained by the case, blaming himself for five needless deaths: 'It was one of the biggest mistakes I have made in my life ... I will regret it until my death, because, had it not been for my action, there would have been only one death, whereas, in the event, there were six in all.'[35] The executions were carried out early on the morning of 6 September. It had a catastrophic effect on republican morale; but for the government, and the wider society, it indicated a reassuring willingness to stand firm in the face of the subversive threat. The choice had been to govern or to abdicate, and de Valera had finally fulfilled the promise he had made to invoke 'the ultimate law' to preserve the security of the state.

Although a decisive note had been struck by the executions, the familiar routine for the 'Standing Counsel to the illegal organisation' continued.[36] In the aftermath of the executions, MacBride was engaged in the defence of Thomas Hunt, a 21-year-old captured following the raid on Rathgar Road. Hunt had 'apparently

---

33 NAI, D/T S12048B, Petitions for the reprieve of Patrick McGrath and Thomas Harte.
34 NAI, D/T S12069, Seán MacBride to Eamon de Valera, 5 September 1940.
35 *Dáil Éireann Debates*, vol. 91, col. 604, 9 July 1943.
36 UCDA, Seán MacEntee Papers, P67/373(4), Text of speech at Clonmel, n. d. [October 1947]

taken no part in the gunfight and had escaped in the confusion', but the address of the safe house where he found shelter was found on Paddy McGrath and raided six days later.[37] Hunt was charged before the Military Court with the murder of Detective Hyland on 21 September but, as MacBride pointed out in his defence, 'the prosecution asked [the Court] to find him guilty of aiding or abetting. The order committing Hunt for trial restricted the Court to trying him on a charge of murder.'[38]

Such technicalities were, MacBride argued, of even greater importance, owing to the restrictions placed on the Court in the matter of sentencing. There is some merit in this argument. Conditions of the most extreme stringency were imposed on defendants before the Court; that the State did not hold itself to the same lofty standards reflects ill on the harsh nature of justice meted out. Of course, the IRA were in no real position to criticise the government on its judicial record, given that they had long been engaged in a process of widespread intimation of juries. However, notwithstanding the resonance of aspects of MacBride's defence to a wider liberal outlook, his argument held no currency in the Military Court, who found Hunt guilty and passed the sentence of death.[39] Hunt, however, was reprieved on the recommendation of Gerry Boland, Minister for Justice, who later claimed that 'that boy was more a tool than anything else. He was the sort of young fellow who got landed in it more by accident than by anything else.'[40] The perception that the true perpetrators of the crime had already received the ultimate penalty undoubtedly contributed to the exercise of clemency in this case.

During this period, MacBride was maintaining his customary equilibrium between his outward appearance as a reputable member of the Bar and the inner reality of continued dabbling with republican politics. A report on the telephone surveillance on Roebuck House in the weeks leading up to the Hunt case contained the following 'peculiar' conversation with an unidentified 'Rory':

> 'Rory' said he thought 'Mac' was coming back for the harvest to which MacBride replied that it would be ridiculous to come all the way back for that. They discussed also a steam engine, coal and water which were required for some unstated purpose.[41]

This clearly coded conversation reveals two things: that MacBride was engaged in suspicious activity of some kind; and that he was aware of the surveillance and therefore treading carefully, perhaps mindful of the pledge he had given the authorities some months earlier to have no contact with the IRA. He continued to present an outwardly conformist façade, appearing at a debate of the Technical Students' Literary and Debating Society at the Technical Institute in Dublin in November 1940, in a rather eclectic gathering, which included parliamentarians Senators Desmond FitzGerald and Frank MacDermott, General Eoin O'Duffy, David Gray and Hanna Sheehy Skeffington. MacBride's contribution that evening,

---

37 Christy Quearney quoted in MacEoin, *The IRA in the Twilight Years*, p. 777.
38 *Irish Times*, 24 September 1940.
39 *Weekly Irish Times*, 28 September 1940.
40 *Dáil Éireann Debates*, vol. 101, col. 1132, 29 May 1946.
41 Irish Military Archives, Cathal Brugha Barracks [IMA], G2/2278, Maud Gonne MacBride file, Seán MacBride telephone censorship, 15 September 1940.

in response to a paper entitled 'Whither Our Nationalism', was to note that 'it was surprising in a paper on nationalism no reference was made to the real grievance of six counties of this country being under the influence of foreign rule against the wishes of the majority of the people'. This was in reaction to FitzGerald's observation that 'common good cannot be attained except through the operation of the law, vested in a law-making authority'.[42] MacBride's comments were arguably a veiled rationale for the IRA's campaign against the state, and indicate the vice-like grip partition continued to exercise over his critical faculties.

Although his interventions were usually tired reiterations of republican mantras, by partaking in such debates, MacBride was attempting to establish his legitimate participation in Irish public life. But the transparency of his apparent conformism was rendered even more starkly by his failure to join the volunteer forces that augmented the Irish Army, particularly from the summer of 1940. These forces proved an especially successful method of integrating still recalcitrant republicans into the state infrastructure, attracting the service of, among others, Ernie O'Malley and Florence O'Donoghue.[43] In the *Irish Press*, the spectacle of former members of the Dublin Brigade of 1919–21 marching together in formation to join up was reported in tones of breathless admiration.[44] MacBride's non-participation, therefore, made him an easy target for some of Seán MacEntee's more scathing remarks during the 1947 Dublin by-election campaign, when he castigated MacBride for his lack of loyal service: 'being a loyal citizen claiming to have accepted the Constitution [MacBride] would have, in view of his past as a super-soldier and super-patriot, given some sort of voluntary service to the Irish nation, even at some cost to his professional career.'[45] Refusal to serve in the new Volunteer reserve was, however, consistent with MacBride's earlier rejection of a rank in the National Army after Fianna Fáil had gained power; for him and for others, the dangers of wartime had not sufficiently altered circumstances to enable such a volte-face.

As the new year began, the IRA were pressurised as never before. The extraordinary legislative measures which had been introduced since the beginning of the war provided the government with unprecedented resources to face down the subversive threat. Although a number of incidents fraught with potential crisis had presented themselves during the previous year, the steeliness of key members of the Fianna Fáil Cabinet – principally Gerald Boland and Seán MacEntee – coupled with de Valera's resolute determination to maintain Irish neutrality above all other

42 *Irish Times*, 18 November 1940; *Sunday Independent*, 17 November 1940.
43 Richard English, *Ernie O'Malley: IRA Intellectual* (Oxford: Oxford University Press, 1998), pp. 52–4. The record of Tom Barry during this period is somewhat obscured. He later claimed that the Irish Army refused to accede to his request that he be permitted to serve as a private and that this, rather than pique at not being awarded a plum position, lay behind his failure to complete his term of service which, in the event, lasted only two months. See Meda Ryan, *Tom Barry: IRA Freedom Fighter* (Cork: Mercier Press, 2005, first published 2003), pp. 310–14 for a sympathetic discussion of this subject.
44 *Irish Press*, 3 July 1940. Former comrades of MacBride in B Company, Third Dublin Battalion who joined the Volunteer reserve at this time included Joseph O'Connor and Seán O'Keeffe.
45 UCDA, Seán MacEntee Papers, P67/373(3), County Dublin by-election Speech at Swords, n. d. [October 1947].

political considerations had steered the government through hunger strike and execution, largely avoiding the pitfalls of martyrdom. There was one significant event, however, which had yet to be resolved: the German spy Hermann Goertz, his identity still unknown to the authorities, remained at large. Since the Held raid the previous May and Iseult Stuart's arrest, Goertz had been sheltered by a network of republican women, all of them faintly enamoured of the German spy. After Iseult's acquittal, it seems that Goertz returned to Laragh, where the two conducted a brief affair.[46] Although he had been put in touch with Stephen Hayes, Goertz retreated from the original scope of his mission – intelligence reports as well as liaising with the IRA north and south of the border to provide the German High Command with details of Allied military installations in Northern Ireland – and focused instead, by his own account, on a series of botched escape attempts by sea and on developing links with members of the Irish political establishment. These were augmented by Goertz's contacts with Major Niall MacNeill, intelligence officer of the 2nd Northern Division to whom he passed information gleaned from republican contacts on British military installations in Northern Ireland. Taken together with the apparent dialoguing of Nazi diplomat Henning Thomsen with Eoin O'Duffy and MacNeill's cousin and superior officer, Hugo MacNeill, this was a highly sinister development.[47] However, despite Goertz's dalliance with establishment figures, he had completely failed in his overall mission. As Mark Hull commented, 'he had not succeeded in directing ... IRA activity to Germany's advantage, and not managed to pass on a single report of any intelligence value – or even to set up a transmitter to make a situation report'.[48] Throughout 1941, in keeping with his initial reaction to Goertz's arrival, MacBride continued to give the spy a wide berth, focusing instead in the early months of the year on a case which remained with him for the rest of his life.

Murder at Marlhill

On 21 November 1940, Harry Gleeson, a farm labourer in Marlhill, near New Inn, Co. Tipperary, discovered the body of Moll Carthy. She had been murdered by two shotgun blasts to the head, the second blowing away the right side of her face. A large Garda operation was launched and, nine days later, Gleeson was arrested and charged with her murder. MacBride was engaged as junior counsel and the trial opened in Dublin on 17 February 1941. Gleeson was found guilty on 27 February; despite the jury's strong recommendation that mercy be exercised on the condemned man, a sentence of death was passed. Gleeson was hanged in Mountjoy Prison on 23 April, after leave to appeal had been refused and

---

46 A. Norman Jeffares, Anna MacBride White and Christina Bridgwater (eds.), *Letters to W. B. Yeats and Ezra Pound from Iseult Gonne: A Girl that knew all Dante once* (Basingstoke: Palgrave, 2004), pp. 152–3; *Sunday Independent*, 18 March 2007 and 31 May 2009.

47 Eunan O'Halpin, *Spying on Ireland: British Intelligence and Irish Neutrality during the Second World War* (Oxford: Oxford University Press, 2008), pp. 177–8. MacNeill's initial approach to Hempel appears to have been officially sanctioned by his military superiors, although in requesting a meeting with the IRA he was drastically contravening the entire ethos of the Irish Army. See also McGarry, *Eoin O'Duffy*, pp. 334–8.

48 Hull, *Irish Secrets*, p. 146.

the government had turned down a petition for reprieve signed by some seven thousand people.[49] The details of the case, which has been the subject of two modern investigations – Marcus Bourke's *Murder at Marlhill* and a 1995 television documentary entitled 'Mystery at Marlhill' – provide a revealing glimpse into the make-up of mid-century Irish society, where social transgressors occupied a liminal space beyond the protection of public respectability, and where the power of the local community to close ranks against both the transgressor and the outsider could result in two violent deaths.

Moll Carthy was the ultimate transgressor: born outside wedlock herself, she openly raised six illegitimate children in New Inn. Each of the children was born of a different local father; the progenitors of the first six children were widely known within the locality, helped by familial resemblances and by Moll Carthy's propensity to give her children names which clearly signalled their fathers' identities.[50] Moll Carthy's initial contravention of social norms was thus compounded by her refusal to hide herself and her children away, and in sending her children to the local school where she insisted that they were 'as good as the rest'. Although her cottage was regularly visited by a series of local men – including, apparently, Gardaí – attempts were systematically undertaken to drive her out of the local community. A parish priest condemned her from the altar; the Gardaí failed in an application to take her children into care; and, as early as 1926, her cottage was set on fire in a case of deliberate arson and attempted murder.[51] She remained in her cottage, however, living off a limited amount of state relief and primarily the kindness of neighbours – including Harry Gleeson, who brought her potatoes from time to time. Moll Carthy's continued presence in the community, therefore, as well as her ongoing 'open-house' policy to local men was an intolerable affront to the carefully regulated conventions of social interaction.

The prosecution case against Harry Gleeson presented his motive as a grubby but familiar combination of illicit sex and land hunger. Gleeson was nephew to the Caesars, a farming couple who had bought into the area of New Inn but who had no children of their own. Although Gleeson was 38 years old, he was utterly financially dependent on his uncle and his entire prospects were bound up with the inheritance of the farm.[52] Gleeson's position was common in rural Ireland throughout the twentieth century: grown men leading the lives of adolescent boys, waiting for their father or uncle to die before they could fully accede to manhood and its attendant privileges of marriage, financial independence, or even a room of one's own. Gleeson, it was alleged by the prosecution, was the father of Moll Carthy's seventh child – who had died aged six months – and, fearing that word would spread of this 'immoral association', which 'would probably deprive him of his probable inheritance of his uncle's farm', he lured Moll Carthy into a field where he was waiting with a shotgun.[53]

49   *Irish Times*, 18–28 February 1941, 19 and 24 April 1941.
50   Marcus Bourke, *Murder at Marlhill: Was Harry Gleeson Innocent?* (Dublin: Geography Publications, 1993), p. 102.
51   *Irish Times*, 5 February 1994.
52   Statement by Harry Gleeson, 25 November 1940, reproduced in Bourke, *Murder at Marlhill*, p. 108.
53   *Irish Times*, 18 February 1941.

The case, thus presented, was no doubt appealing to both judge and jury: a deferred and long-awaited inheritance, an outsider desperate to protect his prospects, and a red-headed 'loose woman'. But the state case had significant inconsistencies, primarily relating to the time of death. Moll Carthy's body temperature indicated that she had been killed on the morning of 21 November not, as alleged, on the evening of 20 November; and no whisper of Gleeson's paternity had ever reached local ears, normally well attuned to such scandal. Moreover, evidence which suggested that the victim had been shot elsewhere and carried to the field in question – lack of blood underneath the head of the deceased, bloodstains on the inside of her clothes which had no corresponding external marks, and dry grass under the body even though it had been raining heavily on the evening of 20 November – were not adequately addressed by the prosecution.[54]

MacBride, to his credit, raised all these points during the course of the defence case, but struggled in the face of near constant interruptions from a hostile judge and a plainly partisan charge to the jury. More sinisterly, MacBride later wrote that 'because most of the people of New Inn were in some way involved with [Moll Carthy], they entered into a conspiracy of silence'.[55] This conspiracy of silence manifested itself in a host of local people refusing to testify on Gleeson's behalf – even the parish priest declined to give a character reference – and widespread obstruction of Gleeson's legal team in their attempts to build a case. This latter was encouraged by local Gardaí, who intimidated witnesses who might have been considered friendly to the accused. More than a conspiracy of silence, however, Marcus Bourke has demonstrated the existence of an active conspiracy to frame Harry Gleeson for the murder of Moll Carthy, a plot in which local people and the Gardaí connived.[56] Although Gleeson had been living in the locality for twenty years, he remained an outsider, and as such was a convenient scapegoat on whom to pin the murder, which had probably been carried out by two, or even three, men on the morning of 21 November. MacBride's draft closing speech to the jury included the observation that Moll Carthy was 'the victim of a perverted sense of morality bred by a civilisation which, nominally based on Christianity, lacks most of its essentials'; Harry Gleeson was another victim of that same perversion, when the people among whom he had lived for two decades firmly turned their backs on the stranger in their midst.[57]

On the eve of the execution, MacBride visited Gleeson in the condemned cell in Mountjoy and afterwards wrote a moving account of the meeting:

> [Gleeson] asked me to let his uncle and aunt and friends know that he did not mind at all dying, as he was well-prepared, and that that he would pray for them as soon as he reached heaven. He was quite calm and happy ... At the end of the interview he stood up and said: 'The last thing I want to say is that I will pray tomorrow that whoever did it will be discovered, and that the whole thing will be like an open book. I rely on you, then, to clear my name.'

54 *Irish Independent*, 21–2 February 1941.
55 Bourke, *Murder at Marlhill*, p. 87.
56 Bourke, *Murder at Marlhill, passim*.
57 *Irish Times*, 5 February 1994.

Gleeson was hanged at dawn the following morning but he remained in MacBride's thoughts for more than thirty years. It had been the first non-political capital case in which MacBride had been professionally involved, and his unswerving belief in the innocence of his client made this case radically different from the political and constitutional cases to which he had been accustomed, and which often hinged on a jury's interpretation of obscure legal technicalities. Equally, Harry Gleeson's simple and unwavering insistence on his innocence contrasted starkly with the sullenly defiant IRA prisoners whom MacBride so often represented.

MacBride's fixation on the Gleeson case was reinforced by his political associ-ation with John Timoney, Gleeson's solicitor, who was elected for Clann na Poblachta in 1948; as party colleagues, the two men often discussed the case, teasing out new theories and new interpretations of evidence which had become imprinted on their minds.[58] The Gleeson case was clearly on MacBride's mind on 21 November 1951 when he introduced an unsuccessful motion to Dáil Éireann for the abolition of the death penalty:

> I know from my own experience that certainly in one case, not a political case, in which I was involved as a lawyer, I had grave doubts as to the accused man's guilt. These doubts have been greatly intensified since, but nothing can be done. It is too late.[59]

While Harry Gleeson's reputation has been somewhat restored by those who reinvestigated the circumstances of the case, and those who, like MacBride, never stopped believing in his innocence, an even more poignant postscript to the case was the committal to industrial schools of four of Moll Carthy's children who had not attained their majority.[60] Their only 'crime' was their illegitimacy and the murder of their mother.

'That spiritless creature'[61]

As the body of Harry Gleeson was laid in quicklime in the yard of Mountjoy, MacBride's momentary diversion from the fluctuations of republican politics came shudderingly to an end. From the spring of 1941, a series of events around the Chief of Staff Stephen Hayes engulfed the IRA in a 'Dostoyevskian world of suspicion' and paralysed it as an effective organisation for the remainder of the year.[62] The roots of the Hayes affair lay in the heightened efficiency of Special Branch in successfully targeting IRA operations and the huge increase in numbers of IRA members in government custody. To a group of northern IRA officers, this pointed irrefutably to a government informer within IRA GHQ. That Hayes remained at large, despite his haphazard approach to his personal security

---

58 C. T. O'Sullivan, 'The IRA takes constitutional action: a history of Clann na Poblachta, 1946–65', MA Thesis (UCD, 1995), p. 22; Bourke, *Murder at Marlhill*, p. 106.

59 *Dáil Éireann Debates*, vol. 127, col. 1165, 21 November 1951.

60 *Irish Times*, 10 May 1941.

61 Tom Doran on Stephen Hayes, quoted in MacEoin, *The IRA in the Twilight Years*, p. 499.

62 Richard English, *Armed Struggle: The History of the IRA* (London: Pan, 2004, first published 2003), p. 53.

and his chronic alcoholism, meant that the shadows of suspicion fell heavily on him. This cabal – Seán McCaughey, Liam Rice, Pearse Paul Kelly and Charlie McGlade – moved into the Dublin organisation, forced Hayes to appoint them to GHQ positions, and began gathering evidence as to his treachery.

Riven by distrust, the IRA proceeded to tear itself asunder. By June, convinced of his guilt, Hayes was arrested by his fellow officers and taken to a series of safe houses in Louth, Wicklow and Dublin where, after protracted interrogation, he was court-martialled and found guilty of conspiring with the Irish government to impede the progress of the IRA and of treachery against the latter organisation.[63] Sentenced to death and desperate to buy time, Hayes began writing his notorious 'confession', a 140-page document which satisfied his captors' every suspicion of his collusion with members of the government and placed the blame for every travail and setback the IRA had suffered – the bombing campaign, the Magazine Fort raid, the bomb at Dublin Castle, even the murders of Gardaí – at their feet, and, particularly at the feet of ministers James Ryan and Tomás Derrig.

Hayes's desperation provided him with fathomless inspiration, and the confession soon turned into an interminable, imaginative arabesque, as Hayes drew on old associates and casual acquaintances from his GAA past to fill the pages. But the document was risible, as much as for its content as for the circumstances under which it was produced. The northern IRA group appear to have been taken aback by the evident scale of the conspiracy revealed in Hayes's confession, and they were slow to decide on a course of action. Seeking counsel from more experienced hands, McCaughey brought parts of the confession to MacBride and Moss Twomey, who clarified details and advised caution. MacBride, in particular, was suspicious of the confession, but instead of viewing it as the desperate act of a desperate man, he saw the hidden hand of the British Secret Service therein, an even more convenient scapegoat for all the vicissitudes which had befallen the IRA since the Russell takeover. Publication of the confession, a move towards which IRA GHQ was already leaning, was discouraged by MacBride: it would, he said, be dangerous to the IRA and useless in terms of discrediting Fianna Fáil.[64] And in the interim, Hayes kept writing.

As the prisoner filled his foolscap pages, another IRA Volunteer faced the firing squad: on 9 August Richard Goss, a 26-year-old from Dundalk, was executed at Portlaoise Prison. He had been convicted before the Special Military Court for shooting at military in County Longford. MacBride, who represented Goss at trial – another indication of the confused IRA policy regarding recognition of the courts – raised the possibility that the wounded soldiers could have been hit in crossfire between police and military; that Goss had not shot a third soldier whom he had captured inside the farmhouse before firing began, and that he had only fired his revolver on hearing the order 'shoot to kill' given to the police

---

63 NLI, MS 33706/2, IRA papers, Special Communiqué issued by the IRA Army Council, 10 September 1941. See also Stephen Hayes, 'My strange story', parts I and II, *The Bell*, vol. xvii, nos 4 and 5 (July–August 1951).

64 M. Meehan, *Finely-tempered Steel: Seán McCaughey and the IRA* (Dublin: Republican Publications, 2007), p. 31; J. Bowyer Bell, *The Secret Army: the IRA* (New Brunswick: Transaction Publications, 2004, first published 1970), p. 208.

and military might also have indicated that this affair was very different from the previous shoot-out on the Rathgar Road.[65] A verdict of guilty was nonetheless returned on Goss and he was sentenced to death. A somewhat muted campaign for clemency was mounted, noticeably less vociferous than previous instances, although the circumstances of Goss's conviction might have been expected to produce some public disquiet.[66] Goss's execution, and the determination of the government to press ahead with an execution even on a relatively minor charge indicates that a new level of determination had been scaled in the campaign to break the IRA as a force in Irish political life. The latter part of the year and the early months of 1942 would see these efforts redoubled, as the very fundamentals of law were set aside to crush the illegal organisation.

On 8 September 1941, the hidden world of double-dealing, brutality and despair, which had been poisonously fermenting since the arrest of Stephen Hayes, imprinted itself upon the public consciousness when Hayes's shackled, manacled and bruised figure lurched into Rathmines Garda Station.[67] Once Hayes had reached the sanctuary of Garda custody, the delicately constructed edifice of the IRA, already built on hollow foundations, rapidly entered a state of total collapse. Large-scale raids and arrests ensued, with most of Hayes's captors taken into custody. More seriously, Hayes's willingness to testify against McCaughey, who had been arrested three weeks earlier when a Special Branch detective recognised him on a Dublin tram, confirmed Hayes's readiness to cooperate with the hated Special Branch and proved him as a traitor. The trial was a sensation, laying bare the inner turmoil of the IRA to a horrified Irish public; Hayes appeared in the witness box – pale, uncomfortable, and still bearing the bruises of his interrogation – across the court from the faintly smiling McCaughey, making the latter's conviction for false imprisonment a foregone conclusion.[68]

But the perniciousness of the Hayes confession applied as much to public confidence in the government as to the morale of the IRA itself. Despite all the successes of the previous year in determinedly pursuing IRA offenders and applying the strictest possible penalties to those convicted before drastically strengthened courts, the Hayes confession threatened to undermine all that had gone before; as the *Round Table* pointed out, 'that it should be possible for such an illegal organisation to carry on its fell work without detection, in the manner described by Hayes, and for circumstantial charges of collusion in its activities to be made against individual Ministers and the Government, is most disquieting'.[69] Although MacBride and others had urged caution, IRA GHQ decided to circulate the confession widely among TDs, Senators and prominent public figures.

65 *Anglo-Celt*, 9 August 1941; MacEoin, *The IRA in the Twilight Years*, pp. 529–30.
66 NAI, D/T, S12127 Richard M. Goss Reprieve Petitions; 'Irish developments and difficulties', *Round Table*, vol. xxxii, no. 125 (December 1941), p. 105.
67 *Irish Times*, 30 December 1974.
68 *Time Magazine*, 29 September 1941. McCaughey was sentenced to death by firing squad; this was later commuted to life imprisonment, to be served at Portlaoise Prison. Although McCaughey refused to recognise the court and all legal representation, MacBride visited him several times in prison prior to the trial, with Con Lehane BL and Cecil Lavery SC. *Irish Times*, 19 September 1941
69 'Irish developments and difficulties', *Round Table*, vol. xxxii, no. 125 (December 1941), p. 107.

Thus, even before court proceedings began, knowledge of its contents, and the charges against the government, was widespread. The authorities were obliged to issue a categorical denial, which had the effect of further piquing public interest in the affair: 'Fantastic though these allegations are, the Government and Ministers named in the document think it well to state categorically that they are wholly untrue and without any shadow of foundation.'[70] Despite these and other denials – Ministers Ryan and Derrig later appeared at the trial of Stephen Hayes for usurping a function of the government to deny in person the allegations against them – the belief persisted among some quarters, not all of them republican in outlook, that Hayes was indeed a government agent.[71] But whereas Hayes continued to maintain until the end of his life that he had never been a government agent – certainly the five-year sentence he received makes it even more unlikely – it appears certain that shortly after he staggered into Rathmines Garda Station, he gave the authorities information which led, on 10 September 1941, to the discovery of the body of Michael Devereux and to the most extraordinary legal manoeuvres in the history of the State.

The Michael Devereux Case

Around the time of the executions of Patrick McGrath and Thomas Harte, another, more secret execution was taking place. Michael Devereux, a 24-year-old lorry driver and IRA member from Wexford, was lured from his home on the night of 23 September 1940, drove his executioners to a safe house in Tipperary and, early the following morning, was shot in the head on the slopes of the Knockmealdown Mountains. An IRA Garda agent had identified Devereux as an informer, whereas Gerry Boland affirmed that 'he had no connection with the police at all'; the more likely scenario is that Devereux 'had got a bad roughing up from detectives after arrest and gave something away in his confusion and fear'.[72] Normal IRA procedure does not appear to have been followed in Devereux's execution: he was not informed of the charge against him and he was not court-martialled. As a Justice official commented, 'to add to the horror he was done to death, without being given any opportunity to see a priest, by a man who had shared his bed for the previous three nights while professing to be his friend and comrade'.[73] Devereux was buried under a cairn of stones on the mountainside, his fate never communicated to his widow. Devereux's body lay undisturbed for almost a year until, in the aftermath of Hayes's escape from his captors, both his dismantled lorry and his body were discovered by a team of Gardaí.[74] The coincidence of these two events

---

70 *Irish Press*, 3 October 1941.
71 David Gray evidently harboured some doubts: see 'Behind the green curtain', chapter XVII.
72 *Irish Times*, 'Gerry Boland's Story – 9', 17 October 1968.
73 NAI, S11534A, IRA Activities in Ireland, 1939–1950, 'Memorandum on the policy of the government with regard to Offences Against the State'. Michael Moroney, 'George Plant and the rule of law: the Devereux affair, 1940–1942', *Tipperary Historical Journal* (1988), pp. 1–12. Plant was a Protestant, a fact perhaps reflected in the Justice memorandum's lamentations that Devereux was sent to his death unshriven.
74 *Irish Independent*, 4 October 1941.

led many contemporary observers to conclude that Hayes gave the Gardaí details of the Devereux murder.[75]

Once Devereux's body had been discovered, four men were taken into custody: George Plant, Joseph O'Connor – an IRA officer who passed on the order for the execution – Michael Walsh and Patrick Davern. Davern and Walsh both made statements to Gardaí detailing the whole affair; these statements were expected to form the basis of the prosecution case against Plant and O'Connor, charged with murder and procuring murder respectively, and Walsh and Davern were listed as witnesses for the state. Inside Mountjoy, however, untold pressures were brought to bear on both men; Pearse Paul Kelly, recently arrested, recalled that the two

> were now suffering remorse of conscience ... We had a long discussion on their problem and the relevant instructions I had sent them after their arrest. The outcome was that they agreed to give the appearance of standing by their statements until they were put into the witness-box at Plant's trial, and then they would withdraw and disown the statements.[76]

At the ensuing trial of Plant and O'Connor, MacBride as counsel for the accused, indicated that his defence strategy would rest on establishing whether Devereux had in fact been a police agent, a tack swiftly rejected: 'the Court could not hold that as justification for murder'.[77] Establishing Devereux as an informer might have gained some ground in an ordinary trial by jury, where the old distaste might have procured if not an acquittal, then leniency; such tactics were, however, unlikely to succeed in the Special Criminal Court. The case collapsed sensationally when Walsh, Davern and a third witness, Simon Murphy, refused to testify, claiming that their statements had been extracted by force. It was a bold ploy on the part of the IRA, and for a brief moment it seemed as though they had out-manouevred the state.

But the government reacted swiftly and more decisively than the republican movement could have imagined. A *nolle prosequi* was entered for Plant and O'Connor, but the two defendants were immediately charged again with the murder of Devereux, along with Walsh and Davern. Under Emergency Powers (No. 41F) Order, the case was immediately transferred to the sterner location of the Military Court; more crucially, the government issued Emergency Powers (No. 139) Order which allowed unsworn, unsigned statements to be admitted as evidence in a court of law, regardless of whether the author of the statement should give evidence or not. It further provided that 'if, on any occasion during the trial before a court to which this order applies, the court considers it proper that it should not be bound by any rule of evidence, whether statutory or at common law, the court shall not be bound by such rule'.[78] This was an unprecedented step, altering at a stroke the basis of law as it had been practised in Ireland. MacBride

75 NAI, D/T S12741, Memorandum to Government, 7 November 1945; Moroney, 'George Plant and the rule of law', pp. 5–6.
76 *Irish Independent*, 'Pearse Paul Kelly – Doing My Time Part II', 21 January 1969.
77 *Irish Times*, 10 December 1941.
78 Emergency Powers (No. 139) Order, quoted in Ó Longaigh, *Emergency Law in Independent Ireland*, pp. 262–3.

quickly launched a legal challenge, seeking habeas corpus and prohibition from trial first in the High Court and then the Supreme Court. Appearing with Cecil Lavery, MacBride submitted that

> a Military Court – whose appointment was at the hands of a political executive, and subject to the whims of a political executive – vested with powers of life and death over others, without trial under any rule of law or rule of evidence, was not in accordance with the object set out in the preamble to the Constitution: the common good.[79]

Without the normal rules of evidence, MacBride argued, the Military Court failed to constitute a judicial tribunal as envisaged in the Constitution and was therefore repugnant. The High Court rejected the arguments, albeit with a tinge of regret: Gavan Duffy noting that 'the Constitution had placed in the hands of the Oireachtas ... authority to suspend judicial control over the other organs of government ... the applicants had come for relief to a Court which had no power to give them relief'.[80] The Supreme Court also refused their appeal; the long-adjourned trial could begin. The failure of MacBride's arguments – erudite in places and closely reasoned – must have been a bitter blow: it might have been expected that the Supreme Court would have been induced to uphold the centuries of legal tradition, which were suspended by the government's order. In rejecting their arguments, the High Court and Supreme Court intimated that, notwithstanding the monstrous encroachment into individual liberties and the rule of law represented by the order, the ultimate law invoked by de Valera in 1940 took precedence.

There was a possibility, however, that the Oireachtas might have provided a mechanism to revoke the order. After the Supreme Court judgement had been delivered, William Norton, leader of the Labour Party, proposed a motion to annul the order: he argued that if such rules of law were to be applied to previous cases in Irish history, then not only the Hayes confession but also the Parnell forgeries would have had to be accepted as fact. Attacking the Military Court in terms not dissimilar to MacBride, Norton described it as 'composed entirely of Army officers who have no legal training and do not purport to have legal training and that is a particularly undesirable type of court to equip with wider powers than are given to highly-trained judges'. Although temperamentally minded to support the government in measures against the IRA, Fine Gael were also perturbed by what had unfolded, John A. Costello commenting that the order 'had shocked both lawyer and layman.' But Boland was unrepentant, bluntly exposing the hard-line government policy:

> Are we to allow crimes to go uninvestigated, are we to allow people to laugh at us and say: 'We will kill whom we like'? I will not stand for that, and the Government will not stand for it... We have to stop [the IRA]; we have to throttle this thing and put it down.[81]

79 *Irish Times*, 15 January 1942.
80 Irish Law Reports, [1942] IR, p. 119.
81 *Dáil Éireann Debates*, vol. 85, col. 1460ff, 28 January 1942.

The mark had been laid down, and the motion failed. At the ensuing eleven-day trial, in which the judicial powers under the new order were invoked, the statements by Walsh and Davern were accepted as evidence. MacBride battled hard for his clients despite the most insurmountable of legal obstacles; in a complimentary account the *Irish Times* described him as having 'maintained a straight fight to the end'.[82] After 45 minutes' deliberation, the Military Court returned a verdict: O'Connor was acquitted (but immediately rearrested and interned) while Plant, Walsh and Davern were all found guilty and sentenced to death by shooting. The sentences for Walsh and Davern were later commuted, but Plant's stood. He was transferred to Portlaoise Prison on 4 March, allegedly with his coffin alongside him in the back of the lorry, where MacBride observed the calmness with which he prepared himself for death: 'he was a particularly nice fellow and seemed to have no fear. The night before his execution he sat up reading, completely composed all night, and went to his death wearing his best suit.'[83] Plant's family, not having been notified, learned of his death on the radio.[84]

'There is no organisation now, it is all broken up'[85]

Plant's execution closed a chapter in the most disastrous development from the IRA's perspective since the Emergency had begun. The suspicions engendered by the Hayes confession, as well as the subsequent government crackdown, led to the almost entire collapse of the organisation in southern Ireland. A further blow had been dealt to wider IRA plans when Herman Goertz was finally arrested in November 1941. In focusing on building links with military and political figures, Goertz had remained somewhat aloof from both the IRA – whose new, tight-lipped northern leadership rather frightened him – and from the series of equally inept spies the *Abwehr* had sent to Ireland in what increasingly appeared to be self-sabotage missions. One, Ernst Weber-Drohl, a former circus strongman who had fathered two children in Ireland on a previous visit, is believed to have contacted MacBride. Carole Carter identified MacBride as MB in Hempel's coded telegrams: 'very anti-British and reliable, yet retains strong sympathies for France and had contacts with the French embassy'.[86] This contact, if indeed it existed, must have been kept to a minimum: throughout the war, MacBride demonstrated a whole-hearted reluctance to associate, openly or otherwise, with German spies of any kind, preferring instead a policy of *attentisme*. When Pearse Paul Kelly, who inherited the shattered IRA after the Hayes debacle, planned to travel to Germany on an arms mission, MacBride and Twomey expressed their disapproval, a position

82   *Irish Times*, 27 February 1942.
83   MacBride quoted in Tim Pat Coogan, *The IRA*, third edn (London: Harper Collins, 1995, first published 1971), p. 158; Pierce Fennell quoted in MacEoin, *The IRA in the Twilight Years*, p. 572. NAI, D/T S 12741
84   Moroney, 'George Plant and the rule of law', p. 11.
85   Response made by Patrick Murphy when charged with membership of an illegal organisation. *Weekly Irish Times*, 18 October 1941.
86   Carole Carter, *The Shamrock and the Swastika: German Espionage in Ireland in World War II* (Palo Alto, California: Pacific Books, 1977), p. 209.

also partly attributable to their rightful distrust of the mercurial Goertz.[87] Despite MacBride and Twomey's reluctance to engage openly with espionage agents, both were still being watched carefully by G2 throughout 1941 and 1942. An undated memorandum recorded:

> The Germans require an organisation headed by men of some standing, past or present in the IRA, to work for a complete sell-out to Germany in the event of an invasion of England. To this end, five have been invited to form a new emergency executive of the IRA. Four of the five are Maurice Twomey, Padraig MacLogan, Seán MacBride and Con Lehane. The name of the fifth man is not known.[88]

An annotation to this memorandum noted that: 'MacBride is of more importance than is generally known.'[89] Despite his most strenuous efforts over the previous three years, MacBride had still not managed wholly to establish his legitimate, democratic credentials. His legal representation of the IRA maintained his position as a 'mob lawyer', tolerated within the political system but never really part of it. Over the coming year, however, MacBride would begin the process of truly disentangling himself from the IRA and its associations with Nazi Germany, and commence the related project of building a successful political career.

---

87 *Irish Independent*, 'Pearse Paul Kelly – Doing My Time Part I', 20 January 1969.
88 IMA, G2/X/0058, IRA General File, 1939–1943.
89 IMA, G2/X/0058, IRA General File, 1939–1943. Comments dated 11 September 1941.

9

'One of the Most Dangerous Men in the Country': 1942–1946

The latter half of the war years was a period of domestic stagnation and deter-mined, if blinkered, introspection for Irish political life, bearing out more force-fully the accuracy of F. S. L. Lyons's observation that Irish society was divorced from the 'fire of life'.[1] This isolation was as much moral as it was political, and was determined equally by the disinterest of the Irish public as it was by the crippling effects of the harsh censorship regime. But there is an important distinc-tion to be made between the Irish experience of war in its earlier and latter stages: whereas the years from the outbreak of war until the end of 1941 were character-ised by internal and external tensions, there initially was a certain vibrancy in Dublin, which revelled – albeit in a muted, Irish fashion – in its status as a neutral capital. John Betjeman, the British press attaché, wrote strikingly of his impres-sions in early 1941: 'And here neutrality, harps, art exhibitions, reviews, libels, backchat, high-tea, cold, no petrol, no light, no trains; Irish language, partition, propaganda, propaganda, propaganda, rumour, counter-rumour, flat Georgian facades – Guinness, double Irish single Scotch, sherry, censors, morals, rain home to all.'[2] By the end of the war, the privations forced by both rationing short-ages and Catholic prurience provided a visiting American soldier with a twisted rationale for Irish neutrality: 'no night clubs – no dancing girls – no wonder you're neutral, you've nothing to fight for'.[3]

Such contemporary accounts reinforce Brian Girvin's observation that 'a certain dullness fell upon the country once the threat of invasion or internal subversion had receded'.[4] The first period of the war was dominated by the dual menaces of IRA violence and seditious contact with German agencies, the latter of which threatened to precipitate a pre-emptive British invasion. The sense of crisis engen-dered by the external threats, both Allied and Axis, dissipated somewhat once the international focus switched from an expected German attack on Britain – which in some manner would have engulfed Ireland – to the Nazi invasion of the Soviet

---

1 F. S. L. Lyons, *Ireland since the Famine* (London: Fontana, 1982, first published 1972), p. 558.
2 Candida L. Green (ed.), *John Betjeman: Letters, Volume 1: 1926–1951* (London: Methuen Books, 1994), J. Betjeman to J. Piper, 10 January 1941.
3 As recalled by Patrick Lindsay, *Memories* (Dublin: Blackwater Press, 1992), pp. 77–8.
4 Brian Girvin, *The Emergency: Neutral Ireland, 1939–1945* (London: Macmillan, 2006), p. 235.

Union in June 1941.[5] Suddenly, Ireland's isolation was rendered even more starkly; those who had calculated their attitudes according to the likelihood of a German victory, MacBride among their number, were forced to reposition themselves in the new American dispensation which appeared certain to dominate post-war politics.

Just as the latter half of the war years has suffered somewhat historiographically by comparison with the more ostentatiously exciting preceding period, so do MacBride's activities lose something of the momentum of 1939–1941. The government crackdown on the IRA, coupled with the debilitating divisions engendered by the Hayes affair, meant that the organisation had entered a period of almost irreversible decline as an armed revolutionary movement. That such a decline had begun, however, should not be interpreted as signifying the end of the IRA as a potentially disruptive force within Irish political life; yet, such were the security and legislative framework in which it was operating that the possibility of mounting a sustained challenge to the state and its instruments had rapidly disappeared. Similarly, for MacBride, the high points of constitutional challenges to the emergency legislation were not to be repeated in this period.

Although his association with the IRA followed largely the same pattern which had been established in the earlier years of the war – representation before the courts, appearances at inquests and coordination of reprieve campaigns – these now assumed the character of sporadic, if forceful, self-contained episodes rather than a sustained agitation as a corollary to a wider political programme. The passions evoked by some of these interventions, for the most part, burned out swiftly, and it was not until the McCaughey inquest and the subsequent public outcry at the conditions in which the prisoner had been held that MacBride was in a position to capitalise politically on wider public disaffection with the government. This, nevertheless, does not suggest that MacBride regarded each of the campaigns and movements with which he was involved as ends in themselves; rather, it is possible from 1942 to trace a new enthusiasm for participation in the political sphere.

Republican Gaze Switches Northwards

The fallout from the Hayes affair had a highly corrosive effect on IRA morale in the south. Whether the Chief of Staff had indeed been a government agent or whether the entire affair had resulted from the paranoia of the northern cabal, neither possibility reflected well on the IRA. The noticeably hardened government attitude toward the organisation – strict emergency legislation and a new determination to see executions carried out – coupled with the traditional Special Branch harrying made the southern state a cold place for republicans. These circumstances, as well as the imprisonment of most of the southern leadership, contributed to a switch of focus within the IRA to operations north of the border. Within the republican mindset, there was a definite rationale to this development, particularly as US army personnel soon arrived to augment the 'foreign' troops

---

5 E. O'Halpin, *Spying on Ireland: British Intelligence and Irish Neutrality during the Second World War* (Oxford: Oxford University Press, 2008), pp. 162–3.

already resident in Northern Ireland. The newly militant attitude of the northern IRA soon expressed itself in violence: two RUC constables were shot dead over the Easter weekend in April 1942, one, Thomas Forbes, a father of ten children, the other a Catholic named Patrick Murphy. The IRA O/C, Thomas Williams, was also wounded.[6] During the course of the latter incident, which was intended as a diversionary operation to allow republican Easter parades proceed unmolested, six IRA men were arrested, later convicted of murder and duly sentenced to death.

Immediately, an enormous campaign for clemency mobilised north and south of the border, with MacBride as chairman of the southern committee. Almost 270,000 signatures were collected for a petition urging mercy, and a series of mass meetings were held in Dublin. In an address on 16 August 1942 in O'Connell Street, MacBride criticised the manner in which the trial had been conducted, claiming that

[of] 430 names of the panel of jurors for the trial, only forty were Catholics. That in itself is a sad commentary on how the jury panel is prepared in Belfast. Contrary to all legal usage, the Crown challenged the few Catholic jurors whose names were picked. It was a clear case of packing the jury.[7]

Such meetings attracted huge attendances; as Kathleen Lynn noted, '[it was] like old times to see that great crowd'.[8] The Dublin government fully supported the agitation for clemency, allowing extensive coverage of meetings, petitions and speeches in support of the condemned men, in stark contrast to the blanket restrictions which were placed on all previous attempts to mobilise public opinion around executions, hunger strikes, and the conditions in which republican prisoners were held. De Valera's last-minute appeal to Churchill to commute the sentences was the pinnacle of a hypocrisy which even outstripped that which had characterised the Barnes and McCormack campaign.[9] IRA prisoners in southern Ireland were subject to a much harsher judicial process than existed in the northern state. MacBride might have critiqued the process of jury selection in Belfast, but the Military Court in Dublin did not even have judges, let alone juries; and the execution of Richard Goss demonstrated that IRA volunteers did not have to commit murder to receive the death penalty, as was the case in Northern Ireland. On all of these grounds, de Valera's plea for clemency was thoroughly hollow. This endemic hypocrisy at the heart of the Irish political establishment did not go unnoticed: Frank MacDermott pointed out in *Time Magazine* that 'we claim an overriding right for Irish nationals to commit crimes of violence in British territory that would be punished with the utmost severity at home.'[10]

6 Public Record Office of Northern Ireland [PRONI], CAB 3A/78B, RUC War History (1) IRA Activities; Richard English, *Armed Struggle: A History of the IRA* (London: Pan, 2004, first published 2003), p. 68; Jim McVeigh, *Executed: Tom Williams and the IRA* (Belfast: Beyond the Pale Publications, 1999), pp. 26–8.
7 *Irish Press*, 17 August 1942. Other members of the committee included Roger McHugh, Con Lehane, Úna Stack, Kathleen Clarke, Kathleen Lynn and Jim Larkin.
8 Library of Royal College of Physicians, Kathleen Lynn Diaries, 16 August 1942.
9 T. P. O'Neill and Lord Longford, *De Valera* (Dublin: Gill & Macmillan, 1970), p. 399.
10 *Time Magazine*, 14 September 1942. See also Dónal Ó Drisceoil, *Censorship in Ireland, 1939–1945: Neutrality, Politics and Society* (Cork: Cork University Press, 1996), p. 240.

MacBride remained at the head of the reprieve campaign, cabling President Roosevelt – whose attention might have been expected to be elsewhere – that 'the execution of any of these men would be an outrage on justice and an affront to the Irish race at home and abroad'.[11] Addressing another crowd in the Mansion House on 'the background to this impending tragedy', he explained:

> Easter Sunday is a day of remembrance and observance by all shades of national opinion in Ireland. In Belfast the demonstrations were banned year after year. It was customary to create a diversion to distract police attention. On this occasion shots were fired harmlessly over a patrol car. The lads were followed into a house and were surrounded. Some came face to face with policemen and with drawn revolvers. Williams was shot probably before the policeman.[12]

In fact, Constable Murphy had been shot five times in the chest and abdomen, Williams receiving one wound to the leg; moreover, as O/C of the IRA unit, he accepted full responsibility for the murder once in custody.[13] Clemency was exercised: on 30 August five of the six men were reprieved, but the sentence on Thomas Williams, who had admitted responsibility, was allowed to stand. In sum, this represented a victory for the reprieve, but the campaign continued on to the execution day of Williams. After the 18-year-old 'added his young life to the army of martyrs for Ireland' early on 2 September, remembrance masses were held and shops and business closed across the southern state. Not all of these closures were voluntary: crowds smashed windows of businesses which remained open, and Gardaí were forced to draw their batons.[14]

The reprieve campaign provided a rallying point for all shades of nationalist opinion in Ireland and was also a possible mechanism through which nationalist Ireland could transfer any residual unease with de Valera's policy towards the IRA. In projecting all the dissatisfaction on to the northern authorities and, by extension, the British 'imperialist' state, nationalist Ireland was able to avoid examining her own record too closely. The IRA were keen to capitalise on the wave of popular sentiment which followed the execution of Williams, who soon became a 'lasting icon' of the republican movement. To this end, MacBride was approached by Hugh McAteer, O/C of the Northern IRA, to write an official account of Williams's life and execution.[15] Although MacBride declined the offer, his heading of the reprieve

---

11   *Irish Times*, 19 August 1942.

12   *Irish Press*, 28 August 1942.

13   PRONI, BELF/1/1/2/178/5, R v Cordner and others, Affadavit of Denis Edgar Coyle of the Royal Victoria Hospital, and Thomas Williams Statement, 7 April 1942. Other voices in the campaign included Henry Harrison, General Sir Hubert Gough, and Sir Shane Leslie. *The Times*, 17 August 1942; *Irish Independent*, 2 September 1942.

14   Library of Royal College of Physicians, Kathleen Lynn Diaries, 2 September 1942; Ó Drisceoil, *Censorship in Ireland*, p. 240; *Irish Times*, 3 September 1942.

15   A number of documents associating MacBride with the IRA leadership surfaced during the trial of Charles Kerins in 1944. One, dated 1 October 1942, read as follows: 'Brian O'Higgins's attitude is, as you say, surprising and difficult to understand. However, we now know that we need not depend on his cooperation in future and need waste no more time upon him. We are certainly discovering who our friends are. By all means ask "Sceilg" to undertake the work, and, if he refuses also, I feel sure that Seán MacBride will be only too happy to do it for us.' *Irish Times*, 5 October 1944. O'Higgins had earlier published a similar volume on

campaign helped to heighten his public profile. An indication that his stock was rising in some Irish political circles came when his name was included among a list of potential Labour candidates for the 1942 local elections, held in August. MacBride's name was not put forward, but Labour's willingness to consider so republican-minded a candidate was part of a wider willingness at party level to engage with the republican constituency, attributable partly to the influx of former Communist Party of Ireland members after December 1941.[16] In the absence of any real inclination on the part of Fine Gael to fundamentally criticise the government's policies vis-à-vis the IRA, Labour were increasingly the voice of opposition, expressing unease with particularly the hard-line approach on prisoner issues and reprieve campaigns. This policy was evidently attractive to voters: Labour's vastly improved performance at the local elections indicated the beginnings of voter dissatisfaction with Fianna Fáil after ten years of unbroken government and the wartime hardship began to tell, and provided a hint of the gains to come in the following year's general election.[17]

Differing Fortunes in the 'Terror Court'

The rush of feeling stirred up by the execution also provided something of a fillip to the IRA both north and south, although neither proved capable of capitalising on it. In Northern Ireland, as the date of the executions approached, a police raid uncovered a large stash of weapons and explosives in County Antrim; in the ensuing shootout an IRA member, Gerard O'Callaghan was killed. Undeterred by this setback, the IRA leadership issued a statement pledging to 'avail itself of the darkest moment in England's history to strike'[18] This statement was the spearhead of a new policy which was intended to concentrate on operations north of the border. Although some attacks were attempted, resulting in the murder of three further policemen, the northern campaign soon fizzled out into 'low-level brutality and largely directionless violence'.[19] In Dublin, although the IRA were still shattered by the debilitating fragmentation of the Hayes affair and heavily reduced in numbers, energies were similarly focused. The restoration of a sense of confrontation with the forces of the state, both northern and southern, brought

---

Barnes and MacCormack, the Coventry bombers. Sceilg, or J. J. O'Kelly, had been editor of the Catholic Bulletin and was one of the obstinate remnants of the Second Dáil. MacBride elaborated on what this cryptic letter meant in a letter to the *Irish Press*, 1 June 1946.

16 Niamh Puirséil, *The Irish Labour Party, 1922–1973* (Dublin: University College Dublin Press, 2007), p. 88. See also Dónal Ó Drisceoil, '"Whose emergency is it?" Wartime politics and the Irish working class', in Dónal Ó Drisceoil and Fintan Lane (eds.), *Politics and the Irish Working Class, 1830–1945* (Basingstoke: Palgrave, 2005), p. 275; and Charles McGuire, *Roddy Connolly and the struggle for Socialism in Ireland* (Cork: Cork University Press, 2008), pp. 171–89.

17 Brian Girvin, 'Politics in wartime: governing, neutrality and elections', in Brian Girvin and Geoffrey Roberts (eds.), *Ireland and the Second World War: Politics, Society and Remembrance* (Dublin: Four Courts Press, 2000), pp. 39–40; Cornelius O'Leary, *Irish Elections, 1918–77* (Dublin: Gill & Macmillan, 1979), p. 35.

18 *Irish Times*, 2 September 1942; Harry White and Uinseann MacEoin, *Harry* (Dublin: Argenta Publications, 1985), pp. 100–1.

19 English, *Armed Struggle*, p. 70.

a renewed viciousness to Irish politics for the remainder of the war years as well as providing MacBride with further platforms to disseminate his critique of government policy and his advocacy of a newly political republican agenda.

Unable to adhere to the GHQ decision to restrict IRA activities to operations in Northern Ireland, the Dublin leaders made a drastically ill-advised decision to target Detective-Sergeant Denis O'Brien, their chief adversary within Special Branch. Perhaps the best known of the 'Broy Harriers', former IRA members who joined the Garda Síochána after Fianna Fáil formed a government, O'Brien was closely associated with the old republican establishment: his brother, Paddy O'Brien had been O/C in the Four Courts, both brothers were 1916 and War of Independence veterans, and another brother was private secretary to Seán Lemass.[20] On the morning of 9 September 1942, three IRA gunmen lay in wait outside O'Brien's home in Rathfarnham; as he drove down the avenue on his way to work, they opened fire with rifles and a machine gun, killing the detective instantly. O'Brien's close ties to senior figures within Fianna Fáil's republican past and present meant that his murder was not only an attack on the preservation of law and order in the state, but a personal blow to many members of the government.

This murder marked a new low in the confrontations between the IRA and Special Branch since the war had begun: where previous killings had occurred during raids and shootouts, this 'deliberate and planned assassination' was testimony to a brutality which was increasingly coming to resemble a vendetta.[21] As well as instigating a new stage in the blood-feud between the IRA and the Gardaí, the murder of O'Brien provided a further opportunity for the de Valera government to demonstrate its unblushing double standards to IRA crimes inside and outside its jurisdiction. The press censor instructed Irish newspapers to describe the crime as murder wherever possible and the perpetrators as murderers, not gunmen. This, as Dónal Ó Drisceoil has shown, was in direct contradiction to the instructions issued less than a week previously, when the opposite terminology was ordered for coverage of the Williams execution. Hence the ostentatious *pietà* presented in the *Irish Times*, with an elaborate description of the dead man's wife cradling her husband's body in her arms, after an operatic account of the murder, prompting David Gray's scornful comment that 'murder by the IRA is murder only in Eire and not when committed north of the border'.[22]

---

20   *Irish Times*, 11 September 1942. O'Brien featured in all of the IRA reverses and humiliations in recent years, from the Hayes debacle to the Devereux affair. As well as forming part of the Special Branch unit which raided Rathgar Road, resulting in the capture and subsequent execution of McGrath and Harte, he was also noted for his prowess in the interrogation room and his willingness to open fire on IRA suspects in the field: he was personally responsible for wounding Liam Rice and Charlie McGlade in recent engagements. White and MacEoin, *Harry*, p. 105; Conor Brady, *Guardians of the Peace* (Dublin: Gill & Macmillan, 1974), p. 237; Michael Moroney, 'George Plant and the rule of law: the Devereux affair, 1940–1942', *Tipperary Historical Journal* (1988), pp. 5–6.

21   Brady, *Guardians of the Peace*, p. 237; Eunan O'Halpin, *Defending Ireland: The Irish State and its Enemies since 1922* (Oxford: Oxford University Press, 1999), pp. 249–50.

22   Gray memorandum on Censorship in Ireland, quoted in Ó Drisceoil, *Censorship in Ireland*, p. 240; *Irish Times*, 10 September 1942.

A catalogue of ugly incidents followed the O'Brien murder, as police intensified efforts to arrest the chief suspects. In Cavan, a raid on a wedding house resulted in the deaths of IRA Volunteer Patrick Dermody and Detective Michael Walsh. A second IRA man, Harry White, escaped injured.[23] The death list further increased on 24 October after another shootout in Donnycarney. This time, Detective George Mordaunt was killed. Harry White again escaped, but Maurice O'Neill was captured. This was an unprecedented series of events: despite the long-standing bitterness between the IRA and the Gardaí, the murder of three policemen in the space of two months evoked memories of an earlier struggle against another force, something the government was determined to avoid. Such heightened domestic tensions – with a general election expected the following year – explain the virulence with which O'Neill was prosecuted in the Military Court. He was charged not with the murder of Detective Mordaunt but with 'firing at detectives with intent to resist arrest'. It was a most unpropitious time to be facing such a charge; not only was the murder of Mordaunt uppermost in the mind of the government and the Court, but the killers of O'Brien had yet to be apprehended. O'Neill was certainly aware of the odds against him, writing to his brother:

> I suppose you saw in the papers that I met my Waterloo last Saturday night. Well, such are the fortunes of war ... I am to be tried under Emergency Powers (41.G). That is a bloodthirsty Bill, there is only one sentence – death or release, so I believe it is the full penalty now for me. There is no good having false hopes, hard facts must be faced.[24]

With less than three days to prepare a defence for a death charge, MacBride gamely represented O'Neill, basing the defence around the suggestion that the police fired the first shot and that O'Neill was merely acting in self-defence. In an unusual move for an IRA defence, O'Neill was put on the stand, giving blunt evidence that his IRA unit was preparing to travel to the North and that the gun he carried was for training purposes only.[25] In MacBride's closing address, he made a final plea for clear heads on the precise nature of O'Neill's charge. 'Everybody deeply regrets the tragedy which resulted in Detective Mordaunt's death and everyone prays that we will be spared similar tragedies,' he said,

> At times, during the cross-examination of the prisoner I felt that conviction was being sought for this and for other tragedies. But the more the court is deeply shocked by the death of Detective Mordaunt the more scrupulously careful it must be not to allow this consideration to weigh against the prisoner.[26]

Such considerations, however, could have no effect on the outcome of the trial. O'Neill had been charged with firing at detectives, that charge had not been disproven, and any charge before the Military Court carried the death penalty. Despite Harry White's recollection that there were 'no efforts made for reprieve or

23   *Irish Press*, 2 October 1942.
24   Maurice O'Neill to Seán O'Neill, 31 October 1942, quoted in MacEoin and White, *Harry*, p. 127.
25   *Irish Press*, 5 November 1942.
26   *Irish Times*, 6 November 1942.

protest meetings', a campaign emanating principally from O'Neill's native county Kerry did make its presence felt in the aftermath of his sentencing. As well as the North Kerry Old IRA, the Kerry County Board of the GAA and Kerry County Council, the South Kerry branch of Fianna Fáil also wrote in the strongest terms to plead for a reprieve.[27] O'Neill's humble origins seem to have had a particular purchase in stirring up county feeling on his behalf; the former Fianna Fáil TD for Kerry, Thomas J. O'Reilly, wrote to de Valera that 'O'Neill was a tool, a simple country "gom", who could neither sponsor nor direct any operation requiring leadership nor, if he had the attainments necessary for leadership, would he have his habitat in such a remote place as the townland of Letter in the parish of Cahirciveen.'[28] Old Fianna Fáil ties to Kerry, wrought in the bloody executions of the Civil War, weighed heavily with certain members of the Cabinet. As with all of the wartime executions, much personal pressure was brought to bear on Gerald Boland:

> I lost some of my oldest friends in Kerry at that time, and one very old friend, but I told him that although we hated the job, we couldn't allow Kerrymen to come up to Dublin and shoot at policemen. If I did that, then we would all have to carry guns.[29]

In the absence of any government inclination to commute the sentence, feelings in Kerry ran high on the night of the execution: Michael McInerney reported later that 'about 100 members of the LDF resigned, shots were fired at the Garda barracks in Tralee and shopkeepers closed their shops for the day'.[30] Despite the failure to secure clemency, and the subsequent execution of O'Neill, the reprieve campaign, with its overtly local focus, can be seen as a precursor to the much wider campaign for the reprieve of Charles Kerins two years later.

O'Neill's execution represented a professional low point for MacBride: he was the fifth IRA prisoner to be executed during the war, and the sixth client of MacBride. The government were still pursuing the IRA with vigour; the organisation itself showed no signs of modifying its policies in face of a transformed international context; and the long hoped-for German victory was becoming a distant prospect. In such a gloomy personal and professional context, therefore, the trial in January 1943 of Maurice Quille was a significant boost. Quille, another Kerry native, had quickly been identified as one of the chief suspects in the murder of Denis O'Brien, a crime for which, for the reasons outlined above, the government

---

27 National Archives of Ireland [NAI], D/T S13004, Maurice O'Neill Reprieve Petitions.

28 National Archives of Ireland [NAI], D/T S13004, T. J. O'Reilly to Eamon de Valera, 9 November 1942. Other appeals included one from the newly elected Eamon Donnelly, abstentionist MP for West Belfast wrote '[It took] 24 years to win Falls – for God's sake don't smash it – reprieve O'Neill.' In fact, Donnelly soon lost his seat, won in the emotive aftermath of the Williams execution, to the Northern Ireland Labour Party, indicating a certain pragmatism on the part of the nationalist constituency of West Belfast. See Henry Patterson, *Ireland since 1939* (Oxford: Oxford University Press, 2002), pp. 34–5; Graham Walker, 'The Northern Ireland Labour Party, 1924–45', in Ó Drisceoil and Lane, *Politics and the Irish Working Class*, pp. 239–42.

29 *Irish Times*, 'Gerry Boland's Story – 9', 17 October 1968.

30 *Irish Times*, 'Gerry Boland's Story – 9', 17 October 1968.

was anxious to secure a conviction. In keeping with the IRA's professed intentions to focus activities north of the border, Quille was arrested in Belfast on 2 October 1942 and, in an effective example of unofficial extradition and the excellent working relationship then existing between the RUC and the Gardaí, was served with an exclusion order, brought to the border and deposited into the arms of the waiting Guards. The case built against Quille, on the surface, appeared strong: there were positive identifications from O'Brien's widow and another Garda, and Quille's connection with the IRA was established by the discovery of subversive material at a boarding house in which he had stayed. With such evidence, and the prospect of the case being heard in the forbidding environs of the Military Court, the state was confident that a conviction was forthcoming.[31]

But as the trial progressed, MacBride exposed major inconsistencies in the identification evidence: one witness claimed that Quille was clean-shaven at the time of the murder, another that he had a moustache; the identification parade was revealed to have been unfairly conducted (all witnesses were shown photographs of Quille beforehand); and there was conflicting testimony regarding the height of O'Brien's assassin (Quille was six feet tall; the man identified by a Garda was 5'7").[32] Crucially, MacBride was able to produce witnesses to testify to Quille's presence in Belfast on the day of the murder: appearing in camera after a pledge had been given that their names would not be passed to the RUC, Sara Malone, Maureen Malone and Mary McGuigan from the Falls Road gave evidence that Quille had been in Belfast on 9 September 1942 and for some time after.[33] There is a hint, however, that Quille's alibi was fabricated; Harry White, later tried on the same charge, remembered that 'the IRA had cobbled together a strong alibi for Quill [sic] and were determined to meet Free State subterfuge with their own'.[34]

It was an intensely frustrating case for the state: there had been at least twenty witnesses to the murder but such was the reluctance still present among the Irish public to testify against the 'illegal organisation', few were willing to come forward. As a chief superintendent commented, 'fear was a great brake on the tongue, and fear resulting from the shooting and from the background of it was operating in the minds of a lot of people who had been at Ballyboden that morning'.[35] MacBride's skilful handling of the evidence, including the testimony of three Garda chief superintendants, was enough to leave a significant doubt in the mind of the Court, and on 20 January Quille was found not guilty. That Quille was immediately arrested on discharge and interned on the Curragh for the remainder of the war did not diminish the sense of jubilation felt within the republican movement; despite appearing in a 'terror court', with rules of evidence heavily stacked against him, MacBride had scored an important personal and professional victory.

31 NAI, D/T S 13075, Statement from the Chief State Solicitor regarding trial of Michael Quille, 4 January 1943.
32 NAI, D/T S 13075, Record of Proceedings of the trial of Michael Quille, 20 January 1943.
33 White and MacEoin, Harry, p. 129. The women received extensive coaching beforehand in Con Lehane's office on Ormond Quay.
34 White and MacEoin, Harry, p. 129.
35 Irish Press, 15 January 1943.

Reorganising the Republican Movement

Stung by the local elections results of 1942 – in Dublin alone Fianna Fáil dropped from twelve seats to two – the government was reluctant to call the long awaited general election.[36] A number of parties were eager to see whether the gains in the previous year's local elections and a general popular discontent with the government – produced especially by wartime shortages, rationing and a highly unpopular wage freeze – would tell at the polls. The state of Irish politics was, therefore, as delicately poised as it had been for a decade, and a sense of new possibilities was in the air.[37] The republican movement was also sensitive to the new alignments currently taking shape within the Irish political establishment; although the tentative steps taken by the recently formed republican party Córas na Poblachta had not resulted in any gains at the local elections, from the spring of 1943 there was a definite trend towards political engagement which had been absent from the movement since the Russell takeover four years previously. Although private discussions must have been taking place for some time, the first public announcement of a *détente* regards political participation came with a one-day conference called by the National Association of the Irish Republican Army Old Comrades on 17 March 1943.[38] Attendees included representatives from the republican movement old and new – Peadar Cowan, Seán Dowling, Maureen Buckley, Roger Sweetman, Roger McCorley, Con Lehane and Mick Fitzpatrick – as well as representatives of the Labour Party. A standing committee was elected at the conference, comprising MacBride as Chairman, Dónal O'Donoghue and May Laverty as Secretaries, and Roger McHugh and Luke Duffy as Honorary Treasurers. The last name is most significant: Duffy was the current secretary of the Labour Party. His attendance at the conference and his nomination as an officer of the standing committee arguably indicated some measure of official Labour approval for the initiative. Despite the readiness to consider political action, however, the conference retreated into the old republican platitudes. The 'minimum demands' adopted were:

- the restoration of a de facto Republic for the whole of Ireland
- the ending of partition under any form
- the economic freedom and social security of the people on the basis of the teaching of Pearse, Connolly and Lalor

36 *Dáil Éireann Debates*, vol. 89 col. 2357, 5 May 1943; see also Girvin, *The Emergency*, p. 241. One of the dangers of holding elections in wartime was the possibility of invasion in the interim period after the dissolution of the old Dáil and before new Dáil was summoned. To avoid this, a special Bill was introduced to adjourn the old Dáil, so as to keep it alive should there by any external threat. See General Elections (Emergency Provisions) Act, 1943 at www.irishstatutebook.ie/1943/en/act/pub/0011/index.htm (accessed 27 January 2009).

37 Michael Price, of the CPI faction within the Labour Party, predicted that the 1943 poll would be 'the most momentous general election since 1922'. Quoted in Puirséil, *The Irish Labour Party*, p. 99. See also Richard Dunphy, *The Making of Fianna Fáil Power in Ireland, 1923–1948* (Oxford: Clarendon Press, 1995), pp. 286–9.

38 *Irish Times*, 19 March 1943. This association appears to be distinct from the National Association of Old IRA. The personnel, alignments and activities of a number of old republican comrades organisations is an area which would merit further research.

- the efficient restoration of the Gaelic language as the language of the nation
and the efficient fostering of Gaelic games and culture
- the restoration and preservation of democratic institutions and the elimination
of bureaucracy and corruption from our public life.[39]

The first four objectives could be found on any republican wish-list since the
Civil War. More interesting, however, is the last demand, which can be considered a precursor to the staunchly anti-corruption, anti-'jobbery' stance of Clann
na Poblachta when it emerged three years later. Usually, this position is attributed
to the damaging fallout of the Locke's Distillery affair; that it was identified as a
policy platform of a new republican party in 1943 might indicate a further degree
of continuity between current and future republican initiatives.[40]

The conference, as well as MacBride's chairmanship, however, should not be
interpreted as a break from the violent strand of republicanism represented by
the IRA; rather, the illegal organisation was intimately associated with the strategies drawn up for this new approach. On 30 March 1943, Hugh McAteer wrote to
Charles Kerins that he was 'very pleased to see by the Press reports that a start has
been made in launching the new Republican party'. He further queried whether
'Seán McBride intends to implement the suggestions I made in my last dispatch,
re contesting of certain seats and attitude of non-hostility towards Labour in
other areas'.[41] The accommodationist attitude towards other parties revealed in
this letter is an interesting development in the hitherto self-absorbed mentality
of extreme republicanism. Subsequent letters between GHQ members McAteer
and Charlie Kerins reveal a more sustained process of reflection and dialogue on
electoral affairs, in a manner unthinkable for the staunchly 'non-political' IRA in
previous years:

> I have come to the conclusion that it would be inadvisable to put forward a
> Republican candidate [in Kerry], as this would split the anti-Fianna Fáil votes,
> with the result that the Fianna Fáil candidates would be re-elected. The present
> Labour and Farmer candidates, though not members of the Army, have very
> sound Republican principles.

MacBride was also involved in this dialectic, apparently expecting a visit from 'the
chief Labour man [in Kerry] – Dan Spring – ... in connection with the formation
of a Republican Party branch'.[42] From the republican point of view, the rationale
for electoral cooperation was simple:

> All the parties have the blood of Republican martyrs on their hands but Fianna
> Fáil are the worst. They murdered Republicans in the name of Republicanism
> and stooped to meaner methods than were ever used by the first Free Staters
> or the English. On that account we want to see them kicked out no matter what
> party takes their place.[43]

39 *Irish Times*, 19 March 1943.
40 On the Locke's Distillery affair, see Eithne MacDermott, *Clann na Poblachta* (Cork: Cork
University Press, 1998), pp. 41–3.
41 *Irish Times*, 5 October 1944. This was another of the documents revealed during the Kerins
trial.
42 *Irish Times*, 5 October 1944.
43 NAI, D/T S 11534A, IRA Activities in Ireland, 1939–1950, copy of *Republican News*, June

The position of Labour regarding the new republican political initiative is equally intriguing, and one which the most recent generation of Labour historians have relatively neglected, concentrating instead on internal party divisions and the strength of the hard-left faction.[44] The possibility that high-ranking members of the Labour Party were engaged in what amounts to electoral cooperation with the republican movement at a time when the party, as a whole, was still unprepared to countenance supporting a Fine Gael government might cast a different light on traditional interpretations of the dynamics and allegiances of party politics in the years preceding the formation of the inter-party government.

The Repositioning of MacBride

During the election campaign, MacBride maintained his distance from Córas na Poblachta, who mismanaged the campaigns of their two best known candidates, Seán Dowling and Simon Donnelly (both well known Old IRA members), by running them in the same constituency, Dublin South.[45] He did, however, enter the fray on behalf of Seán MacCool, a former IRA Chief of Staff interned in the Curragh. Standing as an independent republican in East Donegal, MacCool's campaign played on his imprisonment in an attempt to replicate the success of Joe McGuinness almost thirty years earlier; indeed, a government offer of release on condition that he undertake 'not to take part in subversive activities during the period of his release' was refused.[46] A further attempt to manipulate the emotions of the Irish voting public was MacCool's decision to begin a hunger strike on 22 May. But the strictness of the censorship regime kept this fact out of the public domain until 10 June, when the barest of details relating to his candidature were published.[47] MacBride travelled to Donegal in June 1943 to canvass on MacCool's behalf; and his addresses to election meetings reveal more evidence of an unofficial electoral pact between the republican candidates and the Labour Party:

> Addressing a very large gathering in Letterkenny on Saturday night in support of Sean McCool ... Mr Sean McBride, Dublin, appealed for support for the labour candidate, Mr McElhinney, declaring that the Labour Party had stated definitively that they desired to see the country separated completely from England and re-organised on the basis of an Irish Republic, free from any entanglements with England. In addition, the Labour and Republican policies, so far as

---

1943. The same issue referred to Seán MacEntee as 'a ministerial corner-boy ... a skunk who disowned Pearse and Connolly and (in his court-martial in 1916) declared that but for being late for a train he would be in the British Army in France instead of being mixed up in what he called "that unfortunate insurrection".'

44 Puirséil, *The Irish Labour Party*; Ó Drisceoil, '"Whose emergency is it?"'.

45 Brian M. Walker (ed.), *Parliamentary Election Results in Ireland, 1918–92: Irish Elections to Parliaments and Parliamentary Assemblies at Westminster, Belfast, Dublin, Strasbourg* (Dublin: Royal Irish Academy, 1992), p. 156.

46 NAI, D/T S 1153A, IRA Activities in Ireland, 1939–1950, Memorandum on the policy of the government regarding Offences Against the State, p. 11.

47 *Irish Times*, 10 June 1943. Contrary to Dónal Ó Drisceoil's assertion, MacCool's status both as an internee and hungerstriker was permitted in the newspapers. Ó Drisceoil, *Censorship in Ireland*, p. 241.

economic matters were concerned, offered the same hope to the people of some escape from the ills of the moment and the ills that would obtain after the war ... Mr McBride said that Sean McCool was in prison without trial of any kind because his views were opposed to those of the government. He was now 28 days on hunger strike. He appealed to the electorate to place McCool at the head of the poll because he stood for a nationalism which all the other big parties had forgotten.[48]

In the event, MacCool and all the other republican candidates (including Córas na Poblachta) polled dismally, uniformly losing their deposits. But the two main parties also performed badly in the election: despite another catchy slogan ('don't change horses in midstream'), Fianna Fáil lost ten seats and its overall majority, while Fine Gael lost thirteen.[49] The beneficiaries were, overwhelmingly, Clann na Talmhan and Labour, both parties that appeared to endorse wider republican aims. New Labour TD Roddy Connolly, son of James, made explicitly clear Labour's electoral debt to the republican constituency in his maiden speech:

> it should be obvious to the Minister that the 80,000 extra votes which the Labour Party obtained at the election were, perhaps, due very largely to the fact that quite a number of Republicans, those with Republican traditions, had come over towards the Labour Party, and that their activities had resulted in that accretion of strength. Naturally, if that is so, the Labour Party must become responsive to this new impact on its political make-up.[50]

Labour was responsive to this new impact, arguing vigorously in the Dáil for the release of the hunger-striking prisoners, and setting a precedent for future advocacy of republican issues over the subsequent years.

In the aftermath of the election, MacBride wrote an extraordinary letter to the press, in which he publicly urged the government and the republican movement to 'make a solemn effort, if not reach an understanding, to at least avoid further conflict'.[51] What he viewed as 'essential factors of the present situation' present an insight into his developing political thought and gradual acceptance of both Irish neutrality and the de facto legitimacy of the southern state:

1. that normal political development is impossible until the national and territorial sovereignty of the Irish nation has been achieved;
2. that until the national and territorial sovereignty is achieved this part of the nation must be organised under some form of centralised authority;
3. That that central authority, if properly directed, provides the most effective machinery for the achievement of the national objective.
4. That, as far as this part of the country is concerned, in the present circumstances strict neutrality is the only possible policy, irrespective of the wishes of those who might desire otherwise – on either side.

---

48 University College Dublin Archives [UCDA], Seán MacEntee Papers, P67/542(18), report from *Derry Journal*, 21 June 1943.
49 O'Leary, *Irish Elections, 1918–77*, p. 35; Puirséil, *The Irish Labour Party*, p. 101.
50 *Dáil Éireann Debates*, vol. 91, col. 543, 9 July 1943.
51 *Irish Times*, 3 June 1946. Letter dated 10 July 1943.

The second and third components of this manifesto constitute a crucial shift in MacBride's political outlook: as we have seen, previous political initiatives with which he associated himself were firmly abstentionist, holding steadfast to the principle that the Free State institutions were illegitimate.[52] MacBride's acceptance of their legality was, however, somewhat grudging:

> entering the Dáil does not entail any acceptance of our present national status; the Dáil is merely the central authority under which the Twenty-Six Counties are, for the time being, organised, in the same way as a County Council is the authority charged with the administration of local affairs in a county.[53]

This limited acceptance certainly fell full short of his later claims that, from 1937, he fully supported a 'constitution which invested sovereignty in the people of Ireland'.[54] Despite his assertion that 'past responsibility matters little in this situation', MacBride also included a bitter critique of government policy since the outbreak of war:

> By suppressing all organs of Republican opinion, the Government drove the IRA underground; by destroying the constitutional liberty of the citizen and amending the law for that purpose, altogether apart from the emergency, the Government created a position wherein violence could only but increase; by needlessly ill-treating those it held prisoner ... it created a situation wherein acts of terror became inevitable; by herding hundreds of Republicans into camps like cattle in pens and leaving them there year after year, it destroyed hope and drove men to hunger strike in order to focus attention on their plight.

As well as criticising the failure of the government to include a republican representative in the all-party Defence Council, MacBride further castigated attempts to coax support from republicans through 'pensions, positions and preferments'. Finally, MacBride publicly urged McCool and his comrades to end their hunger strike, not before aiming a few darts at 'the decadence of our political life'.[55] This letter ought to have been the first public intervention MacBride had made in his own right – rather than as the legal representative of an IRA prisoner – since the beginning of the war, but it provoked the ire of Frank Aiken, minister responsible for administering censorship, particularly for suggesting that the Oireachtas was 'a mere County Council with no moral or constitutional right to govern'.[56] The letter was suppressed, finally appearing in print three years later.

In a sense, the letter is best viewed not as a critique of government policy *tout court*, but as an attempt by MacBride to establish his democratic credentials and,

---

52 Richard English, *Radicals and the Republic: Socialist Republicanism in the Irish Free State, 1925–1937* (Oxford: Clarendon Press, 1994), pp. 242–3.

53 *Irish Times*, 3 June 1946. Letter dated 10 July 1943.

54 Seán MacBride, *That Day's Struggle: A Memoir, 1904–1951*, ed. Caitriona Lawlor (Dublin: Currach Press, 2005), p. 123.

55 *Irish Times*, 3 June 1946. Letter dated 10 July 1943. The hunger strike ended on 11 July 1943, apparently after the counsels of MacBride and Con Lehane were heeded. Uinseann MacEoin, *The IRA in the Twilight Years, 1923–1948* (Dublin: Argenta Press, 1997), p. 462, n. 6.

56 *Irish Times*, 4 June 1946. Aiken declared that MacBride was 'prepared publicly to excuse the foulest crimes against the State and people, and thus encourage the men who commit them.'

most importantly, his support for the policy of neutrality, which he was careful to underline – requiring of Republicans that they '[avoid] any act which might directly or indirectly jeopardise neutrality'.[57] It is from this point that a decisive shift in MacBride's position vis-à-vis Irish neutrality can be traced. Previously, as preceding chapters have demonstrated, his attitude was best described as *attentiste*: pinning his hopes on a Nazi victory, MacBride cultivated close links with the German Minister in Dublin while remaining ostensibly on the right side of the law. But when the balance of the war shifted dramatically with US participation and unexpected Soviet resistance to the German advance eastward, MacBride was forced to realign himself now that the awaited New Order no longer looked likely to materialise. The project of rebuilding a career in Irish political life would take precedence over the subsequent years, and he was always anxious to maintain his support for Ireland's neutral stance, declaring in 1946: 'During the war, ideologically, my sympathies were with the democratic powers; by reason of historical factors and by reason of our national status and partition, I supported wholeheartedly the policy of neutrality.'[58]

Life as a Successful Barrister

The remainder of 1943 was, for MacBride, lived at a less brisk pace than the frenetic speed of the previous years. With the IRA largely quiescent – one of the last, and ugliest, outbursts of violence came on 4 July when Jackie Griffiths, an escaped IRA prisoner from Mountjoy, was machine-gunned off his bicycle on Mount Street[59] – the focus switched to less serious matters. In an elegant thumbing of the nose to the strict wartime petrol rationing – which had curtailed normal electioneering the previous month – MacBride and Mac O'Rahilly travelled to Wicklow Circuit Court on O'Rahilly's yacht, a frivolity which merited a front-page mention in the *Irish Times*, in the middle of a more serious article on the compulsory evacuation of a number of French towns.[60]

August brought a happy family event, when MacBride gave away his cousin Sheila MacBride – daughter of the late Joseph MacBride and Eileen Wilson – in marriage to John Durcan, MacBride's colleague at the Bar.[61] On 11 October, MacBride was admitted to the inner bar; his path to 'taking silk' was completed in less than six years, a feat unprecedented in Irish legal history.[62] As Senior Counsel, MacBride initially busied himself with legal cases less fraught with political tensions: representing a Bandon couple in a long-running case with the Munster and Leinster Savings Bank, which was concluded in the bank's favour, with an enormous award of almost £10,000; and he successfully secured an acquittal in

---

57 *Irish Times*, 3 June 1946. Letter dated 10 July 1943.
58 *Irish Times*, 3 June 1946.
59 English, *Armed Struggle*, p. 59; Irish *Independent*, 7 July 1943.
60 *Irish Times*, 9 July 1943.
61 *Irish Press*, 12 August 1943.
62 J. Clancy, M. Connolly and K. Ferguson, 'Alphabetical index to barristers' memorials, 1868–1968', in Kenneth Ferguson (ed.) *King's Inns Barristers, 1868–2004* (Dublin: The Honourable Society of King's Inns in association with the Irish Legal History Society, 2005), p. 234.

the case of an unmarried 29-year-old Galway woman accused of murdering her 13-day-old baby, whose body was never recovered.[63]

The latter stages of 1943 also saw the commencement of a case that would rumble on until 1945: a challenge to the administration of the Military Service Pensions to which IRA or Cumann na mBan members who had served more than three months in the period leading up to 11 July 1921 were legally entitled. Although the history of the Military Service Pensions remains to be written – largely owing to the unavailability of state archive material – it appears that the whole system had attracted controversy from the outset, particularly the defini-tion of 'active service' as understood by the terms of the statutory act.[64] Hours of Dáil business were wasted in almost every session, as deputies entered questions of behalf of constituents who were dissatisfied with the Pension Board decision, or dissatisfied with the delay in reaching a decision; the responsible Minister – in this period, Oscar Traynor as Minister for Defence – customarily replied that he either did not the information to hand, or that he could not interfere with the procedures of the Pensions Board, constituted as a separate and independent body. In October 1943 MacBride appeared in a test case, in which a Cork IRA veteran contested the entire process of judging applications, which, in his case, took more than ten years; this normally followed the sequence of a Referee and an Advisory Committee examining written evidence attesting to the claimant's participation in the Easter Rising or the War of Independence, before arriving at a decision. Part of the problem, MacBride argued before the High Court, was that the sheer number of applications to the Pension Board had not been anticipated; therefore claims were delayed and then dismissed out of bureaucratic expediency rather than any real judgement of the intrinsic merits of each case.[65]

The legal fortunes of the test case fluctuated over the subsequent months, as initial judgements were overturned on appeal. A final decision was handed down from the Supreme Court on 20 December 1944: the Court held that the Refer-ee's reports denying a pension to the test applicants should be quashed, finding that the interpretation of 'continuous active service' and the procedure of hearing evidence, were not in accordance with the stipulations laid down in the original act.[66] This decision had potentially enormous implications for the 48,538 or so

63 *Irish Times*, 9 December 1943; *Irish Press*, 29 November 1943.
64 *Dáil Éireann Debates*, vol. 91, col. 669, 20 October 1943. James Tunney of Labour asked the Minister for Defence 'if he is aware of the widespread dissatisfaction that exists with regard to the administration of the Military Service Pensions Act 1934; that it is widely alleged that men with long and meritorious service with the IRA have not been awarded pensions or awarded pensions not commensurate with their service, and whether, in those circum-stances, he will cause an enquiry to be made into the operation of the Act and particularly in respect of the definition of "active service" as understood by the referee appointed under the Act'.
65 *Irish Times*, 21 October 1943.
66 Irish Law Reports [1945] IR 126. In the background to the Supreme Court case was the government's introduction of an amendment to the Military Service Pensions Act (1934) in order to close off a loophole on which they feared another challenge: the convention that civil servants did not also draw a military service pension. If sustained, this challenge would have serious financial implications. Oscar Traynor, the responsible minister, commented on introduction of the amendment that 'we have decided that we must protect the Exchequer

rejected applications; equally, it was argued, the 11,239 qualifying applications had been administered on flawed procedural grounds.[67] Amid wildly varying estimations of how long it would take the present Pensions Advisory Board to re-examine all the applications, the government moved to introduce legislation to close the loopholes which had existed in the previous Act, although the thorny question of what constituted 'active service' remained problematic.[68] Although the question of Military Service Pensions continued to be the subject of active debate and recurrent questions inside Parliament, it is impossible to critically assess the impact of both the original 1924 and 1934 Acts and the amendments made thereafter without the release of the Pensions Records. It is likely that the records contain a unique insight into the nature of the Irish Revolution and its contested memory, as well the individual participants.

MacBride and the 'American Note' Crisis

Although Ireland had largely remained at a remove from the whirlpool of war after the threat of invasion faded in late 1940, and the fraught question of the Treaty ports receded in importance after 1941, one final crisis erupted in early 1944. Concerned that information about the impending Normandy invasions might be leaked to the Axis powers via their legations in Dublin, on 21 February, the US formally requested the expulsion of Axis diplomats, a request verbally endorsed by the British representative John Maffey some days later.[69] De Valera instantly refused what he viewed as a threatening ultimatum, placed the Irish army on high alert, and drafted a lofty response, delivered some days later and subsequently published.[70] While the long-term effects of the Irish government's refusal to accede to the American request are arguably discernable in Ireland's international isolation in the post-war years – including failure to secure Marshall Aid grants and exclusion from the United Nations until 1955 – the immediate reaction inside Ireland was one of pride that de Valera had not yielded to what was viewed as undue external pressure. The *Irish Times*, the most pro-Allied of all the Irish newspapers, commented approvingly on de Valera's response to the American request: 'Mr de Valera, so far, has handled an appallingly difficult situation not only with diplomatic skill, but also in a statesmanlike way'.[71] De Valera quickly capitalised on this rush of public support by calling a snap election in June

---

against any attempt by these types of persons to drive the proverbial coach and four through these Acts', *Dáil Éireann Debates*, vol. 92, col. 1456, 22 February 1944. These words, presumably, applied equally to those taking the present case.

67 *Dáil Éireann Debates*, vol. 96, col. 66, 14 February 1945.

68 Military Service Pensions (Amendment) Act, 1945, available at www.irishstatutebook. ie/1945/acts.html (accessed 30 January 2009).

69 Girvin, *The Emergency*, pp. 306–11; John P. Duggan, *Herr Hempel at the German Legation in Dublin, 1937–1945* (Dublin: Irish Academic Press, 2003), pp. 190–2; Eunan O'Halpin (ed.), *MI5 and Ireland, 1939–1945: The Official History* (Dublin: Irish Academic Press, 2003), pp. 82–9.

70 *Irish Press*, 11 March 1944. MI5 disapproved of the request, fearing it would jeopardise the excellent security relationship between Irish and British military authorities. Eunan O'Halpin, 'Irish-Allied security relations and the "American note" crisis: new evidence from British records', *Irish Studies in International Affairs*, vol. 11 (2000), pp. 71–83.

71 *Irish Times*, 13 March 1944.

1944, where, despite the lowest turnout since 1923, Fianna Fáil managed to regain their overall majority.[72]

MacBride had also felt impelled to praise de Valera for his management of the affair, writing rather obsequiously that 'if in the course of the present crisis, my services can be of any value to the Government, I shall be at your disposal. If I may be permitted, I should like also to express confidence in the manner in which you have handled the situation.'[73] Keane argues that this letter is further evidence of MacBride's support for neutrality, which she has mistakenly dated from the beginning of the war.[74] As we have seen however, MacBride's apparent conversion to the virtues of Ireland's neutral stance came rather later, with the first public enunciation attempted in 1943. Indeed, much of his activities in the preceding years suggest a much more ambiguous attitude towards neutrality, and imply a certain hedging of bets with regard to the outcome of the war. MacBride's letter to de Valera can perhaps more accurately be interpreted as a very deliberate expression of support for the position of the Irish government vis-à-vis the American note *only*; namely, the refusal to expel the Axis diplomats, one of whom, it should be remembered, was a close family friend. That family allegiances should have coincided so neatly with MacBride's larger project of proclaiming his legitimate credentials and fervent support for neutrality was a happy coincidence. Throughout the remainder of the year, MacBride continued to appear regularly at public debates, where some of his contributions can be seen as testing grounds for policies later adopted by Clann na Poblachta. Once more returning to his *idée fixe* of partition, at the inaugural meeting of the Solicitors' Apprentices' Debating Society in October 1944, he argued that much of the current debate around the question of partition was 'self-complacent', continuing that:

Vested interests had grown up which benefit by reason of the continued existence of partition. These ranged from certain industrialists on the one hand to smugglers on the other hand. It would be the paramount duty of the Government in power to knock on the door of any peace conferences that might be held at the end of the war and to demand the ending of this unnatural and artificial frontier.[75]

It did not enter MacBride's calculations that a resolutely neutral state, which had publicly incurred the displeasure of Britain and America, might not be in a position to make demands of any of victorious nations in the post-war conferences. MacBride did, of course, attempt to barter neutrality in return for an end to partition when the question of NATO membership arose, displaying a certain pragmatism and flexibility, if the problem of rising roughshod over unionist sensibilities remained.[76]

72 Ó Drisceoil, *Censorship in Ireland*, p. 273; O'Leary, *Irish Elections*, p. 37. Divisions within the Labour Party on the communist issue had begun to tell; the formation of a breakaway National Labour Party further fragmented the opposition inside Dáil Éireann.

73 UCDA, Eamon de Valera Papers, P150/2571, S. MacBride to E. de Valera, 23 March 1944.

74 Elizabeth Keane, *Seán MacBride: A Life* (Dublin: Gill & Macmillan, 2007), p. 66.

75 *Irish Independent*, 28 October 1944.

76 See Keane, *Seán MacBride*, pp. 152ff; Ian MacCabe, *A Diplomatic History of Ireland: the Republic, the Commonwealth and NATO* (Dublin: Irish Academic Press, 1991); Bernadette

'At Mountjoy Gaol, young Charlie Kerins was roped'[77]

While MacBride was continuing to formulate new political ideas, and was equally concentrating on non-political legal cases, the elevated passions of the height of the IRA campaign against the state briefly recurred. Early on the morning of 15 June, Kerryman Charles Kerins – the 'chief of staff of a one man army' – was arrested at the home of Dr Kathleen Farrell in Rathmines.[78] Gardaí and government had long been certain that Kerins had given the order for the O'Brien murder if he had not actually carried it out, a belief borne out by Harry White's later recollection that Kerins had warned him to 'stay out of the way' on the morning of the shooting.[79] On 2 October, Kerins's trial for murder opened before the Special Criminal Court: the state's evidence was largely circumstantial, resting on a fingerprint of Kerins found on a bicycle close to the murder scene, weapons and IRA documents discovered at a boarding house in Dublin, and some very shaky identifications. Many of the witnesses who appeared in court refused to identify Kerins and were treated as hostile witnesses by the state, a testament to the fear which still governed public attitudes towards the IRA.[80] After being found guilty, Kerins lambasted the judicial system, declaring: 'If this is an example of de Valera's justice, freedom and democracy, then I should like to know what dictatorship and militarism are.'[81]

Whelan, *Ireland and the Marshall Plan, 1947–1947* (Dublin: Four Courts Press, 2000). Equally, MacBride's determination, once in government, to reinvigorate Dublin's partition policy failed to produce any meaningful advance, resulting instead in alienating not only unionist and British sensibilities, but also irritating the majority of European observers who were forced to endure the tedium of the 'sore thumb' approach.

77   Austin Clarke, 'The last republicans', in *Selected Poems*, ed. H. Maxton (Dublin: Lilliput Press, 1991), p. 66.

78   J. Bowyer Bell, *The Secret Army: the IRA* (New Brunswick: Transaction Publications, 2004, first published 1970), p. 234. Dr Farrell, a long-time republican supporter, was later convicted in the Special Criminal Court of failing to account for her movements on 6 February 1944. Given a three-month suspended sentence, she was defended by MacBride. Her next public appearance was at the head of the Save the German Children Campaign, an organisation set up in 1945 to provide humanitarian support for German Catholic war orphans, but which was suspected of having a 'an anti-British and almost pro-Nazi bias'. See *Irish Times*, 8 July 1944; Mark Hull, *Irish Secrets: German Espionage in Wartime Ireland, 1939–1945* (Dublin: Irish Academic Press, 2003), p. 252; and Cathy Molohan, 'Humanitarian Aid or Politics? The case of the Save the German Children Society', *History Ireland*, vol. 5, no. 3 (Autumn 1997), pp. 7–9.

79   MacEoin and White, *Harry*, p. 104. The murder was actually carried out by Archie Doyle, probably with Michael Quille, who had already been acquitted. Doyle had previously been part of the unit that murdered Kevin O'Higgins in 1927. See Chapter 5. The third man may have been Harry White, who was later convicted of the murder but maintained his innocence, or Liam Burke.

80   For a record of the trial, see the *Irish Times*, 3–11 October. After the state case had been heard, Kerins was again given an opportunity to present a defence; again, declining, he declared scornfully that '[the President of the Court] could have adjourned it for six months as far as I am concerned, as my attitude towards the Court will always be the same'. It was during the course of the trial that documents naming MacBride as associating with the IRA in 1942 were read out.

81   *Irish Independent*, 11 October 1944.

Sentenced to death by hanging, Kerins launched an appeal. He was represented by MacBride and Noel Hartnett, beginning an association that would lead to the formation of Clann na Poblachta. The Court of Criminal Appeal having refused leave to appeal on 15 November, Kerins's legal team applied for permission to appeal to the Supreme Court. Arguing that Kerins's 'trial was not satisfactory and the evidence ... insufficient', MacBride and Lavery submitted that key witnesses – who had given evidence at the trial of Michael Quille for the same offence – were not called. The circumstantial nature of the fingerprint evidence and documents linking Kerins with the IRA was also queried, and finally that the prosecution had been permitted to make a closing speech was severely criticised:

> [It was] the first occasion in the legal history of this country, of Great Britain or of the United States upon which an address for the prosecution was made in the course of a trial of an undefended person charged with a capital offence. Where in the case of minor offences a second or closing speech was made by the prosecution in the case of an undefended man who tendered no evidence, the Court of Criminal Appeal has usually quashed the conviction for that reason.[82]

The Attorney-General refused a certificate to appeal to the Supreme Court, and the execution date of 1 December was allowed to stand.

Immediately, however, a massive campaign for clemency was launched. Eunan O'Halpin's assertion that 'the IRA and their supporters could raise scarcely a whisper of defiance' simply does not correspond with the evidence pointing to an enormous outpouring of feeling around the impending execution.[83] Petitions containing the signatures of such diverse figures as Seán O'Faolain, Harry Kernoff, Seán Keating, Colm Gavan Duffy, Austin Clarke, Eileen Davitt, Rosamond Jacob and Mrs Mellows were received; in total almost 100,000 signatures were collected. A reprieve committee was established, including Con Lehane, Kathleen Lynn, Peadar O'Donnell, Hanna Sheehy Skeffington, Moss Twomey, Roger McHugh and Denis Guiney (a prominent businessman and Fianna Fáil supporter), while a number of local Kerry organisations – including Kerry County Council – also agitated for clemency.[84] But the government took a robust line with the reprieve campaign, refusing to allow any publicity around, for instance, the meeting at the Mansion House on 27 November where a number of Labour TDs spoke. Similarly, attempts to advertise that and future public meetings were suppressed, including a seemingly innocuous appeal to 'all Kerrymen and women living in Dublin' to attend a meeting outside Clery's department store on 30 November.[85] Indicating his close association with the reprieve campaign, MacBride attempted to circum-navigate this censorship by liaising with the Dublin correspondents of the Belfast papers, trying to replicate in inverse the mass mobilisation that had taken place in

---

82 NAI, D/T S 13567/1, Charlie Kerins Reprieve Petitions, Memorandum submitted by Seán MacBride, Cecil Lavery and Con Lehane.

83 O'Halpin. *Spying on Ireland*, p. 258.

84 NAI, D/T S 13567/1, Charlie Kerins Reprieve Petitions; National Library of Ireland [NLI], MS 31756(3), Charles Kerins Reprieve Petititons.

85 NAI, D/T S 13567/1, Charlie Kerins Reprieve Petitions; Ó Drisceoil, *Censorship in Ireland*, pp. 242–3.

the southern state around the Williams execution two years earlier. The northern newspapers – mostly unionist in inclination – were, however, less prepared to engage with republican issues than their southern counterparts.[86]

A debate on the censorship of the campaign was held in the Dáil on 1 December 1944, after Kerins's execution in the early hours of the morning. It was particularly galling to republicans that the British hangman, Albert Pierrepoint, had performed the execution.[87] The Labour Party made strong representations that the clampdown infringed the constitutional rights of Irish citizens to agitate, describing the government actions as 'the methods of tyrannical dictators'.[88] The authorities believed that the reprieve campaign was being used as a front to reorganise the IRA; certainly, attempts were being made to reorganise the republican movement.[89] MacBride had participated in a meeting convened by Patrick McLogan, former MP for Armagh, in October 1944, and a month previously a similar gathering brought together Moss Twomey, Simon Donnelly and Mrs Austin Stack.[90] But these meetings are best interpreted as forging a new political way forward for the republican movement as a whole, not as a reorganisation of the IRA.

That organisation had been thoroughly shattered by the security crackdown throughout the war years; even before the arrest of Kerins, the whole infrastructure of the IRA had broken down. Cognisant of this, the authorities initiated a process of gradual release of the interned prisoners, commencing in the autumn of 1943. This process accelerated through 1944, and by March 1945 only 115 remained in the Curragh.[91] While the Kerins reprieve campaign did succeed in questioning the extent and purpose of censorship in Ireland during the war years, the chances of securing a reprieve for Kerins were always slim. O'Brien's murder was perceived as a personal slight to some members of the Fianna Fáil Cabinet; equally, the

---

86 NLI, Roger McHugh Papers, MS 31756(2), Note on Seán MacBride contacting correspondents of Belfast papers in Dublin. The newspapers targeted were the *Northern Whig*, the *Belfast Telegraph* and the *Belfast Newsletter*.

87 Pierrepoint's autobiography details the extreme secrecy with which he had to conduct his activities in Ireland, travelling under an assumed name. Albert Pierrepoint, *Executioner* (London: Harrap, 1974).

88 *Dáil Éireann Debates*, vol. 95, col. 1420, 1 December 1944. Jim Larkin Junior and Dan Spring had both been suspended from the Dáil the previous evening, when they understandably refused to accept the Chair's ruling that the matter of censorship surrounding the Kerins reprieve campaign was not urgent.

89 De Valera was explicit on this: 'The advertisements were stopped by virtue of our right to maintain order and preserve the State, to prevent organisations getting ahead and using this as a cloak for reorganisation.' *Dáil Éireann Debates*, vol. 95, col. 1459, 1 December 1944. A half-hearted attempt to reconvene the IRA was made in late 1945, swiftly stamped out by the Gardaí. By 1947, the Department of Justice reported that 'The IRA has disintegrated ... it can no longer be regarded as a serious menace to peace and good order.' Quoted in Seosamh Ó Longaigh, *Emergency Law in Independent Ireland, 1922–1948* (Dublin: Four Courts Press, 2006), p. 273.

90 UCDA, MacEntee Papers, P67/550, Notes on IRA Activities, 1941–47, p. 80, and Profile of Seán MacBride.

91 Ó Longaigh, *Emergency Law in Independent Ireland*, p. 302; John Maguire, *IRA Internments and the Irish Government: Subversives and the State, 1939–1962* (Dublin: Irish Academic Press, 2008), pp. 49–50.

Gardaí were determined that someone should be brought to justice for the murder of their colleague. The flimsiness of the evidence linking Kerins to the actual murder was set aside for the wider aim of vengeance. Kerins remains the last republican executed in Ireland, north and south, for a political crime. In 1948 his remains, along with those of all other republicans executed during the war years, were released to his next of kin by the inter-party government, a move undoubtedly pressed by his legal representative, then Minister for External Affairs.[92]

Refugee and Recalcitrant Husband: Francis Stuart in Post-war Europe

As the war moved inexorably towards its conclusion, MacBride was largely concerned with the Military Service Pensions case, still making its way through the courts. Other 'ordinary' (non-political) cases also took up most of his time and energy.[93] The reaction of the Irish government to the end of the war has been well-recorded: de Valera's visit of condolence to the German legation on the death of Hitler coupled with his restrained if self-centred response to Churchill's victory broadcast reinforcing the impression of an introspective political elite unaware of the enormous convulsions which had taken place in Europe and beyond over the previous seven years.[94] Whether the Irish political elite were also unaware of the true brutality of the Nazi regime throughout the war years is a moot point; undeniable, however, is that the authorities attempted to censor reports from Bergen-Belsen.[95] This insistence of moral relativism or moral equivalence between the belligerents – which had governed the Irish censorship regime to the point of farce – was also to be found across Irish society, particularly in republican quarters.[96] The refusal of Irish society to accept the war crimes of the Nazis for fear of morally compromising Irish neutrality created a climate in which republican and nationalist opinion more generally was able to cling to the old Anglophobic certainties, unmoved by the words and images filtering back from mainland Europe. One commentator soon noted the effect of this tendency:

If you had spoken of any of these things to an Irishman at that time, he would

---

92 NAI, D/T S 12540, Memorandum on remains of Richard Goss, 26 July 1948.

93 See, for example, the *Irish Times*, 17 February & 24 April 1945.

94 Dermot Keogh, 'Eamon de Valera and Hitler: an analysis of international reaction to the visit to the German Minister, May 1945', *Irish Studies in International Affairs*, vol. 3, no. 1 (1989), pp. 69–82; Girvin, *The Emergency*, pp. 1–18; Clair Wills, *That Neutral Island: A Cultural History of Ireland during the Second World War* (London: Faber & Faber, 2008), pp. 389–92.

95 Paul Bew, *Ireland: The Politics of Enmity, 1789–2006* (Oxford: Oxford University Press, 2008), p. 474.

96 Despite her long-standing knowledge and condemnation of the persecution of Jews in Germany, Kathleen Lynn confided to her diary on 2 May her admiration of Hitler: 'He was great in many ways.' Library of Royal College of Physicians of Ireland, Kathleen Lynn Diaries, 2 May 1945. Similarly, Hubert Butler recalled in 1978 this ambivalence across wider society: 'There were disapproving letters in the local papers; here in Kilkenny one writer declared that "it was all propaganda" and that the British had used starving Indians to impersonate Belsen inmates ... there was a fancy-dress ball where the First Prize went to The Beast of Belsen.' *Irish Times*, 14 December 1978.

most likely have retorted on you with Amritsar and Bachelor's Walk and Kevin Barry's broken-hearted mother. Ireland, that has missed every great historical experience, has missed this one also, and perhaps we may be thankful – the dreadful 20th-Century experience of the Abyss.[97]

There was one Irish citizen, however, who had deliberately gone to the edge of the abyss. From the moment the war ended, Francis Stuart immediately became a problem both for MacBride and for the Irish government.

Stuart's presence in Germany from early 1940 onwards soon became the subject of acute embarrassment to the Irish authorities. As Brendan Barrington has shown, his propaganda broadcasts, along with those of fellow Irishman William Joyce, were intensely political in tone: despite his avowed support for Irish neutrality, which was of course in German interests, Stuart's broadcasts carried the taint of pro-Nazi sentiment and, as Barrington has demonstrated, were also anti-Semitic.[98] While in Germany, Stuart was almost entirely cut off from his wife and children; communication was difficult and the only real contact his family had with him was to listen to his broadcasts, faint and crackly: 'It's such a comfort for us to hear your voice occasionally when our wireless behaves itself.'[99] Shortly after hostilities in Europe had drawn to a close, Iseult began to make enquiries about facilitating her husband's return to Ireland. Worried that 'he might have been killed or have fallen into the hands of the Russians or French', she met with F. H. Boland of External Affairs in person. The problem of Stuart was clearly one which had been discussed at length in Roebuck House, and MacBride urged his sister not to institute official diplomatic enquiries about her husband, as he may have been attempting to avoid official attention at that time. Iseult was unaware that the Irish government had declined to renew Stuart's Irish passport in March 1943, and Boland didn't enlighten her.[100] Iseult was also unaware that her husband had embarked on a serious extramarital relationship with Gertrud Meisner, a student at Berlin University, with whom he had lived for at least four years in Berlin and Luxembourg. Attempting to escape the chaos of disintegrating Berlin, the couple peregrinated around southern Germany and Austria in the spring of 1945, before Stuart decided to travel to Paris to try and obtain transit visas for himself and Gertrud – whom he had rechristened Madeleine, disliking the guttural German name – to travel to Ireland.[101]

A lengthy triangular correspondence ensued between the Irish legation in Paris, External Affairs in Dublin and the MacBride family, as all parties attempted

97 Arland Ussher, *The Face and Mind of Ireland* (London: Victor Gollancz, 1949), p. 70.
98 Brendan Barrington (ed.), *The Wartime Broadcasts of Francis Stuart: 1942–1944* (Dublin: Irish Academic Press, 2000), pp. 38–53. See also Andreas Roth, 'Francis Stuart's broadcasts from Germany, 1942–4: some new evidence', *Irish Historical Studies*, vol. xxxii, no. 127 (May 2001), pp. 408–22.
99 Irish Military Archives, Cathal Brugha Barracks, Dublin [IMA], G2/0214, Francis and Iseult Stuart file, Iseult Stuart to Francis Stuart, n. d.
100 NAI, DFA, A72, Francis Stuart file, Memorandum of Fred Boland, 12 May 1945.
101 Jerry Natterstad, *Francis Stuart* (London: Associated University Presses, 1974), pp. 65–7; Francis Stuart, 'A Berlin diary' in *States of Mind: Selected Short Prose, 1936–1983* (Dublin: Raven Arts Press, 1984), pp. 31–45; Madeleine Stuart, *Manna in the Morning: A Memoir, 1940–1958* (Dublin: Raven Arts Press, 1984), pp. 60–70.

to ascertain Stuart's precise intentions towards his wife, his mistress and his domicile. Iseult was anxious to send her husband some money; the Irish authorities reluctantly agreed, although underlining that 'Stuart should not assume from the fact of our agreeing to transmit this £15 to him that he enjoys Irish diplomatic protection or that his conduct in 1940, at a particularly dangerous moment in our history has been forgotten.'[102] Shortly after this communication, Boland obtained a detailed dossier on Stuart from G2, Irish Military Intelligence, which asserted that although there was 'no legal evidence on any point to associate him with illegal activities, his history and associations are of a very suspicious nature'.[103] Notwithstanding this assessment, External Affairs continued to facilitate the transfer of money to Stuart throughout the autumn of 1945, an expense which was primarily undertaken by MacBride. In October, he wrote to Joseph Walshe, Secretary of the Department, about providing a regular monthly income for Stuart: 'Whatever [the monthly sum] is, I shall make the necessary financial arrangement and shall reimburse any monies which the Legation may have to advance him.'[104]

Shortly after making their way back to Austria, Stuart and Madeleine were both arrested by the French authorities. They were held in Bregenz-Oberstadt prison for almost six months, their fate unknown to both the Irish authorities and the MacBride family.[105] Still displaying a remarkable amount of forbearance, MacBride paid the debts Stuart had run up at the Irish legation in Paris and instituted some very cautious enquiries with the French authorities.[106] Finally, in May 1946, word arrived that Stuart and Madeleine had been transferred from Bregenz prison to Freiburg, also in the French zone, where they were held under house arrest for a further two months. Iseult was horrified, writing immediately to Boland:

> A French jail, possibly under the control of left-wing elements ... It isn't nice to think of. And Heaven knows how long he may have been in already! I read how my old friend Ezra Pound was driven insane; yet he always seemed so well-balanced, but like Francis, a writer and poet. For such people jail conditions are particularly dangerous.[107]

It was at this point that Madeleine's presence really became problematic. Although it was likely that he would be able to find passage home, Stuart was unwilling to leave Madeleine behind, although he failed to communicate the real reasons for this effectively to his wife. Iseult laboured under the impression that Madeleine had saved Stuart's life during an air-raid in Berlin, and so 'Francis is under some great obligation to her ... apparently she has lost all her people [and] is homeless and destitute.' Iseult was at this point so desperate to get her husband home that she convinced herself that Madeleine could also travel to Ireland, writing that 'if [Madeleine] can't find work, at the worst she could stay here. I had always meant

102 NAI, DFA, A72, Francis Stuart file, Fred Boland to Seán Murphy, 16 August 1945.
103 NAI, DFA A72, Francis Stuart file, Dan Bryan to Fred Boland, 17 August 1945.
104 NAI, DFA, A72, Francis Stuart file, Seán MacBride to Joseph Walshe, 1 October 1945. Some monies were also paid to Stuart by his aunt, Janet Montgomery.
105 See Stuart, *Manna in the Morning*, pp. 71–6 for an account of this imprisonment.
106 NAI, DFA, A72, Francis Stuart file, Seán MacBride to Fred Boland, 30 April 1946.
107 NAI, DFA, A72, Francis Stuart file, Iseult Stuart to Fred Boland, 15 May 1946.

to adopt some German child, we can adopt her instead.'[108]

The situation was rapidly becoming untenable. The Irish authorities, who had behaved admirably towards someone to whom they had no diplomatic obliga-tion, were being placed in a horrendously difficult position; as Boland commented exasperatedly, 'the eternal triangle factor makes the whole thing tiresome and rather hopeless'.[109] Equally, MacBride, who had been bankrolling Stuart for at least a year, was tiring of his brother-in-law's procrastinations and prevarications. Stuart was behaving reprehensibly: accepting money from his brother-in-law and aged aunt to fund his sojourn with his mistress, and taking no responsibility for his wife (who had always struggled with heart disease), his elderly and frail mother, and his teenaged children. In September 1946, Stuart came clean to the Irish authorities, at least, writing formally to the Irish minister in Paris, 'I do not want to return [to Ireland] at present.' Iseult, however, was still in the dark as to his intentions, and in November requested that the French authorities deport her husband; passage was arranged (and paid for by MacBride) on a US plane to Foynes. Finally, in January 1947 Iseult accepted what everyone around her had long come to realise: that Stuart had effectively abandoned his family, that he was intent on building a new life with Madeleine, and that he would never come home.[110]

Although the estranged spouses maintained a strained and rather pitiful corre-spondence, they had only one further meeting. In 1954, Iseult died of the heart disease from which she had suffered since early adulthood, her spirit weakened irrevocably by the death of her mother the previous year. The callous disregard with which Stuart had treated his wife infuriated MacBride, who refused to associate in any way with him after Stuart's eventual return to Ireland, having married his Madeleine, in 1958.[111]

Hunger Strike and Political Mobilisation

While the problems with Stuart continued, MacBride's slow journey towards full political participation took on a new urgency when a new hunger strike burst onto the public consciousness, freed from the strictures of wartime censorship. Seán McCaughey, the northern IRA member who had led the interrogation of Stephen Hayes, had been sentenced to life imprisonment for his part in that affair; and along with a hardcore of dangerous prisoners, he was sent to Portlaoise Prison to serve his sentence. This was evidently a source of discontent: angered at what they viewed as attempts at criminalisation, this group of prisoners, led by McCaughey

108 NAI, DFA, A72, Francis Stuart file, Iseult Stuart to Fred Boland, 29 May 1946.
109 NAI, DFA, A72, Francis Stuart file, Fred Boland to Seán Murphy, 4 November 1946.
110 'Mrs Stuart has realised what she ought to have realised long ago and that, in the light of that realisation, neither she nor the family are any longer particularly anxious to get Francis home.' NAI, DFA, A72, Francis Stuart file, Fred Boland to Seán Murphy, 12 January 1947.
111 In 1990, MacBride told Geoffrey Elborn, who had contacted him seeking an interview for his forthcoming biography of Stuart, that, 'Francis Stuart treated Iseult disgracefully, and I will have nothing to do with you or your book.' Geoffrey Elborn, *Francis Stuart: A Life* (Dublin: Raven Arts Press, 1990), p. 7; A. Norman Jeffares, 'Iseult Gonne', in Warwick Gould (ed.), *Poems and Contexts: Yeats Annual 16* (Basingstoke: Palgrave, 2005) pp. 259–62.

and Tomás MacCurtain, refused to wear prison uniforms, dressing instead in prison blankets fastened with twine, poncho-style. The result of this stand-off was the withdrawal of privileges such as newspapers and visitors, and the keeping of certain prisoners in solitary confinement for long periods.[112] McCaughey seems to have been especially affected by the circumstances of his incarceration, displaying signs of nervous strain and paranoia; given that he had spent over three years in continuous solitary confinement, such a reaction is unsurprising.

These pre-existing tensions were ratcheted even higher after the war ended and most of the republican internees had been released; under the mistaken belief that the Military Court had been disestablished, the prisoners began hunger-striking for release. After five days, McCaughey also began refusing water, and his subsequent deterioration was rapid.[113] There was a crucial difference in the conduct of this hunger strike from that of McNeela and D'Arcy six years previously: the ending of censorship meant that regular updates could be given of the prisoners' conditions, and public meetings could also be reported. McCaughey's plight evidently captured the public imagination, and by 8 May an Oireachtas petition for release was presented to de Valera. Simultaneously, a number of public demonstrations in support of his strike took place, including a baton-charged march on Leinster House, and a work stoppage by turf-cutters in Phoenix Park.[114] McCaughey died on 11 May, after many days in a critical condition; curiously, MacBride was the first to be notified, receiving a telephone call from Maurice Moynihan, secretary to the Taoiseach, in the early hours of the morning, asking him to inform the McCaughey family. Having done so, MacBride drove to Portlaoise with Con Lehane and Noel Hartnett to represent the McCaughey family at the inquest, held later the same day. The dramatic scenes which followed ensured that the McCaughey death was the subject of widespread public and political comment.

The inquest was essentially a battle of wills between MacBride and the Coroner; the latter was determined to confine the inquest to the immediate cause of death whereas MacBride was equally intent on proving that the conditions in which McCaughey was held drove him to hunger-strike. The celebrated exchange in which MacBride forced the prison doctor to admit that he would not keep a dog in the conditions inflicted on McCaughey was quickly followed by a melodramatic withdrawal by McCaughey's legal team and family. Before Lehane's withdrawal, he declared that 'the conditions which exist in this prison ... compare with Buchenwald and Belsen', a ridiculous hyperbole which was much repeated by republican supporters in the aftermath of the inquest. The jury's verdict was, in the circumstances, mild – concurring with the medical evidence as to cause of death while including a rider that 'the conditions existing in the prison were not all that

---

112 Maud Gonne commented reverently to her friend Ethel Mannin that 'they looked like monks'. NLI, Ethel Mannin Papers, MS 17875, Maud Gonne MacBride to Ethel Mannin, 15 May 1946. See also Maguire, *IRA Internments and the Irish Government*, pp. 56–7.

113 Liam Rice described McCaughey after two weeks on hunger strike as 'no more than a skeleton covered by a parchment of skin ... [h]is eyes were dried holes, his sight gone. His tongue was no more than a shrivelled piece of skin between his jaws.' Liam Rice quoted in MacEoin, *The IRA in the Twilight Years*, p. 538.

114 *Irish Press*, 8 May 1946; *Irish Times*, 4 May 1946.

could be desired, according to the evidence furnished'.[115] Before leaving Portlaoise Prison, MacBride served as a pall-bearer alongside an IRA guard of honour at the removal of McCaughey's remains to the Franciscan Church in Dublin, before a funeral Mass in Belfast.[116]

The aftermath of the inquest brought a growing sense of public disquiet, fuelled undoubtedly by the rabble-rousing public meetings which ensued. These were largely held under the auspices of the Republican Prisoners' Release Association, and were addressed by all members of McCaughey's legal team as well as other republican and public figures. It is probable that MacBride saw both in the McCaughey death, aside from any humanitarian concerns which he may have had, and in the outpouring of public feeling in its aftermath, an issue on which he could harness public discontent for political ends. Addressing a meeting on 19 May in O'Connell Street, he underlined that 'the responsibility for the conditions in [Portlaoise] jail rested on the government'.[117]

It was amid this climate, with letters condemning McCaughey's treatment regularly appearing in the press, that a heated debate took place in Dáil Éireann on the question of an inquiry into the conditions in Portlaoise. After a challenge laid down by Michael Donnellan, Gerry Boland delivered a spirited defence of conditions inside Portlaoise – 'I happen to have been in prison several times myself' – before launching into a devastatingly blunt résumé of the threat posed by the IRA during the war. It was the first time that much of this material had made its way into the public domain in its entirety: the Magazine Fort raid, the Emergency Powers Bill, the German parachutists and the Hayes affair. Boland also delivered a blistering attack on MacBride, which if made outside the house would almost certainly have landed him in the libel court: There is a well-known legal gentleman who has severed about one-quarter of his connection with the IRA. He was trusted by them most implicitly. This particular gentleman is an expert on juries ... I am dealing with one of the most dangerous men in the country.'[118] John A. Costello vigorously defended his legal colleague, arguing that MacBride's political associations had nothing to do with the motion at hand and describing him as 'a loyal colleague at the Bar and a man of honour and integrity, so far as my association with him is concerned'.[119] The motion for an inquiry was defeated, amid some disorderly scenes.

115 For a report of the inquest, see the *Irish Times*, 13 May 1946. There may have been some irregularities in the deliberation of the jurors; Maud Gonne wrote to Ethel Mannin that 'the Coroner ... did the unheard-of thing, after the jury retired to consider their verdict, of going into the jury room'. NLI, Ethel Mannin Papers, MS 17875, Maud Gonne MacBride to Ethel Mannin, 15 May 1946.

116 UCDA, MacEntee Papers, P67/550, Notes on IRA activities, 1941–47, p. 93; Máirtín Meehan, *Finely Tempered Steel: Seán McCaughey and the IRA* (Dublin: Republican Publications, 2007), p. 60.

117 *Irish Independent*, 20 May 1946. Another meeting had been held on 15 May at which Con Lehane, Noel Hartnett, Roddy Connolly and Ernest Wood spoke, attracting 3,500 people. NAI, J8/939, Noel Hartnett, Comments in connection with Seán McCaughey case.

118 *Dáil Éireann Debates*, vol. 101, col. 1125ff, 29 May 1946. Boland named MacBride as the 'legal gentleman' to whom he was referring.

119 *Dáil Éireann Debates*, vol. 101, col. 112, 29 May 1946.

The McCaughey case and its attendant publicity provided a focal point around which the burgeoning political engagement among republicans could coalesce. Eithne MacDermott has argued that although the first meeting of Clann na Poblachta took place in July 1946, preparations for its establishment had clearly been underway for some time. As such, the McCaughey case served 'more as a detonator than as a catalyst'.[120] For republican supporters, the criticisms it evoked of the conditions in which republican prisoners were held masked a wider profound dissatisfaction with the entire wartime approach to the IRA. As shown, there was a long-standing desire within the republican movement to find a new political way forward; and while this may have been blocked during the war years by both the intransigence of the IRA and the extraordinary powers given to the government, peace brought new possibilities. For MacBride, the McCaughey case gave him the opportunity again to display his talent for handling an inquest jury, and the public platform from which to really construct his political career. Although Boland, and later MacEntee, sought to smear him by associating him with the wider IRA threat, their tactics largely backfired; by engaging in a long-running public squabble, principally in the letter columns of the press, they allowed MacBride to present himself as a rational, reasoned voice against frenzied and unfair attacks. This public battle also permitted MacBride to both defend his position and elaborate a wider set of criticisms of government policy in what was essentially an election manifesto:

> When the 1937 Constitution was enacted, I considered, like Mr de Valera, that the obstacles to the recognition of the Dáil had been removed, and that Republicans should, therefore, take their place in the councils of the nation. This by no means meant that I agreed with the policy of Fianna Fáil in other respects. Their bid to obtain support by way of pension, bribes and jobbery could, in my view, only bring those associated with it into public contempt. Their continual encroachment upon civil and individual liberty was leading towards dictatorial government and was a bad headline for future Governments, be such Governments Republican, Fine Gael or Labour. Essentially, I am a firm believer in democracy and I felt that their administration was bringing democracy into contempt.[121]

It was the final springboard for a political development which had encompassed youthful revolution, socialist leanings, humanitarian activity and Nazi sympathies, but above all an acute concern for his own personal advancement.

120 MacDermott, *Clann na Poblachta*, pp. 38–9.
121 *Irish Times*, 3 June 1946.

Epilogue

'I have been asked repeatedly to form a political party; I have been asked repeatedly to stand as a candidate; I have so far refrained from doing so for various reasons.'[1] A month after Seán MacBride unblushingly declared his disinterest in party politics in a national newspaper, Clann na Poblachta was launched in Wynn's Hotel on 6 July 1946. The history of the party, including its part in the first inter-party government, has been well served in current historiography, and a brief survey of its principal moments will suffice here.[2] While several authors have noted Clann na Poblachta's development from similarly named previous incarnations of the republican body politic, none have interrogated the crucial difference with the 1946 version: the abandonment of abstention as a political platform. MacBride was elected in the Dublin County by-election of October 1947, topping the poll on the basis of transfers from the Labour and Fine Gael candidates.[3] In the general election of the following February, Clann na Poblachta won ten seats and entered government in Ireland's first coalition; MacBride took the seat of External Affairs and appointed his junior colleague Noël Browne to the Health portfolio.

The government's performance, as it staggered from one crisis to the next, was highly criticised; even the republican high point, the declaration of the Republic of Ireland, was mismanaged and anti-climactic. MacBride's own performance – as party leader and as Minister for External Affairs – has also drawn criticism. As minister, he courted early success, particularly in securing Ireland's place in developing European integration projects, but encountered significant failures in other key areas. The bungling of the Marshall Aid negotiations and the question of Irish entry to NATO were two of the most immediately obvious miscalcula-

1 *Irish Times*, 1 June 1946.
2 See especially Eithne MacDermott, *Clann na Poblachta* (Cork: Cork University Press, 1998; David McCullagh, *A Makeshift Majority: The First Inter-party Government, 1948–51* (Dublin: Institute of Public Administration, 1998); Elizabeth Keane, *An Irish Statesman and Revolutionary: The Nationalist and Internationalist Politics of Seán MacBride* (London: Tauris Academic Studies, 2006); Elizabeth Keane, *Seán MacBride: A Life* (Dublin: Gill & Macmillan, 2007).
3 Brian M. Walker (ed.), *Parliamentary Election Results in Ireland, 1918–92: Irish Elections to Parliaments and Parliamentary Assemblies at Westminster, Belfast, Dublin, Strasbourg* (Dublin: Royal Irish Academy, 1992), p. 167. Patrick Kinane was also elected for Clann na Poblachta in the Tipperary by-election on the same date.

tions; MacBride's obsession with partition was another.[4] Partly attributable to the need to compete with de Valera's anti-partition world tour after his exit from government in 1948, MacBride's insistence on a 'sore thumb' policy with regard to partition did much to negate the value of Irish participation in European and international organisations, at a time when her isolation from the current of world affairs had been sharply wrought. The prospects of Irish unity had, of course, been reduced dramatically by the repeal of the External Relations Act and the exit from the Commonwealth – two measures which MacBride counted among his most significant achievements.[5]

As party leader, MacBride's record was similarly chequered. Shunning 'populist politics', he cultivated the remoteness of de Valera, but without the latter's mystical appeal. More seriously, his External Affairs portfolio was a difficult one for a party leader to carry off: with large amounts of foreign travel, MacBride quickly lost touch, not only with the party's grass-roots but with key sections of the party executive. While his quarrel with Browne attracted the most attention, perhaps the more historically important was MacBride's falling out with Noel Hartnett, an influential figure within the party structures who appears to have played a significant role in fomenting the poisonous dispute which eventually erupted between MacBride and Browne. Although the collapse of the coalition government, once welfarist principles came up against the bulwark of the combined forces of Catholic hierarchy and Irish Medical Organisation, was perhaps unavoidable, MacBride could have saved the party from its imminent electoral collapse. Set unswervingly against his ministerial and party colleague, MacBride allowed personal feelings to colour what ought to have been an unquestioned political decision: leading Clann na Poblachta out of government on such a principled issue would have reasserted his radical credentials within the party and to the electorate.

As it was, the party was almost totally eviscerated in the 1951 general election, with only two deputies retaining their seats: John Tully of Cavan, and MacBride himself in Dublin South-West, filling the last of five seats by the skin of his teeth. He remained in Dáil Éireann until 1957, declining a Cabinet seat in the second inter-party government of 1954; his principal focus from the back benches was

4   Bernadette Whelan, *Ireland and the Marshall Plan, 1947–1957* (Dublin: Four Courts Press, 2000); Till Geiger and Michael Kennedy (eds.), *Ireland, Europe and the Marshall Plan* (Dublin: Four Courts Press, 2004); Ronan Fanning, 'The United States and Irish participation in NATO: the debate of 1950', *Irish Studies in International Affairs*, vol. 1 (1979), pp. 38–48; Ian McCabe, *A Diplomatic History of Ireland, 1948–49: The Republic, the Commonwealth and NATO* (Dublin: Irish Academic Press, 1991).

5   In response to the declaration of the Republic of Ireland Act, the British government passed the Ireland Act. Its position was communicated as follows to the Dublin government: 'It is open, as it has always been open, to the Government of the Irish Republic to provide evidence to the people of Northern Ireland that their interests lie with the people of the Irish Republic rather than with the rest of the United Kingdom. The United Kingdom Government will always be happy to see the development of good feeling between Northern Ireland and the Irish Republic. Meanwhile they are satisfied that no good would come were they to leave in doubt the right of Northern Ireland to remain within the United Kingdom so long as the majority of its people desire this.' National Archives London [NAL], CAB21/1843, Commonwealth Relations Office to United Kingdom Representative in Ireland, 10 May 1949.

Ireland's incipient economic collapse of the late 1950s. MacBride was curiously perceptive on the issue of developmentalism, and has been identified by the principal historian of that period as one of a small band of politicians and civil servants who grasped both the dangers and the potentials of that period.[6] MacBride's withdrawal of support for the second coalition government – ostensibly on economic issues but widely perceived as an act of protest against the government's crackdown on the IRA's border campaign – was his last political act. He lost his seat at the ensuing general election and failed again to regain it in a subsequent by-election.

Although his legal career continued to provide him with an income, in many ways he considered himself too big a fish to be satisfied with the Irish Bar and the provincial circuit. Having retained his interest in European affairs throughout his period out of government, and getting an early taste of the profile to be gained from the international 'trouble-shooting' he attempted with the Makarios affair in 1957, he effected a stunning reinvention as international humanitarian. Much of this was undoubtedly due to a quite genuine concern for human rights and prisoners' issues, given best expression in his membership of Amnesty International from its foundation in 1961.[7]

His energy was boundless: over the subsequent fifteen years, in addition to his position as Secretary-General of Amnesty International, MacBride was Secretary of the International Commission of Jurists, United Nations High Commissioner for the troubled statelet of Namibia, and Chairman of the International Peace Bureau. He was something of a 'sore thumb' himself, cropping up in conflict situations across the world, best exemplified by his failed attempt to resolve the Iranian hostages crisis in 1979.[8] Also a prominent advocate of nuclear non-proliferation, MacBride finally received the sort of international recognition he craved with the Nobel Peace Prize in 1974. But there was a growing anti-Western orientation to his political views, a tendency rewarded in 1977 with the award of the Lenin Peace Prize, an event which prompted one cynical observer to enquire, 'Would it be possible to have an Idi Amin Peace Prize to enable Mr Sean MacBride to complete the treble?'[9] This anti-Westernism – in some ways an extension of his anti-imperialist views a half-century previously – was given full expression in the 1980s, in the controversial *Many Voices, One World* report, a UNESCO commissioned investigation into communications problems particularly in the developing world.[10]

Within Ireland, MacBride remained a senior republican figure, especially on legal matters. Having represented Gerard Lawless in his challenge to the Irish government's use of internment in the first case argued before the European

---

6   Tom Garvin, *Preventing the Future: Why was Ireland so Poor for so Long?* (Dublin: Gill & Macmillan, 2005), pp. 132–7.
7   Tom Buchanan, '"The truth will set you free": the making of Amnesty International', *Journal of Contemporary History*, vol. 37 no. 4 (October 2002), pp. 575–97.
8   *Irish Times*, 23 November 1979.
9   *Irish Times*, 26 October 1977.
10 The report was so controversial that the United States and the United Kingdom both resigned from UNESCO in protest, although both countries later rejoined. The report is available at: http://unesdoc.unesco.org/images/0004/000400/040066eb.pdf (accessed 12 June 2009).

Court of Human Rights, he continued to represent republicans before the Irish courts. Allegedly, also an adviser to the Provisional IRA at certain junctures, he was associated with Desmond Boal, the independent unionist, in an unsuccessful attempt to bring paramilitaries from both sides of the Northern Ireland conflict to the negotiating table.[11] But having accrued international honours and many honorary degrees, he felt sorely the lack of recognition at home. In 1978, Trinity College Dublin awarded him an honorary doctorate: not, pointedly, his alma mater of UCD. In 1983 MacBride offered to stand as President of Ireland but was turned down, indicative of the divisiveness still associated with his name.

His death, on 16 January 1988, attracted tributes from across the Irish political spectrum and received wide coverage in the Irish press; much coverage, it must be said, understatedly stressed the ambivalent nature of his life and legacy in political Ireland. The *Irish Times* noted pointedly that '[h]is international reputation will probably stand the test of time more than his period in domestic politics', while Ronan Fanning, writing in the *Irish Independent*, observed that he 'never altogether broke his connections with the IRA'.[12] Coming two months after the Enniskillen bombing, and at the beginning of a year in which a further 104 people were killed, MacBride's death lay heavily in the shadow of continued paramilitary violence in Northern Ireland. The *Irish Times* prediction was borne out; while MacBride's reputation remains high in international jurist and humanitarian circles – the International Peace Bureau, for instance, awards a Seán MacBride Memorial Prize annually – in Ireland, his is a more troubled legacy.

11 John Maguire, *IRA Internments and the Irish Government: Subversives and the State, 1939–1962* (Dublin: Irish Academic Press, 2008), pp. 143–71; Ronan Sheehan, 'Interview with Seán MacBride', *The Crane Bag*, vol. 2 no. 2 (1978), p. 151.
12 *Irish Times*, 16 January 1988; *Irish Independent*, 16 January 1988.

Conclusion

'He was an ardent patriot ... but a man warped by ambition.'[1] Bob Briscoe's assessment of MacBride – his electoral rival for the favours of Dublin South-West in 1957 – is cuttingly accurate. The distrust surrounding MacBride's later career, evoked in the negative comment on his death in the British press and in some sections of the Irish political establishment, rested in large measure on memories of his earlier record as a republican leader. Existing biographical treatments of MacBride are inadequate in examining his republican activities in the years prior to 1946; similarly, a proper assessment of his place in Irish political life requires a more thorough analysis of his earlier political career. This book has, for the first time, provided a full account of MacBride's early career, around which so much controversy later swirled. In doing so, it has not only filled a number of historiographical gaps – the most notable of which are in the existing biography of MacBride – but has also contributed to wider understanding of a number of important themes within Irish political history.

The Politicised Child

Editorialising on his death, the *Irish Times* commented that '[MacBride's] childhood influences, the very genes within him, were such that he could follow no path other than that which was radical and revolutionary.'[2] The early sections of this book uncover those genes and influences: the exalted parentage, the disastrous marriage, the bitter separation. All of these marked MacBride psychologically, particularly the absence of a father figure. Equally importantly, MacBride's early childhood marked him physically. The childhood in France coloured not only MacBride's accent, but also his concept of Ireland. Always viewing Ireland as an outsider, with no easy access to the shared 'Irish' experiences – which for others might be locality, education, or culture – MacBride's Ireland was viewed through the lens of an exile, with all the misguided zealotry that implies. Even his religion was the intellectually austere French Jesuitism, rather than the devotionally ornate Irish Catholicism. This 'otherness' extended to the timbre of his childhood: the bohemian Parisian apartment, its artistically and politically diverse visitors, the

---

1 Robert Briscoe, *For the Life of Me* (London: Longmans, 1958), p. 184.
2 *Irish Times*, 16 January 1988.

menagerie of exotic pets, and the insistent occultist slant. The boy who left Paris in 1917 was the product of a privileged continental hothouse, ill-prepared for the upheavals of the years that followed.

MacBride's young adolescence was characterised by dislocation, underscored by the dizzying unfamiliarity of the return to Ireland. As before, these dislocations operated on the physical and the psychological plane. The emotional turmoil which must have followed the news of his father's execution gave way to an enormous psychological turnaround. The feared figure of John MacBride was replaced by a revered martyr, whose sacrifice for Ireland set an exalted benchmark. The return to Ireland also signalled the end to MacBride's childhood. Although just 14 years old, the arrest and imprisonment of his mother in 1918 meant that, in a very real sense, he was left to fend for himself. While the kindness of friends ensured that he was never without a home, he was treated as an adult, by friends, family and the authorities. The 'real Ireland' still escaped him, however; shunted about from one country house to another, MacBride's peripatetic existence further distinguished him from his contemporaries. The longed-for Irish education, when it finally came, was similarly eccentric. These were difficult years for the young man: eager to establish himself and desperate to live up to his honoured name, they were largely a period of marking time.

MacBride and the Irish Revolution

Subsequent years, conversely, see MacBride in the thick of action. Ireland's revolutionary struggle was a decisively formative influence on MacBride's adult persona, and the imperatives of these years remained with him for the remainder of his life. An in-depth examination of MacBride's experiences during this period has proved essential to a proper understanding of his later career. Furthermore, an exploration of the impetus behind one activist's participation in 'the scrap'[3] adds to a broader understanding of the impulses of the revolutionary generation. MacBride's narrative during these years has much to recommend itself to the historian. As a junior member of the Irish Republican Army, MacBride's revolution reflects the more common experiences of the rank and file: the interminable drilling, the difficulty of securing weaponry and, in many cases, the monotony of revolution. His subsequent rise through the ranks indicates the opportunities available to an eager young gunman, anxious to prove himself. In that sense, the Irish revolution was an immensely democratic process: any young hothead who had a good fighting record and was ready to kill or be killed for the cause could rise to a leadership position, whether at GHQ or at provincial level. Whether bellicosity alone was the best indicator of suitability for leadership is another matter. The delicacy of MacBride's position is worth restating: he was a triple outsider in the revolutionary circles in which he moved: an outsider to Ireland, to Dublin, and to his IRA company. Although great predictions had always been made of the exalted role he would play in Irish history, undoubtedly shaping his boyish

3 Ernie O'Malley, *On Another Man's Wound* (Dublin: Anvil Books, 1979, first published 1936), p. 336.

self-image, nothing in his life had prepared him for the rough-and-tumble of a working-class IRA company, crouched in the darkness firing at a British armoured car, while his comrade lay dead beside him. For a 17-year-old, it took immense personal fortitude.

From the totality of MacBride's experiences, a number of broader points can be made. The first is the extent to which civilian life carried on, even during the darkest months of 1920s. University College Dublin is a useful example: although a great many students were active in or sympathetic to the IRA, the college authorities steered a careful path for the institution through the troubled and violent political atmosphere and, in the process, educated a great many of the leaders of the new state. Second, MacBride's participation in the defence of Bloody Sunday prisoners underlines the importance of executions in radicalising Irish society, legitimising the IRA campaign, and maintaining support through increasingly turbulent years. More than ambushes and reprisals, which wrought a high civilian toll in lives and property, executions – Kevin Barry most famously, but also Thomas Whelan – produced a groundswell of popular sentiment without which the republican campaign could not have continued. Third, MacBride's posting to 'ginger up' the southern Leinster counties indicates the immense local variation in Ireland's experience of revolution. The Irish revolution was a patch-work affair, the deep hues of Cork, Clare, Tipperary and Dublin contrasting with the paler colours of much of Connaught and Leinster. Knowledge of this variation, and the reactions it provoked, helped to determine the pattern of conflict in the subsequent civil war.

From the truce of 1921, MacBride becomes an increasingly perceptive and privileged observer as well as a participant shaping the course of events. His position at the margins of Collins's entourage brought him close to the core of power in the IRA; his opposition to the Treaty marked him out. Having integrated himself into one social circle, where he was displaying every sign of having been accepted, a political decision cut him off, and he had to reconstruct his repub-lican identity, reinserting himself into alternate circles of power. That he was prepared to do this – the outsider who had always craved acceptance – indicates the depth of feeling which the Treaty provoked; for MacBride, it was not a casual decision but one which struck to the heart of his identity and position within the republican movement. It might equally have been a bid for freedom, an attempt to mark himself out as different both from the Collins following and from his mother, whose political opinions had coloured and shaped his life. In a real sense, opposing the Treaty was, for MacBride, a declaration of personal as well as political independence.

Aside from personal psychology, MacBride's observations on certain aspects of republican strategy leading up to the Treaty are especially acute. First, the emphasis placed by the IRA leadership on continuing to obtain arms throughout the truce gave an unmistakeable signal that hostilities would be resumed; it was a dangerous message to send to the doggedly militant personalities who made up the weaponry departments. Second, MacBride's criticism of the manner in which Collins conducted the negotiations, with evenings punctuated by heavy drinking and boisterous frolics, was not the reaction of a youthful ascetic but rather reflects a wider sentiment across the Irregular side that the Irish delegation had not only been out-thought, out-fought and out-played by their British counterparts, but also contributed to the deficiencies of the final settlement. Furthermore, MacBride's perception that de Valera had relinquished control by not insisting on the return of the London delegation every weekend opens an intriguing counter-factual vista: if Collins and Griffith had met with de Valera and the remainder of the Cabinet every weekend, providing regular updates and diminishing the cloud of personal suspicion, would the course of events have been different?

MacBride's place within the Irregular forces also merits reflection: his swift ascent to the position of Assistant Director of Organisation, at the age of 18, indicates the wider range of possibilities open to those who opposed the Treaty. Rejecting both the authority of central GHQ and the wider authority of the civil government, a host of leadership positions were available within the anti-Treaty IRA. MacBride's appointment may reflect the dearth of older, experienced officers but also reveals the vigour of a clever young man asserting his independence. Although his dogged attachment to the militant and extremist Mellows faction, especially during the heated Irregular convention of June 1922, might suggest a young man drawn to political melodrama, it had real consequences which he was not prepared to shirk. The set-piece attack on the Four Courts was for MacBride of a heightened emotional intensity: political and personal significance combining in an episode which marked the end of the unity of the republican movement. His prison experiences were of a similar pitch; as an eyewitness to the dark heart of Ireland's civil war on 8 December 1922, the executions of the Mountjoy prisoners coloured his memories indelibly. These and other executions might have served their immediate purposes in halting the assassination of Free State deputies and ripping the heart out of republican resistance, but they deepened the hatreds and reinforced republican opposition to the state. Although MacBride continued his republican activities after his escape from prison, his year-long sojourn in France after his marriage can be seen as a delayed response to the emotional turmoil which coloured his life since he left that country nine years previously. France represented an opportunity to re-establish his equilibrium before once again plunging headlong into the republican whirlpool.

Life in the Free State

The post-Civil War period represents MacBride's high point within the IRA, but also most determined his controversial reputation within Irish politics, both constitutional and radical. Having been absent in France for the republican split which produced Fianna Fáil, MacBride returned to an IRA which was even more bereft of leadership and direction. He was a driving force in giving the decimated movement direction, proving an adept and enthusiastic organiser. Such enthusiasm invariably attracted the attention of the authorities: of all the IRA leadership of this period, MacBride was the most insistently targeted, perhaps after Peadar O'Donnell. That MacBride escaped serious punishment at a time when security legislation was being strengthened, when evidence against him often appeared damning, and when IRA policy forbidding recognition of the courts meant that volunteers often received lengthy sentences indicates not only his strength of mind but also his intellectual and legal fortitude.

'He was equally adept at politics or soldiering when it suited him'.[4] Moss Twomey's comment on MacBride's facility for both sides of republican activism was in part an admiring compliment but also indicated something of the suspect position he held within the IRA of the 1920s and 1930s. In a politically divided movement, MacBride was not easily placeable, which may have contributed to doubts surrounding him. Having displayed early signs of deeply held radical convictions, he was a vigorous proponent of the Saor Éire initiative and espoused socialist beliefs from a number of republican platforms. The socialist wing of the IRA therefore saw it as a particularly heinous betrayal when he refused to support the Republican Congress and went so far as to argue against political organisation *tout court*. Equally, the militant traditionalist section of the IRA looked askance on his apparent conversion to republican puritanism, suspecting it to be merely the latest in a series of masks affected for maximum personal advancement. Yet, as argued in Chapter 5, MacBride's devotion to Saor Éire appeared sincere, and only began to falter when it was palpably obvious that the Irish public would not respond to socialist republican overtures. MacBride was politically aware, but not an ideologue; politically astute, and more than a little careerist. Saor Éire and Republican Congress, he accurately perceived, were political culs-de-sac; that he tried to steer the IRA away should not be interpreted as necessarily malign. Chapter 6 details MacBride's early foray into party politics, Cumann Poblachta na hÉireann, which was an unmitigated disaster and served merely to heighten the enmity with which he was viewed across the republican spectrum. Socialist republicans viewed his party as an even more profound betrayal, after he had declared that political organisation was incompatible with the IRA project, while traditionalists considered it more distraction from what ought to be the proper direction of the IRA. Ultimately, the failure of Cumann Poblachta na hÉireann contributed to the strengthening of the militant faction within the IRA and MacBride's eventual marginalisation within the Army Council.

Similar suspicion attended his relations with Fianna Fáil, with the greatest doubt concerning his susceptibility to the powerful influence of de Valera. It is worth pausing to consider this curious relationship through the years under consideration in this book. As a boy, MacBride remembered that 'he had been moved by the magic foreign ring of the very name "de Valera"', and in 1932 he admitted that 'personally I like de Valera very much'.[5] In 1958, the MacBride and de Valera families were tenuously linked, when MacBride's daughter Anna married Declan White, the nephew of Sinéad de Valera.[6] Despite MacBride's frosty relationship with senior Fianna Fáil figures, flaring into open hostility during the 1930s and 1940s, there was always a certain reverence attached to his interactions with de

---

4 Moss Twomey on MacBride, quoted in *The IRA in the Twilight Years, 1923–1948* (Dublin: Argenta Press, 1997), p. 843.

5 National Archives London [NAL], DO130/90, Note of a conversation with Mr MacBride, 23 February 1948; National Library of Ireland [NLI], Joseph McGarrity Papers, MS 17,456, Seán MacBride to Joseph McGarrity, 19 October 1933.

6 *Irish Times*, 6 January 1958.

Valera. Of course, much of this was ascribable to de Valera's uncanny ability to place himself somehow above party politics, but for MacBride it went deeper. De Valera in a more profound sense represented what MacBride was always striving towards but ultimately failed to become.

Like MacBride, born outside Ireland and without a decisive paternal influence, de Valera inscribed himself thoroughly into Irish culture, overcoming the handicaps of a foreign name and unorthodox background. De Valera used the 'chrism of combat' to rise politically, but abandoned violence when it was clear it was hampering political progress.[7] MacBride's tragedy is that when he did that, it was too late. His record had been indelibly tainted by his association with the IRA through years of callous murder and increasing political irrelevance. More pointedly, any comparison of de Valera and MacBride calls into question each man's record of leadership of their respective organisations. While de Valera combined exoticism with the common touch, MacBride was distinctly remote. Equally, where de Valera was a calming influence within Fianna Fáil, minimising conflict to the point of stifling debate, MacBride was at the centre of a number of personal conflicts within both the IRA and Clann na Poblachta.

The 'Emergency'

The final chapters are concerned with MacBride's narrative during the years of the 'Emergency', but also offer reflections on Ireland's wider experiences of war. Although non-belligerent, and one of the few neutral countries at the outset of war which retained that status at its end, the crucible of the war years provided a severe test of many aspects of Irish society and political life. The stability of the core institutions – many of which had been reworked only two years prior to the outbreak of war – was hardened considerably; the capacity of the Irish people to accept all kinds of privations and curtailments of civil liberty in pursuit of a loftier goal was established; and an explicit choice had finally to be made between the dream of Irish unity and the reality of Irish sovereignty. The fetishisation of Irish neutrality provided a rationale for the most vigorous suppression of civil liberties since the Balfour era; not merely republican subversives but the agricultural, entertainment and media industries, as well as personal communications, were all subject to unprecedented state interference in the name of neutrality. 'Neutrality which began as a policy has thus ended by becoming a symbol.'[8]

Although Ireland's political system soon felt the upheavals of post-war dissatisfaction, in common with the rest of Europe, the immediate outpouring of public feeling following de Valera's response to Churchill's victory speech testifies to an overwhelming recognition of the labyrinthine mind which had preserved the southern state from invasion and despoliation: 'Mr De Valera's achievement in keeping his country out of the whirlpool was a consummate piece of statescraft, which Irishmen will always remember with legitimate gratitude.'[9] Equally, the

---

7 C. S. Andrews, *Man of No Property* (Dublin: The Mercier Press, 1982), p. 10.
8 'Ireland and the war', *Round Table*, vol. xxxiv, no. 135 (June 1944), p. 71.
9 Arland Ussher, *The Face and Mind of Ireland* (London: Victor Gollancz, 1949), p. 70; Clair Wills, *That Neutral Island: A Cultural History of Ireland during the Second World War* (London: Faber & Faber, 2007), pp. 391–2.

actions and attitudes of politically engaged individuals are of heightened significance during a period of unprecedented external crisis. Thus Joseph Walshe has
attracted significant recent criticism for what has been viewed as his unduly
pro-Nazi stance; similarly, James Dillon's break with the Fine Gael party on
the question of supporting the Allied war effort has latterly been presented as
displaying a moral integrity and honour otherwise lacking in Irish political life.[10]
But while it is difficult not to view internal events entirely through the external
prism, some attempt must be made to evaluate MacBride on his own terms.

The position of the republican movement during the war years has been a
particular focus of this book. The nature of the IRA threat during the war has
been at times underplayed by current historians whose focus is primarily the IRA's
connection with external agencies, but the closer analysis of the IRA's operations
inside Ireland, as discussed here, has revealed that the organisation posed the most
serious challenge to state authority at any time since the Civil War. The bloodi-
ness and bitterness which characterised any and all interactions with the Gardaí is
similarly akin to the poisoned enmity between republican and state forces during
the Civil War. The violence which erupted on the streets of Dublin, in Rathgar, in
Donnycarney and on Merrion Square, was testimony to the diseased heart of the
Irish state, which contained a festering virus yet to be totally eradicated and which
was sustained by the hypocrisy of official pronouncements on the evils of partition. Throughout this period, MacBride inscribed himself into this official hypocrisy; his public pronouncements on partition fed into this irreconcilable tendency
which continued to survive, albeit rhetorically, at the core of Irish political life.

As shown, the violent single-mindedness of the bombing campaign soon gave
way to a more sinister engagement with agencies of Nazi Germany, a liaison
which implicated MacBride from its very outset. Pro-German sentiment among
Irish republicanism has been represented as merely the logical result of traditional Anglophobia; in recent years one republican has strikingly expressed this
equation: 'During the Second World War, we didn't know how bad the Germans
were ... At the time, anyone that was beating the English, we were for them ...
But how wrong we were. How wrong we were.'[11] However while such an attitude
may have been barely possible for the young, naive countrymen and women who
largely constituted IRA rank and file at the time, it is less sustainable for a well-
educated, urbane, politically conscious professional such as MacBride. By 1938,
ignorance of the cruelty and inhumanity of the Nazi attitude towards the Jews
was impossible. It is perhaps to MacBride's credit that no traces of anti-Semitism
can be found in his record during the war, aside from the deluded imaginings
of a disgruntled crackpot. Certainly, he steered well clear of the more radical
pro-German organisations in Dublin through the period, and little of the taint
of 'freemasonry' and control of world financial institutions can be found in his
writings, unlike other members of his family.

10   Brian Girvin, *The Emergency: Neutral Ireland 1939–45* (London: Macmillan, 2006), pp. 123–6,
     pp. 241–2; Maurice Manning, *James Dillon: A Biography* (Dublin: Wolfhound Press, 1999); Paul
     Bew, *Ireland: the Politics of Enmity, 1789–2006* (Oxford: Oxford University Press, 2007), p. 473.
11   Eileen O'Neill quoted in Joseph O'Neill, *Blood-dark Track: A Family History* (London: Granta
     Books, 2000), p. 160.

But although MacBride advocated an *attentiste* approach, and almost certainly influenced German Minister Eduard Hempel in urging Berlin to avoid over-committing with the hotheads in the IRA, such an approach should not merely be seen as restraining Nazi designs on Ireland from a purely selfless perspective. Rather, MacBride's determination to stay on the right side of the law while both maintaining links with the republican movement and cultivating close ties with Nazi representatives was arguably part of a larger design to manoeuvre himself into a position of great potential if the expected New Order arrived. When the course of the war took a decisive shift in 1941, with both US entry and the flawed Russian invasion dealing an immense blow to Nazi fortunes, MacBride and others were forced to undertake an enormous recalculation, if they hoped to have any political future in Ireland.

The first signs of this personal and political reinvention came in 1943, when MacBride participated in some wider republican attempts to begin a more meaningful political engagement. This was reinforced by his attempt in June 1943 to publicly recast himself as a steadfast supporter of Irish neutrality, and to reinterpret traditionally belligerent republican attitudes towards the state and its institutions. Of course, there is a crucial difference between publicly supporting Irish neutrality in the dark days of 1940 and 1941, when an invasion of some sort appeared imminent, and doing so in the relatively more quiescent months of 1943, when any political observer could see that the course of the war had altered. But MacBride built on this stance for the remainder of the emergency, benefiting from growing public concerns about the government approach to the republican threat. This tendency manifested itself particularly in the 1943 general election, which injected a new bloc of opposition TDs more sympathetic to the republican cause; and once the war had ended, and the gilt-edged opportunity of the McCaughey case had presented itself as the ideal vehicle to mobilise both this public concern and wider dissatisfactions in a new political party, MacBride seized it.

While a significant portion of government hostility towards MacBride was driven both by his own subversive past and knowledge of his current links with Nazi agencies, this resentment was heightened by MacBride's representation of republican prisoners during the war years. His courageous defence, not only of his clients but also of wider civil liberties, at a time when extraordinary powers were granted to the legislation and the judiciary, earned him the unremitting enmity of key members of the Fianna Fáil Cabinet. Ministers like Gerald Boland, Frank Aiken and especially Seán MacEntee were especially incensed by what they viewed as MacBride's attempts to undermine government efforts to preserve Irish neutrality in face of a noxious internal threat; this hostility would play itself out in the 1947 by-election and the 1948 general election. Whereas liberal observers might have been discomfited by the extreme nature of the powers granted to the Special Criminal Court and the Military Court – and there is a case to be made that such powers essentially eroded the rightful administration of justice – that such powers were fit for purpose is incontrovertible. By the end of 1942, the IRA was entirely broken as a revolutionary force in the southern state; such residual cases as did occur were no more than the last gasps of a dying organisation.

MacBride the Man

Through this book, glimpses of MacBride's personal side emerge. Though relatively plentiful as a vulnerable young boy, these glimpses diminish as political activism became the dominant note in his life, largely drowning out what might have been an intriguing alternate persona. He remains a difficult figure to assess personally. His posthumously published memoir is resolutely political: family life, friendships and hobbies scarcely feature. Similarly, outside reminiscences of MacBride are very much structured around his political persona. This political solipsism had a corrosive effect on his personality and his relationships, and ultimately dented his professional success as a politician. Because MacBride was wholly consumed by politics, dominating his whole personality, his politics irrevocably shaped external impressions. Peadar O'Donnell is a useful counterpoint in this instance: O'Donnell was extremely politically oriented, and subscribed to a political ideology which was largely alien to significant sections of Irish republican thought. Yet O'Donnell's ebullient, attractive personality was such that he was able to maintain good personal relations even with those who opposed him politically. As his entire personality was constructed around and constricted by his political outlook, MacBride was unable to build the type of personal relationships essential both to success as a politician and as a person.

Much of MacBride's persona was, of course, heavily influenced by his early years in France and the example of political and private life provided by his parents. The shadow which his childhood cast across his life was heavy; the prescriptive nature of his family background must at times have seemed burdensome. The emotional damage wrought by his parents' separation, the enormous trauma of his father's execution, and the uncertainty of being thrust into adulthood aged 14 took a heavy toll. MacBride's cold, resolutely political orientation may well have been a retreat from the emotional difficulties of these years. The relationship with his mother is also worth further reflection. Maud Gonne lived with MacBride from his birth until her death in 1953, apart from a brief period immediately after his marriage. This physical proximity mirrored a psychological intimacy which must at times have seemed suffocating. MacBride's failure to establish an independent identity – whether this be manifested in politically autonomous positions or physically symbolised by establishing his own household – indicates the enormous psychological space occupied by Maud Gonne. He loomed equally large in her mentality, her early fixation with her 'Bichon' undiminished by the passing years.

But in so far as MacBride's exalted parentage shadowed his life, it also extended the opportunities available to him. On a practical level, his mother's wealth, albeit diminished after the Great War, was an important facilitating factor in his dedication to republican activism until the late 1930s. Where the normal demands of marriage and children might have forced others in his position to earn a living, MacBride was very much subsidised by his mother (and his wife's enterprising nature) until well into his thirties, and through the early lean years at the Bar. Moreover, MacBride's rapid advance through the ranks of the republican movement simply would not have been possible had he not been possessed of an honoured name. Yet as indicated, once MacBride reached the higher echelons of the IRA, his personality was ill-adjusted to the demands of an Irish revolutionary organisation. Todd Andrews remembered that he 'spoke to his equals *de haut en bas*';[12] this sense of superiority – perhaps inculcated by his illustrious parentage and sense of entitlement – made relating to IRA volunteers on a basic level increasingly difficult. Eunan O'Halpin commented that MacBride 'revelled in starting arguments and in winning them':[13] at times he appeared bent on demonstrating his intellectual superiority to the majority of his republican comrades. His insistence on proper preparations and on punctuality also fit badly with the sloppiness which had begun to characterise the IRA in the 1930s.

More fundamentally, however, MacBride had no common ground with the bulk of his comrades in the republican movement. Mention has already been made of his exclusion from the shared 'Irish' experiences which bound large sections of Irish society together – education, locality and culture. This was an increasingly important factor when it came to the Gaelic values which so coloured the Irish republican and revolutionary movement. 'Irish-Ireland' was essentially alien to MacBride, despite the gestures made towards the restoration of Gaelic language and culture in every political manifesto he was party to. In 1985 he admitted that his failure to learn Irish was one of the lasting regrets of his life.[14] The attractions of Gaelic sports similarly eluded him, prompting one of Mártín Ó Cadháin's more celebrated anecdotes: MacBride, holding forth at a republican meeting in 1936, was undeterred by the impatience of republican delegates anxious to attend the All-Ireland Football final. When the source of the disquiet was explained, MacBride's response was: 'So a game of football is more important than the future of the Irish Republic?'[15]

This distance from the meat-and-drink of Irish life also hampered his appeal both to rank-and-file IRA and also to the Irish electorate once he had founded Clann na Poblachta. Whereas MacBride and de Valera shared a certain exoticism which had long appealed to the Irish public, the crucial difference was that de Valera was both of the people and apart from them. De Valera's ability to tap into the Irish mentality – the famed auto-cardio-examination – stemmed from a very real rooting in a common Irish experience: his childhood in rural County Limerick. It was this potent combination of the familiar and the exotic that made de Valera's political appeal so far-reaching; MacBride shared the latter, but crucially lacked the former. This can also help to explain his lack of popularity within the IRA, especially contrasted with such an all-round popular figure as Moss Twomey. Twomey followed much the same political path as MacBride for most of the 1930s – supportive of Saor Éire, opposed to Republican Congress, close to aspects of the Fianna Fáil leadership – yet he was widely regarded as a decent man and a well-liked leader, even after the Republican Congress split. Twomey's widespread appeal stems at least partly from his background in rural Ireland, his familiarity

---

12 Andrews, *Man of no Property*, p. 192.
13 Eunan O'Halpin, *Defending Ireland: the Irish State and its Enemies since 1922* (Oxford: Oxford University Press, 1999), p. 126.
14 *Irish Independent*, 20 August 1985.
15 Related in Brendan Ó hEithir, *Over the Bar* (Dublin: Poolbeg, 1991, first published 1984), p. 212.

and ease with the conventions of the predominantly rural Irish social life, and the sense that he was 'one of the lads': all traits MacBride lacked. So while MacBride's exalted parentage and exotic background initially aided his republican career, ultimately they became increasingly debilitating burdens.

One of the most marked features of MacBride's personality was his propensity for conspiracy theories. As we have seen, these reached their most fantastic heights in his speculations around the truth of Michael Collins's assassination, but this was a thread which wound throughout his life. Much of this tendency was undoubtedly inherited from Maud Gonne, who displayed an unerring ability to identify British or Orange malfeasance in almost every calamity which befell Ireland. MacBride resembled his mother in this regard; for his part it was the British secret service whose dark hand lay behind Irish disaster. His own particular slant is the obsession with the civil service as an institution ridden with spies: as early as 1933 he told de Valera that 'most civil servants are merely British secret service agents'. Fifteen years later, his first act as Minister for External Affairs was to ask the secretary of his department for 'a list of all the British agents working [there]'.[16] Although MacBride may eventually have been reassured of the bona fides of all Iveagh House staff, the secret service obsession remained with him, and was the subject of a lengthy if confused reflection in 1987.[17] In 1978, he suggested that the developing school of historical 'revisionism' was part of a 'psychological war which the British services always encourage'[18] This tendency points to a conspiratorial mind but also relates to his inflated opinion of the British authorities: to him, they were invisibly omnipotent. Such an opinion might suggest a poor self-image, both personally and nationally.

MacBride's physical appearance was unprepossessing, although Brian Inglis did rather wonderfully note that he bore 'a vague resemblance to Boris Karloff'.[19] This resemblance to the famed horror actor evidently struck other observers; to Todd Andrews, MacBride's 'hollow cheeks and deep-set haunted eyes gave him something of the appearance of a character in a gothic novel'.[20] He was fastidious in his dress from an early age, sporting a fancy yellow waistcoat during the height of his activities with B Company, Third Dublin Battalion; similarly, Moss Twomey recalled that at their first meeting in 1922 MacBride wore 'a hard hat and tight-fitting jacket, much in advance of his age'.[21] Sixty years later, this sartorial refinement persisted. Ulick O'Connor recorded after a meeting in 1985 that MacBride was 'dressed in very smart shoes, lovely corduroy coat and a white

16 NLI, Joseph McGarrity Papers, MS 17,456, Seán MacBride to Joseph McGarrity, 19 October 1933; MacBride quoted in Dermot Keogh, *Twentieth-century Ireland: Nation and State* (Dublin: Gill & Macmillan, 1994), p. 186.

17 Seán MacBride, 'Reflections on intelligence', *Intelligence and National Security*, vol. 2, no. 1 (1987), pp. 92–6.

18 Ronan Sheehan, 'Interview with Seán MacBride', *The Crane Bag*, vol. 2, no. 2 (1978), p. 154.

19 *Irish Times*, 6 November 1948.

20 Andrews, *Man of no property*, p. 192.

21 Moss Twomey quoted in Uinseann MacEoin, *Survivors: The Story of Ireland's Struggle as told Through some of her Outstanding Living People Recalling Events from the Days of Davitt, through James Connolly, Brugha, Collins, Liam Mellows, and Rory O'Connor to the Present Time* (Dublin: Argenta Publications, 1980), p. 398.

open collar, silk shirt, very casual. Extraordinary how he manages to catch fashion and blend it to suit his age.'[22] Coupled with this vanity was a degree of social grace and smoothness of manners; it was these features – perhaps stemming from his mother's elevated background – that surprised British observers after 1948. Fearing an atavistic republican caricature, they found instead an urbane modern gentleman. Sir John Maffey, United Kingdom representative in Dublin, was struck by MacBride's 'high culture and marked personality' but was reminded of 'a fiery soul which eating out its way; fretted the pygmy body to decay'.[23] The freneticism with which he approached his working life, from republican activities to the law to politics, left little time for much else; his inability to switch off, even in later life, speaks to an inner drive which excluded everything else.

This invariably included family life, which suffered immeasurably through all these years of activism. MacBride had relocated to Geneva in 1963 to take up the chair of the International Commission of Jurists; his wife Kid remained in Dublin. A quietly independent figure, she had provided the family with much-needed financial security in the 1920s and 1930s, as Maud Gonne's wealth began to dwindle. Largely running the jam factory and earning a supplemental income through the Irish Sweepstakes Agency, MacBride remembered that she was 'a tower of strength'.[24] But they seemed to have grown apart, markedly so after the death of Maud Gonne in 1953, quickly followed by that of Iseult in 1954. By 1968, Kid was writing to a family friend that she had not known if Seán would come home for Christmas; in the event, he did come, bringing with him an unnamed French girl.[25] MacBride's philandering was undoubtedly a factor. Rumours had long circulated about his relationship with Louie Bennett, his secretary who lived in a self-contained flat in Roebuck House; more certain is his long affair with Karin O'Donovan, honorary secretary of the Irish section of Amnesty International and coincidentally daughter-in-law of James O'Donovan of S-Plan infamy.[26] Conor Cruise O'Brien rather mischievously recalled MacBride's nickname among the female international journalists of the 1970s – 'Death takes a holiday' – but such an amorous disposition unquestionably took its toll on the marriage. MacBride was not with Kid when she died suddenly in November 1976; her *Irish Press* obituary noted that she 'did not automatically accept all his views and stands'.[27] MacBride's relationship with his children Anna and Tiernan also underwent periods of strain, reflected in their exclusion from his personal effects in his will.

Despite his self-professed political radicalism – republicanism followed by a determined anti-Western outlook in later years – MacBride remained socially

22 Extract from Ulick O'Connor, *Executions*, in *Sunday Independent*, 17 January 1993.
23 NAL, DO130/90, Note of a conversation with Mr MacBride, 23 February 1948.
24 Seán MacBride speaking in 'Seán MacBride Remembers', RTÉ television documentary, originally broadcast 1989.
25 National Library of Ireland [NLI], Patricia Lynch and R. M. Fox Papers, MS40,327(9), Kid MacBride to R. M. Fox, 16 January 1988.
26 This affair was revealed by Karin's husband, Dónal, who criticised MacBride for failing to visit Karin during her long illness prior to her early death aged 38 in 1967. Dónal O'Donovan, *Little Old Man cut Short* (Bray: Kestrel Books, 1990), p. 70.
27 Conor Cruise O'Brien, *Ancestral Voices: Religion and Nationalism in Ireland* (Dublin: Poolbeg Press, 1994), p. 136; *Irish Press*, 14 November 1976.

conservative. Ostentatious in his religious observance, his blithe insistence on receiving communion at a mass in Strasbourg while Minister for External Affairs, after the Irish delegation had spent the previous evening indulging in rich food and drink, was too much for Fine Gael Senator Thomas Esmonde: 'When I saw that bastard approaching the rails ... I said to myself "Tommy, you may be no saint, but you're a damn sight better than he is," and up I got and followed him and I felt great after it!'[28] MacBride had never been unduly troubled by the moral diktats of the Catholic church, especially after the mass excommunication of Irregulars during the Civil War, and retained a characteristically republican ability to compartmentalise his religious faith from his political opinions and personal peccadilloes. In the 1980s, as efforts were made to liberalise Irish society, MacBride was adamant that the prohibition on divorce was not discriminatory, and equated discrimination against homosexuals with discrimination against drug users, dismissing both as the 'cultural germs of discrimination' which every society possessed.[29] For David Norris, who followed Jeffrey Dudgeon's path to the European Court of Human Rights to obtain a judgement that southern Ireland's prohibition on homosexuality was a violation of the European Convention on Human Rights, MacBride's intolerance still stung some twenty years after his death.[30] In Irish social as in political matters, towards the end of his life MacBride appeared increasingly outmoded.

Political Legacy

'In Seán MacBride's case it has to be recorded, regrettably, that his contribution to the cause of peace at home, to the national debate on the North, was in inverse proportion to his service to peace worldwide.'[31] John A. Murphy's biting tribute to MacBride in the *Seanad* registers the barrenness of his political legacy in Ireland, lit mercilessly by the conflict in Northern Ireland. Viewed in the round, one of the most striking aspects of MacBride's political record in Ireland is his failure to mature politically, over sixty years of political activism. The fundamental political opinions he held as a hotheaded young IRA man are depressingly similar to those he held closer to death, typified by his contribution to *Ireland after Britain*.[32] A glimmer of insight appeared in 1971, with his declaration that 'our constitution is biased. If we seriously desire national unity we will have to revise it to make it acceptable to non-Catholics. Mr Paisley is not far wrong when he says it should be scrapped.'[33]

28 As quoted in Máire Cruise O'Brien, *The same Age as the State* (Dublin: O'Brien Press, 2003), p. 213.
29 Peadar Kirby, 'Minorities in Ireland: an interview with Seán MacBride', *The Crane Bag*, vol. 5, no. 1 (1981), p. 62.
30 See Norris's spirited denunciation of MacBride: David Norris, 'Seán MacBride: the assassin's cloak', in Myles Dungan (ed.), *Speaking Ill of the Dead* (Dublin: New Island Press, 2007), pp. 152–66.
31 *Seanad Éireann Debates*, vol. 118, col. 545, 20 January 1988.
32 Interview with Seán MacBride in Martin Collins (ed.), *Ireland after Britain* (London: Pluto Press, 1985), pp. 26–32.
33 NLI, Seán O'Mahony Papers, MS44,110(1), Clipping from Evening Herald, 3 December 1971.

But this rare moment of political self-awareness was short-lived, soon replaced by the old mantras of British withdrawal. His contribution to the New Ireland Forum of 1985 has been described as 'a Bela Lugosi performance'; his outdated advocacy of a Swiss canton-style democratic arrangement for the united Irish state – a platform derived from Alfred O'Rahilly – included a dismissal of the 'two nations' argument and again centred on British withdrawal.[34] Throughout his political life, MacBride was incapable of properly comprehending the Northern question. In this he was not alone within Irish nationalism, however; even Peadar O'Donnell, an Ulsterman, conceptualised the northern question as 'the same people with different relatives' rather than recognising the inherent validity of Ulster unionist identity.[35] MacBride subscribed to the nationalist theory that British withdrawal would lead automatically to Irish unity and end unionist 'false consciousness'. This insistence that the solution to the Northern Irish conflict lay in London rather than on the island of Ireland reflects the blinkered perspective he brought to bear on the conflict.

That MacBride's political vision appears increasingly irrelevant to contemporary observers, and that he has no great monument in Irish political or public life, does not however mean that his early career has not deserved closer analysis. As a youthful revolutionary he represented the idealism and vigour which drove the Irish republican movement; his experiences of provincial variation away from the melting-pot of Dublin and Munster deepens the pattern already delineated by a number of important local studies, and reinforces the importance of regional culture in determining the multiple ways in which Ireland experienced revolution. But if MacBride's War of Independence tends to confirm already existing historical interpretations – advanced in particular by Peter Hart – then his narrative after 1921 provides a compelling new insight into republican mentality, through the Civil War and in the early years of the Irish Free State. As a key republican leader of the 1920s and 1930s, MacBride helped to shape the direction of the IRA, and exemplified some of the shifts in political outlook that the organisation underwent through a turbulent decade from 1925 to 1935. Whereas MacBride's rejection of socialist priciples after the fiasco of Saor Éire and subsequent lack of an overarching political ideology has been interpreted as political shallowness, this book has argued that MacBride's resistance to socialist enterprises after 1931 stemmed from a hard-headed recognition that this political philosophy was alien to large sections of Irish society. This growing political realism culminated in MacBride's break with active republicanism in 1937, later cemented by his acceptance of the validity of that year's Constitution. As a barrister through the war years, he was an increasingly lonely voice in arguing for the upholding of civil liberties in the face of stiffening security legislation. In foregrounding MacBride's representation of IRA prisoners before the domestic courts, while keeping a firm eye on

34 R. F. Foster, *Luck and the Irish: A Brief History of Change, 1970–2000* (London: Allen Lane, 2007), p. 127; *Irish Times*, 5 October 1983.

35 Quoted in Richard English, 'The same people with different relatives? Modern scholarship, unionists and the Irish nation', in Richard English and Graham Walker (eds.), *Unionism in Modern Ireland: New Perspectives on Politics and Culture* (Basingstoke: Macmillan, 1996), p. 220.

external events, this book has allowed wartime republican politics to be viewed in the round. There was, however, a darker side to MacBride's Emergency: the shade of collaborationism stained his record as an advocate, and his leadership of the IRA through a particularly callous series of murders in 1935 and 1936 meant that, for many observers, the sincerity of his conversion to constitutional politics was questionable. In sum, his republican career prior to his foray into domestic and international politics offers an appropriate and thought provoking lens through which to analyse the IRA as a revolutionary movement in decline, while illuminating the dangers – real and perceived – posed by the IRA to successive Free State governments. Despite his undoubted idiosyncrasy and the uniqueness of his personal narrative, the principles and paradoxes of MacBride's republican activism illuminate much of the political culture of his time.

Bibliography

Primary sources

1 *Seán MacBride memoirs and interviews*

Seán MacBride, *That Day's Struggle: A Memoir 1904–1951*, ed. Caitriona Lawlor (Dublin: Currach Press, 2005).

'Seán MacBride Remembers', RTÉ television documentary, originally broadcast 1989.

Seán MacBride, 'Reflections on intelligence', *Intelligence and National Security*, vol. 2, no. 1 (1987), pp. 92–6.

Interview with Seán MacBride in Martin Collins (ed.), *Ireland after Britain* (London: Pluto Press, 1985), pp. 26–32.

Seán MacBride, *A Message to the Irish People* (Cork: Mercier Press, 1985).

Interview with Seán MacBride in John Pilger and Michael Coren (eds.), *The Outsiders* (London: Salem House, 1985), pp. 5–14.

Seán MacBride, review of Dermot Keogh's *The Vatican, the Bishops and Irish Politics, 1919–39, Irish Press*, 18 October 1982.

Peadar Kirby, 'Minorities in Ireland: an interview with Seán MacBride', *The Crane Bag*, vol. 5, no. 1 (1981), pp. 800–5.

Seán MacBride, chapter in Uinseann MacEoin, *Survivors: The Story of Ireland's Struggle as Told through some of her Outstanding Living People recalling Events from the Days of Davitt, through James Connolly, Brugha, Collins, Liam Mellows, and Rory O'Connor to the present time* (Dublin: Argenta Publications, 1980), pp. 105–33.

Ronan Sheehan, 'Interview with Seán MacBride', *The Crane Bag*, vol. 2, no. 1 (1978), pp. 296–303.

2 *Manuscript Material*

Bureau of Military History (copies in National Archives of Ireland)
Seán Murphy Witness Statement, WS 204
George Irvine Witness Statement, WS 265
Maud Gonne MacBride Witness Statement, WS 317
Oscar Traynor Witness Statement, WS 340
Dorothy McArdle Witness Statement, WS 457

Dermot O'Sullivan, Witness Statement, WS 508
Norbert O'Connor Witness Statement, WS 527
Joseph O'Connor Witness Statement, WS 544
John Donnelly Witness Statement, WS 626
Joseph Dolan Witness Statement, WS 663
Michael Noyk Witness Statement, WS 707
Dan McCarthy Witness Statement, WS 722

John J. Burns Library, Boston College
M. J. MacManus Papers
Molly Flannery Woods Papers

Irish Military Archives
Irish Military Intelligence (G2) Papers

Library of Royal College of Physicians, Dublin
Kathleen Lynn Diaries

National Archives of Ireland
Department of An Taoiseach Papers
Department of Foreign Affairs Papers
Department of Justice Papers

National Archives, London
Cabinet Papers
Colonial Office Papers
Dominion Office Papers
Home Office Papers
Security Service Personal Files
Security Service Policy Files
Security Service Subject Files
War Office Papers
W. E. Wylie Papers

National Library of Ireland
Account by Simon Donnelly of Attack on Four Courts
Fred Allan Papers
Frank Gallagher Papers
Niall Harrington Papers
Irish Republican Army Papers
Irish Republican Army Papers (Civil War)
Fred Johnson Papers
Liam Lynch Papers
Patricia Lynch and R. M. Fox Papers
Ethel Mannin Papers
Joseph McGarrity Papers
Roger McHugh Papers
Michael Noyk Papers
Florence O'Donoghue Papers

Seán O'Mahony Papers
Celia Shaw Diary
Hanna Sheehy Skeffington Papers

New York Public Library
International Commission for Political Prisoners Papers
William Maloney Collection, Irish Historical Papers
John Quinn Papers

Public Record Office of Northern Ireland
Belfast Crown and Peace Papers, Criminal Jurisdiction
Cabinet Papers

Queen's University Belfast
The British in Ireland, Series 1: Colonial Office Files [microfilm]

University College Dublin Archives
Frank Aiken Papers
Ernest Blythe Papers
Eithne Coyle-O'Donnell Papers
Eamon de Valera Papers
Desmond FitzGerald Papers
Sighle Humphries Papers
Seán MacEntee Papers
Richard Mulcahy Papers
Ernie O'Malley Papers
Moss Twomey Papers

United States National Archives and Records Administration
Political Affairs: Ireland [microfilm]

Papers in Private Possession
David Gray, 'Behind the green door', copy in the possession of Paul Bew

3 Newspapers and periodicals

An Phoblacht
An Phoblacht-Republican News
The Anglo-Celt
Freeman's Journal
Irish Independent
Irish Law Times
Irish Press
Irish Times
London Review of Books
Manchester Guardian
Meath Chronicle
Nenagh Guardian
New York Times
Poblacht na hÉireann-War News

Republican Congress
Round Table
Southern Star
Sunday Independent
Sunday Press
Sunday Telegraph
Sunday Tribune
Time Magazine
The Times
Weekly Irish Times

4 Reference Material and Official Publications

Abbot, Richard, *Police Casualties in Ireland, 1919–1922* (Cork: Mercier Press, 2000).
Acts of the Oireachtas and Statutory Orders of Ireland, available at: www.irishstatutebook.ie.
Bunreacht na hÉireann, available at: www.taoiseach.gov.ie/upload/static/256.htm.
Census of Ireland, 1911, available at: www.census.nationalarchives.ie/.
Clancy, John, Michael Connolly and Kenneth Ferguson, 'Alphabetical index to barristers' memorials, 1868–1968', in Kenneth Ferguson (ed.) *King's Inns Barristers, 1868–2004* (Dublin: The Honourable Society of King's Inns in association with the Irish Legal History Society, 2005), pp. 127–321.
Dáil Éireann Debates
Documents on German Foreign Policy, 1918–1945: Series D, vol. VIII: The War Years (London: Her Majesty's Stationery Office, 1954).
Fanning, Ronan, Michael Kennedy, Dermot Keogh and Eunan O'Halpin (eds.), *Documents on Irish Foreign Policy, Volume 1: 1919–1922* (Dublin: Royal Irish Academy, 1998).
Hansard, fifth series, vols 106–8
Irish Law Reports
    [1928] IR 451
    [1940] IR 470
    [1941] IR 68
    [1942] IR 119
    [1945] IR 126
O'Halpin, Eunan, Dermot Keogh, Michael Kennedy, Caitriona Crowe and Ronan Fanning (eds.), *Documents on Irish Foreign Policy: Volume 6, 1939–1941* (Dublin: Royal Irish Academy, 2008).
Oxford Dictionary of National Biography, available at: www.oxforddnb.com/public.
Seanad Éireann Debates
Sinn Féin Rebellion Handbook (Dublin: The Irish Times, 1917).
UNESCO report *Many Voices, One World*, 1980, available at: http://unesdoc.unesco.org/images/0004/000400/040066eb.pdf.
Walker, B. M. (ed.), *Parliamentary Election Results in Ireland, 1918–92: Irish Elections to Parliamentary Assemblies at Westminster, Belfast, Dublin, Strasbourg* (Dublin: Royal Irish Academy, 1992).

5 *Memoirs and other Contemporary Material*

Andrews, C. S., *Dublin made me* (Dublin: Lilliput Press, 2001, first published 1979).

Andrews, C. S., *Man of no Property* (Dublin: The Mercier Press, 1982).

Barrington, Brendan (ed.), *The Wartime Broadcasts of Francis Stuart: 1942–1944* (Dublin: Irish Academic Press, 2000).

Beckson, Karl, 'Arthur Symons' "Iseult Gonne": a previously unpublished memoir', in Warwick Gould (ed.), *Yeats Annual 7* (Basingstoke: Macmillan, 1990), pp. 202–4.

Bowman, John, '"*Entre nous*": some notes by Erskine Childers on the making of the Anglo-Irish Treaty, 1921', in P. Fox (ed.), *Treasures of the Library, Trinity College Dublin* (Dublin: Royal Irish Academy, 1986), pp. 222–9.

Briscoe, Robert, *For the Life of Me* (London: Longmans, 1958).

Browne, Noël, *Against the Tide* (Dublin: Gill & Macmillan, 1986).

Byrne, Patrick, *Memories of the Republican Congress* (London: Connolly Association, n.d.).

Connolly-O'Brien, Nora, *We shall Rise Again* (London: Mosquito Press, 1981).

Dalton, Charles, *With the Dublin Brigade, 1917–1921* (London: Peter Davies Ltd, 1929).

Deasy, Liam, *Brother against Brother* (Dublin: Mercier Press, 1982).

English, Richard and Cormac O'Malley (eds.), *Prisoners: The Civil War Letters of Ernie O'Malley* (Dublin: Poolbeg Press, 1991).

Gilmore, George, *The Irish Republican Congress* (Cork: Cork Workers' Club, 1974, first published 1935).

Gilmore, George, *The Republican Congress 1934* (Dublin: Dóchas Co-op. Society Ltd, n.d.).

Green Candida, L. (ed.), *John Betjeman: Letters, Volume 1: 1926–1951* (London: Methuen Books, 1994).

Hayes, Stephen, 'My strange story', parts I and II, *The Bell*, vol. xvii, nos 4 and 5 (July–August 1951).

Healy, T. M., *Leaders and Letters of my Day: Volume II* (London: Thornton Butterworth, 1928).

Hogan, James, *Could Ireland become Communist? The Facts of the Case* (Dublin: Cahill, 1935).

Hogan, James, 'Memoir, 1913–1937', in Donncha Ó Corráin (ed.), *James Hogan: Revolutionary, Historian and Political Scientist* (Dublin: Four Courts Press, 2001), pp. 186–202.

Jeffares, A. Norman, Anna MacBride White and Christina Bridgewater (eds.), *Letters to W. B. Yeats & Ezra Pound from Iseult Gonne: A Girl that knew all Dante Once* (Basingstoke: Palgrave, 2004).

Kavanagh, Matt, 'Events in Wicklow, 1920', *Capuchin Annual* 37 (1970), pp. 589–93.

Kelly, John, and Ron Schuhard (eds.), *The Collected Letters of W. B. Yeats, Volume IV*: 1905–1907 (Oxford: Oxford University Press, 2005).

Kelly, John (general ed.), *The Collected Letters of W. B. Yeats*, available at: www.nlx.com/titles/titleii7.html.

Lindsay, Patrick, *Memories* (Dublin: Blackwater Press, 1992).

Londraville, Janis and Richard Londraville (eds.), *Too Long a Sacrifice: The Letters of John Quinn and Maud Gonne* (London: Associated University Presses, 1999).

MacBride, Maud Gonne, 'Yeats and Ireland', in Stephen Gwynn (ed.), *Scattering Branches: Tributes to the Memory of W.B. Yeats* (London: Macmillan, 1940), pp. 15–34.

MacBride, Maud Gonne, *A Servant of the Queen: Reminiscences* (London: Gollancz, 1974, first published 1938).

MacKenzie, Patrick, *Lawful Occasions: The old Eastern Circuit* (Cork: Mercier Press, 1991).

Moynihan, Maurice, *Speeches and Statements by Eamon de Valera, 1917–73* (Dublin: Gill & Macmillan, 1980).

NanKivell, Joice and Sydney Loch, *Ireland in Travail* (London: John Murray, 1922).

Napoli-McKenna, Kathleen, 'In London with the Treaty delegation: personal recollections', *Capuchin Annual*, 38 (1971), pp. 317–21.

Nolan, W., 'Events in Carlow, 1920–21', *Capuchin Annual* 37 (1970), pp. 583–4.

O'Brien, Conor Cruise, *Memoir: My Life and Themes* (London: Profile, 1998).

O'Brien, Conor Cruise, *Ancestral Voices: Religion and Nationalism in Ireland* (Dublin: Poolbeg, 1994).

O'Brien, Máire Cruise, *The Same Age as the State* (Dublin: O'Brien Press, 2003).

O'Brien, William and Desmond Ryan (eds.), *Devoy's Postbag, 1871–1928* (Dublin: Academy Press 1979, first published 1953).

Ó Broin, Leon, *Just like Yesterday: An Autobiography* (Dublin: Gill & Macmillan, 1986).

O'Connell, J. J., 'The role of Dublin in the War of Independence' in *Iris Droing Átha Cliath 1939: Dublin Brigade Review* (n. p., n.d.[1939]).

O'Connor, Frank, *An only Child* (London: Penguin, 2005, first published 1961).

O'Connor, Ulick and Richard Ingrams (eds.), *A Cavalier Irishman: the Diaries of Ulick O'Connor, 1970–1981* (London: John Murray, 2001).

O'Donnell, Peadar, *The Gates flew Open* (London: Jonathan Cape, 1932).

O'Donnell, Peadar, *There will be Another Day* (Dublin: Dolmen Press, 1963).

O'Donnell, Peadar, *Monkeys in the Superstructure: Reminiscences of Peadar O'Donnell* (Galway: Salmon Publishing, 1986).

O'Donovan, Dónal, *Little old Man cut Short* (Bray: Kestrel Books, 1998).

Ó hÉithir, Brendán, *Over the Bar* (Dublin: Poolbeg, 1991, first published 1984).

O'Faolain, Seán, *Vive Moi! An Autobiography* (London: Rupert Hart-Davis, 1965).

O'Halpin, Eunan (ed.), *MI5 and Ireland, 1939–1945: The Official History* (Dublin: Irish Academic Press, 2003).

O'Hegarty, P. S., *The Victory of Sinn Féin: How it Won it and how it Used it* (Dublin: University College Dublin Press, 1998, first published 1924).

O'Kelly, D., 'The Dublin scene', in *With the IRA in the Fight for Freedom: 1919 to the Truce* (Tralee: the Kerryman, n. d.).

O'Malley, Cormac and Anne Dolan (eds.), *No Surrender Here!: The Civil War Papers of Ernie O'Malley, 1922–1924* (Dublin: Lilliput Press, 2007).

O'Malley, Ernie, *On Another Man's Wound* (Tralee: Anvil Press, 1979, first published 1936).

O'Malley, Ernie, *The Singing Flame* (Dublin: Anvil Books, 1997, first published 1978).

O'Neill, Joseph, *Blood-dark Track: A Family History* (London: Granta Books, 2001).

Quinn, P., 'The Battle of Brunswick Street', in *Dublin's Fighting Story, 1916–21: Told by the Men who Made it* (Tralee: The Kerryman, n.d.).

Phelan, Jim, *Churchill can unite Ireland* (London: Victor Gollancz, 1940).

Pierrepoint, Albert, *Executioner* (London: Harrap, 1974).

Prendergast, Seumas, 'Personal memories of Magazine Raid – December, 1939', *Carloviana* (January 2002), pp. 50–3.

Roche, R., 'Events in Wexford – 1920', *Capuchin Annual*,37 (1970), pp. 574–5.

Sheehy, Eugene, *May it please the Court* (Dublin: Fallon Books, 1951).

Steele, Karen (ed.), *Maud Gonne's Irish Nationalist Writings: 1895–1946* (Dublin: Irish Academic Press, 2004).

Stuart, Francis, 'Frank Ryan in Germany', parts I and II, *The Bell*, vol. xvi, nos 2 and 3 (November and December 1950).

Stuart Madeleine, *Manna in the Morning: A Memoir, 1940–1958* (Dublin: Raven Arts Press, 1984).

Sturgis, Mark, *The Last Days of Dublin Castle: The Mark Sturgis Diaries*, ed. Michael Hopkinson (Dublin: Irish Academic Press, 1999).

Ussher, Arland, *The Face and Mind of Ireland* (London: Victor Gollancz, 1949).

White, Anna MacBride and A. Norman Jeffares (eds.), *Always your Friend: The Gonne–Yeats Letters, 1893–1938* (London: Hutchinson, 1992).

White, Harry and Uinseann MacEoin, *Harry* (Dublin: Argenta Publications, 1985).

Winter, Ormonde, *Winter's Tale: An Autobiography* (London: Richards Press, 1955).

Yeats, W. B., *Memoirs*, ed. Denis Donoghue (London: Macmillan, 1974, first published 1972).

Young, Ella, *Flowering Dusk: Things Remembered Accurately and Inaccurately* (London: Dobson, 1945).

6 *Literature*

Bulfin, William, *Rambles in Eirinn* (Dublin: Gill & Son, 1907).

Clarke, Austin, *Selected Poems*, ed. Harry Maxton (Dublin: Lilliput Press, 1991).

O'Connor, Ulick, *Executions* (Dingle: Brandon Press, 1992).

Stuart, Francis, *Black List Section H* (Dublin: Lilliput 1995, first published 1971).

Stuart, Francis, *States of Mind: Selected Short Prose, 1936–1983* (Dublin: Raven Arts Press, 1984).

Voynich, E. L., *The Gadfly*, available at Project Gutenburg: www.gutenberg.org/files/3431/3431–h/3431–h.htm#2HCH0026.

Yeats, W. B., *The Major Works*, ed. Ed Larrissey (Oxford: Oxford University Press, 1997).

Secondary Sources

7 *Books and articles*

Augusteijn, Joost, *From Public Defiance to Guerrilla Warfare: The Experience of Ordinary Volunteers in the Irish War of Independence, 1916–1921* (Dublin: Irish Academic Press, 1996).

Augusteijn, Joost (ed.), *The Irish Revolution, 1913–1923* (London: Palgrave, 2002).

Balliett, C. A., 'The lives – and lies – of Maud Gonne', *Éire-Ireland*, vol. 14 (Fall 1979), pp. 17–44.

Barton, Brian, *From Behind a Closed Door: Secret Court Martial records of the 1916 Easter Rising* (Belfast: Blackstaff Press, 2002).

Bell, J. Bowyer, *The Secret Army: The IRA* (New Brunswick: Transaction Publications, 2004, first published 1970).

Bellenger, Aidan, OSB, 'An Irish Benedictine adventure: Dom Francis Sweetman (1872–1953) and Mount St Benedict, Gorey', in W. J. Shiels and D. Wood (eds.), *The Churches, Ireland and the Irish: Papers Read at the 1987 Summer School Meeting at the 1988 Winter Meeting of the Ecclesiastical History Society* (London: Basil Blackwell Ltd, 1989), pp. 401–15.

Bew, Paul, *Conflict and Conciliation in Ireland, 1890–1910: Parnellites and Radical Agrarians* (Oxford: Clarendon Press, 1987).

Bew, Paul, Ellen Hazelkorn and Henry Patterson, *The Dynamics of Irish Politics* (London: Lawrence & Wishart, 1989).

Bew, Paul, *Ireland: the Politics of Enmity, 1789–2006* (Oxford: Oxford University Press, 2007).

Binchy, Daniel, 'Adolf Hitler', *Studies*, vol. xxii (March 1933), pp. 29–47.

Bobotis, Andrea, 'Rival maternities: Maud Gonne, Queen Victoria and the reign of the political mother', *Victorian Studies* (Autumn 2006), pp. 63–83.

Bourke, Marcus, *Murder at Marlhill: Was Harry Gleeson Innocent?* (Dublin: Geography Publications, 1993).

Bowman, John, *De Valera and the Ulster Question, 1917–1973* (Oxford: Clarendon Press, 1982).

Brady, Conor, *Guardians of the Peace* (Dublin: Gill & Macmillan, 1974).

Breathnach, Caoimhín S., 'Maud Gonne MacBride (1866–1953): an indomitable consumptive', *Journal of Medical Biography*, vol. 13, no. 4 (2005), pp. 232–40.

Buchanan, Tom, '"The truth will set you free": the making of Amnesty International', *Journal of Contemporary History*, vol. 37, no. 4 (October 2002), pp. 575–97.

Campbell, Colm, *Emergency Law in Ireland, 1918–1925* (Oxford: Clarendon Press, 1994).

Cardozo, Nancy, *Maud Gonne: Lucky Eyes and a High Heart* (London: Gollancz, 1979).

Carey, Tim, *Mountjoy: The Story of a Prison* (Cork: Collins Press, 2000).

Carter, Carole, *The Shamrock and the Swastika: German Espionage in Ireland in World War II* (Palo Alto, California: Pacific Books, 1977).

Cole, Robert, *Propaganda, Censorship and Irish Neutrality in the Second World War* (Edinburgh: Edinburgh University Press, 2006).

Columb, Frank, *The Shooting of More O'Ferrall* (Cambridge: Evod Academic Publishing Co., 1997).

Condon, Janette, 'The patriotic children's treat: Irish nationalism and children's culture at the twilight of empire', *Irish Studies Review*, vol. 8, no. 2 (2000), pp. 167–78.

Coogan, Tim Pat, *Michael Collins* (London: Arrow Books, 1990).

Coogan, Tim Pat, *The IRA*, third edition (London: Harper Collins, 1995, first published 1971).

Cronin, Mike, *The Blueshirts and Irish Politics* (Dublin: Four Courts Press, 1997).

Cronin, Mike, 'The Blueshirts in the Irish Free State, 1932–1935: the nature of socialist republican opposition and governmental opposition', in Tim Kirr and Anthony McElligot, *Opposing Fascism: Community, Authority and Resistance in Europe* (Cambridge: Cambridge University Press, 2004, first printed 1999), pp. 80–96.

Cronin, Seán, *The McGarrity Papers* (Tralee: Anvil Books, 1972).

Curran, J. M., *The Birth of the Irish Free State 1921–1923* (Alabama: University of Alabama Press, 1980).

Davis, Fergal F., *The History and Development of the Special Criminal Court, 1922–2005* (Dublin: Four Courts Press, 2007).

Dolan, Anne, 'Killing and Bloody Sunday, November 1920', *Historial Journal*, vol. 49, no. 3 (2006), pp. 789–810.

Douglas, R. M., 'The pro-Axis underground in Ireland, 1939–1942', *Historical Journal*, vol. 49, no. 4 (2006), pp. 1155–83.

Douglas, R. M., *Architects of the Resurrection: Ailtirí na hAiséirghe and the Fascist 'New Order' in Ireland, 1942–1958* (Manchester: Manchester University Press, 2009).

Duffy, Colm Gavan, 'George Gavan Duffy', *Dublin Historical Record* (March 1983), pp. 90–106.

Duggan, J. P., *Herr Hempel at the German Legation in Dublin, 1937–1945* (Dublin: Irish Academic Press, 2003).

Dunphy, Richard, *The Making of Fianna Fáil Power in Ireland, 1923–1948* (Oxford: Clarendon Press, 1995).

Elborn, Geoffrey, *Francis Stuart: A Life* (Dublin: Raven Arts, 1990).

English, Richard, 'Socialism and republican schism in Ireland: the emergence of the Republican Congress in 1934', *Irish Historical Studies*, vol. xxvii, no. 105 (May 1990), pp. 48–65.

English, Richard, '"Paying no heed to public clamour": Irish republican solipsism in the 1930s', *Irish Historical Studies*, vol. xxviii, no. 112 (1993), pp. 426–39.

English, Richard, *Radicals and the Republic: Socialist Republicanism in the Irish Free State* (Oxford: Clarendon Press, 1994).

English, Richard, 'The same people with different relatives? Modern scholarship, unionists and the Irish nation', in Richard English and Graham Walker (eds.), *Unionism in Modern Ireland: New Perspectives on Politics and Culture* (Basingstoke: Macmillan, 1996), pp. 220–35.

English, Richard, *Ernie O'Malley: IRA Intellectual* (Oxford: Clarendon Press, 1998).

English, Richard, 'Socialist republicanism in independent Ireland, 1922–49', in Mike Cronin and John Regan (eds.), *Ireland: The Politics of Independence, 1922–49* (London: Macmillan, 2000), pp. 84–97.

English, Richard, *Armed Struggle: The History of the IRA* (London: Pan, 2004, first published 2003).

English, Richard, *Irish Freedom: The History of Nationalism in Ireland* (London: Macmillan, 2007).

Fairfield, Letitia (ed.), *The Trial of Peter Barnes and others (The IRA Coventry Explosions of 1939)* (London: William Hodge, 1952).

Fanning, Ronan, 'The United States and Irish participation in NATO: the debate of 1950', *Irish Studies in International Affairs*, vol. 1 (1979), pp. 38–48.

Fanning, Ronan, 'The response of the London and Belfast governments to the declaration of the Republic of Ireland, 1948–9', *International Affairs*, vol. 58, no. 1 (1981).

Fanning, Ronan, '"The rule of order": Eamon de Valera and the IRA, 1923–40', in J. P. O'Carroll and J. A. Murphy (eds.), *De Valera and his Times* (Cork: Cork University Press, 1983), pp. 160–72.

Farrell, Michael, 'The extraordinary life and times of Seán MacBride: Part I', *Magill*, vol. 6, no. 3 (Christmas 1982).

Ferriter, Diarmaid, *Judging Dev: A Reassessment of the Life and Legacy of Eamon de Valera* (Dublin: Royal Irish Academy, 2007).

Fisk, Robert, *In Time of War: Ireland, Ulster and the Price of Neutrality, 1939–1945* (Dublin: Gill & Macmillan, 1983).

Fitzpatrick, David, *Politics and Irish life: Provincial Experiences of War and Revolution* (Cork: Cork University Press, 1998, first published 1977).

Fitzpatrick, David, *The Two Irelands, 1912–1939* (Oxford: Oxford University Press, 1998).

Fitzpatrick, David, *Harry Boland's Irish Revolution, 1887–1922* (Cork: Cork University Press, 1999).

Foley, Conor, *Legion of the Rearguard* (London: Pluto Press, 1992).

Foster, R. F., *W. B. Yeats: A Life: I: The Apprentice Mage, 1865–1914* (Oxford: Oxford University Press, 1997).

Foster, R. F., *W. B. Yeats: A Life: II: The Arch Poet, 1915–1939* (Oxford: Oxford University Press, 2003).

Foster, R. F., *Luck and the Irish: A Brief History of Change, 1970–2007* (London: Allen Lane, 2007).

Foxton, David, *Revolutionary Lawyers: Sinn Féin and the Crown coUrts in Ireland and Britain, 1916–1923* (Dublin: Four Courts Press, 2008).

Foy, Michael, *Michael Collins's Intelligence War: The Struggle between the British and the IRA, 1919–1921* (Stroud: Sutton, 2006).

Garvin, Tom, 'The aftermath of the Civil War', *The Irish Sword*, vol. xx, no. 82 (1997), pp. 387–95.

Garvin, Tom, *1922: The Birth of Irish Democracy* (Dublin: Gill & Macmillan, 2005, first published 1996).

Garvin, Tom, *Preventing the Future: Why was Ireland so Poor for so Long?* (Dublin: Gill & Macmillan, 2005).

Geiger, Till and Michael Kennedy (eds.), *Ireland, Europe and the Marshall Plan* (Dublin: Four Courts Press, 2004).

Girvin, Brian, 'Politics in wartime: governing, neutrality and elections', in Brian Girvin and Geoffrey Roberts (eds.), *Ireland and the Second World War: Politics, Society and Remembrance* (Dublin: Four Courts Press, 2000), pp. 24–46.

Girvin, Brian, 'The republicanisation of Irish society, 1932–48', in Jacqueline R. Hill (ed.), *A New History of Ireland, Volume 7: 1921–84* (Oxford: Oxford University Press, 2003), pp. 127–60.

Girvin, Brian, *The Emergency: Neutral Ireland 1939–45* (London: Macmillan, 2006).

Goulding, George M., *George Gavan Duffy: A Legal Biography* (Dublin: Irish Academic Press, 1982).

Greaves, C. Desmond, *Liam Mellows and the Irish Revolution* (London: Laurence & Wishart, 1971).

Griffith, Kenneth and Timothy O'Grady, *Curious Journey: An Oral History of Ireland's Unfinished Revolution* (London: Hutchinson, 1982).

Hammill, Jonathan, 'Saor Éire and the IRA: an exercise in deception?', *Saothar*, vol. 20 (1995), pp. 56–66.

Hanley, Brian, 'The Volunteer Reserve and the IRA', *The Irish Sword* vol. xxi, no. 83 (1998), pp. 93–8.

Hanley, Brian, 'Moss Twomey, radicalism and the IRA: a reassessment', *Saothar*, vol. 26 (2001), pp. 53–60.

Hanley, Brian, *The IRA, 1926–1936* (Dublin: Four Courts Press, 2002).

Hanley, Brian, '"Just an battalion of armed Catholics"? The IRA in Northern Ireland in the 1930s', in Joost Augusteijn and Marian Lyons, *Irish history: A Research Yearbook, no. 1* (Dublin: Four Courts Press, 2002), pp. 1–23.

Hart, Peter, *The IRA and its Enemies: Violence and Community in Cork, 1916–1923* (Oxford: Oxford University Press, 1998).

Hart, Peter, *The IRA at War, 1916–1923* (Oxford: Oxford University Press, 2005, first published 2003).

Hart, Peter, *Mick: The Real Michael Collins* (London: Macmillan, 2005).

Healy SJ, James, 'The Civil War hunger-strike, October 1923', *Studies* (Autumn 1923), pp. 213–26.

Hogan, Daire, 'The Society, from independence to 1960', in E. G. Hall and Daire Hogan (eds.), *The Law Society of Ireland, 1852–2002: Portrait of a Profession* (Dublin: Four Courts Press, 2002), pp. 73–96.

Hogan, Gerard, 'The Supreme Court and the reference of the Offences Against the State (Amendement) Bill 1940', *The Irish Jurist*, vol. xxxv (2000), pp. 238–79.

Hopkinson, Michael, 'Review article: biography of the revolutionary period: Michael Collins and Kevin Barry', *Irish Historical Studies*, vol. xxviii, no. 111 (May 1993), pp. 310–16 [expanded and republished as 'Biography and Irish history', in Allan Blackstock and Eoin Magennis (eds.), *Politics and Political Culture in Britain and Ireland, 1750–1850: Essays in Tribute to Peter Jupp* (Belfast: Ulster Historical Foundation, 2007), pp. 195–208].

Hopkinson, Michael, *Green against Green: The Irish Civil War* (Dublin: Gill & Macmillan, 2004, first published 1988).

Horgan, John, *Noël Browne: Passionate Outsider* (Dublin: Gill & Macmillan, 2000).

Hull, Mark, 'The Irish interlude: German intelligence in Ireland, 1939–1943', *Journal of Military History*, no. 66 (July 2002), pp. 695–718.

Hull, Mark, *Irish Secrets: German Espionage in Ireland, 1939–1945* (Dublin: Irish Academic Press, 2003).

Humphreys, Madeline, *The Life and Times of Edward Martyn: An Aristocratic Bohemian* (Dublin: Irish Academic Press, 2007).

Innes, C. L., *Women and Nation in Irish Literature and Society 1880–1935* (Hemel Hempstead: Harvester Wheatsheaf, 1993).

Jackson, Alvin, *Ireland, 1798–1998* (Oxford: Blackwell Publishers, 1999).

Jeffares, A. Norman, 'Iseult Gonne', in Warwick Gould (ed.), *Poems and Contexts: Yeats Annual 16* (Basingstoke: Palgrave, 2005), pp. 197–278.

Jeffery, Keith, *Field Marshal Sir Henry Wilson: A Political Soldier* (Oxford: Oxford University Press, 2006).

Jordan, Anthony, *Major John MacBride: MacDonagh and MacBride and Connolly and Pearse* (Westport: Westport Historical Society, 1991).

Jordan, Anthony, *Seán MacBride: A Biography* (Dublin: Blackwater Press, 1993).

Joye, Lar, '"Aiken's slugs": the reserve of the Irish Army under Fianna Fáil' in Joost Augusteijn (ed.), *Ireland in the 1930s: New Perspectives* (Dublin: Four Courts Press, 1999), pp. 143–62.

Keane, Elizabeth, *An Irish Statesman and Revolutionary: The Nationalist and Internationalist Politics of Seán MacBride* (London: Tauris Academic Studies, 2006).

Keane, Elizabeth, *Seán MacBride: A Life* (Dublin: Gill & Macmillan, 2007).

Kehoe, A. M., *History-makers of Twentieth Century Ireland: Carson, Craig, Griffith, Collins, Cosgrave, de Valera, Brookeborough, Lemass, O'Neill, MacBride* (Dublin: Mentor Publications, 1989).

Kennedy, Michael, 'Our men in Berlin: some thoughts on Irish diplomats in Germany, 1929–39', *Irish Studies in International Affairs*, vol. 10 (1999), pp. 53–70.

Keogh, Dermot, *The Vatican, The Bishops and Irish Politics, 1919–39* (Cambridge: Cambridge University Press, 1986).

Keogh, Dermot, 'Eamon de Valera and Hitler: an analysis of international reaction to the visit to the German Minister, May 1944', *Irish Studies in International Affairs*, vol. 3, no. 1 (1989), pp. 69–82.

Keogh, Dermot, 'Mannix, de Valera and Irish nationalism', in John O'Brien and Pauric Travers (eds.), *The Irish Emigrant Experience in Australia* (Dublin: Poolbeg, 1991), pp. 196–225.

Keogh, Dermot, *Twentieth-century Ireland: Nation and State* (Dublin: Gill & Macmillan, 1994).

Keogh, Dermot, *Jews in Twentieth-century Ireland: Refugees, Anti-Semitism and the Holocaust* (Cork: Cork University Press, 1998).

Keown, Gerard, 'The Irish Race Conference, 1922, reconsidered', *Irish Historical Studies*, vol. xxxii, no. 127 (May 2001), pp. 365–76.

Kiely, Kevin, *Francis Stuart: Artist and Outcast* (Dublin: The Liffey Press, 2007).

Kissane, Bill, 'Defending democracy? The legislative response to political extremism in the Irish Free State, 1922–39', *Irish Historical Studies*, vol. xxxiv, no. 134 (November 2004), pp. 156–74.

Kissane, Bill, *The Politics of the Irish Civil War* (Oxford: Oxford University Press, 2005).

Laffan, Michael, *The Resurrection of Ireland: The Sinn Féin Party, 1916–1923* (Cambridge: Cambridge University Press, 1999).

Lee, J. J., *Ireland, 1912–1985: Politics and Society* (Cambridge: Cambridge University Press, 1989).

Linklater, Andrea, *An Unhusbanded Life* (London: Hutchinson, 1979).

Lynch, Robert, *The Northern IRA and the Early Years of Partition, 1920–1922* (Dublin: Irish Academic Press, 2006).

Lynch, Robert, 'Donegal and the joint-IRA offensive, May-November 1922', *Irish Historical Studies*, vol. xxxv, no. 138 (November 2006), pp. 184–99.

Lynch, Robert, 'The people's protectors? The Irish Republican Army and the "Belfast Pogrom", 1920–1922', *Journal of British Studies*, vol. 47, no. 2 (2008), pp. 375–91.

Lyons, F. S. L., *Ireland since the Famine* (London: Fontana, 1982, first published 1971).

Macardle, Dorothy, *The Irish Republic* (Dublin: The Irish Press, 1958, first published 1937).

MacCabe, Ian, *A Diplomatic History of Ireland: the Republic, the Commonwealth and NATO* (Dublin: Irish Academic Press, 1991).

McCarthy, John Paul, *Kevin O'Higgins: Builder of the Irish State* (Dublin: Irish Academic Press, 2006).

McCartney, Dónal, *UCD: A National Idea: The History of University College Dublin* (Dublin: Gill & Macmillan, 1999).

McConville, Seán, *Irish Political Prisoners, 1848–1922* (London: Routledge, 2003).

McCoole, Sinéad, *No Ordinary Women: Irish Female Activists in the Revolutionary Years, 1900–1923* (Dublin: O'Brien Press, 2004, first published 2003).

McCracken, Dónal P., *Forgotten Protest: Ireland and the Anglo-Boer War* (Belfast: Ulster Historical Foundation, 2003, first published 1989).

McCracken, Dónal P., *MacBride's Brigade: Irish Commandos in the Anglo-Boer War* (Dublin: Four Courts Press, 1999).

McCullagh, David, *A Makeshift Majority: The First Inter-party Government, 1948–51* (Dublin: Institute of Public Administration, 1998).

MacDermott, Eithne, *Clann na Poblachta* (Cork: Cork University Press, 1998).

MacEoin, Uinseann, *The IRA in the Twilight Years, 1923–1948* (Dublin: Argenta Press, 1997).

MacEoin, Uinseann, *Survivors: The Story of Ireland's Struggle as Told Through Some of her Outstanding Living People Recalling Events from the Days of Davitt, through James Connolly, Brugha, Collins, Liam Mellows, and Rory O'Connor to the present time* (Dublin: Argenta Publications, 1980).

MacEvilly, Michael, 'Seán MacBride and the republican motor-launch *St George*', *The Irish Sword*, vol. xvi (1984–1986), pp. 49–57.

McEvoy, F. J., 'Canada, Ireland and the Commonwealth: the declaration of the Irish republic, 1948–9', *Irish Historical Studies*, vol. xxiv, no. 96 (November 1985).

McGarry, Fearghal, *Irish Politics and the Spanish Civil War* (Cork: Cork University Press, 1999).

McGarry, Fearghal, *Frank Ryan* (Dundalk: Historical Association of Ireland, 2002).

McGarry, Fearghal, '"Too damned tolerant": republicans and imperialism in the Irish Free State' in Fearghal McGarry (ed.), *Republicanism in Modern Ireland* (Dublin: University College Dublin Press, 2003), pp. 61–85.

McGarry, Fearghal, *Eoin O'Duffy: A Self-made Hero* (Oxford: Oxford University Press, 2005).

McGarry, Fearghal, *The Rising: Ireland, Easter 1916* (Oxford: Oxford University Press, 2010).

McGee, Owen, *The IRB: The Irish Republican Brotherhood from the Land League to Sinn Féin* (Dublin: Four Courts Press, 2005).

McGladdery, Gary, *The Provisional IRA in England: The Bombing Campaign, 1973–1997* (Dublin: Irish Academic Press, 2006).

McGuire, Charles, *Roddy Connolly and the Struggle for Socialism in Ireland* (Cork: Cork University Press, 2008).

McKee, E., 'Church-state relations and the development of Irish health policy: the mother-and-child scheme, 1944–53', *Irish Historical Studies*, vol. xxv, no. 98 (November, 1986), pp. 159–94.

McMahon, Deirdre, *Republicans and Imperialists: Anglo-Irish Relations in the 1930s* (London: Yale University Press, 1984).

McMahon, Paul, 'British intelligence and the Anglo-Irish truce, July–December 1921', *Irish Historical Studies*, vol. xxxv, no. 140 (November 2007), pp. 519–40.

McMahon, Paul, *British Spies and Irish Rebels: British Intelligence and Ireland, 1916–1945* (Woodbridge: Boydell & Brewer, 2008).

McNamara, Kevin, *The MacBride Principles: Irish-America strikes Back* (Liverpool: Liverpool University Press, 2009).

McVeigh, Jim, *Executed: Tom Williams and the IRA* (Belfast: Beyond the Pale Publications, 1999).

Maguire, John, *IRA Internments and the Irish Government: Subversives and the State, 1939–1962* (Dublin: Irish Academic Press, 2008).

Mahon, Tim and J. J. Gillogly, *Decoding the IRA* (Cork: Mercier Press, 2008).

Manning, Maurice, *James Dillon: A Biography* (Dublin: Wolfhound Press, 1999).

Matthews, Kevin, *Fatal Influence: The Impact of Ireland on British Politics, 1920–1925* (Dublin: University College Dublin Press, 2004).

Maume, Patrick, *The Long Gestation: Irish Nationalist Life 1891–1918* (Dublin: Gill & Macmillan, 1999).

Meehan, Máirtín, *Finely-tempered Steel: Seán McCaughey and the IRA* (Dublin: Republican Publications, 2007).

Meenan, James (ed.), *Centenary History of the Literary and Historical Society of University College Dublin, 1855–1955* (Tralee: The Kerryman, 1956).

Molohan, Cathy, 'Humanitarian Aid or Politics? The case of the Save the German Children Society', *History Ireland*, vol. 5, no. 3 (Autumn 1997), pp. 7–9.

Moroney, Michael, 'George Plant and the rule of law: the Devereux affair, 1940–1942', *Tipperary Historical Journal* (1988), pp. 1–12.

Mulvihill, Margaret, *Charlotte Despard: A Biography* (London: Pandora, 1989).

Murray, Patrick, *Oracles of God: The Roman Catholic Church and Irish Politics, 1922–37* (Dublin: University College Dublin Press, 2000).

Murphy, John A., 'Irish neutrality in historical perspective', in Brian Girvin and Geoffrey Roberts (eds.), *Ireland and the Second World War: Politics, Society and Remembrance* (Dublin: Four Courts Press, 2000), pp. 9–23.

Natterstad, Jerry H., *Francis Stuart* (London: Associated University Presses, 1974).

Nic Dháibhéid, Caoimhe, '"This is a case in which Irish national considerations must be taken into account": the breakdown of the MacBride-Gonne marriage, 1904–1908', *Irish Historical Studies*, vol. xxxvii, no. 146 (Nov. 2010), pp. 64–87.

Nolan, Aengus, *Joseph Walshe: Irish Foreign Policy 1922–1946* (Cork: Mercier Press, 2008).

Norris, David, 'Seán MacBride: the assassin's cloak', in M. Dungan (ed.), *Speaking Ill of the Dead* (Dublin: New Island Press, 2007), pp. 152–66.

O'Brien, Gerard, *Irish Governments and the Guardianship of Historical Records, 1922–1972* (Dublin: Four Courts Press, 2004).

O'Brien, Mark, *De Valera, Fianna Fáil and the* Irish Press (Dublin: Irish Academic Press, 2001).

Ó Broin, Leon, *Revolutionary Underground: The Story of the Irish Republican Brotherhood, 1858–1925* (Dublin: Gill & Macmillan, 1976).

O'Connor, Emmett, *Reds and the Green: Ireland, Russia and the Communist Internationals, 1919–1943* (Dublin: University College Dublin Press, 2004).

Ó Corráin, Donncha (ed.), *James Hogan: Revolutionary, Historian and Political Scientist* (Dublin: Four Courts Press, 2001).

O'Donovan, Dónal, *Kevin Barry and his Time* (Dublin: Glendale, 1989).

Ó Drisceoil, Dónal, *Censorship in Ireland, 1939–1945* (Cork: Cork University Press, 1996).

Ó Drisceoil, Dónal, 'Jews and other undesirables: anti-Semitism in neutral Ireland during the Second World War', in Ethel Crowley and Jim Mac Laughlin (eds.), *Under the Belly of the Tiger: Class, Race, Identity and Culture in the Global Ireland* (Dublin: Irish Reporter Publications, 1997), pp. 65–92.

Ó Drisceoil, Dónal, *Peadar O'Donnell* (Cork: Cork University Press, 2001).

Ó Drisceoil, Dónal, '"The Irregular and Bolshie situation": republicanism and communism, 1921–36', in Fearghal McGarry (ed.), *Republicanism in Modern Ireland* (Dublin: University College Dublin Press, 2003), pp. 42–60.

Ó Drisceoil, Dónal, '"Whose emergency is it?" Wartime politics and the Irish working class', in Dónal Ó Drisceoil and Fintan Lane (eds.), *Politics and the Irish Working Class, 1830–1945* (Basingstoke: Palgrave, 2005), pp. 262–80.

O'Faoláin, Seán, *The Life-story of Eamon de Valera* (Dublin: Talbot Press, 1933).

O'Faoláin, Seán, *De Valera* (Harmondsworth: Penguin, 1939).

Ó Gráda, Cormac, *Jewish Ireland in the Age of Joyce* (Princeton: Princeton University Press, 2006).

O'Halpin, Eunan, *Defending Ireland: The Irish State and its Enemies since 1922* (Oxford: Oxford University Press, 1999).

O'Halpin, Eunan, 'Irish-Allied security relations and the "American note" crisis: new evidence from British records', *Irish Studies in International Affairs*, vol. 11 (2000), pp. 71–83.

O'Halpin, Eunan, 'British intelligence, republicans and the IRA's German links' in Fearghal McGarry (ed.), *Republicanism in Modern Ireland* (Dublin: University College Dublin Press, 2003), pp. 108–31.

O'Halpin, Eunan, *Spying on Ireland: British Intelligence and Irish Neutrality during the Second World War* (Oxford: Oxford University Press, 2008).

O'Leary, Cornelius, *Irish Elections, 1918–77* (Dublin: Gill & Macmillan, 1979).

Ó Longaigh, Seosamh, 'Emergency law in action, 1939–1945' in Dermot Keogh and Mervyn O'Driscoll (eds.), *Ireland in World War Two: Diplomacy and Survival* (Cork: Mercier Press, 2004), pp. 63–80.

Ó Longaigh, Seosamh, *Emergency Law in Independent Ireland, 1922–1948* (Dublin: Four Courts Press, 2006).

O'Malley, Kate, *Ireland, India and Empire: Indo-Irish Radical Connections, 1919–64* (Manchester: Manchester University Press, 2008).

O'Neill, T. M., 'Handing away the trump card? Peadar O'Donnell, Fianna Fáil and the non-payment of land annuities campaign, 1926–32', *New Hibernia Review*, vol. 12, no. 1 (spring 2008), pp. 19–40.

O'Neill, T. P. and Lord Longford, *De Valera* (Dublin: Gill & Macmillan, 1970).

O'Toole, Fintan, 'A portrait of Peadar O'Donnell as an old soldier', *Magill* (February 1983), pp. 27–30.

Parkinson, Alan, *Belfast's Unholy War: The Troubles of the 1920s* (Dublin: Four Courts Press, 2004).

Pašeta, Senia, 'Nationalist responses to two royal visits to Ireland, 1900 and 1903', *Irish Historical Studies*, vol. xxxi (1999), pp. 488–504.

Patterson, Henry, *The Politics of Illusion: Republicanism and Socialism in Modern Ireland* (London: Hutchinson, 1989).

Patterson, Henry, *Ireland since 1939* (Oxford: Oxford University Press, 2002), pp. 34–5.

Puirséil, Niamh, *The Irish Labour Party: 1922–73* (Dublin: University College Dublin Press, 2007).

Radcliff, S. C., 'The destruction of the Public Records Office in Dublin', *Historical Research*, vol. 2, no. 4 (June 1924), pp. 8–9.

Raymond, R. J., 'Ireland's 1949 NATO decision: a reassessment', Éire-Ireland, vol. xx, no. 3 (Fomhar, 1985).

Regan, John M., *The Irish Counter-revolution: Treatyite Politics and Settlement in Ireland* (Dublin: Gill & Macmillan, 2001, first published 1999).

Regan, John M., 'Michael Collins, General Commanding-in-Chief, as a historiographical problem', *History*, vol. 92, no. 307 (June 2007), pp. 318–46.

Roth, Andreas, 'Gunrunning from Germany to Ireland in the early 1920s', *The Irish Sword*, vol. xxii, no. 88 (2000), pp. 290–320.

Roth, Andreas, 'Francis Stuart's broadcasts from Germany, 1942–4: some new evidence', *Irish Historical Studies*, vol. xxxii, no. 127 (May 2001), pp. 408–22.

Ryan, Meda, *Tom Barry: IRA Freedom Fighter* (Cork: Mercier Press, 2005, first published 2003).

Saddlemyer, Ann, *Becoming George: The Life of Mrs W. B. Yeats* (Oxford: Oxford University Press, 2002).

Schabas, W. A., 'Ireland, the European Convention on Human Rights and the personal contribution of Seán MacBride', in John Morison, Kieran McEvoy and Gordon Anthony (eds.), *Judges, Transitions and Human Rights* (Oxford: Oxford University Press, 2007), pp. 251–74.

Smith, M. L. R., *Fighting for Ireland? The Military Strategy of the Irish Republican Movement* (London: Routledge, 1995).

Steele, Karen, *Women, Press & Politics during the Irish Revival* (New York: Syracuse University Press, 2007).

Stephan, Enno, *Spies in Ireland* [translated from the German by A. Davidson] (London: Macdonald Press, 1963).

Tóibín, Colm, 'Issues of truth and invention', *London Review of Books*, 4 January 2001.

Townshend, Charles, *The British Campaign in Ireland: 1919–21: The Development of Political and Military Policies* (Oxford: Oxford University Press, 1975).

Townshend, Charles, 'The Irish Republican Army and the development of guerrilla warfare', *English Historical Review*, vol. 94 (1979), pp. 318–45.

Townshend, Charles, *Political Violence in Ireland: Government and Resistance since 1848* (Oxford: Clarendon Press, 1983).

Townshend, Charles, *Easter 1916: The Irish Rebellion* (London: Penguin, 2006).

Valiulis, Maryann, *Portrait of a Revolutionary: General Richard Mulcahy and the Founding of the Irish Free State* (Dublin: Irish Academic Press, 1992).

Walker, Graham, '"The Irish Dr Goebbels": Frank Gallagher and Irish republican propaganda', *Journal of Contemporary History* vol. 7 (1992), pp. 149–65.

Walker, Graham, 'The Northern Ireland Labour Party, 1924–45', in Dónal Ó Drisceoil and Fintan Lane (eds.), *Politics and the Irish Working Class 1830–1945* (Basingstoke: Palgrave, 2005), pp. 229–45.

Ward, Margaret, *Unmanageable Revolutionaries: Women and Irish Nationalism* (Dingle: Brandon Press, 1983).

Ward, Margaret, *Maud Gonne: Ireland's Joan of Arc* (London: Pandora, 1990).

Ward, Margaret, *Hanna Sheehy Skeffington: A Life* (Cork: Attic Press, 1997).

Whelan, Bernadette, *Ireland and the Marshall Plan, 1947–1947* (Dublin: Four Courts Press, 2000).

Whelan, Yvonne, 'The construction and destruction of a colonial landscape: monuments to British monarchs in Dublin before and after independence', *Journal of Historical Geography*, vol. 28, no. 4 (2002), pp. 508–33.

Wills, Clair, *That Neutral Island: A History of Ireland during the Second World War* (London: Faber & Faber, 2008).

Wills, Clair, *Dublin 1916: The Siege of the GPO* (London: Profile Books, 2009).

8 Unpublished theses

McHugh, J. P., 'Voices of the rearguard: a study of *An Phoblacht*: Irish republican thought in the post-revolutionary era, 1923–1937' (MA thesis, UCD, 1983).

McQuade, James, 'The Irish Republican Congress – 1934' (MSocSc thesis, QUB, 1988)

O'Callaghan, Liam, 'The history of the death penalty in Ireland since the Civil War (MPhil thesis, UCC, 2003).

O'Sullivan, C. T., 'The IRA takes constitutional action: a history of Clann na Poblachta, 1946–65' (MA thesis, UCD, 1995).

Index

Printed and bound by CPI Group (UK) Ltd, Croydon, CR0 4YY

09/06/2025

14685806-0001